ex libris

DEREK SHORTHOUSE

LATIN GREEK ENG. LIT. POLITICS HISTORY LOCAL GOVT. CHRISTIANITY KTλ

heluonis librorum

GLADSTONE, WHIGGERY AND
THE LIBERAL PARTY
1874–1886

DEDICATION

To my Mother, and to the Memory of my Father.

Gladstone, Whiggery and the Liberal Party 1874–1886

T. A. JENKINS

CLARENDON PRESS · OXFORD

1988

Oxford University Press, Walton Street, Oxford OX2 6DP
Oxford New York Toronto
Delhi Bombay Calcutta Madras Karachi
Petaling Jaya Singapore Hong Kong Tokyo
Nairobi Dar es Salaam Cape Town
Melbourne Auckland
and associated companies in
Beirut Berlin Ibadan Nicosia

Oxford is a trade mark of Oxford University Press

Published in the United States
by Oxford University Press, New York

© T. A. Jenkins, 1988

British Library Cataloguing in Publication Data
Jenkins, T. A.
Gladstone, Whiggery and the Liberal
Party 1874–1886.
1. Liberal Party—History   2. Great
Britain—Politics and government—
1837–1901
I. Title
324.24106'09   JN1129.L42
ISBN 0-19-820129-X

Library of Congress Cataloging-in-Publication Data
Jenkins, T. A. (Terence Andrew), 1958–
Gladstone, Whiggery, and the Liberal Party, 1874–1886 / T. A.
Jenkins.
p.   cm.
Bibliography: p.   Includes index.
1. Gladstone, William Ewart, 1809–1898.   2. Whig Party (Great
Britain)—History—19th century.   3. Liberal Party (Great Britain)—
History—19th century.   4. Great Britain—Politics and
government—1837–1901.   I. Title.
DA563.5.J46   1988   941.081—dc19   87–28113
ISBN 0-19-820129-X

Set by Rowland Phototypesetting Ltd
Bury St Edmunds, Suffolk
Printed in Great Britain by
Biddles Ltd, Guildford and King's Lynn

ACKNOWLEDGEMENTS

This book is based largely upon the private papers of politicians of the period, most of which have now been deposited in public institutions. I am therefore indebted to the archivists and staff of numerous libraries and record offices, and in particular to those of the British Library, the Bodleian Library, and the Cambridge University Library, for access to these collections.

For access to and permission to quote from documents in which they own the copyright, I am grateful to the following: The Duke of Devonshire and the Trustees of the Chatsworth Settlement; the Marquis of Ripon Trust; the Earl of Derby, M C; the Earl Fortescue; the Earl of Halifax; the Earl of Kimberley; the Earl of Northbrook; the Earl of Selborne; the Earl of Shelburne and the Trustees of the Bowood Manuscripts; the Viscount Esher; Sir Richard Dyke Acland, Bt.; Sir John Dilke, Bt.; Sir William Gladstone, Bt.; Major Kingscote; Mr Keith Adam; Mr Patrick Gordon-Duff-Pennington, M B E; Mrs Gilbert Elliot and the Trustees of the National Library of Scotland; the hon. Mrs Crispin Gascoigne; Mrs Grace James; the Librarian of the House of Commons; the University of Birmingham; the University of Sheffield; the Lincolnshire Archives Office, and the Northamptonshire Record Office.

I would like to thank the Cambridge University Press for permission to use in this book material from an article of mine which was published in the *Historical Journal* in 1984.

The research for the dissertation on which this book is based was initially funded by the Department of Education and Science, and I have since received financial assistance from Corpus Christi College, Cambridge, the Cambridge Historical Society, and the British Academy.

Finally, I would like to express my thanks to Dr Paul Gurowich and Dr Boyd Hilton, who have offered valuable advice on parts of the book, and to Professor Richard Shannon and Dr Peter Clarke, who examined the original dissertation. I have also benefited in various ways from conversations with Mr Graham Goodlad and Mr John Spain. Above all, I am under an immense debt of gratitude to Professor Derek Beales, my research supervisor, who has continued to provide encouragement and support during the difficult period in which this book was completed.

                                                              T.A.J.

CONTENTS

A NOTE ON REFERENCES

The abbreviation BL Add. MSS is used throughout to denote the British Library Additional Manuscripts series. NLS MSS refers to the National Library of Scotland Manuscripts series. In references to primary sources only the first folio number of the document is given. The place of publication of printed works is London unless otherwise stated.

Introduction

W. E. Gladstone's attempt to carry a measure of home rule for Ireland in 1886 split the Liberal party and led to the formation of an alliance between the dissentient Liberals and the Conservatives which was to dominate the political scene for twenty years. The purpose of this book is to re-examine the background to what was clearly an event of profound importance to late nineteenth-century British politics, but it seeks to do so not merely by tracing the 'origins' of the Liberal schism, but by establishing a broad chronological context within which the home rule crisis of the mid-1880s can be rendered intelligible. One compelling reason for adopting this approach is the need, in my opinion, to restore the role of 'Whiggery' to its true significance in Liberal politics, and, in the process, to offer a reassessment of Gladstone's leadership of the party. This study begins, therefore, with the fall of Gladstone's first ministry in February 1874, his subsequent resignation of the Liberal leadership, and his replacement by the Whig duumvirate of Granville and Hartington. The forces of Radicalism, represented at the highest level by such men as Bright, Chamberlain, and Dilke, will not be ignored, but set in their proper place as one aspect—a crucial one, to be sure—of the relationship between Gladstone and the Whigs.

The emphasis placed in this book upon 'Whiggery' stems from a view of the nature of the Victorian Liberal party and, more broadly, of Liberal politics, which differs from those presented in the existing literature. According to the more traditional of these views, which continues to find favour with students of Radicalism, the Liberal party was chronically divided, with substantial Whig and Radical 'wings' which were bound to pull apart, and which were only prevented from doing so for so long because of the unique cohesive influence of Gladstone.[1] Alternatively, there is the view put forward in an influential book by Professor Vincent, which holds that the

---

[1] T. W. Heyck, *The Dimensions of British Radicalism: The Case of Ireland, 1874–1895* (Illinois, 1974), 90, 115. For a similar view of the Liberal party, see Michael Barker, *Gladstone and Radicalism: The Reconstruction of Liberal Policy in Britain, 1885–94* (Hassocks, 1975), 11–24.

Liberal party, in the 1860s, and apparently beyond, was essentially a rather vague 'community of sentiment', and that the majority of Liberal MPs were men 'whose common Liberalism amounted to little more than a common good nature'.[2] Vincent argues that there was no distinct Liberal creed or programme and that the few intra-party groups that did exist 'were small and not necessarily troublesome'.[3] The back-bench Whigs, in particular, accounted for only a tiny proportion of the parliamentary party.[4] Consequently, the idea of a confrontation between 'two large blocs of Whigs and Radicals' is dismissed as a myth, part of the rhetoric employed by Chamberlain in the 1870s to further his own ends.[5] The bulk of MPs from all social and economic backgrounds were, it seems, merged together into a docile, politically indeterminate, 'Liberal plain'.[6] Vincent's view has been endorsed by Professor Hamer, who, in attempting the only general survey of Liberal politics in the late nineteenth century, felt justified in disregarding the Whigs almost entirely.[7]

It would seem desirable, since this book departs from the prevailing historiography of the Liberal party in assigning a much more important role to 'Whiggery', to attempt to elucidate the meaning of that term, and then to examine both its presumed antithesis, 'Radicalism', and that still more elusive concept, 'Liberalism'.

Professor Vincent's belief that 'Whiggery' was virtually non-existent rests upon his analysis of the Liberal front bench, those whom he calls the 'Public men'. In his view, when men entered Liberal Cabinets they left their social and economic backgrounds behind them (sharing as they all did a high ideal of administrative purity), and although most Cabinet ministers were connected to the aristocratic and landowning classes, they tended to be the 'poor cousins' or else derived part of their income from non-landed

---

[2] John Vincent, *The Formation of the British Liberal Party, 1857–68* (1976 edn., Hassocks), 257–8. Although Professor Vincent is dealing mainly with the 1860s, his analysis of the parliamentary party extends to 1874, and he also states (p. xlvii) that it is possible to obtain a 'fairly comprehensive view of nineteenth century Liberalism from one decade of its heyday alone'.

[3] Ibid. 257–8.

[4] Ibid. 20–5. According to Vincent, only twenty-seven members from 'historic' Whig families sat in the parliaments between 1859 and 1874.

[5] Ibid., pp. xlviii, 3–4, 20.

[6] Ibid. 25–7.

[7] D. A. Hamer, *Liberal Politics in the Age of Gladstone and Rosebery* (Oxford, 1972), p. xiv.

sources, with the result that they actually shared a 'fellow-feeling for the resentment of others' towards those classes.[8] However, while Vincent is undoubtedly right to stress the prevailing administrative ethic on the Liberal front bench, we should not suppose that this affected in any way their aristocratic outlook. To say, as Vincent does, that men like Palmerston, Russell, and Clarendon were first and foremost town politicians may be true, but no one would ever have doubted that their sympathies were entirely aristocratic. Granville's wealth may have come from the iron industry rather than from landownership, but as one of his colleagues observed, 'no man was ever more thoroughly aristocratic in manners and character of mind; as well as by birth'.[9] Similarly, as the character portrait in Chapter 3 will show, it would be a serious mistake to think that because the property to which he was the heir was industrial as well as agricultural, Hartington's intellectual make-up was altered by one degree.

The 'Whiggery' that, I would suggest, still existed, and that contemporaries certainly believed existed, in the Liberal party of the 1870s and 1880s was a tradition of aristocratic leadership. It was still an immense advantage to be able to enter politics at any early age, as the case of Hartington illustrates: elected to the House of Commons at the age of 24, he was given junior office at 30 and attained Cabinet rank at 33. What had changed over the years was that these 'Whigs' had lost much of the petulance and cliquishness of their early nineteenth-century predecessors like the Greys and Russells. The virtual monopoly of office after the Corn Law crisis of 1846 had established the Whig-Liberal party,[10] with its advocacy of free trade and its belief in the efficacy of gradual reform, as the party of responsible administration, and 'Whiggery' had therefore developed a reputation for sound and dispassionate government by

---

[8] Vincent, *Formation of Liberal Party*, pp. 11–20. Vincent depicts the Whig peerage as a group largely remote from the rest of the Liberal Party.

[9] Lord Derby's diary, 1 Jan. 1883, Derby MSS.

[10] The generic term 'Liberal', reflecting shared principles of liberty and toleration in civil and religious matters, gradually came into fashion during the 1830s and 1840s as a substitute for the old labels of 'Whig' and 'Reformer', and the crisis of 1846 seems to mark the decisive point. For instance, *The Times* began to talk of 'the Liberals' (e.g. 9 Feb. 1846, p. 7, 8 June 1846, p. 5), and whereas *Dod's Parliamentary Companion* for 1845 listed only seventy-five MPs as Liberals, the edition for the new parliament in 1847 listed 163, and shows that very few newly elected MPs were using the old labels, with the result that these had virtually died out by 1857. Of course, the acceptance of a common name did not necessarily make the party any more homogeneous than before.

absorbing into its ranks men of talent from a variety of backgrounds. Of the 'Whigs' who were flourishing in the 1870s, Hartington, Granville, and Spencer represented a more or less untainted Whiggery, but Lords Kimberley and Ripon were descended from Tory families, while Argyll and Selborne were both Peelites, and Northbrook was from a financial family. 'Whiggery' was so all-inclusive that contemporaries continued to refer to it as though it meant virtually the whole of the Liberal front bench.[11]

The close identification of 'Whiggery' with the official wing of the Liberal party is of crucial importance for our understanding of its relationship to the rest of the parliamentary party. Contemporaries frequently referred to 'the Whig and moderate party', or 'the Whigs and moderate Liberals', or 'the Whigs and moderate men', indicating that while the aristocratic Whigs were still thought of as a distinct group who supplied much of the party's front-bench material, they were for this same reason regarded as the central nucleus of a much broader phenomenon, 'moderate Liberalism'. For all practical purposes the term 'Whig' was synonymous with 'moderate Liberal',[12] embracing the majority of MPs who were not 'Radicals'. 'Whiggery', in other words, was indistinguishable from that section of the party whom Professor Vincent argues constituted the 'Liberal plain'. The common outlook shared by the official Whigs and the bulk of moderate Liberal MPs[13] explains why it was that there was no regular, organized 'Whig section' on the back benches. 'Whig' revolts against the party leadership did take place, but they were *ad hoc* affairs (prompted by the issues of foreign policy in 1878 and Irish policy in 1880–2), and were generally resorted to with considerable reluctance. Moreover, such revolts were capable of attracting wide-

[11] For example, Hartington's private secretary, observing the attacks on the Beaconsfield administration by the Liberal front bench, wrote of the 'amiableness of the present set of Whigs', Reginald Brett's diary, 18 Dec. 1878, Esher MSS, 2/5. Cf. Dilke's Diary, 23 Nov. 1880, BL Add. MSS 43924: 'If we extinguish the present Whigs, and become the next Whigs ourselves . . .'. Men like Childers and Goschen were certainly hard to distinguish from their more truly aristocratic 'Whig' colleagues. Even individual Radicals like Forster came to look more and more Whiggish once they had joined the front bench. John Bright was an obvious exception, as he was promoted to the front bench because of the weight he carried as a Radical leader.
[12] It will be noticed that, for stylistic reasons, I have myself used the terms 'Whig' and 'moderate' as though they were synonymous.
[13] A point that has been noted by Hugh Berrington, 'Partisanship and Dissidence in the Nineteenth Century House of Commons', *Parliamentary Affairs*, 21 (1967–8), 361–2.

spread support or sympathy from within the Liberal party, and this demonstrates how misleading is Vincent's application of a very narrow definition to the back-bench Whigs—those who were descended from 'historic' Whig families.[14] Such a definition has little real meaning in any case, for few families could boast a record of uninterrupted affiliation to the Whig or Liberal party, and since the term Whig had not been used, earlier in the nineteenth century, to denote exclusively the representatives of 'historic' Whig families,[15] there seems no reason to confine the label just to those whose ancestors had been martyred two hundred years earlier or had been supporters of Charles James Fox, or to those who were descendants of the fecund Lord Gower of the mid-eighteenth century (himself originally a Tory).

Some measure of the Whigs' potential constituency may be gained from an analysis of the social composition of the parliamentary Liberal party as it stood after the general election in February 1874. Of the 241 MPs who remain after the necessary adjustments have been made,[16] we find that twenty-six were members of the nobility, that is to say, they were the heirs, younger sons, or brothers of peers of the realm. Lord Kensington, an Irish peer, is counted in this group. A further twenty-one MPs were baronets, sixteen of them possessing substantial landed estates which were entered in John Bateman's survey of *The Great Landowners of Great Britain and Ireland* (1879 and 1883 editions),[17] and six more MPs were the sons of baronets. A total of fifty-five MPs may therefore be classed as members of the 'titled aristocracy'. Bateman also listed thirty-six other Liberals as 'great landowners', and an additional thirteen, who did not so qualify, were listed as the heads of families in *Burke's Landed Gentry* (6th edition, 1879).[18] If the above categories of aristocrats, great

---

[14] Vincent, *Formation of Liberal Party*, pp. 20–5.

[15] In the 1830s, *Dod's Parliamentary Companion* used the term to describe anyone who was a general supporter of the Grey and Melbourne ministries.

[16] All of the Irish home rulers, nominal or committed, have been excluded from the reckoning. *Dod's Parliamentary Companion* for 1874 mistakenly listed two Conservatives (Elcho and Wilmot) as Liberals and omitted one Liberal (Cardwell) who was elected but then raised to the peerage. The effect of election petitions was to deprive eight Liberals of their seats, but five new members were returned at the ensuing by-elections.

[17] Bateman drew a minimum qualifying line of 3,000 acres or a rental of £2,000 p.a. for an entry in his book.

[18] Twenty-five of the thirty-six 'great landowners' were listed by Burke as members of the landed gentry.

landowners, and landed gentry are taken as an approximation to the strength of what might be called the 'aristocratic-landowning' section of the Liberal party, we have a total of 104 MPs, or about 43.1 per cent of the parliamentary party. The second main social group was made up of those MPs who, according to their entries in *Dod's Parliamentary Companion*, either were, or had been, engaged in industry or commerce. This group includes not only manufacturers and merchants, but also mine and quarry owners, railway directors, shipowners, brewers, engineers, and a wholesale stationer. A total of eighty-four MPs, or 35.2 per cent of the parliamentary party, could thus be counted as belonging to the 'industrialists and merchants' group, although eighteen of these (21 per cent) overlapped with the 'aristocratic-landowning' group.[19] This overlap reflects not only the fact that successful businessmen were acquiring landed estates, but that it was by this time considered desirable to reward them with hereditary titles (although usually only a baronetcy).[20] A third group, members of the legal profession, accounted for fifty-six Liberals (23.2 per cent of the parliamentary party),[21] but the overlap here with the 'aristocratic-landowning' section was even more considerable, amounting to nineteen (34 per cent) of the 'lawyers'. Indeed, it is certain that a fair number of these 'lawyers' never practised their profession. There can be no suggestion, of course, that political divisions within the parliamentary Liberal party were related simply to the social and economic background of MPs, and the official Whigs had in any case to act as leaders of the party as a whole rather than of one section, as the study of the Granville–Hartington leadership in Chapter 3 shows clearly. It is sufficient, for our present purpose, to observe that the aristocratic and landowning classes, those who were most likely to be sympathetic to the Whig tradition

---

[19] I have had to exclude from the above figures a number of MPs who are not easy to categorize. These include eight men from financial families (a diverse group, including Rothschild, Goschen, Lubbock, and Kinnaird), five members or ex-members of the army (no other information being available about them), two working-men's representatives, two doctors of medicine, a chemist, an accountant, a university professor, a farmer, a land agent, an ex-publisher, and an ex-Congregationalist minister. There are also a handful of MPs for whom no information could be found in the reference works consulted.

[20] See Granville's letters to Gladstone, 8 Aug., 23 Sept., 13 Oct. 1869, in Agatha Ramm (ed.), *The Political Correspondence of Mr Gladstone and Lord Granville, 1868–1876* (Camden Society, 81–2; 1952), i. 43, 59, 67.

[21] Fifteen Queen's Counsel, thirty-six other barristers, and five solicitors or attorneys. Based on *Dod's Parliamentary Companion*.

of leadership, still formed the largest social group within the parliamentary Liberal party in 1874, and continued to do so until 1885.

Clearly, the Whigs must be accorded a more central place in Liberal politics than has been allowed by other scholars. The Whigs in fact retained a clear notion of their traditional political function, which was to act as the leaders and educators of 'the people', keeping in check the pressures emanating from Radicalism and extra-parliamentary agitation, and guiding those energies into constructive, but safe, channels. Hartington, in a speech at Accrington in December 1883, gave the classic description of this regulating function:

I confess I am not dissatisfied with the position that the Whig party have in former times occupied, and that I believe they occupy at the present time. I admit that the Whigs are not the leaders in popular movements, but the Whigs have been able, as I think, to the great advantage of the Country, to direct, and guide, and moderate those popular movements. They have formed a connecting link between the advanced party and those classes which, possessing property, power and influence, are naturally averse to change, and I think I may claim that it is greatly owing to their guidance and to their action that the great and beneficial changes, which have been made in the direction of popular reform in this Country, have been made not by the shock of revolutionary agitation, but by the calm and peaceful process of constitutional acts.[22]

In private, it could safely be admitted that a coalition between the Whigs and the Conservatives would be undesirable because it would put an end to the 'tacit understanding between the leaders on both sides' which had so much to do 'with the smooth working of our complex political system', and because the violence and bitterness which such a coalition would introduce into the party system could only be to the ultimate advantage of the Radicals.[23]

By the very nature of things, then, 'Whiggery' had to be a relative concept. Although contemporaries still spoke of 'Whig principles', these were really of a historic nature, relating to the need to limit both

[22] Cited by Bernard Holland, *Life of Spencer Compton, Eighth Duke of Devonshire, 1833–1908* (1911), i. 405–6. See also the interesting comments in Bernard Mallet, *Thomas George, Earl of Northbrook: A Memoir* (1908), 32–3.

[23] Ethel Drus (ed.), *A Journal of Events during the Gladstone Ministry, 1868–1874, by John, First Earl of Kimberley* (Camden Miscellany, 21; 1958), 1, entry for 8 Dec. 1868. Cf. Lord Spencer to Lord Elcho, 21 Jan. 1867, in Peter Gordon (ed.), *The Red Earl: The Papers of the Fifth Earl Spencer, 1835–1910*, i (Northants Record Society, 31; 1981), 59–61.

the sovereign and the democratic power, and to promote civil and religious freedom. A far more vital 'Whig principle' was the continuing belief in the capacity of the traditional ruling class to govern.[24] Lord Coleridge, in his observation of the House of Lords in 1877, was struck by:

The intense 'feudalism' of our great Liberal chiefs, such as the Duke of Argyll, combined with very free opinions on all things which don't touch themselves . . . Granville, who represents them very well, is, I think, very careless about *what* is done, so long as *they*, the great nobles, have the doing of it; and he is firmly resolved, I think, that they *shall* have the doing of it from that proud yet perfectly natural and unaffected belief in themselves and their power, as a fact in the Country.[25]

In practice, the Whigs necessarily obtained their definition of themselves partly by reaction to the activities and opinions of the advanced section of the Liberal party, and the essential characteristic of 'Whiggery' was a remarkable absence of doctrinaire thinking, as Sir Alfred Pease, the self-styled 'last of the Whigs', recalled: 'They believed that Government was a practical thing, and did not exist to furnish a spectacle of uniformity nor to comply with logic, arithmetic, or the theories of visionary politicians.'[26] Even when their inclinations appeared to be essentially conservative, this was compensated for by a strong sense of their inherited Liberal traditions, and by an element of political pragmatism.

---

[24] This point is illustrated nicely by the young Reginald Brett's letter to his friend Albert Grey, the heir to one of the great Whig titles, who had recently graduated from Cambridge: 'What by tradition you ought to be is the noblest position for a man in this Country—a Whig. You may be a republican in France and a supporter of tyranny in Egypt and yet perfectly consistent with your principles—for your motto should be . . . "I am content to govern and *will* govern while I am endeavouring to teach and instruct". A Whig has no fear of the people or of party cries. He merely says of all reforms "Prove your case and I go with you: until then I am content to rule, but will help you and think well of your opponents"', 5 Jan. 1874, Grey MSS, 222/5.

[25] Lord Coleridge to Sir William Heathcote, 8 June 1877, in E. H. Coleridge, *Life and Correspondence of John Duke, Lord Coleridge, Lord Chief Justice of England* (1904), ii. 267–8.

[26] Alfred E. Pease, *Elections and Recollections* (1932), p. xiii. Curiously enough, Pease was a member of the Quaker banking family. The essentially practical nature of Whig administrators is reflected in the way one of them, who had been an Indian Viceroy, justified his acquiescence in the Irish Land Act of 1881: 'under the circumstances I confess I see no other way out of the difficulty . . . Perhaps . . . from having had to put aside the abstract doctrines of Political economy not infrequently in India, I am become rather lax in my views', Northbrook to Halifax, 30 July 1881, Hickleton MSS, A4/54a.

It was generally recognized, albeit with some reluctance, that politicians had to come to terms with the new 'democracy' created by the Conservatives in 1867, and adapt themselves to the methods which a more broadly based and increasingly complex political system demanded. One striking illustration of this process of adaptation is the way that, during the second half of the 1870s, leaders like Hartington found themselves making more and more frequent appearances on the public platform, in response to the expectations of an enlarged electorate and, more specifically, of the new constituency organizations. There were important implications, too, for the formation of policy. After a speech made by Hartington in 1877, on the question of Scottish Church disestablishment, Lord Halifax, one of the most sagacious of the older generation of Whigs, expressed his belief that:

> many of us old public men must make up our minds to see public questions dealt with in a very different fashion from the days of our youth. The people generally were ignorant in those days and the old Whigs were far in advance of the people . . . Now the people are more educated—all public questions are fully and universally discussed in the press as soon as they can be considered and before they can be taken up by the heads of parties. It may not be wise to *say* it, but in practice it cannot be helped. Public opinion will direct the course of public men—it may to a great extent be formed by them—but able writers in the public press will do much more than any man can do in Parliament.[27]

Evidently, the Whigs were conscious of the power of extra-parliamentary forces which were to some extent beyond their control, but, while this suggests that an exclusively 'high political' approach to late nineteenth-century history has certain limitations, it would be equally misleading to assume a crudely deterministic relationship between 'high' and 'low' politics. In fact, the process by which politicians tried to gauge what those outside their own sphere felt and wanted was highly impressionistic and imprecise, as is shown by their difficulty in interpreting the electoral vicissitudes of our period. Although it is now common to think of the period between the second and third reform acts as the 'classic age of the two-party system', the notion of a natural 'swing of the pendulum' —successive general elections producing large majorities first for one party, then the other, so that they alternated in office—was very slow

[27] Halifax to Lord Fortescue, 'Christmas day 1877', Fortescue MSS, FC 126.

to enter into contemporary thinking.[28] To contemporaries, it appeared that the Conservatives' 'leap in the dark' in 1867 had injected a regrettable degree of instability into the political system,[29] but the difficulty which politicians experienced in trying to comprehend the ways of the new 'democracy' played an important part in sustaining highly subjective interpretations of the fluctuations in party fortunes, which could sometimes work to the Whigs' advantage. The Conservative electoral victory in 1874, for instance, was believed to mark the end of 'Gladstonian Liberalism' and the beginnings of a new dispensation in which a Whig leadership was best suited to the Liberal party. The equally unexpected Liberal victory in 1880 destroyed this illusion and brought 'Gladstonianism' back to the fore, but the party's failure to secure the widely anticipated landslide majority in 1885 was considered to have strengthened the position of the Whigs, which had come under threat from 'Chamberlainite Radicalism'.

Moreover, the Whigs were able to justify the influence which they exerted within the Liberal party by appealing to an allegedly substantial body of 'moderate opinion' in the country as a whole. Thus, according to the *Edinburgh Review*, a long-established organ of Whiggery, the Whigs represented the 'left centre' of politics, reflecting 'the principles and opinions of the great mass of intelligence and liberality in the Country'—namely, a devotion to the principle of freedom, tempered by an equally strong aversion to 'rash and violent innovations'. The Whigs, therefore, represented 'not a clique or coterie of aristocratic statesmen but the pith and marrow of the nation'.[30] For this reason, the *Edinburgh Review* asserted, 'in the Whig party lies the centre of gravity of Liberal politics in England', for without this 'central nucleus, guiding and controlling the rest', the process of gradual reform would come to a halt and the Liberal party would in all likelihood 'crumble into noisy powerless sections'.[31]

---

[28] The term 'swing of the pendulum' does not appear to have been commonly used until 1885; see e.g. the leading article in the *Pall Mall Gazette*, 24 Nov. 1885, p. 1.

[29] 'However what Demos may do, I think the wisest man cannot foretell. What seems pretty certain is that he is sure before long to veer round entirely. Uncertainty and instability are a growing danger in English politics', Kimberley to Ripon, 3 Sept. 1881, BL Add. MSS 43522, fo. 269.

[30] [Henry Reeve], 'Plain Whig Principles', *Edinburgh Review*, 151 (Jan. 1880), 257–80.

[31] [Reeve], 'The Past and the Future of the Whig Party', ibid. 139 (Apr. 1874), 544–73. For a further statement, see [Reeve], 'A Whig Retort' ibid. 155 (Jan. 1882), 279–90.

The Whigs claimed, in other words, to represent the 'national' element in Liberal politics,[32] and Hartington frequently invoked this against the 'faddists', groups such as the Liberation Society and the United Kingdom Alliance, whose activities sometimes threatened to disrupt the unity of the party: 'Let me remind you that political party is an engine not merely for the carrying of this or that reform—not merely for removal of this or that abuse; it is an engine the object of which is to form the opinion and guide the destinies of the nation.'[33]

If the Whig tradition of leadership demanded a strategy of remaining within the Liberal party in order to exercise a restraining influence over the Radicals, the prospects for pursuing this successfully were greatly assisted by the lack of coherence amongst the Radicals themselves. This is not to deny the existence of a substantial body of Liberal MPs who were more or less resentful of the established political élite,[34] and who claimed to stand, in some special sense, for certain ideals of justice and humanity—notably with regard to 'oppressed nationalities'—and for the moral elevation of the individual.[35] All too often, however, such attitudes bred suspicion of any assertion of authority by the State, both in domestic and more especially in foreign affairs, which led to a purely negative and destructive outlook providing no basis for the policy of a government. What was missing was a clear Radical, as distinct from Liberal, philosophy which might have provided a positive basis for

[32] Cf. G. C. Brodrick, 'Liberals and Whigs', *Fortnightly Review*, 137 (May 1878), 729–40.
[33] Hartington at Keighley, *Manchester Guardian*, 4 Nov. 1876, p. 8.
[34] It is certainly a mistake to minimize the strength of Radicalism in the way that Professor Vincent has for the parliaments sitting between 1859 and 1874. Vincent claims that in these three parliaments together only fifty-four out of 456 Liberal MPs sitting for English constituencies can be regarded as Radicals, of whom twenty were 'secular Radicals' of the Cobden and Bright variety, and thirty-four were 'militant businessmen', mostly Dissenters like Samuel Morley, who had 'a sense of mission' (we are not told how this distinguishing characteristic is ascertained). Vincent, *Formation of Liberal Party*, pp. 3, 28–39. The major weakness in Vincent's analysis of the parliamentary party is that he treats as entirely separate categories from the Radicals both the lawyers, who, he claims, had a close affinity with the aristocratic establishment and were concerned only with professional advancement, and the Scottish, Welsh, and Irish MPs, whom he depicts as being preoccupied with parochial issues. Ibid. 3, 39–53.
[35] For an illustration of this mentality, see A. Tilney Bassett, *The Life of the Rt. Hon. John Edward Ellis, M.P.* (1914). We find in such men a strong emphasis on the improvement of the individual through education and sobriety, rather than through collectivist measures.

political action, a point that is reflected in the fact that contemporary definitions of 'Radicalism' or a 'Radical' usually amounted to nothing more than 'Liberalism very much alive' or 'one who is in earnest'.[36] As T. H. S. Escott, a journalist ally of Joseph Chamberlain, observed, 'Liberalism and Radicalism are only varying modes of the same political agency. The difference between them is one, not of principle, but of chronology.'[37] The literal overthrow of the ruling élite was never a realistic objective, and there is little evidence to suggest that most Radicals even desired to see the Whigs driven out of the Liberal party. Dr Heyck, who claims that this was their objective, is less than convincing when he relies upon a quotation of Richard Cobden to prove his case, for as Professor Vincent has rightly argued, Cobden's 'system' of politics, based upon hostility towards aristocratic government in all its manifestations, was never generally embraced by Radical Liberals.[38]

Far from being an irresistible force destined to sweep the Whigs into oblivion (or the Conservative party), Victorian Radicalism was itself prone to grave weakness through its frequent lack of any clear objective on which to focus its energies. Except on those occasions when an emotive—but entirely negative—cry such as opposition to 'Beaconsfieldism' could be raised, the energies of Radicalism were liable to be diffused, and the vision of its adherents restricted, by the tendency for individual MPs, and more especially for groups in the constituencies, to become preoccupied with specific 'fads', such as temperance reform, Church disestablishment, non-denominational education, opposition to the Contagious Diseases Acts, or opposition to compulsory vaccination. The so-called 'revolt of the Nonconformists' against the Gladstone ministry during the early 1870s, when the supporters of the National Education League, the Liberation Society, and the UK Alliance withheld their votes from Liberal by-election candidates who would not give the required pledges, provides a clear illustration of the determination of the 'faddist'

---

[36] F. W. Hirst, *Early Life and Letters of John Morley* (1927), ii. 226; J. Davidson, *Eminent Radicals In and Out of Parliament* (1880), 9–18 (quoting Gladstone). It is interesting to note that in *Dod's Parliamentary Companion* for 1874, only six MPs are actually described as 'Radicals'. About a score of others are listed as 'advanced Liberals', while many more, subscribing to similar views on particular policies, were content with the appellation 'Liberal'.

[37] T. H. S. Escott, *Politics and Letters* (1886), 63.

[38] Heyck, *Dimensions of Radicalism*, p. 6; Vincent, *Formation of Liberal Party*, pp. 31–5.

groups, at times, to put their own cause before the interests of the party as a whole.[39] It was largely because of their individual association with one of a variety of specific causes that the rivalry and jealousy amongst Radical M Ps was so intense, while the competition between the various sectional organizations, beyond Westminster, to gain priority for their own 'fad' also created friction.[40] Furthermore, what is often overlooked, there was considerable rivalry and hostility between the provincial cities: Manchester, Birmingham, Leeds, Bradford, and Newcastle each had its own distinct identity and powerful sense of civic pride and independence, with which its 'Liberalism' was closely bound up.

The central theme of Joseph Chamberlain's career in Liberal politics may be seen as the attempt to transcend the narrow, sectional organizations of Radicalism and its parliamentary representatives by establishing a broadly based Radical movement appealing to a wide range of advanced opinions. This concern was reflected, of course, in the creation of the National Liberal Federation in 1877: a collection of local Liberal organizations, supposedly democratic in their structures, uniting together to decide upon a common programme which could then be presented to the official party leaders.[41] But Chamberlain's efforts to impose order and discipline upon the Radical factions and so create a formidable weapon with which to strengthen his own position within the existing Liberal hierarchy were themselves probably doomed to failure because of the very nature of the materials with which he was trying to work. 'Chamberlainite Radicalism' was, after all, in essence Birmingham Radicalism trying to dictate policy to the rest, as Chamberlain's letter to one of his henchmen, during the preparations for the foundation of the National Liberal Federation, shows very clearly: 'I think it is a great mistake to ask Manchester and Leeds to join Birmingham in starting the Federation . . . if these two associations are joined with us they will seriously hamper our action, and they will claim equal representation on all the committees of the federation, and this would render

[39] For the activities of the National Education League and the UK Alliance in the years 1871–3, see D. A. Hamer, *The Politics of Electoral Pressure* (Hassocks, 1977), 122–39, 179–99. For the Liberation Society, see S. M. Ingham, 'The Disestablishment Movement in England, 1868–74', *Journal of Religious History*, 3 (1964–5), 38–60.
[40] See Hamer, *Liberal Politics*, pp. 1–33.
[41] Ibid. 46–54.

prompt and united action an impossibility in the future'.[42] As a Sheffield MP rightly suspected, Chamberlain's idea was that 'Birmingham is to pull the strings of the Liberal Boroughs, and the puppets are to dance in response to the wires', and that therefore issues would be taken up, or neglected, 'as Birmingham deems desirable, and Chamberlain moves Birmingham'.[43] The proud Liberalism of the great northern cities was never to take kindly to dictation of this sort, and the resulting hostility partly explains why Chamberlain lost control of the National Liberal Federation in 1886. Chamberlain was never successful in establishing a commanding position for himself over an organized Radical 'wing' of the Liberal party, and in fact, the elderly and inert John Bright continued to enjoy far greater personal influence and prestige in the country as a whole.[44] The tendency among biographers and historians to exaggerate the extent of Chamberlain's power, and to dwell upon the antagonistic side of his relations with the Whigs, has served to obscure the crucial point that (along with most other Radicals) he generally recognized the need to co-operate with them.

With the considerable flexibility of 'Whiggery' and the lack of clear purpose in 'Radicalism', it is perhaps unsurprising to note the absence of any very clear definition of 'Liberalism' itself. At times, this vagueness could be a source of some embarrassment to the party. During the protracted general election campaign of 1885, for example, the *Pall Mall Gazette* derived much amusement from its efforts to discover the essential tenets of the Liberal creed. In a leading article on 19 August, the Revd George Brooks described how he had asked a number of prominent Liberals what they thought the fundamental principles of 'Liberalism' were, where these principles were best stated, and who the chief exponent of them was. Most, including Gladstone, Bright, Hartington, Morley, Cowen, Derby,

---

[42] Chamberlain to Jesse Collings, 2 Mar. 1877, Chamberlain MSS, JC5/16/64. In the event, Leeds did participate in the inauguration of the National Liberal Federation, but the Manchester-based National Reform Union continued to operate independently for some years: H. J. Hanham, *Elections and Party Management* (1978 edn., Hassocks), 147–54. London and Scotland also had separate associations, ibid. 139, 159. As late as 1884, only a minority of English and Welsh borough organizations were affiliated to the National Liberal Federation, ibid. 139.

[43] A. J. Mundella to Robert Leader, 5, 23 June 1877, Mundella-Leader MSS, 6P/67. In another letter, dated 20 June, ibid., Mundella reported that Chamberlain's activities had aroused much resentment amongst Liberal borough MPs.

[44] Cf. Roland Quinault, 'John Bright and Joseph Chamberlain', *Historical Journal*, 28 (1985), 623–46.

and Forster, declined to prepare a reply, on the grounds that they were too busy. Forster, however, did add that 'if you ever take part in practical politics you will find that you will not have time for abstract definitions, and you will also be surprised that the request to give these should be made by a stranger'. Among the other negative replies was one from Goschen, who observed that 'The question as to the fundamental principles of any political party is one of unending controversy, and I do not think it can be treated or that it has been treated in the precise and scientific form which your letter suggests. If there were any work in which the principles of Liberalism were fully and clearly stated, I would have directed you to it, but I know of none.' Lord Sherbrooke (Robert Lowe), in typically forthright manner, wrote that 'I am unable to answer the questions which you ask me, for the simple reason that no two people agree as to what Liberalism is, or where it is to be found. Till that is discovered all inquiries of this kind are merely beating the air.' W. S. Caine's classic reply, on a postcard, was as follows: 'To make it easy for men to do right, and difficult to do wrong—this is the fundament of true Liberalism.' Only the Duke of Argyll provided a full reply, though he emphasized that he could 'only answer for my own understanding of a word which in itself is necessarily very vague': he stressed the principle of liberty and opposition to tyranny, but in any case preferred the term 'Liberality'—'that habit and disposition of mind which keeps our reason and our hearts open to all suggestions from the past and to all aspirations from the future, tending to promote the welfare and happiness of all mankind'.[45]

Brooks's article, and the correspondence in the *Pall Mall Gazette* arising from it, seems to have provided the stimulus for an attempt by Andrew Reid, a Liberal propagandist, to remedy the deficiency of definitions of 'Liberalism' in a book, *Why I am a Liberal*, published in October 1885. The result cannot be said to be philosophically enlightening, but Reid's collection of definitions does point to one conclusion, that for most active Liberals, their 'Liberalism' was more an attitude of mind than a set of doctrines with a clearly agreed application to current problems. The most common idea was that society was in a constant state of evolution, with 'progress' being considered both inevitable and essential if society was to prosper: as Chamberlain put it, 'Progress is the law of the world—Liberalism is

---

[45] *Pall Mall Gazette*, 19 Aug. 1885, pp. 1–2.

the expression of this law in politics'.[46] 'Progress', in this sense, was generally understood to involve the securing of equal political rights (not to be confused with equality) to all classes, the removal of restrictions upon individual liberty, and the widest possible extension of the right to self-government.[47] The Liberal party was the best instrument for ensuring social progress, as it alone was capable of transcending the interests and prejudices of the various classes in the State and of acting instead in the interests of the nation as a whole.[48] There was an underlying belief in the essential goodness of 'the people', or at least in their capacity for improvement, but it was also clearly understood that the masses needed guidance from their social superiors, a belief exemplified in Gladstone's own maxim that 'The principle of Liberalism is trust in the people, qualified by prudence.'[49] Professor Blackie presumably had the same idea in mind when he suggested to the *Pall Mall Gazette* that Liberalism represented 'liberty and progress' and Conservatism 'authority and stability', and that good government was to be found 'in the balance of the two forces'.[50] It appears, then, that few Liberals shared John Stuart Mill's Utopian belief in the ultimate creation of an ideal State based on a rational consensus of Liberal principles and the elimination of class barriers,[51] most being content simply with the prospect of continual improvement expressed in Shaw Lefevre's dictum that Liberalism was 'necessarily progressive, for its aims advance as it succeeds in approaching them'.[52]

Neither of the existing perspectives on Liberal politics, the one assuming a schismatic destiny, the other seeing little more than a

---

[46] Andrew Reid (ed.), *Why I am a Liberal* [1885], 15. Cf. the definitions by Lord Dalhousie, p. 42, Lubbock, pp. 71–3, Playfair, pp. 79–80, Stansfeld, pp. 93–6.

[47] Ibid., definitions by Broadhurst, p. 35, Hopwood, pp. 60–1, Shaw Lefevre, pp. 83–4. Cf. Hartington's speech at Darwen, *The Times*, 26 Oct. 1885, p. 7.

[48] Ibid., definitions by Heneage, p. 56, Shaw Lefevre, pp. 83–4. Cf. Hartington's speech at Nelson, *The Times*, 2 Nov. 1885, p. 8. According to Lord Selborne, who would have concurred with the Duke of Argyll, 'If Liberality in politics (I hate all *isms*) means anything, it means a principle sufficiently disinterested and large minded to prefer the interests of the Country to those of party, and patriotism to the very poor ambition of office', Selborne to Arthur Elliot, 24 Jan. 1886, Elliot MSS.

[49] Reid, *Why I am a Liberal*, p. 13.

[50] *Pall Mall Gazette*, 22 Aug. 1885, p. 6.

[51] For an exception, see Robert Wallace, 'The Philosophy of Liberalism', *Nineteenth Century*, 9 (Feb. 1881), 302–23. Even Wallace, however, believed there was a need for a leisured ruling class, and that inequality could be justified on utilitarian grounds. He became a Liberal MP in 1886.

[52] Reid, *Why I am a Liberal*, pp. 83–4.

bland 'community of sentiment', seems, then, to provide us with an adequate framework for comprehending the subject in all its complexity. The special emphasis given in this book to Whiggery, however, showing both the reality of its existence and the tenacity of its hold upon a part of Liberalism, offers an alternative line of approach. Whereas Professor Hamer, by disregarding the Whigs and concentrating on Gladstone and the Radicals, depicted Liberal politics as a debate between the various 'faddist' groups as to what priority should be given to their respective causes, with leaders like Gladstone and Chamberlain trying to find issues which would overcome these sectional differences,[53] a more comprehensive examination of Liberal politics would show that the real debate was about the desirability or practicability of reforms, and the pace at which they were to be implemented. It is therefore more meaningful to regard the Liberal party as an organism, constantly evolving out of the tension between conflicting forces, but with no fixed, ultimate objective. If there was haziness about the 'Liberalism' to which all were attached, this lay not so much in the vagueness or benignity of the political views held by individuals or groups, but in the bond that held together such a diversity of opinions. The crucial question in Liberal politics was where to find the common ground on which contending sections, each claiming to embody 'Liberal principles' and perhaps having little sympathy with the aims of others, yet each needing the support of the others if there was to be any chance of gaining power and carrying any measures at all, could agree to co-operate for immediate political purposes.

In practice, a solution was usually found in the frank recognition of differing opinions within the party—'Some of us may think the time is come for measures which others believe to be not yet ripe for execution. Some may wish to go further and faster than others'[54] —accompanied by appeals for mutual toleration and by warnings of the fatal consequences if any one group tried to impose its views upon the Liberal party prematurely.[55] Lyon Playfair employed characteristic Liberal imagery to express these sentiments in a speech during the 1885 general election campaign, which was noted by a

---

[53] Hamer, *Liberal Politics*, pp. 1–78.

[54] [J. A. Hardcastle], 'Principles and Prospects of the Liberal Party', *Edinburgh Review*, 147 (Jan. 1878), 274–300. Cf. Hartington's speech at Mansfield, *The Times*, 5 Dec. 1885, p. 7.

[55] Cf. Hartington at Nelson, *The Times*, 2 Nov. 1885, p. 8.

companion: 'Liberals were not disunited. Like trains on a railway, they had pilot engine, driver Joseph Chamberlain, stoker Jesse Collings; express, drivers John Morley and Dilke; then came fast train—steady driver, Hartington, good Liberal hands, Harcourt, others. All Liberals along the road could find seats in fast or slow.'[56] Naturally, mutual self-interest did much to ensure united action, as is illustrated by the way local 'Whigs' and 'Radicals' shared the Liberal representation in the two-member constituencies which were prevalent until 1885.[57] But one should not underestimate the forces of tradition and sentiment, derived from past battles and triumphs (and the body of party mythology thus generated), which helped to promote a sense of common identity amongst Liberals of all shades, and inculcated a belief in their own moral and administrative superiority.[58] However, *pace* Professor Hamer, there was no question of the competing forces within 'Liberalism' being reduced to order, or a 'system':[59] on the contrary, it was necessary for 'Liberalism' to remain vague if the Liberals were to remain a viable force in politics. The absence of any precise definition of 'Liberalism' was potentially a great source of strength, for it enabled the party to embrace a wide diversity of opinions which, while making a certain degree of disunity almost unavoidable, acted at the same time as a powerful influence against disintegration.

[56] Playfair at Kettering, 22 Nov. 1885, in F. A. Channing, *Memories of Midland Politics, 1885–1910* (1918), 39.

[57] Thus, J. J. Colman felt constrained by the 'fair and honourable understanding' between the Whigs and Radicals of Norwich from coming forward as a second Radical candidate, in 1874, until it became clear that the Whigs had no man of their own: Helen C. Colman, *Jeremiah James Colman: A Memoir* (1905), 268. For the situation in Scarborough, where the rivalry between Whigs and Radicals was overcome in time for the 1880 general election, see J. Newton, *W. S. Caine, M.P.: A Biography* (1907), 66. In the more industrialized county constituencies, the representation was sometimes shared between a landowner and the urban Liberals, as was the case with the Fitzwilliam family and the Liberals of Wakefield in the southern division of the West Riding: Charles Milnes Gaskell to Lord Halifax, 8 Aug. 1884, Hickleton MSS, A4/169.

[58] This was particularly apparent in 1880 with the denunciations of 'Beaconsfield-ism'. In 1906 and 1923, the defence of free trade could still provide a valuable rallying cry for Liberals of every variety.

[59] Hamer, *Liberal Politics*, pp. 1–33.

I

Gladstone: Religion, Politics, and the Leadership of the Liberal Party

In recent years, historians have shown a greater awareness of the relevance of Gladstone's early religious thought for an understanding of his political career. Dr Matthew and others have suggested that the key to the apparent contradiction of Gladstone's transformation from High Church Tory to leader of the Liberal party and close associate of the Nonconformists is to be found in the invalidation of his youthful ideals about the relationship between Church and State.[1] Having been thwarted in his original wish to enter the Church, Gladstone published a book, *The State in its Relations with the Church* (1838), embodying the notion of Britain as an organic society whose identity owed much to the beneficial moral influence of its official religion, which proclaimed his commitment, as a Tory politician, to the defence of the Anglican Church. Experience as a minister in Peel's government soon demonstrated, however, that this theory was inapplicable to the complex reality of British society, which was liable to throw up such perplexing issues as education in factories and the Maynooth grant, and Gladstone was compelled to recognize that adaptability was a necessary part of the politician's

---

[1] Strictly speaking, this explanation can be traced back to Gladstone's own apologia, *A Chapter of Autobiography* (1868). The first modern scholarly work on the subject was A. R. Vidler, *The Orb and the Cross: A Normative Study in the Relations of Church and State with Reference to Gladstone's Early Writings* (1945). Cf. H. C. G. Matthew (ed.), introduction to vol. iii of *The Gladstone Diaries* (Oxford, 1974), and the same author's essay, 'Gladstone, Vaticanism and the Question of the East', in D. Baker (ed.), *Studies in Church History* (Oxford, 1978), 417–42; Deryck Schreuder, 'Gladstone and the Conscience of the State', in P. Marsh (ed.), *The Conscience of the Victorian State* (Hassocks, 1979), 73–130; Perry Butler, *Gladstone: Church, State and Tractarianism—A Study of his Religious Ideas and Attitudes, 1809–1859* (Oxford, 1982); Boyd Hilton, 'Gladstone's Theological Politics', in M. Bentley and J. Stevenson (eds.), *High and Low Politics in Modern Britain* (Oxford, 1983), 28–57; Agatha Ramm, 'Gladstone's Religion', *Historical Journal*, 28 (1985), 327–40. There is also an excellent article, demonstrating the political relevance of Gladstone's religious attitudes, by J. P. Parry, 'Religion and the Collapse of Gladstone's First Government, 1870–1874', ibid. 25 (1982), 71–101.

craft. This liberation from the intellectual strait-jacket of his early years marked the beginning of that process of 'growth', which John Morley identified many years ago as the principal feature of Gladstone's political career.[2]

The fact that Gladstone never found an alternative guiding creed to his discredited theory of Church–State relations poses a serious problem, however, for it is by no means clear that his subsequent political career was sustained by anything more than personal ambition and opportunism. Walter Bagehot, in a classic essay, expressed the view that, while Gladstone had proved that he had a 'susceptible nature' which would 'not live out of sympathy with his age', this could only have been achieved at the expense of 'the first principles of belief' and 'the best landmarks of consistency'. Gladstone had therefore shown himself to be 'essentially a man who cannot impose his creed *on* his time, but must learn his creed *of* his time'.[3] Indeed, his immersion in questions of practical politics left the impression, among some who knew him later in his career, that his mind had altogether lost its theoretical bent. As James Bryce recalled, 'Like Pitt and Peel, Mr Gladstone had a mind which, whatever its original tendencies, had come to be rather practical than meditative. He was fond of generalisations and principles, but they were always directly related to the questions that came before him in actual politics.'[4] This apparent secularization of his political work formed the basis of A. R. Vidler's charge that Gladstone had failed to rise above the optimistic, materialist assumptions of *laissez-faire* Victorian Britain and leave a legacy of political wisdom for future generations: 'As it was, his faith as a Christian and his faith as a Statesman were not sufficiently integrated.'[5] Some recent historians have gone much further, and postulated a 'divide between the religious self and the political self' in support of their assertion that Gladstone's religion had no bearing at all upon his actions as a politician.[6]

Of course, it is scarcely credible that Gladstone could have been

[2] John Morley, *Life of William Ewart Gladstone* (1903), i. 207–8.
[3] Walter Bagehot, 'Mr. Gladstone', in *Biographical Studies* [ed. R. H. Hutton] (1881), 84–115. This essay was originally published in the *National Review* for 1860.
[4] James Bryce, *Studies in Contemporary Biography* (1903), 465.
[5] Vidler, *Orb and Cross*, pp. 153–5.
[6] Andrew Jones, 'Where "Governing is the Use of Words"', *Historical Journal*, 19 (1976), 251–6—a review of A. B. Cooke and John Vincent, *The Governing Passion: Cabinet Government and Party Politics in Britain, 1885–86* (Hassocks, 1974).

suffering from the form of 'schizophrenia' diagnosed by Dr Jones; and Dr Hilton has recently affirmed, in a stimulating essay, that Gladstone's religion was integrally related to his political work. He may have had to relinquish the idea that his purpose in politics was to maintain the privileged position of the Anglican religion, but Gladstone came to see politics instead as the arena in which to discover God's intentions for the world.[7] However, while it is clearly important to establish the way in which Gladstone's mind worked, there still remains the possibility, as Dr Hilton concedes, that Gladstone's religion merely served to cloak his political ambition, and that 'God's will' was being confused with the will of Gladstone.[8] I would suggest that there was indeed a contradiction between Gladstone's secular and religious impulses, but that this was obscured in his own mind in such a way that the political problems with which he became preoccupied served as substitutes for his discredited theological ideals. Contemporaries were invariably struck by the great earnestness with which Gladstone addressed every conceivable subject,[9] and he appears to have had a peculiar manner of infusing secular, political questions with an intense religious fervour, to the point where he became obsessed with them. The zeal which he displayed, during the 1850s and 1860s, in pursuing the fiscal policies initiated by his political mentor Peel is a conspicuous example of this tendency. As Dr Matthew has observed, Gladstone 'came to invest the general concept of free trade with the moral role in the nation's ethical progress earlier attributed to the established Church', and thus 'saw economic progress linked to religion in achieving moral and social development'.[10] In learning to adapt to the reality of conditions in nineteenth-century Britain, then, Gladstone developed an unconscious habit of impregnating political exigencies with his religious enthusiasm in such a way that the political impulse acquired an air of moral righteousness which

---

[7] Hilton, 'Gladstone's Theological Politics', pp. 29–30.

[8] Ibid. 39. This problem is also recognized by Schreuder, 'Gladstone and the Conscience of the State', pp. 82–3.

[9] When Gladstone visited Knowsley, in the autumn of 1881, his host noted that 'There is something odd in the intense earnestness with which he takes up every topic . . . since the days of old Lord Brougham, I have heard nothing like his restless and eager volubility . . . His face is very haggard, his eye wild: a lady who saw much of him said "He has the eye of a madman"', Lord Derby's diary, 29 Oct. 1881, Derby MSS.

[10] Matthew, *Gladstone Diaries*, iii, p. xxxvii.

blinded him to the fact that the original motivation had been political. Conflicting impulses, personal and political, were thus synthesized so as to create the impression that they had been brought into accordance with the facts of a given situation, and conveniently, though always with perfect sincerity, Gladstone was able to make what happened to be politically opportune seem morally right also. Such was the conclusion to which Lord Cranborne (later the third Marquis of Salisbury) was drawn, in a *Quarterly Review* article of July 1866:

> His ambition has guided him in recent years as completely as it ever guided any Statesman of the century; and yet there is not even a shade of untruth in the claim made for him by his friends that he is wholly guided by his convictions. The process of self-deceit goes on in his mind without the faintest self-consciousness or self-suspicion . . . the process by which the mind is made to accept the most advantageous or most convenient belief, is with him automatic and unconscious.[11]

The interpretative difficulties that can arise from Gladstone's capacity for self-deception are examplified by *A Chapter of Auto-biography* (1868), an attempt to justify his decision to press for the disestablishment of the official Church in Ireland. As far back as the 1840s, Gladstone explained, he had reached the conclusion that the position occupied by the Church of Ireland was theoretically indefensible.[12] Nevertheless, for many years afterwards, he had taken care to do nothing that might hasten the movement for disestablishment, because he considered that the time was not ripe for an effective measure—indeed, he had voted against various motions for inquiry and change. In 1865, however, in his response to a motion for disestablishment by L. L. Dillwyn, Gladstone had finally revealed his personal opinion on the subject, and, though he still maintained that immediate action was impossible, he had conceded that this would be 'the question of the future'. His view of the situation, as he later gave it in *A Chapter of Autobiography*, was as follows:

> agreeing with Mr. Dillwyn as to the merits of the case, I held, as I have ever held, that it is not the duty of a Minister to be forward in inscribing on the Journals of Parliament his own abstract views; or to disturb the existence of a great institution like the Church of Ireland, until he conceives the time to be come when he can probably give effect to his opinions. Because the question

[11] Cited by Schreuder, 'Gladstone and the Conscience of the State', p. 84.
[12] W. E. Gladstone, *A Chapter of Autobiography* (1868), 16.

was not within the range of practical politics, agreeing with his sentiment, I voted against his motion.[13]

No doubt Gladstone believed in his assertion that he had not anticipated Irish disestablishment coming to the forefront of politics in his own political lifetime (though 'this argument was to become wearisomely familiar, during the later phase of his career, with respect to several other issues), but the fact remained that, by his speech on Dillwyn's motion, he had effectively identified himself with this particular cause. Moreover, he had felt it his 'duty' to bring the 'remote question' of Irish disestablishment before his constituents at Oxford University,[14] a move which served to hasten his propulsion into the arms and hearts of the advanced section of the Liberal party. When we consider the political context in which Gladstone was acting, in 1865, where there were obvious advantages in building up support amongst the Radicals so as to consolidate the inheritance which seemed likely to be his when Palmerston and Russell departed from the scene, it is difficult to resist the conclusion that Gladstone's conduct was designed—perhaps unconsciously —to secure the fulfilment of his political ambitions.[15] This conclusion is strengthened, of course, when we remember that, in 1868, the 'remote question' of Irish Church disestablishment suddenly became 'ripe' for settlement, at a time when Gladstone badly needed a unifying issue with which to draw the Liberal party together, after the chaos caused by the reform crisis.

Contemporary suspicions of opportunism on Gladstone's part prompted him to write a second apologia, in 1886, justifying his attempt to carry a bill which would have granted home rule to Ireland.[16] The circumstances on this occasion were somewhat different from those of 1868, for, as Gladstone explained, he was not implementing a policy long before accepted in principle, but responding to a new and unforeseen situation. He therefore refuted the

[13] Ibid. 22.

[14] Ibid.

[15] It is even more difficult to resist this conclusion when we remember Gladstone's equally dramatic declaration on the franchise question in 1864 (related to his newly found affinity with the virtuous working classes), and the fact that, during the early 1860s, he had been cultivating links with moderate Nonconformists over such issues as Church rates. Cf. Morley, *Gladstone*, ii. 121–37, and G. I. T. Machin, 'Gladstone and Nonconformity in the 1860s: The Formation of an Alliance', *Historical Journal*, 17 (1974), 347–64.

[16] W. E. Gladstone, *The Irish Question*, i: *History of an Idea*; ii: *Lessons of the Election* (1886).

suggestion that he had either changed his mind on the question of home rule, or else had concealed his real opinion from his colleagues:

It was no consequence from my not having condemned Home Rule, that I had either not considered it, or had adopted it. What is true is, that I had not publicly and in principle condemned it, and also that I had mentally considered it. But I had neither adopted nor rejected it; for the very simple reason, that it was not ripe either for adoption or rejection. It had not become the unequivocal demand of Ireland: and it had not been so defined by its promoters, as to prove that it was a safe demand.[17]

The problem with this explanation is that a great many people disagreed with Gladstone's conclusion that the Irish agitation for home rule had reformed its character, and that the measure could now be conceded with safety. It suited Gladstone's purposes, though, to recognize that the Irish people were expressing their settled wish by constitutional means, and that he was bound to act at once: 'The real test may be stated in one word: the ripeness or unripeness of the question . . . The first political juncture which made action permissible, also made it obligatory.'[18]

Gladstone's belief in the importance of the timing of political initiatives, which comes out clearly from both of his apologias, has important implications for our understanding of his relationship with the Liberal party—whose purpose it was to be, to a greater or lesser extent, the party of reform—and his own conception of his role as its leader. His position was elaborated in a famous and often-quoted memorandum, written near the end of his life:

I am by no means sure . . . that Providence has endowed me with anything that can be called a striking gift. But if there be such a thing entrusted to me, it has been shown, at certain political junctures, in what may be termed appreciations of the general situation and its result. To make good the idea, this must not be considered as the simple acceptance of public opinion, founded upon the discernment that it has risen to a certain height needful for a given work, like a tide. It is an insight into the facts of particular eras, and their relation one to another, which generates in the mind the conviction that the materials exist for forming a public opinion, and for directing it to a particular end.[19]

[17] Ibid. 8.
[18] Ibid. 22.
[19] This memorandum is printed in John Brooke and Mary Sorensen (eds.), *The Prime Minister's Papers: W. E. Gladstone*, i: *Autobiographica* (1971), 136. For examples of the way in which this memorandum is frequently used, cf. D. A. Hamer, *Liberal Politics in the Age of Gladstone and Rosebery* (Oxford, 1972), 68–9; E. D. Steele, 'Gladstone and Ireland', *Irish Historical Studies*, 17 (1970–1), 58–88.

It was this divine 'gift' which, in his own estimation, distinguished Gladstone from the Whigs and Radicals with whom he worked. Not for him the belated and half-hearted gestures, made in the face of mounting pressure for a particular reform, that passed for Whig statesmanship; but nor was it any part of Gladstone's notion of leadership to attempt to build an agitation upon some abstract principle, bearing no relation to political practicability. If Gladstone ever adopted a 'Radical' position, therefore, he believed that it was done on his own terms, and that he provided the momentum with which to sustain the movement.

It must be doubted, however, whether historians have been justified in placing great reliance upon Gladstone's retrospective memorandum as the basis of their interpretations of his leadership. I would argue that, in fact, this memorandum was nothing more than an elaborate rationalization, enabling Gladstone to accommodate his personal and political needs with the appearance of consistency. The four instances he gave where his 'gift' of insight had operated —two of the great successes earlier in his career, the budget of 1853 and Irish Church disestablishment in 1868, and two controversial, unsuccessful, and highly personal issues near the end, Irish home rule in 1886 and the desire for a dissolution on the question of the House of Lords in 1894—raise strong suspicions that he was seeking to refute the charge of opportunism by reference to a single, consistent principle of action, in order to vindicate the last years of his leadership. Furthermore, the guidelines laid down in the retrospective memorandum were so conveniently flexible that any action could have been justified by reference to them. On the one hand, Gladstone was able to allow his conservative instincts to prevail, when this happened to be politically convenient, on the grounds that a particular question was not 'ripe' for settlement. During the period of his second administration (1880–5), we find several illustrations of Gladstone's inclination to put off major questions whenever this was possible: he was relieved, for instance, to think that Church disestablishment in England was becoming increasingly remote;[20] the reform of the House of Lords he was similarly content to relegate to the far-distant future, beyond his own political lifetime,[21] and, as

[20] e.g. D. W. R. Bahlman (ed.), *The Diary of Sir Edward Walter Hamilton, 1880–1885* (Oxford, 1972), ii. 793 (entry for 10 Feb. 1885).
[21] e.g. Gladstone to Sir Arthur Hamilton-Gordon, 5 Dec. 1884, BL Add. MSS 44321, fo. 221.

late as the autumn of 1884, his attitude to Irish home rule was that it
was probably the biggest issue with which politicians would have to
deal—in ten years' time.[22] The events of 1868 and 1885–6, on the
other hand, suggest that great questions had a habit of becoming
'ripe' for settlement very rapidly, when they suited Gladstone's
tactical purposes.

In addition to these reservations about the validity of his retrospective memorandum, one can also point to occasions on which
Gladstone clearly was following public opinion, rather than forming
it. Professor Shannon, in his celebrated study of the Bulgarian
agitation of 1876, showed that Gladstone only became involved in
this protest movement once it was clear that 'public opinion' had
been aroused,[23] and, in a recent essay, he has gone further and
suggested that it was the absence of any 'virtuous passion' on
questions of foreign policy, before the late 1870s, which delayed the
formulation of a distinct set of Gladstonian principles until the
Midlothian campaign of 1879.[24] Another example, from the same
period, which has been completely overlooked by historians as well
as by Gladstone, might be added. In July 1878, with the Beaconsfield
administration apparently in the ascendant, Gladstone was seriously
contemplating action on the question of Scottish Church disestablishment. According to the account by Alexander Taylor Innes, a
prominent campaigner for the cause, he met Gladstone in the lobby
of the House of Commons:

he drew me away to a quieter spot, which turned out to be the corridor of the
House of Lords, deserted at that hour. There under the wall paintings which
record the struggles of the English historic past, he made a proposal . . . Mr
Gladstone no longer disguised from himself that he was coming back into
politics; even a year before, a letter to me showed that his interest was
equally divided between Scotland and Bulgaria. As usual he was eager for
immediate action. At that moment the question of religious census was in the
air, and what had occurred to him was whether a Church census for
Scotland, supplemented by statistics of Church membership and Church

---

[22] Cf. Sir Algernon West, *Recollections, 1832 to 1886* (1899), ii. 206–7 (diary
entry for 7 Oct. 1884); Bahlman (ed.), *Hamilton Diary*, ii. 620 (entry for 20 May
1884).

[23] Richard Shannon, *Gladstone and the Bulgarian Agitation 1876* (1975 edn.,
Hassocks).

[24] Richard Shannon, 'Midlothian: 100 Years After', in Peter J. Jagger (ed.),
*Gladstone, Politics and Religion: A Collection of Founder's Day Lectures delivered at
St Deiniols Library, Hawarden, 1967–83* (1985), 88–103.

attendance, might not give him the required mandate. The recent bye-elections, he pointed out, had been favourable to Liberalism, and in the event of our agreeing to the census proposal, he was prepared himself to bring it forward (whether before or after the approaching General Election I do not now remember).[25]

In the event, it proved impossible to secure unity among the Free Church groups in Scotland, and Gladstone was forced to conclude that the question of disestablishment was not yet 'ripe' for settlement.[26] Nevertheless, the point remains that, on this occasion, he was apparently willing to put himself at the head of a reform movement once it was clear that there would be sufficient support for it, rather than acting from an 'appreciation of the general situation' and seeking to form a public opinion. Of course, the anomalous position which he occupied at this time, owing to his 'retirement' in 1875, and his subsequent involvement in the Bulgarian agitation, must reinforce our suspicion that Gladstone's interest in an initiative on Scottish Church disestablishment was bound up with an instinctive urge to restore his authority over the Liberal party.

If the reliance placed by historians on Gladstone's memorandum has led to a rather indulgent assessment of his motives, that document has been no less effective in creating confusion with regard to the nature of his relationship with the Liberal party. The impression has been conveyed of Gladstone as someone above, rather than of, party, for it was implicit, in his method of 'forming a public opinion, and . . . directing it to a particular end', that he saw his role as that of an educator, guiding the Liberal party along a certain path, but without coercing it, until the desired conclusion was reached. Thus, according to Professor Hamer, Gladstone did not believe in establishing unity by imposing his leadership upon the party, but looked instead for a unity which was spontaneous; if this could not be achieved, then he would leave the party to resolve its own problems.

---

[25] A. Taylor Innes, *Chapters of Reminiscence* (1913), 126–7. The date of his meeting with Gladstone is established by his letter of 18 Oct. 1878, BL Add. MSS 44548, fo. 70. On 2 Dec, 1877, Gladstone had written to Innes that 'I think the future course of the question is in the hands of the Scottish Liberals and Nonconformists, and that if they are tolerably united it will march. There is not a crying grievance, but there is a total want of positive case'; Innes, *Reminiscences*, p. 124. Innes noted this incident in his book, he said, because it had been omitted from the official lives of Gladstone and Principal Rainy, ibid. 133. His inability to remember when Gladstone had intended to raise the question of a census may have been designed to avoid embarrassment.

[26] Ibid. 133.

And yet, we are told, when Gladstone judged that a particular question was 'ripe' for settlement, and accordingly gave a lead on it—without previously consulting his followers, and leaving it to them to decide whether or not to support him—such action might itself produce that 'spontaneous' unity which he required.[27] Such a fine distinction between the imposition of leadership and the nurturing of a spontaneous party unity is hardly convincing, and it fails to allay the legitimate suspicion that the exacting standard of discipline which Gladstone demanded from his party concealed an inability to tolerate resistance to his leadership. Indeed, I would argue that Gladstone's memorandum and the scholarly work emanating from it have obscured the exceptionally autocratic nature of his leadership.

It can easily be seen how the dictatorial tendency in Gladstone was related to the earlier developments in his religious thought. Once Gladstone had been forced to abandon his ideal of the State as the trustee and propagator of the values of an homogeneous Christian society, he was led to the conclusion that the only fitting repositories for those values lay in the Churches and the Christian people of the country. As Professor Schreuder has observed, 'This transference of conscience in politics from State to nation also interestingly paralleled the formal shift in Gladstonian allegiance from toryism to liberalism . . . The Christian idealist of the 1830s had presumed that moral progress lay in ethical authority emanating from above; the emerging Christian Statesman of mid-century saw ethical advances reflecting the liberty of the mass of individual consciences in the nation.'[28] Gladstone himself later conceded that he had been slow to learn 'the great fact that liberty is a great and precious gift of God, and that human excellence cannot grow up in a nation without it'.[29] By the 1860s, however, with the apparent success of free trade, and the maintenance of political stability in spite of the extended franchise of 1832, the equation between freedom and progress had been fully absorbed into his thinking, and he was prepared to recognize that even the Nonconformists, whom he had previously regarded as a discordant element in society, had a role to play, in conjunction with the established Church, in nurturing the moral conscience of

[27] Hamer, *Liberal Politics*, pp. 59–60.
[28] Schreuder, 'Gladstone and the Conscience of the State', p. 101. Cf. Hilton, 'Gladstone's Theological Politics', p. 46.
[29] Gladstone's memorandum, 12 July 1892, in Brooke and Sorensen (eds.), *The Prime Minister's Papers: W. E. Gladstone*, i: *Autobiographica*, pp. 33–8.

the people. Consequently, in Professor Schreuder's words, Gladstone looked to 'a moral constituency in the nation out of which the politics of edification and progress could be developed . . . by 1868 he was acutely aware of the possibilities of drawing moral power out of the respectable individuals who composed the broad mass of Victorian society'.[30]

It was by means of a characteristically tortuous process that Gladstone convinced himself of the moral virtues of the common man, but this important revelation was to provide him with the means to assert his authority over the Liberal party while reinforcing the sense in which he stood above it. Having invested 'the people' with his own notions of Christian morality, it became natural for Gladstone to base his appeal to 'the nation' on supposedly 'national' issues, while treating the Liberal party as a mere 'instrument by which a great work is to be carried out'.[31] As Professor Hamer has pointed out, this tendency to see his duty as being to the nation, rather than to party, and of seeking to establish organic unity amongst the Liberals by guiding them into cohesion on some 'great cause', was especially marked after the electoral disaster of 1874 and his (temporary) resignation of the leadership.[32] However, as this book will seek to show, Gladstone's increasing identification with the virtuous masses, beyond parliament and London 'society', also served as a weapon with which to combat a recalcitrant ruling class, including the Whig element within the Liberal party, who were failing in their duty to keep in step with opinion 'out of doors'—or rather, as it may well seem, with Gladstone's opinions.[33] His growing intolerance of the ruling class, apparent in his conduct over the Eastern Question and his triumphant campaigns in Midlothian, had become firmly entrenched, by 1886, as a private mythology of 'the classes' against 'the masses'.

Gladstone's intolerance of disunity amongst the Liberals, and his

---

[30] Schreuder, 'Gladstone and the Conscience of the State', pp. 101–2.

[31] Gladstone to Granville, 23 May 1877, in Agatha Ramm (ed.), *The Political Correspondence of Mr Gladstone and Lord Granville, 1876–1886* (Oxford, 1962), i. 42.

[32] Hamer, *Liberal Politics*, pp. 63–8.

[33] Gladstone always had a strong sentimental attachment to the aristocracy; cf. Lord Acton to Mary Gladstone, 24 Apr. 1881, in Herbert Paul (ed.), *Letters of Lord Acton to Mary Gladstone* (1904), 95; Lewis Harcourt's diary, 7 Dec. 1882, Harcourt MSS; and yet he still remained somewhat distanced from them. See the remarks by Peter Stansky, *Gladstone: A Progress in Politics* (1981), 14–17.

predilection for 'great causes', were indicative of certain shortcomings in his leadership which became openly apparent during the
reform crisis, following the defeat of Russell's ministry in 1866, and
which reappeared after the demise of his own government in 1874.
On the former occasion, he had responded vehemently to the
divisions in the Liberal party, speaking of the desirable effect of a
purge of the ranks, and making clear his own belief that the party
should be left leaderless until it had resolved its own problems.[34]
Clearly, in spite of his undoubted talents, Gladstone was temperamentally too impatient, and insufficiently conciliatory in his manner,
to be suitable as the leader of a party in which cracks needed to be
repaired and wounds healed. Such was the impression gained by
some of his colleagues in the ministry of 1868–74. Lord Kimberley,
for instance, surveying the plight of the government after the ministerial crisis of March 1873, noted that 'Our old programme is
completely exhausted: and Gladstone is not the man to govern
without "measures", nor is he at all suited to lead a party in
difficulties. He must have a strong current of opinion in his favour.'[35]
Similarly, Lord Selborne, writing several months after the fall of the
government, observed that Gladstone's mind seemed to be 'too
one-sided and vehement, and to want accuracy, equability, and the
sense of proportion and breadth', and that this made it 'hardly
possible for him to be a Minister, except when it is the time for some
"heroic" measures, for which he can excite public enthusiasm'.[36]
   In 1874, certainly, there was little evidence of public enthusiasm
for 'heroic' measures. Gladstone had taken the political world
(including his own party) by surprise with his sudden announcement,
on 24 January, that parliament was to be dissolved, and that he
would be seeking a mandate from the electorate for a set of fiscal
proposals which included the abolition of the income tax.[37] This
bold attempt to regroup the scattered forces of Liberalism around a

---

[34] Cf. Maurice Cowling, 'Derby, Disraeli and Fusion, October 1865 to July 1866',
Historical Journal, 8 (1965), 58; Gladstone to Russell, 2 Nov. 1867, in G. P. Gooch
(ed.), *The Later Correspondence of Lord John Russell, 1840–1878* (1925), ii. 362–3.

[35] Ethel Drus (ed.), *A Journal of Events during the Gladstone Ministry, 1868–74,
by John, First Earl of Kimberley* (Camden Miscellany, 21; 1958), 37. Entry for 18
Mar. 1873.

[36] Selborne to Sir Arthur Hamilton-Gordon, 6 Sept. 1874, in Roundell, Earl of
Selborne, *Memorials: Personal and Political, 1865–1895* (1898), i. 334.

[37] See Morley, *Gladstone*, ii. 478–90. It is interesting that Gladstone should have
excluded his financial plan of 1874 from the list of those occasions when he had used
his gift of 'insight'.

great reforming measure ended in disaster, however, and with the advent of Disraeli's government, a disillusioned Gladstone refused to make any further commitments to his party. Indeed, in January 1875, he took the step of resigning the leadership of the Liberal party altogether. This decision has been explained in terms of Gladstone's belief that the differences between the Liberal party and himself, particularly on questions relating to religion, were irreconcilable, and it has been suggested that, in any case, his paramount concern for spiritual matters had finally asserted itself over the rather sordid business of politics.[38] A re-examination of Gladstone's position between the election defeat of February 1874 and his resignation will show, however, that there was no such simple partition between Gladstone's religion and his political conduct, that each acted upon the other, and that, in fact, Gladstone may not have intended his withdrawal from the party leadership to be permanent.

It was perhaps understandable that, in February 1874, Gladstone should have been hesitant to commit himself, for a necessarily prolonged period, to the task of rebuilding the strength of a party which had failed to unite around his finance proposals.[39] Consequently, at a dinner for the retiring Cabinet on 16 February, he announced to his colleagues his intention not to lead the party. This was how Lord Aberdare interpreted Gladstone's meaning:

Gladstone is resolutely bent on retiring from the leadership of the party —until it has settled its differences and has acquired as keen a sense of the duties of followers as of those of leaders. He still feels and bitterly resents the insults and outrages to which he was exposed in 1866–8 and he has a lively sense of the disloyalty of the party during the last 3 years. He wishes them to enjoy the blessings of anarchy for a while in order that they may learn to appreciate the necessity of party obedience.[40]

There was no assumption, here, that Gladstone's withdrawal from the party leadership would be permanent, but rather that, having sufficiently punished the Liberals for their disloyalty, he would

[38] The view that Gladstone's true interests were outside politics is emphasized by Philip Magnus, *Gladstone* (1954), 191, 229, 232. For Gladstone's sense of isolation from his party on religious questions, see Matthew R. Temmel, 'Gladstone's Resignation of the Liberal Leadership, 1874–1875', *Journal of British Studies*, 16 (1976), 153–77.

[39] For Gladstone's view of the state of the Liberal party, see the fragment dated 12 Feb. 1874, cited by Morley, *Gladstone*, ii. 498.

[40] Aberdare to Ripon, 19 Feb. 1874, BL Add. MSS 43535, fo. 82.

decide to resume his position.[41] Granville, the leader in the House of Lords, doubtful of Gladstone's ability to retire altogether from active politics, therefore endeavoured to ensure that he made no impetuous statement about his future intentions.[42] Similarly, Sir Thomas Dyke Acland, one of Gladstone's oldest friends, urged him, when they met on 3 March, to say nothing that might discourage the hope that he would agree eventually to lead the party again, and he expressed himself well pleased with Gladstone's reticence at the opening of the new parliament on the fifth:

I have been constantly thinking over what you said and I do think . . . that the Liberals (I do not say the party for is it now a party?) ought not to take umbrage if you hesitate to commit yourself to a renewed lease of responsibility of which you cannot now measure the dimension under altered circumstances. I also feel very strongly the truth of what you said that till the impulse comes from without, and the objects on which the Country desires us to concentrate are plain, we have no adequate bond of union which enables us to press upon you.[43]

Gladstone's public letter to Granville on 12 March, explaining that he needed to rest, that he would only attend the House of Commons occasionally during the parliamentary session, and that he would reconsider his position before the beginning of the 1875 session,[44] was therefore received with general satisfaction by the Liberal press, and it was widely supposed, even by his former Cabinet colleagues, that after a period of repose he would again take up the reins of leadership.[45]

Indeed, events during the 1874 session of parliament raised the possibility that Gladstone might be tempted to launch a new

[41] Abraham Hayward wrote to Lady Emily Peel on 27 Feb. that 'I had a long talk with Gladstone yesterday. He thinks the party in too heterogeneous a state for regular leadership; that it must be let alone to shake into consistency. He will attend till Easter, and then quit the field for a time. He does not talk of permanent abdication', Henry E. Carlisle (ed.), *A Selection from the Correspondence of Abraham Hayward, Q.C., from 1834 to 1884* (1886), ii. 258.

[42] Granville to Northbrook, 3 Mar. 1874 (typescript), Northbrook MSS, vol. 22.

[43] Acland to Gladstone, 7 Mar. 1874, BL Add. MSS 44092, fo. 124. Acland's letter of 4 Mar., ibid., fo. 122, establishes the date of their meeting.

[44] Gladstone to Granville, 12 Mar. 1874, in Agatha Ramm (ed.), *The Political Correspondence of Mr Gladstone and Lord Granville, 1868–1876* (Camden Society, 81–2; 1952), ii. 449–50. In fact, Gladstone had originally intended to delay his decision until the end of the 1875 session; cf. Hartington to the Duke of Devonshire, 9 Mar. 1874, Devonshire MSS, 340.572.

[45] Cf. *Daily News*, 13 Mar. 1874, p. 4; *Daily Telegraph*, 14 Mar. 1874, p. 4; Forster to Granville, 13 Mar. 1874, PRO 30/29/56; Ripon to Northbrook, 27 Mar. 1874 (typescript), Northbrook MSS, vol. 22.

initiative on the question of disestablishment. Firstly, the government introduced a Scottish Church Patronage Bill, which proposed to abolish all lay patronage in the Church of Scotland and hand control of it over to the congregations. This measure was strongly opposed by the Free Churches in Scotland, who demanded disestablishment as an essential precondition for any settlement of a matter which pre-dated the schism of 1843.[46] The government's bill was also condemned as provocative by Gladstone, in the House of Commons, and he called for an alternative measure acceptable to all the Church groups in Scotland.[47] He did not go so far as to advocate disestablishment, but he evidently considered that events might well lead in that direction.[48]

Within a few days of the debate on the Scottish Church Patronage Bill, Gladstone was involved in a second controversy, this time concerning the bill introduced by the Archbishop of Canterbury which aimed at establishing stricter control over ritualistic practices within the Church of England.[49] Gladstone's fierce opposition to the Public Worship Regulation Bill proved futile, as he received little support from his own party for his 'six resolutions',[50] but he remained convinced that further Erastian interference in ecclesiastical matters would pose a serious threat to the survival of the Church of England as the established Church. If parliament were to continue to support the efforts of the Anglican hierarchy to impose a stricter uniformity on the clergy, Gladstone personally believed that disestablishment would be the best thing for the Anglican Church, though he maintained that he had no intention of promoting such a policy himself.[51] Nevertheless, his attitude towards English Church disestablishment was ominously reminiscent of his position with regard to disestablishment in Ireland in the mid-1860s, a fact which caused great consternation among some of his closest friends and

[46] For the agitation in Scotland, see P. C. Simpson, *The Life of Principal Rainy* (1909), i. 275–81.

[47] Gladstone, 6 July 1874, 3 Hansard, ccxx, cols. 1113–30.

[48] In a letter to W. P. Adam, the new Liberal chief whip, Gladstone referred to 'the paper of the Scottish Disestablishment association which may prove to be an important one', 3 Sept. 1874, Blairadam MSS, 4/431. Unfortunately, I have not been able to trace this paper.

[49] See J. Bentley, *Ritualism and Politics in Victorian Britain: The Attempt to Legislate for Belief* (Oxford, 1978).

[50] Gladstone, 9 July 1874, 3 Hansard, ccxx, cols. 1372–92.

[51] Gladstone to Lord Harrowby, 1 Oct. 1874, in D. C. Lathbury (ed.), *Correspondence on Church and Religion of William Ewart Gladstone* (1910), i. 396.

colleagues.[52] After a visit to Hawarden, in November, Arthur Hamilton-Gordon reported to Lord Selborne that:

I found him quite unable to talk or think of anything except religious or ecclesiastical question . . . I don't think he is *quite* so determined not to take office again, as he was. He consented to contemplate the possibility of his being once more Prime Minister. He spoke very strongly as to last year's ecclesiastical legislation. Till then, he had (he said) regarded disestablishment as a disordered dream;—it had, he thought, been rendered less 'nebulous' by it. The thing I most disliked . . . in relation to this subject, was that he had been contemplating the difficulties, 'the almost insuperable' difficulties, of such a measure, in a *practical* light; saying, e.g. that the compensation to private patrons could be hardly less than £13,000,000.[53]

The political implications of Gladstone's changing perspective on disestablishment had been recognized by Radicals such as T. B. Potter, who was in contact with him during the debates on the Public Worship Regulation Bill, and who quite explicitly hoped that Gladstone would emerge as the leader of a rejuvenated Liberalism on their platform of 'religious liberty'.[54] Whether Gladstone would really have been tempted by this idea, if it had appeared likely to have a unifying influence upon the Liberal party, is impossible to tell, but a letter from his intimate confidant Lord Wolverton, written after the approach from Potter, is suggestive: 'Things seem to be working as you expected and as they should, but you know better than I do *how* far the smoother water is still off.'[55] This was Gladstone's dilemma, however, for if, as must have seemed certain, a decisive move on the question of disestablishment proved to be premature, with the Liberals unable to act together, then he would be reducing himself to the position of leader of only a section of the party—a step he had resolved never to take.[56] In other words, disestablishment could hardly be considered a matter that was 'ripe' for settlement.

It was at this point that Gladstone's facility for confusing religious and political impulses provided him with a badly needed diversion from the perplexities of the political situation. During the autumn of 1874, he became involved in a theological controversy which had the effect of accentuating his personal sense of isolation from the Liberal

[52] e.g. Selborne to Hamilton-Gordon, 6 Sept. 1874, in Selborne, *Memorials, 1865–1895*, i. 334.

[53] Hamilton-Gordon to Selborne, 17 Nov. 1874, ibid. i. 357–8.

[54] T. B. Potter to Gladstone, 5, 20 Aug. 1874, BL Add. MSS 44282, fos. 41, 45.

[55] Wolverton to Gladstone, 23 Aug. 1874, BL Add. MSS 44349, fo. 32. Unfortunately, only a few of Gladstone's letters to Wolverton have survived.

[56] Cf. Gladstone's fragment, dated 12 Feb. 1874, in Morley, *Gladstone*, ii. 498–9.

party. His violent condemnation of the Public Worship Regulation Bill had created a rift between himself and his largely Erastian Liberal colleagues, and this was widened when his concern to rebut allegations that he held Anglo-Catholic sympathies led him to clarify his attitude in an article on 'Ritual and Ritualism' for the October edition of the *Contemporary Review*. Dr Matthew has shown that this article was deliberately stiffened up to include an attack upon Catholics in the United Kingdom for their subservience to the Vatican,[57] and the attack was then followed up, even more trenchantly, in a pamphlet, *The Vatican Decrees in their Bearing on Civil Allegiance: A Political Expostulation*, published in November, in which he denounced the declaration (in 1870) of papal infallibility. Dr Matthew has seen Gladstone's subsequent resignation of the Liberal leadership as proof of the 'retrospective nature of his expostulation',[58] but the extraordinary manner of his outburst —quite wilfully alienating the Catholic Irish MPs, and embroiling himself in an old theological quarrel with Cardinal Manning— suggests a desire, possibly unconscious, to reinforce his sense of isolation from contemporary British politics by perpetuating his differences with former supporters.

In fact, Gladstone's preoccupation with theological matters was of great importance to him politically, for it created an entirely separate rationale for his desire not to resume the leadership of the Liberal party. The real purpose of this spiritual diversion, however, was that it enabled Gladstone to avoid taking a step that might lead him and his party in the direction of English Church disestablishment. In England, at least, the question of disestablishment could not be considered 'ripe' for settlement, and because Gladstone was unwilling to do anything that might help to bring the matter on, he felt that his personal views on the subject precluded him from acting as leader of the Liberal party while there remained a chance that disestablishment could be averted. As he explained to Granville, on 7 December.

the religious question generally—which we could manage while we were in power—has now passed out of our hands, and is a great difficulty in *my* way. What, in this province, the next session may bring about, I cannot tell. But the Church of England has been brought to the brink of a most serious crisis,

[57] Matthew, 'Gladstone, Vaticanism and the Question of the East', pp. 434–5. Gladstone's revision of his article followed a visit to Dr Dollinger in Sept. Dollinger was involved in the Bonn conference of the 'old Catholic' movement, seeking a reunited Catholic Church, something Gladstone had always sympathized with.

[58] Ibid. 437.

which may take the form of schism, disestablishment, or both. It is I believe still avoidable: but only by an amount of selfcommand, highmindedness, and circumspection, on the part of the highest Church authorities, very different from that which they exhibited during the last session. While this question remains unclosed, any *strapping* up of the relations between the party and me can only I fear constitute a new danger.[59]

Gladstone's theological diversion served a dual purpose, though, for while his anti-Catholic rhetoric isolated him from the moderate Liberals and the Irish, it gave great encouragement to the Nonconformists, opening up the prospect of a *rapprochement* after the difficulties of the early 1870s. T. B. Potter wrote, in October, to express the delight of the Nonconformists with the Vatican decrees pamphlet, and at the conference of the Liberation Society at Bristol, late in November, speakers claimed to perceive in Gladstone's pamphlet principles that led logically to Church disestablishment, and the hope was openly expressed that he was on the verge of another great 'conversion'.[60] The significance of a possible reconciliation between Gladstone and the Nonconformists may have been that, while he had no intention, as yet, of gratifying their wishes with regard to English Church disestablishment, he had no idea of self-sacrifice for the sake of the Church of Scotland. Again, Gladstone did not want to be personally responsible for forcing on disestablishment, but he may have been inclined to bide his time and wait for the issue to come to a head. The day before his letter to Granville, Gladstone wrote to W. P. Adam (who was associating himself with the Scottish disestablishment movement) that he thought it unwise to accept a proposed acknowledgement, from the Free Churches, for his role in the opposition to the Patronage Bill, but that 'We ought now I think for a time to watch the question as it works itself out in Scotland'.[61] The Duke of Argyll may well have been entitled to his suspicion that, though Gladstone had probably not resolved upon a policy of disestablishment for England, 'he is quite ready so far as Scotland is concerned'.[62]

[59] Gladstone to Granville, 7 Dec. 1874, in Ramm (ed.), *Gladstone–Granville Correspondence, 1868–1876,* ii. 461–2. This may have been the meaning behind Wolverton's observation, in a letter of 11 Dec., that 'few really see the exact position or weigh the *risk* against the general feeling of *relief* which a flag in your hands would afford', BL Add. MSS 44349, fo. 46.
[60] Potter to Gladstone, 14 Oct. 1874, BL Add. MSS 44282, fo. 53. For a report on the Liberation society conference, see *The Times,* 26 Nov. 1874, p. 7.
[61] Gladstone to Adam, 6 Dec. 1874, Blairadam MSS, 4/431.
[62] Argyll to Selborne, 21 Dec. 1874, in Selborne, *Memorials, 1865–1895,* i. 359–60.

Further support for the suggestion that Gladstone may have been contemplating an eventual return to the Liberal leadership, under more auspicious circumstances, is provided by his attitude towards the appointment of a successor to lead the Liberal party in the House of Commons. During the 1874 session of parliament, while Gladstone had supposedly been resting, the Liberals in the Commons had had no one acknowledged leader (that function had been shared between several former Cabinet ministers), and it appears that, even when he decided to resign, Gladstone expected this arrangement to continue. A draft of his letter of resignation, shown to Granville by Wolverton on 5 January 1875, prompted Granville to protest that Gladstone's attitude would make it 'impossible that any individual, or any combination of two or three should have any authority' on the Commons front bench, and that the effect on party discipline would be highly injurious.[63] Wolverton, in his report to Gladstone, noted that Granville 'seemed to me to think much of the *Constitutional* difficulty of the position, if there was no leader of opposition for the ordinary and daily work', and he went on to suggest that the resignation letter might 'be a little strengthened in the allusion to your support for a leader for daily work—interim or otherwise—if the party select one', although Wolverton added his own opinion that 'They will not do so while you are possible, of this I am sure, but it is just possible some might think of it in the first instance.'[64] In his public letter of resignation, addressed to Granville, Gladstone may have adopted Wolverton's suggestion,[65] but even so, he still doubted whether an appointed leader for the party in the House of Commons was necessary. He believed that the Liberals had to undergo 'a kind

[63] Granville to Gladstone, 5 Jan. 1875, in Ramm (ed.), *Gladstone–Granville Correspondence, 1868–1876*, ii. 463–4.

[64] Wolverton to Gladstone, 7 Jan. 1875, BL Add. MSS 44349, fo. 53.

[65] The original draft of Gladstone's resignation letter has not survived, but one of the many fragments relating to this period in the Gladstone papers may well be the passage in question: 'Under these circumstances it is for others rather than for me to take the lead in considering what arrangements may be requisite for the regular conduct of Parliamentary business for the convenience and advantage of the Liberal party . . . it will be my duty to conduct my own proceedings with the fullest regard to such arrangements', BL Add. MSS 44762, fo. 148. Compare this with his formal resignation letter: 'I need hardly say that my conduct in Parliament will continue to be governed by the principles on which I have heretofore acted: and, whatever arrangements may be made for the treatment of general business, and for the advantage or convenience of the Liberal party, they will have my cordial support', Gladstone to Granville, 13 Jan. 1875, in Ramm (ed.), *Gladstone–Granville Correspondence, 1868–1876*, ii. 464–5.

of schooling' before their internal cohesion could be restored,[66] and, when complications arose concerning the selection of his successor, Gladstone expressed quite clearly his opinion that 'the party can do for a time without a leader in the Commons . . . it has peccant humours to purge, and bad habits to get rid of, and it is a great question whether this can or cannot best be done without first choosing a leader'.[67]

However, in spite of Gladstone's doubts, his former colleagues, anxious to avoid a repetition of the chaos of the 1874 session,[68] went ahead with the selection of a new leader for the House of Commons. Many, including Granville, nevertheless doubted whether Gladstone could remain detached from active politics permanently, and, while no one could have anticipated the remarkable come-back of 1879–80, it was clear that the seeds of future difficulties had been sown.[69] This feeling was expressed by one of Gladstone's oldest friends, from his Oxford days, Frederic Rogers, Lord Blachford: 'I suppose for the present he is full of something or somethings or other. But will he not soon become *désœuvré* and take to prowling round the political pen, from which he has excluded himself and snuffing for an entrance? And when he begins to snuff it will not be long before he makes a rush—an ugly one—at the door.'[70] Gladstone's attitude, between the electoral defeat of February 1874 and his 'retirement' in January 1875, had certainly not indicated an absolute determination to resign the Liberal leadership irrevocably, and the fact that he was to remain in the House of Commons suggested that he had established a convenient position for himself, leaving him free from the responsibilities of leading the whole party, and free to become involved in any sufficiently attractive political cause when the occasion suited him.

[66] Gladstone to Halifax, 20 Jan. 1875, Hickleton MSS, A4/88.

[67] Gladstone to Granville, 27 Jan. 1875, in Ramm (ed.), *Gladstone–Granville Correspondence, 1868–1876*, ii. 468.

[68] Cf. Goschen to Granville, 5 Jan. 1875, PRO 30/29/28, and Forster to Granville, 12 Jan. 1875, PRO 30/29/25A, for the feeling that the arrangement during the 1874 session must not be repeated.

[69] 'Gladstone will assuredly return some day. So think his old colleagues. He cannot resist the temptation of a good fight', A. J. Mundella to Robert Leader, 19 Mar. 1875, Mundella–Leader MSS, 6P/65. Cf. Granville to Sir Thomas Dyke Acland, 4 Feb. 1875: 'you talk as if he were really gone—a fact in which I do not believe, however much he may himself think so', A. H. D. Acland (ed.), *Memoirs and Letters of . . . Sir Thomas Dyke Acland* (privately printed, Oxford, 1902), 319.

[70] Blachford to Dean Church, 17 Jan. 1875, in G. E. Marindin (ed.), *Letters of Frederic, Lord Blachford* (1896), 360.

2
The Whig Revival, 1874–1875

The general election of 1874 inflicted a heavy blow upon the ambitions of Gladstone and the pretensions of Radicalism. Contrary to the assumption of most contemporaries that the Liberal ministry would survive, though with a reduced parliamentary following,[1] the Conservatives were, in the event, returned to power with their first overall majority since 1841. This unexpected result was interpreted as a sign that the country was now satiated with reforms and had no wish for a further period of great legislative activity. Indeed, Gladstone himself was held responsible for aggravating, by his unpredictable behaviour, the widespread unease that existed regarding the future policy of a Liberal government.[2] At the same time, the elections had highlighted the continuing problems posed by the 'crotchet-mongers' or 'faddists', groups such as the National Education League and the United Kingdom Alliance, each of whom had pressed the claims of their own particular cause to the extent of making it a test question on which basis alone they decided whether or not to support a Liberal candidate. The consequent harassment of candidates was roundly condemned by the press,[3] and the National Education League was singled out for particular criticism, with allegations that it had alienated many moderate voters fearful for the security of the Church of England.[4] It may well be that contemporaries somewhat exaggerated the extent of the damage done to the

---

[1] Cf. *Daily Telegraph*, 26 Jan. 1874, p. 4; *Pall Mall Gazette*, 3 Feb, 1874, p. 4; *Manchester Guardian*, 6 Feb. 1874, p. 4; Lord Kimberley's Journal, 21 Feb. 1874, in Ethel Drus (ed.), *A Journal of Events during the Gladstone Ministry, 1868–74, by John, First Earl of Kimberley* (Camden Miscellany, 21; 1958), 43.

[2] Cf. *Manchester Guardian*, 18 Feb. 1874, p. 5. For the view of a defeated Whig, hostile to Gladstone, see E. P. Bouverie to Earl Fortescue, 10 Feb. 1874, Fortescue MSS, FC 129.

[3] Cf. *The Times*, 29 Jan. 1874, p. 9; *Pall Mall Gazette*, 29 Jan. 1874, p. 1; *Daily News*, 4 Feb. 1874, pp. 4–5.

[4] *Leeds Mercury*, 14 Feb. 1874, p. 7.

Liberal cause by 'faddist' abstentions,[5] but whatever the case, to many observers, surveying the Liberal wreckage after the general election, it seemed that a 'period of inward discipline and searching of the heart' was now required.[6] The consequences of the selfish actions of the Radical 'crotchet-mongers' had demonstrated clearly that their various 'fads' could never, by themselves, provide an adequate basis for a 'national' Liberal party, and they had to learn that they formed only one wing of that party and could not expect to be able to impose their ideas upon the whole of it.[7]

There was little doubt in the minds of most Liberal leaders that the Conservative triumph represented a fundamental shift in the balance of political power and could not be dismissed as a freak result. Accordingly, it was thought unlikely that the Liberal party would regain power for some considerable time. Childers, for instance, gave the Conservatives ten years in office, provided they were prudent.[8] The situation was assessed with characteristic Whig ambiguity by Granville: 'For those who desire a speedy recovery of office, nothing can be more gloomy.'[9] In fact, the position was perceived to be so serious that some had doubts about the future viability of the Liberal party as an instrument of government. Halifax reported to Northbrook that his colleagues were 'not very hopeful . . . as to the future of the Liberal party . . . One really does not see the materials for a future Government.'[10] For, as Cardwell explained, 'The truth is that our party has never been a party, except *ad hoc*, for some special purpose. Such was the Irish Church . . . The only man who could

[5] There is no easy way of verifying the claim made some years later by Francis Adams that abstentions by supporters of the National Education League had cost the Liberals twenty seats: *History of the Elementary School Contest in England* [1882] ed. Asa Briggs (Hassocks, 1972), 300. The UK Alliance was usually prepared, in practice, to support Liberals who took a 'neutral' line on the temperance question: D. A. Hamer, *The Politics of Electoral Pressure* (Hassocks, 1977), 191–2. It should be noted that the Liberation Society did not make disestablishment a test question in 1874: S. M. Ingham, 'The Disestablishment Movement in England, 1868–74', *Journal of Religious History*, 3 (1964–5), 53.

[6] *Manchester Guardian*, 21 Feb. 1874, p. 5.

[7] Ibid. See also *Leeds Mercury*, 7 Feb. 1874, p. 7. A. J. Mundella reported to Robert Leader on 7 Feb. that 'A very distinguished man of the moderates said to me today, "the next 5 years will be spent in educating the nonconformists". He meant in teaching them to be tame and submissive', Mundella–Leader MSS, 6P/64.

[8] Childers to Sir Andrew Clarke, 5 Apr. 1874, in Spencer Childers, *Life and Correspondence of the Right Hon. Hugh C. E. Childers, 1827–1896* (1901), i. 227–8.

[9] Granville to Northbrook, 3 Mar. 1874 (typescript), Northbrook MSS, vol. 22.

[10] Halifax to Northbrook, 20 Feb. 1874, ibid.

have kept together the so-called party, formed from such materials, for so long a time, was Gladstone.'[11]

It appeared, then, as if the alliance of Whigs, Radicals, and Irish Liberals welded together by Gladstone in 1868 was now in disarray, with the Irish and the Radical Nonconformists evidently bent on asserting their separate interests and identities. Early in March 1874, the Irish home rulers (who had stood separately from the Liberals during the general election) actually decided to form an independent party, electing their own parliamentary committee and appointing their own whips (though they continued to receive the Liberal whip as well).[12] The prominence of ecclesiastical questions during the 1874 session of parliament made the prospects for future united action between the Radical Nonconformists and the remainder of the Liberal party equally uncertain. It was seen in the last chapter how Gladstone's speech on the Scottish Church Patronage Bill and his subsequent involvement in the dispute over the Public Worship Regulation Bill gave encouragement to those Nonconformists who looked to him to take the initiative on the question of Church disestablishment. By the end of the session, Gladstone's conduct had left Kimberley wondering whether 'we should have a break-up of parties: next session will show'.[13] During the autumn, all the signs were that the Nonconformists would be as intransigent as ever, as they prepared to continue their agitation for disestablishment and declared their intention of making this a test question in elections.[14] Ominously, Joseph Chamberlain, in an article for the October edition of the *Fortnightly Review*, was arguing that disestablishment and disendowment would be the foremost question in British politics and that it should be regarded as a rallying cause for all Radicals.[15]

In one sense, it was as a reaction to the difficulties of the Gladstone ministry in its last years, and to the fragmentary state of the Liberal party during and after the general election of 1874, that the notion of a revival of 'Whiggery' began to take a hold in political circles. Appropriately enough, it was that most ambitious and barometrical

---

[11] Cardwell to Northbrook, 19 Feb. 1874, ibid.
[12] David Thornley, *Issac Butt and Home Rule* (1964), 212–19, 251–60.
[13] Kimberley to Northbrook, 9 Aug. 1874 (typescript), Northbrook MSS, vol. 22. Cf. Argyll to Northbrook, 28 July 1874, ibid.
[14] See *The Times*, 5 Nov. 1874, p. 7, for a report on the Liberation Society's conference and public meeting at Manchester.
[15] 'The Next Page of the Liberal Programme', *Fortnightly Review*, 16 (Oct. 1874), 405–29.

of politicians, Sir William Harcourt, a former Radical back-bencher before becoming Solicitor-General in Gladstone's ministry in 1873, who emerged as the prophet of the new 'Whiggery'. Convinced of the damage being done to the Liberal party by Gladstone's leadership and the conduct of the extreme Radicals, and seeing also the opportunity this created for him to further his own career, Harcourt had resolved, just prior to the dissolution in January 1874, to 'hoist[. . .] the good old Whig flag'.[16] Following the election defeat, he took the lead in protesting about Gladstone's refusal either to make any commitment to the party or to permit it to be reorganized with a new chief whip. Harcourt therefore wrote to Hartington urging him to assume the leadership:

I have again looked through the list of M.P.s and I send you the names of about 80 (making together with the late government about 100) of persons who would take an active and steady interest in my opinion in said effort to reinstate and reorganise the Liberal Party if you would come forward . . . I have had a long talk with [Sir Henry] James and he is very eager to support. I know no-one who is better acquainted with the mechanism of Party management in and out (especially out) of the House. He like myself is greatly disgusted at the *mot d'ordre* which has evidently been given out from Carlton Gardens by *both the G's* [Gladstone and Granville] to [perpetuate] the state of chaos as much as possible and to prevent all attempts to rally—partly I imagine to *punish* the party and partly to procure a restoration.[17]

Predictably, this intrigue was a failure, as Hartington was unlikely to jeopardize his chances of eventually succeeding to the leadership by appearing to be trying to force Gladstone out.[18] Nevertheless, Harcourt continued to pursue his vendetta against Gladstone, boldly standing up to him, on one famous occasion, during the Commons debate on the Public Worship Regulation Bill.[19] This attack upon Gladstone's ritualist sympathies was renewed in a speech at Oxford,

[16] Harcourt to Mrs Thomas Hughes, 4 Jan. 1874, in A. G. Gardiner, *The Life of Sir William Harcourt* (1923), i. 265. Harcourt had made a speech at Oxford, on New Year's Day, attacking the Radicals, ibid. 263–4.

[17] Harcourt to Hartington, n.d. [19 Feb. 1874], Devonshire MSS, miscellaneous. See also a letter dated 'Thursday', ibid.

[18] Granville warned Hartington of the obvious dangers to his long-term prospects of becoming leader if he was seen to be 'a nominee of William Harcourt', Granville to Hartington, 20 Feb. 1874, Devonshire MSS, miscellaneous. See also Granville's letter of 5 Mar., ibid. Cf. Hartington's reply to Harcourt, 20 Feb. 1874, Harcourt MSS, Box 78, in Gardiner, *Harcourt*, i. 271.

[19] Gardiner, *Harcourt*, i. 273–9.

in December, an eloquent defence of the 'Whig tradition . . . the inheritance of the Liberal party', in which he also urged the Liberals to eschew the extreme views and quack remedies of the faddists and rely instead on those 'moderate' opinions of the Whigs 'which . . . constitute the staple political sentiments of the English nation'.[20] Privately, Harcourt was convinced that Gladstone was about to make a declaration against the Church of England, and he therefore asserted the need for the moderates to act to ensure that the ex-Premier and the Radicals never again ruled the Liberal party or held office.[21]

The proclaimed 'Whig' revival naturally gained vital credibility from the announcement of Gladstone's resignation in January 1875, and the selection of Hartington as the new leader in the House of Commons. For a time there had been the prospect of an embarrassing and damaging public contest for the leadership between Hartington and W. E. Forster, whose supporters, fearing a Whig plot, were demanding a meeting of the parliamentary party to settle the matter.[22] Fortunately, such a calamity was averted, for although Forster enjoyed considerable support in the parliamentary party—as on so many occasions, the party did not divide on 'Whig–Radical' lines—[23] it became painfully clear that he could not command the allegiance of the Radical Nonconformists, who had not forgiven him for the Education Act of 1870.[24] It was partly for this reason that the Liberal front bench were almost unanimous in their opposition to

[20] 'A Speech Addressed to his Constituents in the Corn Exchange, at Oxford, on December 21, 1874, by Sir W. V. Harcourt, Q.C.' (1875). Harcourt received many letters praising his speech, see e.g. those by the Duke of Westminster, 8 Jan. 1875, Harcourt MSS, Box 206, Duke of Bedford, 11 Jan. 1875, and Lord Penzance, 14 Jan. 1875 (typescripts), ibid., Box 727.
[21] Cf. Harcourt to Goschen, 4 Jan. 1875, Harcourt to Fitzmaurice, 6 Jan. 1875 (typescripts), Harcourt MSS, Box 727, in Gardiner, *Harcourt*, i. 285–6.
[22] Playfair to Granville, 15 Jan. 1875, PRO 30/29/28, in Lord Edmond Fitzmaurice, *The Life of Granville George Leveson-Gower, Second Earl of Granville, K.G., 1815–1891* (1905), ii. 145–6. Apart from Playfair, Forster's most influential supporters included Fawcett, Mundella, and Trevelyan. Their correspondence may be found in the Playfair and Mundella papers.
[23] Cf. *The Times*, 2 Feb. 1875, p. 9. A list drawn up by the chief whip gave Hartington only a slight lead, 52 to 46, among those MPs whose views were known: Blairadam MSS, 4/414.
[24] See the *Leeds Mercury*, 21. Jan 1875, p. 5, for the verdict of the United Nonconformist Committee at Crewe, and the *Daily News*, 22 Jan. 1875, p. 6, for the resolution passed by the executive committee of the National Education League.

Forster.[25] Once again, the intransigence of the Radical Nonconformists served to emphasize their political impracticability, for
they were prepared to accept the Whig Lord Hartington rather than
support a man with more advanced opinions, because the latter was
deemed to be a traitor on one specific issue.[26] Hartington thus
emerged as the only candidate capable of maintaining party unity,[27]
and, with Granville prudently withholding a letter expressing Hartington's willingness to stand down rather than force a contest, it was
left to Forster to state publicly his intention of withdrawing.[28] At a
meeting of Liberal MPs at the Reform Club on 3 February, therefore,
Hartington was unanimously endorsed as the new leader in the
House of Commons.[29]

The effect of the bombshell of Gladstone's retirement upon political opinion in London had been dramatic, producing, in the words of
the special correspondent of the *Leeds Mercury*, 'one of the most
remarkable changes of political sentiment that has occurred within
my experience':

Scarcely a day passes that I do not find Liberals who were the most
enthusiastic advocates of Mr. Gladstone's various reforms hinting that the
time for sweeping measures is at least for the present gone by, that the
Country wants repose, that it is unwise to court further constitutional
change, and that as a necessary consequence we may look forward to a long
period of moderate Liberalism and moderate Conservatism alternating with
each other as in the days of Lord John Russell and Lord Derby. Further, there
seems to be a disposition to recognise those advanced Liberals who are
dissatisfied with this prospect, as a sort of Extreme Left, whose alliance
would be more dangerous than their opposition. Impatient Radicals may

---

[25] The *Daily News*, 4 Feb. 1875, p. 4, stated that only Cardwell was prepared to
support Forster. For the feeling against Forster, cf. Lowe to Granville, 25 Jan. 1875,
PRO 30/29/28; Halifax to Northbrook, 21 Jan. 1875 (typescript), Northbrook MSS,
vol. 23.

[26] See J. Guinness Rogers's letter to the *Daily News*, 23 Jan. 1875, p. 5.

[27] Adam, the chief whip, wrote to Granville on 20 Jan. that there was a 'strong
feeling in favour of unity' among the Liberal MPs he had seen, PRO 30/29/28. Cf. the
subsequent letters to the chief whip from W. H. Gladstone, 24 Jan. 1875, Blairadam
MSS, 4/413, and Sir Harcourt Johnstone, 26 Jan. 1875, ibid. 4/414.

[28] Cf. Hartington to Granville, 22 Jan. 1875, PRO 30/29/22A/2; Granville to
Hartington, 23 Jan. 1875, Devonshire MSS, 340.595. Granville had also received a
letter from Playfair, bearing the same date as Hartington's, concluding that Forster
would have to withdraw because of the animosity of the Nonconformists, PRO
30/29/28.

[29] The *Times*, 4 Feb. 1875, p. 8, gave a list of 137 MPs who were present.

call this a return to Whiggism, but it is only my business to describe to you a direction of public sentiment which is unmistakeable.[30]

Such feelings were even to be found expressed in an advanced Liberal newspaper like the *Daily News*, which admitted that 'There is no use in shirking facts. We are probably entering upon a period which . . . is destined to be marked by a succession of moderate Liberal and moderate Conservative Administrations such as those of Lord Melbourne and Sir Robert Peel, Lord John Russell and Lord Derby, Lord Aberdeen and Lord Palmerston.'[31]

There was a general belief that politics in Britain was entering a new phase, or, to be more precise, was re-entering an older one. The Liberal alliance of the 1860s had apparently broken down, and Gladstone himself, who might have been the focus for a reunion of all the disparate elements, was obviously unwilling to accept this role and had made a decision to retire which was assumed to be irrevocable.[32] Viewed in this light, it was not unreasonable to suppose that the period of great reforms associated with the Liberal ministry of 1868–74 had been an aberration, the product of special circumstances, which could not be regarded as a part of the natural order of things.[33] This was reflected in the repeated analogy with the situation in 1841, when, after passing a number of major reforms, the Whig party had become debilitated and unpopular, and was soundly defeated at a general election.[34] Thus, the prognosis appeared to be a reversion to the more 'normal' political dispensation that had existed between 1841 and 1868, when the various sections of the 'Liberal party' had been only loosely bound together and often acted independently,[35] and when the (supposed) narrowness of the field of political contention between the Liberal and Conservative parties had enabled the moderate wings of each to predominate, with 'Lord

---

[30] *Leeds Mercury*, 16 Jan. 1875, p. 7.

[31] *Daily News*, 29 Jan. 1875, p. 4.

[32] Cf. *The Times*, 15 Jan. 1875, p. 9, and the *Leeds Mercury*, 18 Jan. 1875, p. 3, for the view that Gladstone's decision was final.

[33] e.g. *Daily News*, 22 Jan. 1875, p. 4. For an earlier view, see the *Daily Telegraph*, 10 Mar. 1874, p. 6. It should be noted that the *Telegraph* was still, at this stage, a Gladstonian paper.

[34] e.g. *Daily News*, 22 Jan. 1875, p. 4. For an earlier view, see *The Times*, 13 Feb. 1874, p. 9.

[35] The *Daily News*, 3 Feb. 1875, p. 4, made the comparison with the situation in the time of Palmerston (1859–65), *The Times*, 2 Feb. 1875, p. 9, with the Radicals and Russell from 1841–6.

Palmerston's long regime of Liberalism with a nightcap on its head'[36] proving well suited to the requirements of the age.

The dismal position was summed up, from an advanced Liberal point of view, by the *Fortnightly Review* in February 1875: 'Mr. Gladstone's formal retirement completes the eclipse of the party of progress . . . imagination and courage are for the hour at a discount. Intellectual energy and political inventiveness are as much at a discount as either fervour or conviction.' As a result, the controlling influence in politics was left in the hands of a large central group of members of both parties, 'the modern Whigs, whether calling themselves Conservatives or Liberals', who cared little for reform though 'they pretend that they do'. Nevertheless, it had to be recognized that, in this, the 'Whigs' were an accurate reflection of the opinions of the majority of the British public:

The theory that the Government of the day is always Whig, even when it is carried on by nominal Conservatives, is good enough for the mere official politician. Of a neighbouring Country it is said, that France is always left centre. The same is true of England. The great body of the English voters, so far as they have political ideas or interests at all, are left centre. They have a general feeling that the world ought to be made a little better, while they listen sometimes with profound apathy, sometimes with faint intellectual interest, usually with the bitterest suspicion and the most resentful distrust, to every proposal for making it better, and every hint that it is time to begin . . . Our people soon weary of political improvement. They can only tolerate very scanty doses, each little dose being followed by a prolonged and rather stertorous slumber.[37]

'Whiggery', then, had come to be identified with the official or administrative wings of both the Liberal and Conservative parties, embodying their respective claims to be the natural representatives of that large body of moderate opinion in the country, and commanding, for that reason, the support of the majority of party members. Thus the *Edinburgh Review* could affirm its belief 'that the great bulk of the nation is Whig, that the majority of the late Parliament was Whig, including men of note on both sides of the House, and that under another name the majority of the present House is only intent on following similar principles of government under any other leader'. Gladstone's ministry had been rejected, it was argued,

[36] *Daily Telegraph*, 22 Jan. 1875, p. 4.
[37] [John Morley], 'The Liberal Eclipse', *Fortnightly Review*, 17 (Feb. 1875), 295–304.

'not . . . so much by any violent change of opinion in the Country as by its own personal and administrative unpopularity', and the lesson to be learned was clearly that success for the Liberal party in the future would be determined by the strength of its appeal to the 'left centre'.[38]

It is in this sense that we may say that 'Whiggery' was once again in the ascendant within the Liberal party, having been ousted only temporarily by Gladstone, as it was seen to represent the only possible direction for a 'national' Liberal party to pursue in the prevailing political conditions. This view is reflected in the correspondence of various back-benchers at the time of the leadership crisis. Cowper Temple, for example, saw the need to 'help the moderate section of the Liberal party to keep the ascendancy under which alone it [the party] can become powerful in the present state of the public mind'.[39] Similarly, Samuel Laing thought it was necessary to 'satisfy the public that we are safe, and can be relied upon to do nothing that is sensational', and that it was therefore 'essential that we should rally our broken party on the old constitutional Whig nucleus'.[40] Hussey Vivian believed that the selection of Hartington as leader would 'give confidence to many of the old Whig section who have felt of late that things were going rather too fast: our Party in fact wants a little steadying',[41] and Francis Foljambe (a Whig supporter of Forster), doubtful that the Liberal party could ever again act with the Radical Nonconformists, warned of the dangers of making any concessions to them: 'Any policy adopted, any "cry" raised—not for the benefit of the Country, but to unite disaffected members of a party, would in my opinion, not only in itself be highly unpatriotic, but would recoil upon its inventors with fatal effect.'[42]

[38] [Henry Reeve], 'The Past and Future of the Whig Party', *Edinburgh Review*, 139 (Apr. 1874), 544–73. Cf. *Pall Mall Gazette*, 6 Feb. 1874, p. 1.
[39] Hon. W. Cowper Temple to Harcourt, 28 Jan. 1875, Harcourt MSS, Box 206.
[40] Laing to Adam, 27 Jan. 1875, Blairadam MSS, 4/414.
[41] Vivian to Adam, 26 Jan. 1875, ibid. Of course, not everyone felt the same way about the prospect of Hartington as leader. William Rathbone wrote to Adam on 25 Jan. that the party needed a 'vigorous leader': 'I do not believe in "Palmerstonianism" for the Liberal party in office; but in opposition, it appears to me to be simply death', ibid. 4/413.
[42] Foljambe to Adam, 27 Jan. 1875, ibid. 4/414. Thomas Brassey subsequently advised Hartington that 'The difficulty is to keep the left wing of the party in order, and to conciliate such men as Leatham, Richard, and *id genus omne*, without surrendering the principles of common sense to their extravagant demands', 6 Feb. 1875, Devonshire MSS, 340.609.

The appointment of Hartington reflected, as we have seen, the belief that his leadership offered the best hope for maintaining at least some degree of party unity. Whether the effort to achieve this was possible, however, remained in considerable doubt, and Hartington himself had had reservations about accepting the responsibility. He had expressed to Gladstone the opinion that, if the latter carried out his plan to retire, 'there could not at present be any regular leadership',[43] and for some time Hartington seriously toyed with the idea that it would be better for the 'Whigs and moderate Liberals' and the Radicals (as well as the Irish home rulers) to act separately, with their own leaders. As he explained to Granville:

> I think that there is hardly an important question on which the Whigs and Radicals will not vote against each other; 'Dissent', 'Household Suffrage in Counties', 'Education', 'Land Laws', &c: and the position of a nominal leader seeing his flock all going their own way without attending to him, will not be comfortable. If each section had its own leader and its own organisation, it seems to me that there might be more real union and co-operation on points where we could agree, than if we were nominally united; when each section would complain and quarrel every time the party organisation was not used to support its views.[44]

Although in the end Hartington succumbed to Granville's advice that the party wanted a leader,[45] it is unlikely that his talk of recognizing the divided state of the Liberals was merely a testing of the political water. Apart from the fact that others were speaking in similar terms, quite independently of Hartington,[46] his attitude is consistent with his forthright speech at Lewes on 27 January, indicating quite clearly the style and limitations of the leadership that he thought the circumstances permitted, which must rank as the most remarkable declaration of willingness to lead a political party

[43] Hartington to Granville, 13 Jan. 1875, PRO 30/29/22A/2.
[44] Hartington to Granville, 21 Jan. 1875, ibid., in Fitzmaurice, *Granville*, ii. 150–1. This letter expanded on an earlier one dated the 18th. See also Hartington to Harcourt, 17 Jan. 1875, Harcourt MSS, Box 78, in Gardiner, *Harcourt*, i. 289, and Hartington to the Duke of Devonshire, 18 Jan. 1875, Devonshire MSS, 340.584.
[45] Granville to Hartington, 19 Jan. 1875, Devonshire MSS, 340.590. See also Harcourt's letters to Hartington, dated 15 and 19 Jan., urging him to hoist the Whig flag and prevent a disruption of the party, ibid. 340.585 and 587.
[46] Edward Ellice also thought that the Whigs and Radicals should appoint their own leaders, because of the 'irreconcilable differences' between them on certain questions: Ellice to Adam, 29 Jan. 1875, Blairadam MSS, 4/413, while T. B. Potter had wondered, 'Can the Liberal party *ever* be reunited upon Ecclesiastical [questions]?', Potter to Adam, 16 Jan. 1875, ibid. 4/414.

ever made. Hartington freely acknowledged that the Conservative government was more in tune with public feeling, and he admitted that he had 'no particular fault to find' with them. Indeed, he thought that 'the Liberal party to which we belong are [*sic*] now probably for a considerable period removed from office, and I cannot say that I regret it', for although he did not 'for one moment believe that we have reached finality in reforms . . . it is clear to everyone that the people of this Country are not prepared for great and extensive organic change'. It was, however, 'desirable, if possible, to keep the Liberal party together', in Hartington's opinion, because when the time did finally come for further reforms to be made, it would be 'better that they should be made by the Liberals than by the Conservative party'. He therefore advised his audience to 'work and wait . . . in order that you may re-organise and reconstitute the great Liberal party'. But it was necessary for the various sections to realize that the way to secure their objectives was not by setting up their 'crotchets' as test questions, but by accepting that they must seek to convert public opinion by means of persuasion and argument. 'That seems to me to be the Liberal principle of carrying reforms we want to carry—to try to persuade people of their justice and truth, but not to endeavour to force them upon unwilling constituencies and unwilling candidates.' On this condition, Hartington argued, it would be possible for all Liberals to retain their own freedom of action, while at the same time they might 'for all useful purposes . . . remain a united party'.[47]

Clearly, Hartington had only very limited expectations of what his leadership could achieve for the time being. Nevertheless, his maxim that 'Liberal reforms ought to be made by Liberal Statesmen' reflected the Whig belief that, while the Liberal party was likely in future to fill a more limited and sometimes passive role in politics, it was still prudent to maintain a distinct two-party system and so preserve the Whigs' restraining influence over the Radicals. Conservative governments undoubtedly had their place in the new

[47] Hartington at Lewes, *The Times*, 28 Jan. 1875, p. 10. It is also worth noting a later speech in which Hartington referred to his attitude at the time he became leader: 'I accepted the office with no very high ambition and no very exalted hopes . . . I did not think . . . that I would be called upon to do more than keep together, if possible, a small band of moderate Liberals, who might, so to speak, preserve the traditions of the party, and who might keep together a sort of staff of the Liberal party in order that it might be put into requisition when occasion required', Hartington at Glasgow, *Manchester Guardian*, 8 Nov. 1877, p. 5.

dispensation, because there were times when this was what the public wanted. It was to be hoped, therefore, that they would be content to behave as a truly Conservative party, and not succumb to the temptation to usurp the position of the Whigs by outbidding them for the support of the Radicals, as they had done in 1867. The size of the Conservatives' parliamentary majority was at least reassuring in this respect.[48] Not anticipating an early return to power, the Whigs at least hoped that in their efforts to rebuild a 'national' Liberal party, fit to take office on a sound political basis and able to contain its Radical section, they would not be undermined by periodic bouts of Disraelian adventurism.

[48] Cf. Ripon to Northbrook, 27 Mar. 1874 (typescript), Northbrook MSS, vol. 22; Spencer to Dufferin, 19 Mar. 1874, in Peter Gordon (ed.), *The Red Earl: The Papers of the Fifth Earl Spencer, 1835–1910*, i: *1835–1885* (Northants Record Society, 31; 1981), 122–3.

3
The Whig Leadership and the Liberal Party, 1875–1879

For over five years, from February 1875 until after the general election in April 1880, the Liberal party was led by the Whigs Lord Granville and Lord Hartington. Granville, the leader in the Upper House, was continuing in a position which he had held for a number of years in the 1850s and 1860s, and again since 1870. 'Suave in manner . . . intimate with men and things at home and abroad, schooled in diplomacy, practised in administration, popular everywhere, an able and ready speaker',[1] his seniority—he had not only held the foreign and colonial secretaryships but had also been the royal choice for Prime Minister in 1859—made it natural that he should be regarded as the leader of the party as a whole. Hartington, the heir of the Duke of Devonshire, aged only 41 and very much an unknown quantity, presented a stark contrast: to the *Gentleman's Magazine* he appeared to be 'a hard working, conscientious, stolid man, wearing all the polish he was capable of receiving from high education and social intercourse, but withal somewhat surly in manner, greatly impressed with the vast gulf that is fixed between a Marquis and a man to the despite of the latter, innocent of the slightest spark of humour, guiltless of gracefulness of diction, and free from the foibles of fanciful thought'.[2] To this man fell the formidable task of following Gladstone as leader of the Liberal party in the House of Commons.

The fact that the Whig duumvirate survived for so long has not saved it from neglect at the hands of scholars interested primarily in tracing Gladstone's progress back to the leadership, or in studying the activities of the Radicals with whom his success is associated.[3]

[1] The Candidates for the Leadership', *Gentleman's Magazine*, 235 (Oct. 1874), 443.
[2] Ibid. 442–3.
[3] The most important work here is by Richard Shannon, *Gladstone and the Bulgarian Agitation 1876* (1975 edn., Hassocks). The limitations of the fixation with Gladstone and the Radicals are well illustrated by D. A. Hamer, *Liberal Politics in the Age of Gladstone and Rosebery* (Oxford, 1972).

Generally speaking, the internal debate about the strategy and future role of a political party confronted with the unaccustomed prospect of a long period in opposition has been overlooked on the assumption that the Liberals were simply waiting for Gladstone to come back and rescue them.[4] Even when a detailed study of the Liberals in opposition was finally published, in 1978, the Granville–Hartington leadership was still depicted in conventional terms, as hesitant, ineffectual, increasingly unacceptable to the Radicals, and therefore incapable of maintaining party unity.[5] The object of this chapter is to show that the preoccupation with Gladstone and the Radicals, and the failure to take into account the prevailing climate of political opinion described in the last chapter, has seriously distorted the historiography of the Liberal party during the second half of the 1870s. In fact, it will be seen that the forces behind the rival strategies of 'Gladstonianism' and 'Whiggery' were much more evenly balanced than hitherto supposed, and that it is therefore possible to draw a very different picture of the relations between the Whig leadership and the Radical section.

I

Hartington's belief, expressed at the time he assumed Gladstone's position, that the Liberal party could only be kept together on a very light rein, was amply confirmed by the experiences of the 1875 session of parliament. Whereas the various social reforms introduced by the Conservatives offered little scope for criticism, the opposition themselves were still divided on resolutions brought forward by individual Radical members on such issues as county franchise, and temperance reform. Only the government's proposal to tamper with one of the legislative achievements of the Gladstone ministry, by permitting payments to be made by officers wishing to exchange regiments—seen by Liberals as part of an attempt to restore the system of purchasing commissions, abolished by Cardwell—seems to have provoked an organized attack by the Liberal front-bench,

---

[4] One writer has recently stated that in 1875 the Liberal party 'left its conductor and courier waiting, without route or map, for the driver to return', Michael Bentley, *Politics without Democracy, 1815–1914* (1984), 218–19.

[5] John P. Rossi, 'The Transformation of the British Liberal Party: A Study of the Tactics of the Liberal Opposition, 1874–1880', *Transactions of the American Philosophical Society*, 68 (Dec. 1978).

during the committee stage on 16 March. Generally speaking, however, as Kimberley reported to the Viceroy of India, it appeared that 'A great torpor has come over the nation, and . . . seems likely to continue', and while Hartington had made a promising start in his new position, 'Our party is so demoralised that, were he a heaven-born leader, he could do little at present to mend our fortunes.'[6] As the chief whip, W. P. Adam, admitted, the Liberals were not sufficiently united to be able to take advantage of any mistakes the government made, and all that could be done in the circumstances was to 'bide our time'.[7]

Bearing in mind the precarious state of Liberal unity, and the fact that gratuitous assaults upon government policies were unlikely to make much of an impact, because of the size of the Conservatives' parliamentary majority, it is understandable that Hartington should have been reluctant to give a firm lead unless he felt that he was on strong ground and could be sure that the party would respond. He resisted calls to take action, at the beginning of the 1876 session, for example, over the government's decision to purchase the Khedive of Egypt's shares in the Suez Canal, because, as the chief whip had advised him, 'the measure is popular in the constituencies, and members do not wish to take an unpopular side'.[8] For most of the time, Hartington was content to play a supervisory role, often delegating much of the parliamentary work to his more zealous, self-appointed lieutenants, Harcourt and James,[9] while reserving his own interventions for those occasions when the circumstances demanded that he should lead. Thus, Hartington moved an amendment to the Royal Titles Bill, on 16 March 1876, and in August of the same year he moved a resolution condemning the amendments made by the government during the committee stage of its Elementary

---

[6] Kimberley to Northbrook, 5 Sept. 1875 (typescript), Northbrook MSS, vol. 23.
[7] Adam to Northbrook, 2 Aug. 1875, ibid.
[8] Hartington to Gladstone, 18 Feb. 1876, BL Add. MSS 44144, fo. 203.
[9] This was apparent e.g. during the debate on Whitbread's amendment on the slave circular question (24 Feb. 1876) and on James's motion of censure over the government's handling of the Royal Titles Bill (11 May 1876). Prior to the 1876 session, Harcourt and James successfully fought for admission to the meetings of the opposition leadership, which were summoned by Granville and held at his home in Carlton House Terrace. These meetings usually consisted of ex-Cabinet ministers, but some were more restricted while others were broadened to include men with specialist knowledge of certain subjects, such as Dilke, Fawcett, Playfair, and Grant Duff. After a fire at Carlton House Terrace, in Mar. 1879, the meetings were transferred to Devonshire House and summoned by Hartington, but by the beginning of the 1880 session Carlton House Terrace was back in business.

Schools Bill, which seemed to pose a threat to the school boards created by Forster's act of 1870.[10]

In the circumstances, most contemporaries seem to have felt that Hartington had made a remarkably good start in his new position. Speaker Brand noted in his diary, at the end of the 1875 parliamentary session, that Hartington's leadership had been characterized by 'good temper, firmness [and] moderation', and that 'when the occasion offered, he has been quick to strike a telling blow upon his adversaries'.[11] Another favourable estimate of Hartington at this time was made by Henry Lucy, a leading political journalist, who observed that:

Hartington, after the trial of a Session and a recess, stands much higher in public opinion than he did when the bare honour of leadership was thrust upon him. He has maintained throughout the Session a quiet, manly, and modest demeanour which won the respect and esteem of the House. He was always there when wanted, and he was never there when he had better have stayed away . . . As a speaker he has greatly improved in clearness of diction and ease of delivery . . . What Hartington had to say on the current events of the Session was always sensible, and was sometimes conspicuously wise.

One of the most refreshing features of Hartington's leadership, in Lucy's view, was his honesty—'He never truckles even to his own supporters . . . He never stoops to subterfuge.' Hartington, he concluded, was a man 'whose name and personal character are a tower of strength to his party, and whose leadership is a pledge that its policy will be straightforward and intelligent, bold if need be, manly and true always'.[12] One interesting measure of Hartington's success was the fact that no one now looked to Forster as an alternative leader.[13]

[10]   16 Mar. 1876, 3 Hansard, ccxxviii, cols. 75–86: 3 Aug. 1876, ibid. ccxxxi, cols. 438–46.

[11]   Speaker Brand's diary, 12 Aug. 1875, Hampden MSS.

[12]   Henry Lucy, *A Diary of Two Parliaments* (1885–6), i. 112–13 (entry for 1 Aug. 1875). For a Radical testimonial on Hartington's leadership, see Dilke's address to the electors of Chelsea, Jan. 1876, in S. Gwynn and G. M. Tuckwell, *The Life of . . . Sir Charles W. Dilke, Bart, M. P.* (1917), i. 196.

[13]   Lucy, *Diary of Two Parliaments*, i. 111–12, recorded the suspicion, shared by many Liberals, that Forster had designs on Hartington's position (to be fair, there was always a possibility that Hartington might be elevated suddenly to the House of Lords), and that his speeches during the 1875 session on the county franchise and on imperial federation were part of a bid for the leadership. One reason for Forster's diminished prospects, as Lucy noted, was his personal unattractiveness. The destruction of his papers renders Forster in many ways a rather shadowy figure, both at this time and after his resignation from Gladstone's ministry in May 1882, whose motives and ambitions may never be entirely clear.

Furthermore, it is possible to discern signs of greater Liberal unity during the 1876 session, as major divisions on the slave circular question and the Royal Titles Bill took place virtually on straight party lines (excluding the Irish home rulers from consideration), while complete unanimity was achieved in favour of Osborne Morgan's resolution to allow non-Anglican services for Dissenters buried in Church of England cemeteries.[14] Unfortunately for the Whig leaders, fresh difficulties were soon to confront them as public attention began to concentrate on the revival of the 'Eastern Question'—the position of the Ottoman Empire in Eastern Europe. The effect of this was to accentuate the divisions within the Liberal party and thus create an opening for Gladstone, who emerged as the principal critic of Disraeli's foreign policy and as a potential focus for discontented, or more blatantly opportunistic, Radicals.

Any attempt to assess Gladstone's motives must take into account the essential point that, in spite of his formal resignation of the Liberal leadership, he had never really retired from politics. A cursory glance at the sessions of 1875 and 1876 is enough to show that he frequently participated in parliamentary debates, often in accordance with the views of his former colleagues, as was the case with his speech on the regimental exchanges question, in March 1875, and with his speeches a year later during the debate on the Royal Titles Bill, in which he played a prominent part.[15] On a subject for which he felt a special responsibility, finance, Gladstone saw no reason why he should not take his own line, and he informed Hartington, in May 1875, of his plan to move a series of resolutions which 'shall be understood as my own individual proceeding'.[16] Gladstone also pressed the official leaders to take action themselves, if he thought the circumstances were favourable: in the case of the government's purchase of the Suez Canal shares, for example,

[14] Morgan's resolution was defeated by 279 votes to 248, on 3 Mar. It was then taken up in the Lords, by Granville, where it secured 92 votes in a division on 15 May. A strong turnout of Liberal peers was also achieved on 3 Apr. when 91 voted for Shaftesbury's amendment to the Royal Titles Bill.

[15] 16 Mar. 1875, 3 Hansard, ccxxii, cols. 1904–11; 16 Mar. 1876, ibid. ccxxvii, cols. 1736–46.

[16] Gladstone to Hartington, 23 May 1875, Devonshire MSS, 340.620. Cf. Gladstone's animated speech in the House of Commons on Northcote's National Debt plan, 7 May 1875, 3 Hansard, ccxxiv, cols. 290–314. In the event, he did not proceed with the resolutions, but moved an amendment on 8 June, ibid. cols. 1554, 1558–9.

Gladstone urged upon Hartington his view that 'there is probably an amount of opinion, greater than I had supposed, which might be worked up to the point of giving a very *serious* character to the proceedings'.[17] Furthermore, when Hartington declined to act on this occasion, Gladstone was prepared to go his own way, forcing a parliamentary debate on the subject, early in the 1876 session, which proved to be a fiasco for the Liberal party.[18]

Gladstone's involvement in the 'Eastern Question', from the summer of 1876, therefore has to be considered in the light of his evident compulsion to intervene again in politics whenever he saw a favourable current of popular opinion. As Professor Shannon has shown, in his seminal work on the events of 1876, although reports of the atrocities committed by the Turkish authorities on their Christian subjects in Bulgaria had been filtering through to England since May, Gladstone had not associated himself with the early efforts to organize a protest movement and was only drawn in during the second half of August, when extensive newspaper coverage of the atrocities and popular demonstrations in the provinces convinced him that the potential existed for a mass agitation.[19] In a famous letter to Granville, he explained that 'Good ends can rarely be attained in politics without passion: and there is now, the first time for a good many years, a virtuous passion.'[20] The day before he wrote to Granville, Gladstone had started work on a pamphlet, *Bulgarian Horrors and the Question of the East*, which sold 200,000 copies within a month of its publication on 6 September; three days after this, he was addressing a popular demonstration at Blackheath.[21]

The essential characteristics of Gladstone's ambiguous and uncomfortable position in relation to the official Liberal leaders, which were to persist until he finally resumed the leadership in April 1880, may be detected in his own explanation of his conduct during the autumn of 1876. Firstly, in spite of his conspicuous identification with the Bulgarian atrocities campaign, Gladstone was unwilling to admit that this altered in any way his position *vis-à-vis* Granville and Hartington. For instance, he wrote to Adam to decline the suggestion

---

[17] Gladstone to Hartington, 14 Feb. 1876, Devonshire MSS, 340.657.

[18] See Rossi, *Liberal Opposition*, p. 24.

[19] Shannon, *Bulgarian Agitation*, pp. 36–112.

[20] Gladstone to Granville, 29 Aug. 1876, in Agatha Ramm (ed.), *The Political Correspondence of Mr Gladstone and Lord Granville, 1876–1886* (Oxford, 1962), i. 3.

[21] For Gladstone's speech at Blackheath, see *The Times*, 11 Sept. 1876, p. 10.

of a banquet in his honour at Edinburgh, pleading that 'I am a follower and not a leader in the Liberal party and nothing will induce me to do an act indicative of a desire to change my position. Any such act would be a positive breach of faith on my part.'[22] It might well seem that Gladstone was preparing a convenient position for himself, in which he would be free to act without the responsibilities of leadership, but to his own way of thinking, as he told Granville, he was merely 'an outside workman, engaged in the preparation of materials, which you and the party will probably have to manipulate and then to build into a structure'.[23]

Secondly, the simultaneous realization that the failure of Granville and Hartington to act as he wanted them to was causing him to be 'dragged out of . . . retirement',[24] heightened into indignation at the hostility exhibited towards the Bulgarian agitation by the political élite and the metropolitan press (which resulted in an apparent reaction by 'public opinion' during October and November),[25] had the predictable consequence of prompting Gladstone to see his moral crusade on the Eastern Question in class terms. It appeared to him that opinion among the 'upper ten thousand' was lagging behind that being expressed by the country as a whole, and so, increasingly, Gladstone found a sense of moral rapport developing between himself and 'the people'. Thus, in a letter to the chief whip, lamenting the 'spread of what I may call Fitzwilliamism', he maintained that 'all the heart of the Liberal party is with the great work of emancipation'.[26] Similarly, to Granville, he argued that the reaction against the Bulgarian agitation was confined to 'the clubs and Upper Circle', and that 'of the people's interest and unchanging sentiments' he had 'no doubt'.[27] Disappointed by the lack of response from the official leaders, Gladstone's involvement in the agitation deepened, and, on 8 December, he appeared as the main speaker at the National Conference on the Eastern Question, held at St James's Hall, Piccadilly.[28]

[22] Gladstone to Adam, 4 Oct. 1876, Blairadam MSS, 4/431.
[23] Gladstone to Granville, 7 Oct. 1876, in Ramm (ed.), *Gladstone–Granville Correspondence, 1876–1886*, i. 13–14.
[24] Gladstone to Bright, 27 Sept. 1876, BL Add. MSS 43385, fo. 257.
[25] Cf. Shannon, *Bulgarian Agitation*, pp. 239–50.
[26] Gladstone to Adam, 30 Oct. 1876, Blairadam MSS, 4/431. See *The Times*, 24 Oct. 1876, p. 9, for the letter from Earl Fitzwilliam, arguing that it was the duty of all to stand by the government, and criticizing Gladstone's inflammatory language.
[27] Gladstone to Granville, 19 Nov. 1876, in Ramm (ed.), *Gladstone–Granville Correspondence, 1876–1886*, i. 22–3.
[28] Shannon, *Bulgarian Agitation*, pp. 258–62.

The revival of the Eastern Question placed the Whig leaders in an impossible position, trapped in no man's land, for while the 'patriotic' style in which the government conducted its foreign policy secured for the Conservative party the 'Palmerstonian' tradition of asserting Britain's influence in European affairs and protecting the Ottoman Empire from Russian encroachment, the emergence of Gladstone as the principal critic of that policy also demonstrated the vulnerability of the Whigs' hold on their left flank. Such a situation left the Whigs with little hope of developing a distinctive policy of their own, as they were understandably reluctant to indulge in a purely factious opposition to a government of whose conduct many of them generally approved, but equally aware that failure to differentiate their own position from that of ministers would leave little hope for maintaining even a semblance of Liberal unity.

After visiting Constantinople (September–October 1876), Hartington was convinced, like Forster, who had just completed a similar trip, that autonomy for the 'Christian' provinces of Eastern Europe was impracticable, that no reforms could be imposed upon the Sultan without armed intervention by the European Powers, and that the Powers were no longer disposed to act with one another in any case.[29] In his speech at Keighley on 3 November, therefore, Hartington took a very cautious line, refraining from any attack on the aims and methods of the British government and confining his criticisms to its refusal to endorse the Berlin memorandum of May.[30] He was prepared to assert that the Turks were incapable of self-reform and had to be pressured into making concessions by the 'Concert of Europe', but significantly, Hartington declined to comment on the question of what methods of coercion should be applied

[29] Hartington to the Duke of Devonshire, 25 Sept. and 11 Oct. 1876, Devonshire MSS, 340.674, 676, extracts printed in Bernard Holland, *Life of Spencer Compton, Eighth Duke of Devonshire, 1833–1908* (1911), i. 179–81. For Forster's view, see the letter to his wife in T. Wemyss Reid, *The Life of the Rt. Hon. W. E. Forster* (1888), ii. 139–41, and his letter to R. H. Hutton of the *Spectator*, 11 Oct. 1876, ibid. 147–51; see also his speech at Bradford, *Manchester Guardian*, 9 Oct. 1876, pp. 6–7. As Shannon, *Bulgarian Agitation*, p. 119, has noted, Forster's trip to Constantinople may well have been designed as a means of asserting his own position against Hartington.

[30] Even this criticism was somewhat inconsistent with his previous views. He had actually approved of the government's rejection of the Berlin memorandum at the time: Hartington to Granville, 28 June 1876, PRO 30/29/26A. Cf. Granville's speech in the Lords on 26 June, 3 Hansard, ccxxx, cols. 417–18. Note also Hartington's highly 'Palmerstonian' views expressed on 8 Feb. 1876, after the government's cautious endorsement of an earlier European initiative, the Andrassy note: ibid. ccxxvii, cols. 70–88.

by the Powers. With regard to the Bulgarian agitation itself, Hartington was suitably ambiguous, praising it for making clear to the
government that 'they could not rely upon the support of the people
of this Country in the maintenance of the Turkish Government
unless they could show adequate means for the reform of abuses, for
the protection of the Christians, and adequate security against the
recurrence of such outrages'.[31] In private, however, Hartington's
opinions were far more trenchant. With a meeting of the Powers due
to take place at Constantinople, he was opposed to Mundella's
planned National Conference on the Eastern Question as he could
see no reason 'why . . . any moderate man is to pledge himself to the
"release of the provinces from the direct rule of the Porte"'.[32]
Gladstone's participation in the National Conference was obviously
vexing for Hartington, who thought that 'the Whigs and moderate
Liberals in the House are a good deal disgusted', and feared that if
Gladstone 'goes on much further, nothing can prevent a break-up of
the party'.[33] As for the Conference itself, it had simply ignored, in
Hartington's opinion, all the difficulties of the situation. He had no
wish to see Britain embroiled in a war for the sake of Turkey, but he
was also deeply suspicious of Russian intentions, and thought it
might become necessary for Britain to take steps to prevent her from
extending her territory and influence in Eastern Europe.[34]

During the early months of the 1877 session of parliament,
therefore, the opposition leadership was careful not to commit itself
to any specific policy. The best course for the Liberals to pursue,
Hartington advised Harcourt, was to concentrate its criticisms upon
the failure of the government to act in concert with the other
European Powers when it refused to sign the Berlin memorandum.[35]
This strategy had the double advantage of providing the Liberals

[31] *Manchester Guardian*, 4 Nov. 1876, p. 8.
[32] Hartington to Granville, 26 Nov. 1876, PRO 30/29/22A/2, in Holland,
Devonshire, i. 183–4.
[33] Hartington to Granville, 18 Dec. 1876, PRO 30/29/22A/2, in Holland,
Devonshire, i. 185–7.
[34] Ibid. Hartington expressed these views in an even more forthright manner in a
letter to Spencer on 12 Nov. 1876, in Peter Gordon (ed.), *The Red Earl: The Papers of
the Fifth Earl Spencer, 1835–1910*, i: *1835–1885* (Northants Record Society, 31;
1981), 127–9.
[35] Hartington to Harcourt, 14 Feb. 1877, Harcourt MSS, Box 78. Cf. the speeches
made a few days earlier, following this line, by Granville (8 Feb.), 3 Hansard, ccxxxii,
cols. 15–32, and by Hartington (8 Feb.), ibid., cols. 72–92. For a later speech taking a
decidedly 'Palmerstonian' line, see Kimberley (20 Feb.), ibid., cols. 684–9.

with a text for criticizing the government, on which they could all easily unite, that also happened to be entirely retrospective, as the Whigs no longer believed a concerted policy of action by the Powers to be possible. Accordingly, as Hartington explained to Gladstone, the Liberals ought to be content to sit tight and avoid being drawn into making any declaration of policy while diplomatic efforts to resolve the situation were continuing.[36]

Gladstone's position at this time reveals the ambiguity of his relationship with the popular agitation over the Eastern Question. In fact, his views on the subject were much more limited than many supporters in the country would have supposed, for, as Professor Shannon has pointed out, the reference in his pamphlet on the 'Bulgarian Horrors' to the removal of the Turks from Europe 'bag and baggage' meant only the removal of the central Turkish administration, not of the Turkish population: Gladstone, in other words, still wished to maintain the 'territorial integrity' of the Ottoman Empire.[37] The curious result of this ambiguity was that, while Gladstone threatened to bring forward a series of resolutions in parliament calling for the European Powers to coerce the Turks into conceding reforms,[38] he always seemed to hesitate about taking such a step, in spite of the fact that an impressive vote in the House of Commons might have influenced the diplomatic proceedings.[39] Instead, Gladstone delayed his decision to move the 'five resolutions' until the worst possible moment, two days after the Russians had unilaterally declared war on Turkey (24 April).[40] It was rather gratuitous to talk of a concert of Europe forcing the Turks to implement reforms at just the time when such a prospect was at its most distant, and there must be a strong suspicion that, albeit

[36] Hartington to Gladstone, 3 Mar. 1877, BL Add. MSS 44144, fo. 223, in Holland, *Devonshire*, i. 193–4. Cf. Hartington's speech during the debate on a motion by Fawcett calling for guarantees by the Turkish government, 23 Mar. 1877, 3 Hansard, ccxxxiii, cols. 408–14.

[37] Shannon, *Bulgarian Agitation*, pp. 109–10. Cf. Gladstone's original speech on the Eastern Question in the Commons (31 July 1876), 3 Hansard, ccxxxi, cols. 172–202.

[38] Gladstone to Granville, 28 Jan. and 24 Feb. 1877, in Ramm (ed.), *Gladstone–Granville Correspondence, 1876–1886*, i. 29, 30–1.

[39] Cf. Dilke's memoir, 6 Jan. 1877, in Gwynn and Tuckwell, *Dilke*, i. 216; Harcourt to Fitzmaurice, 25 Jan. 1877 (typescript), Harcourt MSS, Box 727, in A. G. Gardiner, *Life of Sir William Harcourt* (1923), i. 316. Hartington was angered at the way Gladstone had encouraged Fawcett to forward a motion without himself voting for it: Hartington to Granville, 23 Mar. 1877, PRO 30/29/22A/2.

[40] For the text of the resolutions, see 3 Hansard, ccxxxiv, cols. 101–2.

unconsciously, it was the irrelevance of the policy Gladstone was advocating that made it easier for him to bring it forward. Moreover, by choosing this moment to take independent action, Gladstone was imperilling the fragile unity of his party.

The 'five resolutions' were not only extremely embarrassing for the official leaders, who had no wish to raise a definite issue while the future was so uncertain, but they were seen by Hartington as a serious threat to his authority in the House of Commons.[41] With virtually the whole of the Liberal front bench in agreement, it was resolved, at a meeting on 2 May, to oppose the resolutions by putting up Sir John Lubbock to move the 'previous question'. Furthermore, much to Gladstone's disgust, this decision was fed to the press, while at the same time great pressure was put on back-bench MPs to follow the official line.[42] For some days, a break-up of the Liberal party seemed to be unavoidable,[43] until finally, on 5 May, Gladstone agreed to a compromise whereby the second resolution was modified and the controversial third and fourth ones were dropped altogether.[44] He was still able to make his planned speech in the Commons,[45] but his former colleagues, while regretting the absence of concerted action by the Powers, merely emphasized the need for Britain to maintain her neutrality so that she might help to mediate when the Russo-Turkish war ended.[46]

Significantly, then, when confronted with a determined resistance from the Whigs, Gladstone had been forced to back down. Hartington's letter to Granville, shortly after this episode was over, illustrates very forcefully his view that the authority of their leadership had been at stake:

the explanation of recent divisions appears to me very simple and to be just this: that upon the Eastern Question Mr. G. has taken the lead, and is looked

---

[41] Hartington to Granville, 30 Apr., 1 May 1877, PRO 30/29/26A.

[42] See the *Daily News*, 3 May 1877, pp. 4–5, for the official leaders' decision; Gladstone to Argyll, 4 May 1877, in John Morley, *Life of William Ewart Gladstone* (1903), ii. 564, for Gladstone's complaints about the deliberate leak and the pressure on MPs. The *Manchester Guardian*, 4 May 1877, p. 7, carried a report that Hartington might resign if a majority of Liberal members defied him.

[43] See the London correspondent of the *Leeds Mercury*, 5 May 1877, p. 7.

[44] Rossi, *Liberal Opposition*, p. 53.

[45] 7 May 1877, 3 Hansard, ccxxxiv, cols. 402–39.

[46] Hartington (14 May), ibid., cols. 923–38; Forster (10 May), ibid., cols. 688–701; Goschen (11 May), ibid., cols. 807–18; Harcourt (14 May), ibid., cols. 876–86.

upon by a large portion of the party as their leader. Whether if you, I, or others were out of the way, he could unite the party upon the subject, is not the question. While we remain responsible for the management of the party in Parliament, Mr. G. cannot expect that we should entirely subordinate our opinions and judgment to his, and unless we do, it seems inevitable that one section of the party will follow his lead, and the other ours.
[. . .]
As to the recent Resolutions . . . I fail to see how the split could have been avoided, *unless* we were prepared to follow instead of to lead. Mr. G. may think that the compromise come to at last might have been adopted at the beginning; but I think that, unsatisfactory as it was, it could only have been accepted by us after the protest on behalf of our independence, which was made by our announced intention of voting for the previous question on the Resolutions taken as a whole.[47]

There can be little doubt that, if Gladstone had forced his resolutions to a final issue, the Liberal party would have been seriously divided. In fact, according to several Radicals, the party was split more or less half and half between the supporters of Hartington and of Gladstone.[48] The only partial analysis that we have of the division in the party is one made by Dilke, when he was compiling his memoir in the 1890s. He exaggerated, however, in arguing that the most striking fact about the situation was the way both the Whigs and the Radicals were split on the issue. It is true that his memoir lists the names of about a dozen supporters of Gladstone who could be defined as 'Whigs', in a social sense, and a few others who had announced their intention of abstaining, but the presence of most of the individuals on this list is unsurprising and merely serves to emphasize that not all 'Whigs' held 'Whiggish' opinions. The great majority of 'Whigs' and moderates did, it is clear, follow the front bench. Of greater interest is the number of MPs regarded by Dilke as 'Radicals' who, for various reasons, were unwilling to follow Gladstone. These included most of the prominent figures in the so-called 'peace party': John and Jacob Bright, Henry Richard, and Sir Wilfrid Lawson (T. B. Potter was an exception), who were not prepared to countenance any policy that might involve Britain in the use of

[47] Hartington to Granville, 25 May 1877, PRO 30/29/22A/2, in Holland, *Devonshire*, i. 198–200.
[48] Cf. Dilke's memoir, 3 May 1877, BL Add. MSS 43933, fos. 82–91; Mundella to Robert Leader, 4 May 1877, Mundella–Leader MSS, 6P/67; Fawcett in the House of Commons, 14 May 1877, 3 Hansard, ccxxxiv, cols. 918–23.

military force, even against the Turks. Joseph Cowen and his followers, such as E. A. Leatham, also supported Hartington, though Dilke
put this down to personal hatred of Gladstone. But other individual
Radicals from below the gangway whose opposition to Gladstone
surprised Dilke included J. K. Cross, Fitzmaurice, and Trevelyan.[49]
The main lesson from Dilke's analysis would seem to be that, even on
a major issue like the Eastern Question, the differences among the
Liberals could, for any number of reasons, cut across and therefore
blur the recognized political distinctions.

The débâcle over the five resolutions did nothing, of course, to
prevent Gladstone from causing further trouble to the official Liberal
leaders. On the contrary, the effect of this set-back was merely to
reinforce his sense of alienation from the political élite, and so draw
him into a closer alignment with the Radicals. It was no coincidence
that, at the end of May, he attended the inaugural conference of
Chamberlain's National Liberal Federation.[50] Writing to Granville,
to defend his acceptance of Chamberlain's invitation to speak at
Birmingham, Gladstone complained of 'the party lukewarmness on
the aristocratic side', and argued that there was a great need for an
electoral reorganization of the Liberal party. It was in this context of
his enthusiasm for new ways of cultivating the popular support
which he believed existed for his own political stance, in the immediate aftermath of the set-back over the five resolutions, that Gladstone
expressed his often-quoted 'opinion . . . that the vital principle of the
Liberal party, like that of Greek art, is action, and that nothing but
action will ever make it worthy of the name of a party'.[51]

The difficulties experienced by the Liberal leadership in finding a
suitable stance on the Eastern Question, and the additional problem
posed by Gladstone's inability to resist the urge to lead an assault
upon the foreign policy of the Beaconsfield administration, resulted
in a virtual breakdown of party discipline during the tumultuous
parliamentary session of 1878, when the belligerent postures of the
government—determined to prevent Russia from imposing her own

---

[49] Dilke's memoir, 3 May 1877, BL Add. MSS, 43933, fos. 82–91, partially
printed by Gwynn and Tuckwell, *Dilke*, i. 221, 223–4.
[50] See Shannon, *Bulgarian Agitation*, pp. 268–71, for the connection between the
failure of the five resolutions and Gladstone's appearance at Birmingham.
[51] Gladstone to Granville, 19 May 1877, in Ramm (ed.), *Gladstone–Granville
Correspondence, 1876–1886*, i. 40. Note also Gladstone's letter of 23 May, ibid. i.
42, arguing that 'as in so many other cases, the Liberal party alone is the instrument by
which a great work is to be carried on'.

peace terms upon Turkey—threatened to lead to war. With the Russo-Turkish conflict nearing its bloody end, parliament was recalled early, for 17 January, and was quickly confronted with a request for an emergency vote of credit, of six million pounds, for military precautions. This placed the opposition leaders in an invidious position, as there were obvious dangers in appearing to obstruct ministers during a period of national emergency, but equally serious problems, from the point of view of party morale and unity, if nothing was done. Consequently, there was a sharp division of opinion at the meeting of the Liberal leaders on 29 January: Gladstone, Bright, Harcourt, Argyll, Stansfeld, and Granville were in favour of a hostile resolution, Hartington, Goschen, and Childers were against outright opposition, while Forster, typically, wavered.[52] In the end, it was agreed that Forster, and not Hartington, should move an amendment declaring simply that the existing circumstances did not justify the granting of additional financial resources for military preparations.[53]

Events during the following few days quickly revealed the hollowness of the opposition's stance, however. Reports that Russia and Turkey had agreed to an armistice were still unconfirmed,[54] and, as fears grew that the Russian forces might still be advancing, it became apparent that many on the Liberal side were doubtful of the wisdom of proceeding with Forster's amendment. Two back-benchers, Fitzmaurice and Cartwright, drafted a letter to Hartington suggesting (on the optimistic assumption that an armistice had actually been agreed to) that a compromise might be arranged whereby both the government's vote of credit and the opposition's amendment would be dropped. At a meeting with some opposition 'wire-pullers' (including Lord Wolverton) at Lady Waldegrave's house on 3 February, Cartwright noted that 'everyone was animated with a desire that something could be devised to bring about an extrication from a discussion that we felt to have become inexpedient'. Hartington

---

[52] See the accounts in Goschen's diary, 29 Jan. 1878, in Hon. A. D. Elliot, *Life of George Joachim Goschen, First Viscount Goschen, 1831–1907* (1911), i. 183, and in Childers to Sir Andrew Clarke, 1 Feb. 1878, in Spencer Childers, *Childers*, i. 251–2. Before this meeting, Hartington had written to Granville threatening to resign because of differences with his colleagues: 29 Jan. 1878, PRO 30/29/22A/2, in Holland, *Devonshire*, i. 204–6.

[53] See Forster's speech in the Commons, moving the amendment, 31 Jan. 1878, 3 Hansard, ccxxxvii, cols. 729–50.

[54] Goschen's diary, 2 Feb. 1878, in Elliot, *Goschen*, i. 185.

arrived later to discuss the possibilities.[55] The publication of Fitz-maurice's letter in *The Times*, the following morning (apparently Hartington had advised against this, preferring that the suggestion be made during the parliamentary debate itself), aroused the interest of Goschen, and of Forster himself, though Granville had doubts whether the government would allow the opposition off the hook so easily.[56] Then, on 6 February, the Liberals were thrown into a complete panic when a report was circulated that the Russians were advancing on Constantinople,[57] and at a meeting of the opposition leaders, the following day, it was agreed, even by Gladstone and Bright, that Forster's amendment should be withdrawn.[58] More revealing still was the fact that this decision was adhered to even after it became known, during the course of the debate in parliament on that day, that the rumour was untrue. The end result was a serious split in the party, with ninety-four Liberals voting against the Speaker leaving the chair after the second-reading stage of the address (nine others were paired against), ten Liberals voting with the government, and the remainder following their leaders and abstaining.[59] Worse still was to follow, for when the government announced the next day that it had sent the fleet through the Straits to protect British lives and property, Hartington intervened in the debate for the first time to announce his approval of this move and to state that the opposition would not now oppose the vote of credit.[60] This naturally outraged many Liberal MPs, and Gladstone and Bright themselves were among the 113 who opposed the emergency

[55] W. C. Cartwright's diary, 3 Feb. 1878, Cartwright MSS, 6/13. See *The Times*, 4 Feb. 1878, p. 8, for Fitzmaurice's letter.

[56] Goschen's diary, 4 Feb. 1878, in Elliot, *Goschen*, i. 185–6. Goschen went on to lament the fact that 'Matters are changing for the worse with us every day. Numbers of members can scarcely make up their minds to vote with us. Meetings are held against us in many parts of the Country. We are clearly unpopular. Hartington and I foresaw all this. It is miserable to think how great a mistake it has been. No news of armistice or of signature of peace.'

[57] Forster's diary, 6 Feb. 1878, in Wemyss Reid, *Forster*, ii. 191–2.

[58] Forster's diary, 7 Feb. 1878, ibid. ii. 192.

[59] The figures for this division, and all the others in this chapter, are my own calculations, and do not take into account the Irish home rulers. Dr Rossi is clearly mistaken when he states (*Liberal Opposition*, p. 66) that 'only a handful of Radicals' defied the Liberal leaders on this occasion.

[60] 8 Feb. 1878, 3 Hansard, ccxxxii, cols. 1339–51. Hartington was remarkably unrepentant about his action, merely discussing with Granville 'whether anything should be said, or done, short of resignation' to restore his authority: Hartington to Granville, 9 Feb. 1878, PRO 30/29/22A/2.

vote of credit at the committee stage, in defiance of their leaders' policy of abstention, while thirteen voted with the government.

It seems reasonable to suggest that the extent of the division in the Liberal party in February 1878 was aggravated by the inconsistency of the leadership itself, which had angered many MPs. This was perfectly understandable, for, once it was clear that the Russian forces were not advancing, there was really nothing to justify the decision to drop an amendment that had been considered worthy of parliament's attention a week earlier, other than the fact, as we have seen, that the Liberal leaders had lost their nerve and had been looking for an excuse to back out of a position which some of them had argued strongly against taking up in the first place. Furthermore, as with the crisis over the five resolutions, the division in the Liberal ranks did not resolve itself simply into one between 'Whigs' and 'Radicals', because the question at stake, in February 1878, was not whether it was right for the government to protect Britain's interests in the Eastern Mediterranean, but whether Beaconsfield's aggressive policy of seeking an emergency vote of credit—part of a strategy of bluffing the Russians in order to force them to the negotiating table—was best designed to achieve a peaceful settlement of the Eastern Question. A more accurate impression of the rift in the Liberal party may be gained from the fact that of the 128 members who opposed the vote of credit in either of the divisions on 7–8 February, sixty-two played no part in subsequent revolts against the official leaders. On 9 April, sixty Liberals, including Gladstone and Bright, voted for an amendment by Sir Wilfrid Lawson, opposing the government's decision to call out the reserves, after the Whigs had chosen not to move an amendment.[61] Then, on 27 May, shortly after the defeat of a mild amendment by Hartington criticizing the transfer of Indian troops to Malta, on constitutional grounds,[62] thirty-three Liberals effectively opposed the grant of funds necessary for the

[61] Cf. Hartington to Granville, 31 Mar. 1878, Pro 30/29/22A/2, hoping that it would be possible to avoid an amendment. It should be noted that Gladstone had not wanted the Radical amendment to be moved—Mundella to Robert Leader, 14 Apr. 1878, Mundella–Leader MSS, 6P/68—but felt compelled to support it because of 'my relation to the mass of feeling and opinion out of doors, in concert with which I have worked all along', Gladstone to Granville, 12 Apr. 1878, in Ramm (ed.), *Gladstone–Granville Correspondence, 1876–1886*, i. 71. A disgusted Granville thought Gladstone's vote 'one of the heaviest possible blows to the discipline of a party', Granville to Hartington, 10 Apr. 1878, Devonshire MSS, 340.752.

[62] For Hartington's speech, 20 May 1878, see 3 Hansard, ccxl, cols. 264–80. His amendment was defeated, 347: 226.

upkeep of the Indian troops by voting against the motion for the House to enter into committee of supply. In all, seventy-four Liberal MPs (including those who acted as tellers) acted against the official line, and sixty-six of these had also rebelled against the party leaders in February.[63]

It must surely have been an immense relief for the Whigs when the Eastern Question drew to a close, in the summer of 1878, after the Russians agreed to submit the treaty of San Stefano, which she had imposed upon Turkey, to a Congress of the European Powers at Berlin. Beaconsfield's triumphant return from the Congress in July, boasting 'peace with honour', finally deprived the opposition of what little credibility remained to it,[64] and though Hartington made the half-hearted gesture of moving three resolutions criticizing specific aspects of the treaty of Berlin (dubbed by Beaconsfield as 'congratulatory regrets'), there was never any intention of challenging the government's conduct as a whole. It was probably indicative of his real feelings that, in his opening speech, Hartington should have altogether forgotten to mention the third of his resolutions. Clearly, he himself hoped that the Eastern Question could now be left to settle down without any further interference by the great Powers.[65] The demoralized state of the Liberal party was reflected in the division, 338 to 195 in the government's favour, on 2 August: only 184 Liberals attended to cast their vote for Hartington's resolutions, though a further twenty-one were paired in their favour, but eight voted with the government and twenty-six were absent unpaired.

The Times, not without justice, described the debate on the treaty of Berlin as 'a half-hearted attack upon a position which the assailants felt they could not win, and from which they did not care to dislodge the occupants'.[66] This would appear to sum up quite accurately the Whig leaders' perception of their limited room for manœuvre throughout the period dominated by the Eastern Question. John Bright may have been entitled to his suspicion that the

---

[63] See Appendix I.

[64] Cardwell wrote gloomily to Halifax, at this time, that 'In truth there is no effective Opposition, nor any great disposition to create one. The government has us all at its feet', 12 July 1878, Hickleton MSS, A4/154.

[65] Hartington (29 July 1878), 3 Hansard, ccxlii, cols. 527–49. For another favourable estimate of the treaty of Berlin, see Childers to Sir Andrew Clarke, 11 July 1878, in Spencer Childers, *Childers*, i. 254.

[66] *The Times*, 3 Aug. 1878, p. 9.

opposition leaders' own policy was 'so like that of the Government as not to be easily distinguished from it',[67] but it is easy to overlook the crucial point that, in their tentative response to the 'jingoism' of the Beaconsfield administration, the Whigs were seen to represent more accurately than Bright or Gladstone the kind of responsible opposition that the country expected. What the Whigs were anxious to avoid was any imputation that they were indulging in factious opposition at a time of national emergency, and the vehemence of Gladstone's demagogic attacks upon the ministry was therefore considered to be immensely damaging to the reputation of the Liberal party in the eyes of the country. It is significant, for example, that after the National Conference on the Eastern Question, in December 1876, Hartington's view was that 'Gladstone *might* be supported in the Country at a general election, though I doubt it'.[68] Similarly, during the winter of 1877–8, when talk of war with Russia was in the air, Hartington was convinced that public opinion would be strongly behind any request by the government for an emergency vote of credit,[69] and he therefore felt that, for the Liberal party, 'the magnanimous and patriotic line will be the best'.[70] Indeed, by the spring of 1878, Russophobia appeared to be so rampant in the country that even Radicals who had backed Gladstone, like Mundella and Chamberlain, were compelled to admit that if the government were to call a general election, the Liberals would be routed.[71] Far from restoring the fortunes of the Liberal party by their attacks upon the government, then, Gladstone and his Radical associates were considered by many to be an electoral liability.

It is worth remembering, too, that when the Whig leaders came into conflict with Gladstone and the Radicals, a large proportion of Liberal MPs, in most cases the majority, followed the line laid down by the official leadership. Whatever Hartington may have felt about the disloyalty of the ex-Premier's conduct, he never for one moment supposed that Gladstone could unite the party on his

[67] Bright's diary, 5 Apr. 1878, in R. A. J. Walling (ed.), *The Diaries of John Bright* (1930), 406–7.

[68] Hartington to Granville, 18 Dec. 1876, PRO 30/29/22A/2, in Holland, *Devonshire*, i. 185–7.

[69] Hartington to Harcourt, 19 Dec. 1877, Harcourt MSS, Box 78; also 27 Dec. 1877 (typescript), ibid., Box 720.

[70] Hartington to Lady Waldegrave, 1 Jan. 1878, Strachie MSS, WW 23.

[71] Mundella to Robert Leader, 30 Mar. 1878, Mundella–Leader MSS, 6P/68; Chamberlain to Collings, 2 Apr. 1878, Chamberlain MSS, JC5/16/81.

policy.[72] In the case of the crisis over the five resolutions, for example, it is clear that a great many supporters of the Liberal front bench were appalled by Gladstone's move. A. J. Mundella, one of Gladstone's supporters, noted with regret that 'a lot of our men are raging against him', and the London correspondent of the *Manchester Guardian* reported that, while some of the more extreme Radicals were hoping to see Gladstone return as leader, this was 'an anticipation in which the majority of Liberals do not share, and which very few above the gangway hope to see realised'.[73] Furthermore, after his climb-down over the resolutions, one journalist, Henry Lucy, wrote that Gladstone appeared to have 'undermined and hopelessly blown up' his position,[74] whereas Hartington's caution and good sense had strengthened his reputation in the House of Commons. By the end of the 1877 session, according to Lucy, it seemed that 'As the influence of Hartington has increased the influence of Gladstone, in the House of Commons at least, has declined.' There was 'a strong personal animosity towards Gladstone existent in the House . . . by no means confined to the Conservative benches', which was attributable to his own 'restlessness, uncertainty, self-contradiction, and general reck-lessness of conduct'. As a result, in Lucy's judgement, Gladstone's 'present position may be best defined by the fact that whilst three years ago his retirement from the leadership of the Liberal party appeared to be a calamity never to be recovered from, a proposition for his return at the present time would, if submitted for the approval of members who sit on the opposition benches, be voted down by a majority of three to one'.[75]

Nor were the Whig leaders without sympathizers in the Liberal press. The Radical *Daily News* may have criticized their lack of fire and accused them of failing to uphold Liberal principles for fear of making a bad showing in the division lobby,[76] but these complaints were counterbalanced by the approbation given to the Whigs by other weighty dailies like the *Manchester Guardian* and the *Leeds Mercury*. The *Guardian*, for instance, deplored Gladstone's conduct

[72] Cf. Hartington to Spencer, 12 Nov. 1876, in Gordon (ed.), *Spencer*, pp. 127–9; Hartington to Granville, 18 Dec. 1876 and 25 May 1877, PRO 30/29/22A/2, in Holland, *Devonshire*, i. 185–7, 198–200.
[73] Mundella to Robert Leader, 28 Apr. 1877, Mundella–Leader MSS, 6P/67; *Manchester Guardian*, 5 May 1877, p. 7.
[74] Lucy, *Diary of Two Parliaments*, i. 235 (entry for 8 May 1877).
[75] Ibid. i. 315–16, entry for 13 Aug. 1877. For another report on Hartington's growing political stature, see Speaker Brand's diary, 14 Aug. 1877, Hampden MSS.
[76] *Daily News*, 3 May 1877, pp. 4–5; 4 May 1877, p. 8; 8 Feb. 1878, p. 4.

at the time of the crisis over the five resolutions,[77] and subsequently defended the Whigs against the censure of the *Daily News* by repudiating the notion of opposition for opposition's sake.[78] Similarly, both the *Guardian* and the *Mercury* sprang to the defence of Hartington and Forster when they withdrew the amendment against the emergency vote of credit: 'We cannot believe that there will be any general disposition to condemn Lord Hartington and Mr. Forster because in deciding upon their duty as Liberals they have not forgotten that they were Englishmen.'[79]

The Whig leaders' concern lest a hastily conceived and essentially factious opposition to the government's foreign policy should 'alarm the moderate Liberals'[80] is further vindicated by the demonstration of the strength of back-bench feeling at the time of the ministerial announcement of the calling out of the reserves in April 1878. Incensed by Radical efforts to put pressure on Granville and Hartington to move a hostile amendment,[81] a counter-demonstration was got up by MPs above the gangway. According to Chamberlain, 'Hayter, member for Bath, Norwood of Hull, Beaumont of Durham and others, have been obtaining signatures to a kind of pledge to vote for the Government in the event of any amendment being put—it is said that at least 100 members have assented to this document. Unfortunately the defections are not confined to men of this stamp.'[82]

[77] *Manchester Guardian*, 9 May 1877, p. 5 The *Leeds Mercury*, 3 May 1877, p. 4, 8 May 1877, p. 4, had taken a more restrained line, but lamented the prospect of a split and was immensely relieved when this was avoided. The attitude of the *Scotsman* is also instructive, as an example of the unwillingness of the anti-war section of Liberal opinion to support Gladstone's resolutions: see the leading articles on 4 May 1877, p. 4; 5 May 1877, p. 6; 7 May 1877, p. 4.
[78] *Manchester Guardian*, 2 June 1877, p. 7.
[79] *Leeds Mercury*, 11 Feb. 1878, p. 3 Cf. *Manchester Guardian*, 8 Feb. 1878, pp. 4–5. The editor of the *Mercury*, Wemyss Reid, was of course a staunch supporter of Forster. The *Scotsman*, taking the same pacific line as before, was therefore strongly opposed to the vote of credit, but refrained from criticizing the Whigs: see the leading articles of 8 Feb. 1878, p. 4; 9 Feb. 1878, p. 6.
[80] Granville to Adam, 25 Dec. 1877, Blairadam MSS, 4/966.
[81] On 3 Apr. Bright led a deputation from 120 provincial towns to see the Whig leaders: Bright's diary, 3 Apr. 1878, in Walling, *Bright Diaries*, p. 406. In the Commons, a group of some thirty Radicals were holding meetings, chaired by L. L. Dillwyn; see Leonard Courtney to his sister, 10 Apr. 1878, in G. P. Gooch, *Life of Lord Courtney* (1920), 138–9.
[82] Chamberlain to Collings, 5 Apr. 1878, Chamberlain MSS, JC5/16/82. Mundella had earlier reported to Robert Leader that 'Nearly all the moderate men above the gangway are resolved not to vote against the Government', 3 Apr. 1878, Mundella–Leader MSS, 6P/68. Cf. W. C. Cartwright's diary, 3 Apr. 1878, Cartwright MSS, 6/13.

Much to Bright's disgust, the meeting of the opposition leaders on 5 April decided on a policy of abstention.[83] In spite of this decision, however, when Sir Wilfrid Lawson pressed an amendment opposing the government's action outright, twenty-five Liberals still entered the ministerial lobby. Harcourt's report to Hartington on the division list, while playing down the seriousness of the defection, is nevertheless illustrative of the leadership's priorities:

I think on the whole considering the difficulty of the situation you have no cause to be dissatisfied with the division list. The small number voting with the Government I think justifies the 'walking away' policy. I don't find above twenty [*sic*] of whom half were names we could always have reckoned on such as:—Cowen, Macduff, Samuda, Mure, R. Duff, W. Foster, Stafford, Rothschild, Lorne, Ralli, Yeaman, F. Goldsmid. The only 'good men and true' I regret to see there are the Brasseys, F. Foljambe, C. Cotes and T. Hankey.

Besides these there are a few nondescripts of the priggish order like E. Fitzmaurice (who regards himself as a great foreign statesman), Tavistock and Sir E. Watkin.

So that in the Whig and moderate party you may regard yourself as well followed.

The list of Lawsonites is very much what might have been expected.

There are a few men who voted under pressure of constituents being strongly against the amendment and having sworn nothing should induce them to support it like Backhouse, Holms (who told me five minutes before the division he would not vote), Leatham, Leith and Lush, J. Pease . . .

If Gladstone and Bright had abstained, I do not think Lawson would have had twenty votes. Still if you take our Whip at 240 in number you may consider that against 80 men who took their own line 160 followed your example which considering the state of the party ought I think to be satisfactory to you.[84]

If anything, Harcourt was being unduly complacent, for the Whig defections on 9 April, when considered in conjunction with smaller revolts in February and August, which have already been noted, and also one in May against Hartington's resolution criticizing the movement of Indian troops, were indicative of the existence of a group of moderates who were dangerously close to becoming estranged even from the Whig leadership of Hartington and Granville. Similarly with the peers, Henry Reeve had reported early in the year

[83] Bright's diary, 5 Apr. 1878, in Walling, *Bright Diaries*, pp. 406–7.
[84] Harcourt to Hartington, 10 Apr. 1878 (typescript), Harcourt MSS, Box 720.

that 'the disposition of many of the moderate Whigs such as Lord Morley, Duke of Bedford, Duke of Cleveland etc is to support the foreign policy of the Government'.[85] Indeed, two long and obviously well-informed reports by the London correspondent of the *Manchester Guardian* show that during the autumn and winter of 1878, when Liberal popularity had apparently reached its nadir, moves were afoot to form a third party. The initiative seems to have come, in the first instance, from Liberal peers who felt that the government's policy was either insufficiently anti-Russian or not sufficiently pro-Turkish. Twenty or thirty such peers were reported to have taken part in 'actual negotiations . . . principally in two of the great Whig houses in Scotland', with a view to reviving 'the old Whig party, with recognised leaders on the Palmerstonian lines so far as regards continental politics, but acting occasionally with Liberals on domestic questions'.[86]

In the second article for the *Manchester Guardian*, which was published during the emergency parliamentary session summoned to debate the Afghan war in December 1878, it was reported that the movement in favour of a third party had 'developed considerable activity among members of the Lower House', and that its 'chief promoters were connected with the late Government'. It was also suggested, however, that the thirty or so conspirators in the Commons were motivated by somewhat different considerations from those of the peers, one being 'an increasing objection which prevails among the moderate Liberals to be led by the new Birmingham school of politicians, and equally to resent what I may call the platform activity of the tail of the party'. The London correspondent of the *Guardian* did not think it 'desirable to name the promoters of the movement at this early stage; suffice it to say, they are well known men. The presence of two or three of these in this new departure will some day cause considerable surprise to those Radicals who at the present moment receive a certain amount of encouragement and patronage from them.'[87]

The article of 10 December is of considerable interest for what it

---

[85] Reeve to T. Longman, 12 Jan. 1878, in J. K. Laughton, *Memoirs of the Life and Correspondence of Henry Reeve* (1898), ii. 254–5. Early in Feb. Lord Fortescue resigned as chairman of the North Devon Liberal association: *The Times*, 4 Feb. 1878, p. 8.

[86] *Manchester Guardian*, 21 Oct. 1878, p. 5. It may safely be assumed that the Duke of Sutherland was one of the ringleaders in this movement.

[87] Ibid. 10 Dec. 1878, p. 5.

shows of the wider tensions within the Liberal party generated by Joseph Chamberlain's efforts (which will be discussed later) to establish a new form of electoral organization in the constituencies and use that organization to promote a pro-Gladstonian line on the Eastern Question. As regards the individual M Ps who may have been involved in the discussions about the setting up of a third party, it is impossible to be entirely sure, but it is quite likely that one of those whose participation might have surprised some Radicals was Lord Edmond Fitzmaurice, who had rebelled against Hartington on the question of the calling out of the reserves in April, and who evidently feared that Chamberlain was intent on using his new organization to drive the Whigs out of the Liberal party.[88] Another MP with a Radical reputation who might be suspected was G. O. Trevelyan: he was certainly making anti-Chamberlain noises in December 1878, and may well have been the mysterious 'T' who discussed the possibility of a coalition government with Lord Carnarvon, the former Conservative Colonial Secretary.[89] The possible identities of the 'chief promoters', who had been 'connected with the late Government', make for even more fascinating speculation, of course, but two names stand out. One is Forster, who had just been engaged in a battle with the Bradford Liberal association, which had been reorganized along Birmingham lines.[90] The other is G. J. Goschen, whose case is perhaps the most interesting of all. Goschen was one of the few moderate Liberals who could genuinely be described as doctrinaire, having continued to stand out against a reform of the country franchise after Hartington had committed the Liberal party to it in 1877, for fear of the implications of 'democracy' for the principles of *laissez-faire*.[91] It is unlikely that Goschen really thought he could still organize a political party on anti-democratic lines, but it does seem

---

[88] For Fitzmaurice's fears about the 'caucus', see Shannon, *Bulgarian Agitation*, p. 269. In July 1878, he expressed the opinion that, if only he could feel more confidence in the government's handling of foreign affairs, he would be inclined to 'support them and let the old Liberal party go, where perhaps it is bound in any case, to the devil', Fitzmaurice to W. C. Cartwright, 22 July 1878, Cartwright MSS, Box 5, fo. 229. And yet Fitzmaurice's views on domestic issues were notably advanced, for he favoured disestablishment, secular education, and an extensive reform of the electoral system: see his speech at Swindon, *The Times*, 25 May 1877, p. 7.

[89] Cf. Brett's diary, 10 Dec. 1878, Esher MSS, 2/5; Carnarvon's diary, 8 Dec. 1878, BL Add. MSS 60912.

[90] M. Ostrogorski, *Democracy and the Organisation of Political Parties* (1902), i. 194–203.

[91] See Elliot, *Goschen*, i. 157–65.

that he was trying to draw Hartington into an alignment with him in opposition to the 'ultra-democratic' section of the Liberal party.[92] An entry in Goschen's diary, quoted by his biographer, provides a tantalizing glimpse of the position into which he was moving, early in 1878: 'Long talk with Cotes [MP for Shrewsbury] about moderate men. He declares they are in a majority. I am coming to the conclusion that a schism must come. We cannot be dragged any further by Gladstone and Bright. We are compromised by them every moment. This is my ruling idea.'[93] Unfortunately, in the absence of Goschen's papers, it is not possible to trace his activities in 1878 any further,[94] but it is well to remember the presence of Goschen, and the desire that the Liberal party might be organized on some basis other than that being dictated by the 'Birmingham school' of Radicals.[95]

The inability of the Liberals to present a united front on the Eastern Question, in the period 1876–8, naturally served to affirm the Whigs' belief that it would be some considerable time before the party could form a credible alternative government.[96] Indeed, this assumption underlay the strategy of the Whig leadership throughout. A typical remark by Granville, in a letter to Gladstone in October 1876, was: 'supposing the improbable event of a Tory breakdown, what a state our party is in for a reconstruction of a Liberal Government'.[97] Granville could not 'conceive anything less desirable' than the premature removal of the Conservatives from

---

[92] It is interesting to note Goschen's description of the meeting, in Jan. 1878, when he backed Hartington in opposing the rejection of the government's request for a vote of credit: 'Row with Harcourt. He holds me personally responsible for separating Hartington from Liberal party. My reply. Result—Forster is to move a mild amendment. Hartington to sum up. My fear of being left in the lurch, etc', Goschen's diary, 29 Jan. 1878, ibid. i. 183. The hostility between Goschen and Harcourt, who were competing for influence over Hartington, is reflected in Harcourt's expressions of delight at Goschen's suicidal folly in voting against the county franchise motion: Harcourt to Granville, 30 June 1877, PRO 30/29/29.

[93] Elliot, *Goschen*, i. 187. It is not clear whether the date of this entry is 20 Feb. 1878, or later.

[94] There is a suggestion, though, that Goschen's decision not to stand again for the city of London was prompted by disagreement with his constituents: see the *Pall Mall Gazette*, 12 Aug. 1878, p. 2.

[95] Matthew Arnold wrote to his sister Jane Forster, after a visit to Seacox Heath in Jan. 1879, that 'It was very pleasant at Goschen's, and pleasant too to see the movement towards what I call real ideas in politics spreading among the younger men', G. W. E. Russell (ed.), *Letters of Matthew Arnold, 1848–1888* (1901), ii. 181.

[96] e.g. Kimberley to Halifax, 25 Sept. 1876, Hickleton MSS, A4/151.

[97] Granville to Gladstone, 4 Oct. 1876, in Ramm (ed.), *Gladstone–Granville Correspondence, 1876–1886*, i. 12.

office.[98] As he observed in a letter to Harcourt, at Christmas 1877, 'The only dark spot is the possibility at which you hint of an immediate break up of the ministry . . . the pear is certainly not yet ripe for us . . . it will take a long course of discredit really to break up the Conservative party.'[99] The experiences of the 1878 session were not such as to encourage a more optimistic assessment of the prospects for a strong Liberal government,[100] and even after the special session summoned for December of that year to debate the invasion of Afghanistan, the state of the party had not improved quite as dramatically as Dr Rossi has suggested.[101] It is true that the Radical section eventually united behind the leadership on this occasion, but Rossi is wrong to state that no Liberals entered the government's division lobby: nine MPs did so, and a further eighteen, some of them with previous records of rebelliousness, were absent unpaired. Moreover, the division in the House of Lords was a great disappointment for Granville, as the Liberal amendment received only sixty-five votes (including those of one bishop and three dissident Conservatives), with fourteen pairs.[102] The fear still persisted that Liberal opposition to the government might be taken too far, and that the continuing violence of Gladstone's language was likely, as Hartington put it, to 'cause a reaction' in the country in the Conservatives' favour.[103] Even Northbrook, one of the foremost critics of the government's Central Asian policy, in his assessment of the situation by the spring of 1879, was imbued with a sense of the fragility and delicacy of the Liberal party's position in relation to public opinion: 'I think that the opposition will be wise to be quiet. The Country is, I fear, more with than against the Government; attacks will be put down to party spirit and a desire for office, and do our cause, in my opinion, more harm than good. The Country seems to me to have lost for a time its common sense and its conscience.

[98] Granville to Argyll, 14 Oct. 1876, PRO 30/29/22A/4. Cf. James to Harcourt, 13 Aug. 1876, Harcourt MSS, Box 86.

[99] Granville to Harcourt, 25 Dec. 1877, Harcourt MSS, Box 84.

[100] Granville to Hartington, 7 Oct. 1878, Devonshire MSS, 340.776.

[101] Rossi, *Liberal Opposition*, pp. 86–8.

[102] See Lord Ripon's diary, 11 Dec. 1878, BL Add. MSS 43641, for Granville's disappointment at the Liberals' showing. Halifax subsequently wrote to Granville regretting the desertion by the old Whig families: 11 Dec. 1878, PRO 30/29/26. The Duke of Sutherland, and Lords Fitzwilliam and Fortescue, opposed the Halifax amendment. Cf. Duke of Somerset to Granville, 7 Dec. 1878, ibid. declining to vote for it.

[103] Hartington to Harcourt, 2 Jan. 1879, also 5 Jan. 1879, Harcourt MSS, Box 78.

There are some symptoms of a reaction, but I am afraid not enough to secure any general support or sympathy to those who may try to oppose the popular feeling.'[104] Granville, who was predicting, in the autumn of 1878, that when the general election came the Conservatives would 'retain a formidable majority',[105] remained convinced, at the beginning of 1879, that 'the Liberal party is not in a satisfactory position for taking office'.[106]

II

There is no doubt that, up to 1878, the dissensions within the Liberal party arising from the government's controversial but apparently popular foreign policy imposed limits on the effectiveness of the Whig leadership. However, we should not allow this to divert our attention from the fact that simultaneously, with regard to domestic policy, efforts were being made by the Whig leaders to accommodate the views of the Radical section of the party. By 1879 an agreed programme of reforms may be said to have existed, comprising county franchise and redistribution, the reform of county government, and unspecified reforms of the land laws, with certain other issues left 'open'.

The official Liberal leaders were, by nature, far less conservative in their attitudes to reform than is usually supposed. Although the traditional 'Whig principles' of constitutional government, individual liberty, and religious toleration continued to be espoused by the *Edinburgh Review*, these were treated, in so far as they retained any practical relevance, as part of a common political heritage to which appeals could be made at appropriate moments, rather than as a set of working principles for the regular conduct of government. In terms of domestic reform, therefore, it was never apparent that 'Whig principles' meant anything more than a desire to maintain sufficient control over the Liberal party so as to be able to regulate the pace at which the process of reform proceeded, and notions of 'honour' and 'duty' ensured a considerable degree of flexibility and open-mindedness on many questions.

[104] Northbrook to Argyll, 15 Mar. 1879, Northbrook MSS, vol. 19.
[105] Granville to Derby, 10 Sept. 1878, Derby MSS.
[106] Granville to Derby, 8 Jan. 1879, ibid.

Hartington's is a particularly interesting case here. The public impression he conveyed was that of a profoundly apathetic and inert nature, capable of being animated only by the mention of 'the turf', and this has probably done much to encourage the conventional view of the inadequacy of the Whig leadership. And yet it was Hartington, by virtue of his position as leader in the House of Commons, who was primarily responsible for the initiatives made in Liberal reform policy. Lord Derby, when entertaining him at Knowsley in October 1879, suspected that there might be something misleading about Hartington's reputation, which he thought might be 'only the result of a naturally lethargic habit', and which 'in some respects . . . may be useful: it would be impossible to suspect Lord H. of intriguing for office, or of using factious means of trying to push himself'.[107] Derby's suspicions were later confirmed by Reginald Brett, who became Hartington's private secretary at the beginning of 1878. Brett was dismissive of 'the mythical Hartington . . . the man who loves pleasure to the exclusion of work, who is *altogether* without personal ambition, whose mind turns away from long and serious contemplation of dull subjects. All this is fiction.' On the contrary, 'Apart from politics he has no *real* interest in life; and cut off from them he would be in reality as bored as he appears to be by them'.[108] In Brett's view, the key to Hartington's apparent apathy and sur- liness lay in the fact that he had been 'robbed of a public school, and consequently has been forced to go through life with certain chambers of the heart and mind hermetically sealed'.[109] As a result, G. W. E. Russell later recalled, Hartington was 'absolutely selfish; and he did not, as others of the same temperament have often done, attempt to conceal the selfishness under an air of courtesy or consideration. He had no manners. He observed no social usages. If

[107] Lord Derby's diary, 24 Oct. 1879, Derby MSS.
[108] Brett to W. T. Stead, 22 Apr. 1886, in M. V. Brett (ed.), *Journals and Letters of Reginald, Viscount Esher* (1934), i. 125–6. A similar impression was recorded by Sir Alfred Pease: 'The public had, and writers still have, the idea that he was slow, heavy and bored, but this notion arose merely from his appearance, features and attitudes. He would sit during a debate for hours with his hat over his eyes, his legs stretched out and his hands in his pockets. He was really very industrious, got to the bottom of questions, argued soundly, and was a bold reformer when he had decided reform was desirable and practical', Alfred E. Pease, *Elections and Recollections* (1932), 109.
[109] Brett to Stead, 22 Apr. 1886, in M. V. Brett, *Esher*, i. 125–6. Cf. Brett's diary, 3 Jan. 1878, Esher MSS, 2/4: 'He is said to be lacking in human kindness.' It may well be relevant that, apart from never attending a public school, Hartington had been motherless since the age of 7.

he was engaged to dine at eight, he came at nine. If you asked him a question, he either stared in stony silence or else drawled a monosyllable which sounded like "Whor?" and meant "What?" '[110]

It seems that with Hartington, consciousness of the importance of his social rank (magnified perhaps as a result of an isolated childhood) combined with a highly developed sense of the political responsibilities which this entailed were revealed to the world in the form of a condescending aloofness which one biographer described as an air of 'you-be damnedness'.[111] That is to say, the duties he was called upon to fulfil by virtue of his high station were acknowledged grudgingly (but one suspects that he would have complained far more if he had not been asked to perform them), and though he executed them conscientiously, they were always done on his own terms, out of a sense of *noblesse oblige*. The relevance of this for our purpose is that Hartington's attitude not only prescribed no limits to the extent to which reforms pursued by constitutional means might be taken, but actually encouraged a considerable degree of open-mindedness on various issues, as Lord Derby discovered:

[with regard to land reform] . . . he made it plain to me that he had not arrived at any definite conclusion. Indeed he said so plainly enough, admitting that he had no idea what would be pressed by the Liberal party . . . As to the Irish business he was still more vague . . . India . . . he admitted that he knew nothing about . . . [the Duke of Argyll] said it was quite true that he had not studied these matters nearly enough, that he was a good deal in the hands of Adam, the Liberal Whip, who told him the party expected this.[112]

Hartington's aristocratic, highly detached concept of leadership had the advantage of being well suited to the realities of the political situation facing the Liberals after 1874. As we have seen, he had been doubtful, at the time of Gladstone's resignation, whether it was practicable to maintain a single, united Liberal organization, and when it fell to him to attempt this, he had had no expectations of early success. In his speech at Lewes, Hartington had recognized that

[110] G. W. E. Russell, *Portraits of the Seventies* (1916), 86. Cf. Alfred Lyttelton to Brett, 8 Nov. [1878?], Esher MSS, 10/1, after an encounter in a country house: 'It was the first time that I had met Hartington, who is one of the queerest fellows I have ever seen. He has no manners at all, but it must be said that his rudeness is splendidly impartial—he was rather affable to me, I only mean relatively, that is to say he would answer five times out of six if I spoke to him whereas he frequently deigned no reply even to ladies.'
[111] Henry Leach, *The Duke of Devonshire* (1904), 146.
[112] Lord Derby's diary, 26 Oct. 1879, Derby MSS.

the most that could reasonably be hoped for, in the circumstances, was an uneasy equilibrium, based on mutual toleration by the various sections of the party and a *laissez-faire* attitude by the leaders, and sustained by a frank acknowledgement of the dismal short-term political outlook. The formula outlined at Lewes was accordingly repeated in speeches at Bristol and Sheffield, at the end of 1875: the country was prosperous and content, and had little desire for political change; rather than trying to force unwelcome measures upon the country, therefore, the Liberal party had to take the opportunity to re-examine and order its ideas, through discussion and reflection, in preparation for the time when political changes were desired; during this time, no section of the party was to be asked to make any sacrifices, and all were to be free to promote their opinions by legitimate methods, provided that no attempt was made by any one section to impose its views upon the rest.[113] Significantly, these speeches appear to have been well received by many Radicals as proof of Hartington's growing stature as a party leader, and as heralding closer union between the various Liberal sections.[114]

By holding out to the various groups within the Liberal party the prospect of the attainment of their objectives, through their own efforts, Hartington was able to maintain a semblance of unity without making any unnecessary and possibly compromising commitments. During a tour of Scotland in November 1877, for example, it was therefore possible for him to comment on the question of disestablishment in a way satisfactory to his audience. Observing that the disestablishment of the English Church was not a matter of practical politics, he added that it was very doubtful 'whether there is any numerous body who suppose that here either is this question ripe for solution'. He hoped, therefore, that Scottish disestablishment would not be made a test question at future elections. But, as far as Hartington was concerned, while 'I will be no party to stimulate agitation in this Country upon this subject nor . . . will I be a party to any attempt to repress discussion', and he was prepared to say that 'when, if ever, Scotch opinion, or even Scotch Liberal opinion, is fully formed upon this subject . . . the Liberal party . . . will be prepared to

---

[113] Hartington at Bristol, *Manchester Guardian*, 15 Nov. 1875, p. 6, and at Sheffield, ibid., 16 Dec. 1875, p. 8.
[114] Henry Fawcett to Harcourt, 2, 31 Dec. 1875, Harcourt MSS, Box 206; Mundella to Robert Leader, 21, 24 Dec. 1875, Mundella–Leader MSS, 6P/65. Mundella had been responsible for organizing the meeting at Sheffield.

deal with this question on its merits and without reference to any other considerations'.[115] In a speech at Glasgow the following evening, the feelings of the temperance reformers were similarly placated. Hartington was 'quite willing to admit that social and economic reform of the type of the Permissive Bill may, some day or other, become the duty of the Liberal party', although 'that time has not yet come'. In this case, he was rather more guarded than with disestablishment, because 'I am not myself, and I don't think it probable I shall be, an advocate of the Permissive Bill', but nevertheless, 'I fully accord to the advocates of that bill and of similar measures the perfect right to endeavour to induce their Countrymen to agree with the opinions they hold on the subject'.[116]

It should be emphasized that Hartington's willingness to keep an open mind about many of the political issues of the day did not indicate that he had any particular wish to see them resolved in the way the 'faddists' hoped. There was no question of him pursuing a subject any further than was absolutely necessary. Privately, for instance, he maintained that his remarks on Scottish disestablishment at Edinburgh had 'been made too much of', and he expressed to Abraham Hayward his fear 'of the Liberals being disappointed where he fell short, as he should do, of their expectation'.[117] The art of Whiggery, it seems, lay not so much in following the 'democracy' as in trying to stifle the impulse for reform as far as possible, firstly by relying on the natural conservatism of the masses to ensure that many subjects never became ripe for settlement, and secondly, failing this, by exerting their own vitiating influence in order to confine the extent of an unavoidable measure as far as possible within safe boundaries.

A point of far greater importance is that these gestures by the Whigs towards their advanced Liberal supporters, and the more definite commitments which were given on certain subjects, were conceived not simply as a way of keeping them in good humour, but, in all probability, as a means of drawing them away from Gladstone at a time when his vociferous opposition to the government's foreign policy was threatening to cause a breach in the party ranks. Of

---

[115] Hartington at Edinburgh, *Manchester Guardian*, 7 Nov. 1877, p. 8.
[116] Hartington at Glasgow, ibid., 8 Nov. 1877, p. 5.
[117] Hayward to Lord Carlingford, 6 Dec. 1877, in Henry E. Carlisle (ed.), *A Selection from the Correspondence of Abraham Hayward, Q.C., from 1834 to 1884* (1886), ii. 285.

course, it was perfectly proper that the Whigs should have tried to do this, as Gladstone had consistently refused to accept the logic of his conduct by resuming the responsibility for leading the party. But it was certainly something more than a coincidence that, at the end of June 1877, just a few weeks after the crisis over Gladstone's five resolutions, Hartington should have changed his position and, for the first time, given official party backing to Trevelyan's annual motion for the extension of the borough franchise to the counties—a move which secured a vastly improved Liberal vote for the proposal, since 'many Whigs and moderate men rallied to Hartington'[118]—at a time when a demonstration of unity was badly needed.[119] Furthermore, it was in the autumn of the same year that Hartington made his speech at Edinburgh, on Scottish disestablishment, as well as the speech at Glasgow in which, apart from his remarks on the temperance question, he also stressed the official leadership's commitment to reforms in the county franchise, local government, and (more vaguely) the land laws.[120] Hartington's reaction, shortly after his Scottish campaign, to Gladstone's visit to Ireland and renewed interest in Irish matters is also worthy of note as an indication of the direction which his leadership was beginning to take: 'It will be very mischievous, I think, if Mr. Gladstone goes in strongly for the agitation [regarding the Fenian prisoners], and it might be best for us all, Government and Opposition, if he could be anticipated . . . As to Local Government, I have not the remotest idea what Mr. Gladstone's views about it are; and I should doubt very much whether he goes further than I should like to go.'[121]

Hartington's reluctant determination to assert his own leadership, when possible, in order to appease the Radicals and forestall any further Gladstonian revolts, was confirmed during the emergency parliamentary session in December 1878, which was summoned following the government's decision to launch an invasion of Afghanistan. At the outset, Hartington had been his usual, cautious self, preferring, in spite of the growing indignation among those of

[118] Speaker Brand's diary, 29 June 1877, Hampden MSS.
[119] For the success of this move, cf. Harcourt to Granville, 30 June 1877, PRO 30/29/29; *Manchester Guardian*, 2 July 1877, p. 5. The motion was defeated by 276 votes to 220, with the minority including some twenty-five home rulers: 3 Hansard, ccxxxv, cols. 585–8. Only three Liberals, Foster, Goschen, and Lowe, voted against the motion.
[120] *Manchester Guardian*, 7 Nov. 1877, p. 8; 8 Nov. 1877, p. 5.
[121] Hartington to Granville, 23 Nov. 1877, PRO 30/29/22A/2.

his colleagues with previous responsibility for the administration of India, to wait until more information was available, and being opposed to any hostile motion on the address.[122] Gladstone, on the other hand, having already delivered an intemperate attack on the government's policy in a speech at Greenwich on 30 November, was obviously intent on a full-scale assault and wanted to move an amendment to the address himself, when the official leaders decided not to do so.[123] It appeared as if the old difficulties of the Eastern Question were about to be repeated all over again, and after Hartington's initial lack-lustre speech on the address, indicating the opposition leadership's acceptance that war was necessary in the existing circumstances, rumours were afloat of a Radical plot to overthrow him.[124] However, on the final night of the subsequent debate on a motion by Whitbread (who had been put up by the Liberal front bench), to which Gladstone had earlier contributed a powerful speech,[125] Hartington surprised everyone with the force with which he criticized the government for its handling of the situation in Afghanistan.[126] Brett noted that his chief's speech 'pleased our extreme left amazingly', and one of them, A. J. Mundella, reported enthusiastically that 'Hartington made an entirely new departure last night. He smote the Government *hip and thigh*. Gladstone spoke to me in *high praise* of his speech which was really of a very high order.'[127]

During the 1879 session, Hartington further enhanced his reputation with the Radicals by making an important speech in a debate on the agricultural distress which was afflicting the country in the wake of a series of bad harvests and the growth of cheap foreign imports.

[122] Cf. Hartington to Granville, 17, 20, and 28 Nov. 1878, PRO 30/29/22A/2. The fullest, but not entirely reliable, account of the Liberal party and the Afghan question is that in Rossi, *Liberal Opposition*, pp. 77–90. Whigs like Halifax, Northbrook, Argyll, and Lord Lawrence had been incensed by the so-called 'Cranbrook despatch' of 20 Nov., a letter by the Indian Secretary blaming previous Liberal administrations for the situation that had arisen in Afghanistan. The text of this may be found in the *Annual Register* for 1878, pp. 253–9.

[123] See Lord Ripon's diary, 2 Dec. 1878, BL Add. MSS 43641, recording a meeting of the Liberal leaders.

[124] Ibid., 7 Dec. 1878. Cf. Brett's diary, 9 Dec. 1878, Esher MSS, 2/5. For Hartington's speech on 5 Dec., see 3 Hansard, ccxliii, cols. 95–111.

[125] 10 Dec. 1878, 3 Hansard, ccxliii, cols. 541–71.

[126] 14 Dec. 1878, ibid., cols. 807–29.

[127] Brett's diary, 14 Dec. 1878, Esher MSS, 2/5; Mundella to Robert Leader, 14 Dec. 1878, Mundella–Leader MSS, 6P/68. See also Speaker Brand's diary, 17 Dec. 1878, Hampden MSS.

Hartington's intervention was evidently calculated to encourage and give a lead to his party on the land question, for he had originally contemplated moving an amendment of his own.[128] In his speech, on 4 July, he welcomed the Conservative proposal for a Royal Commission on agricultural distress but urged the government to make the terms of reference as wide as possible: Hartington advocated a full inquiry into the system of land tenure, to discover to what extent the existing laws created an artificial situation, and he was prepared to consider the need for changes in the laws of entail and settlement, as well as the possibility of a measure to facilitate cheaper land transfer, which might encourage smaller proprietors.[129]

It is an interesting reflection on the state of Radical 'thinking' by 1879 that the cautious and qualified initiative made by Hartington on the land question easily went far enough to satisfy their expectations. Few even among the Radicals were arguing for anything more than 'free trade' in land at this stage,[130] and it was not until the early 1880s that more extreme panaceas began to be seriously discussed. A closer examination of the position of the Radicals themselves during the period 1875–9 is now necessary in order to show why it was that the modest programme of domestic reforms put forward by the Whigs—land-law reform, county franchise and redistribution, and the reform of county government—provided an acceptable basis for Radical co-operation.

III

It was seen in Chapter 1 that Gladstone's resignation had been a serious set-back for those Radicals who had hoped for a dramatic 'conversion' to English Church disestablishment which might restore the cohesion of the Liberal party on a more advanced basis. John Bright, the father figure of Radicalism, was consequently forced

---

[128] Brett's diary, 29 June 1879, Esher MSS, 2/5.

[129] 3 Hansard, ccxlvii, cols. 1520–33. But note his speech at Radnor, *Manchester Guardian*, 6 Sept. 1879, p. 8, in which he emphasized the qualifications contained in his parliamentary utterance.

[130] See the *Manchester Guardian*, 29 Oct. 1879, p. 8, for the speeches by Fawcett and John Holms, the MPs for Hackney. All that was being advocated here was a measure to give the landowner absolute powers of sale. Cf. the pamphlet by Shaw Lefevre, 'Freedom of Land' (1880), published in the National Liberal Federation's practical politics series.

to admit that 'The party . . . is weakened and for a time destroyed, and I cannot see for it any immediate and early restoration.'[131] Although his speech at Birmingham during the ensuing leadership crisis triggered off speculation that he was about to launch an extra-parliamentary crusade on the disestablishment question, it is doubtful whether Bright any longer possessed the energy for such an undertaking, and his decision to chair the meeting at the Reform Club which endorsed Hartington as the new leader was itself an indication that he had no such intention.[132] The fact was that Bright saw little enough scope, in the short term, for co-operation between the various Radical groups, as the complaints expressed in a letter written at the end of the year show: 'Our forces are scattered, and there is little *sagacity* among the most earnest men. I fear the "fanaticisms" and "crazes" of sections of the party will prevent any combined action.'[133] Bright remained convinced, as he explained to Thorold Rogers, that 'The Church question & the land question are by far the greatest questions before us', but, because the former was dependent 'more on explosive materials within, than on action & assault from without', he foresaw 'no early, & no sure, if remote, success from placing it in the front of the battle', while as for the latter, 'that is an economical question, and the public, whilst well off, may be unwilling to look at it'. Besides, there was the problem of who was to give the lead on this subject: 'Where are the men to rouse and instruct the people? The Free Trade victory was won mainly by the teaching and the labour of a few men. The last Suffrage Bill was made unavoidable by the labour of a few. The land question may be carried by like methods of action, but I see scarcely anyone who understands it, & least of all among those who aspire to lead the working men.'[134]

For a time in the mid-1870s, it appeared possible that the energy and organizing power which the diverse forces of Radicalism so badly needed might be supplied by Joseph Cowen, who had been an MP for Newcastle since January 1874. In many respects, Cowen seemed admirably well equipped for the role of leader of Radical

---

[131] Bright to Granville, 15 Jan. 1875. PRO 30/29/28, in Fitzmaurice, *Granville*, ii. 142–3.

[132] Bright's letter to Granville, ibid., suggests that he had had no idea of getting up an agitation on the disestablishment question. For newspaper reaction to his speech at Birmingham on 25 Jan., cf. *The Times*, 27 Jan. 1875, p. 9; *Daily Telegraph*, 26 Jan. 1875, p. 4; *Pall Mall Gazette*, 26 Jan. 1875, p. 1.

[133] Bright to W. H. Northy, 26 Dec. 1875, BL Add. MSS 44877, fo. 53.

[134] Bright to J. E. Thorold Rogers, 28 Aug. 1875, Thorold Rogers MSS, fo. 149.

Liberalism, combining as he did a strong personal base in the north-east of England with impeccable Radical credentials on a wide range of issues (he was far in advance of most Radicals on many issues, as is evidenced by his consistent sympathy for the demands of the Irish home rulers, during the period 1874–86). In 1874 he launched a new organization in Newcastle, the Northern Reform League, with a programme including universal suffrage, triennial parliaments, the payment of MPs, a 'better apportionment of representatives to population', the extension of polling hours, and the payment of necessary election expenses by the ratepayers, and with an objective of assisting the return of 'advanced Liberals' to the House of Commons.[135] Ill health prevented Cowen from playing a very active part during the parliamentary sessions of 1874 and 1875, but his eloquent speech on the third reading of the Royal Titles Bill (23 March 1876) was considered to have been the great success of that session, indicating that a new Radical star was rising rapidly, and encouraging the hope among some Radicals that he might assume their leadership.[136] Cowen's fatal weakness, however, was to be his independent-mindedness, which made it impossible for him to act consistently with any one group of politicians, and which led him to take up a belligerently anti-Russian line over the Eastern Question that was out of step with the prevailing sentiment in Radical circles. The subsequent feud between Cowen and the Newcastle Liberal Association[137] blighted the remainder of a parliamentary career that had opened with so much promise.

In July 1876, another provincial Radical politician was to enter the House of Commons who undoubtedly aspired to the leadership of a revitalized general Radical movement. Even at the height of the 'revolt of the Nonconformists' in the early 1870s, Joseph Chamberlain, the president of the National Education League and mayor of Birmingham, had been conscious of the limitations of Radical Nonconformity, and had sought to widen its horizons by embracing the causes of the working men, such as the agricultural labourers.[138]

---

[135] A circular is printed by S. Maccoby (ed.), *The English Radical Tradition, 1763–1914* (1952), 179–80.
[136] Cf. Lucy, *Diary of Two Parliaments*, i. 168–9 (entry for 12 Aug. 1876); E. R. Jones, *Life and Speeches of Joseph Cowen, M.P.* (1885), 41–2.
[137] Ostrogorski, *Democracy and Political Parties*, i. 234–40.
[138] See J. L. Garvin, *Life of Joseph Chamberlain*, i. (1932), 148–51, for Chamberlain's programme of 'Free Schools, Free Church, and Free Land', adumbrated early in 1872.

The Liberals' defeat in 1874 merely confirmed his belief that the Nonconformist objective of full religious equality could only be achieved in conjunction with the working classes, whose own specific grievances had received little sympathy from the Nonconformists: 'I feel that this narrowness in respect to general politics, on the part of many of the rank & file of Dissent, will be fatal to the success of our special aims, unless we can induce & make a more generous recognition of the claims of the masses.'[139] Accordingly, in arguing the case for disestablishment and disendowment as the best rallying cry for the entire Radical movement, Chamberlain was careful to emphasize that this should be treated not as a sectional but as a 'national' question, relevant to the interests of the working men as well as to the Nonconformists—for example, by presenting the Church of England as an obstacle to all social reforms, and by pointing out that the funds released through disendowment could be used to provide free education for all.[140]

It was becoming increasingly clear by 1876, however, that disestablishment was unsuitable as a focus for united Radical action, and Bright himself publicly criticized Chamberlain's preoccupation with the issue.[141] Following his entry to the House of Commons, therefore, a shift was discernible in Chamberlain's strategy away from the use of a spearhead policy and in favour of an attempt to broaden his political base through an initiative in party organization. This change of emphasis was made easier by the fact that, during the 1876 session, the Conservatives had carried an act making elementary education virtually compulsory, which, in Chamberlain's estimation, had pushed the education question into the background for the time being and made the National Education League redundant.[142] Chamberlain's determination to try to ride all the Radical horses is indicated by the articles which he published in the

---

[139] Chamberlain to Henry Allon (editor of the *British Quarterly Review*), 13 Feb. 1874, in A. Peel (ed.), *Letters to a Victorian Editor* (1929), 43–4.

[140] 'The Next Page of the Radical Programme', *Fortnightly Review*, 16 (Oct. 1874), 405–29. Chamberlain's close associate John Morley, the editor of the *Fortnightly*, was also keenly interested in disestablishment as a single great unifying question: see D. A. Hamer, *John Morley: Liberal Intellectual in Politics* (Oxford, 1968), 81–111.

[141] Richard Jay, *Joseph Chamberlain: A Political Study* (Oxford, 1981), 33.

[142] Cf. Chamberlain to Morley, 11 July 1876, Chamberlain MSS, JC5/24/112; Chamberlain to Holyoake, n.d. [July 1876], in J. McCabe, *Life and Letters of G. J. Holyoake* (1908), ii. 177.

Fortnightly Review, in January and February 1877, the first dealing with 'Free Schools', which he continued to tie to the question of disestablishment and disendowment, the other dealing with 'Municipal Public Houses'—an obvious bid for the support of the United Kingdom Alliance.[143] It is also noticeable that in public speeches made around this time Chamberlain varied his 'programme' to suit his audience, so that when he addressed the Agricultural Labourers' Union, for example, the emphasis was placed upon county franchise, county government, and other rural reforms, while issues like disestablishment were to follow later.[144] In accordance with the new strategy, the decision was taken, early in 1877, to dissolve the National Education League and substitute for it a federation of local Liberal associations, dominated by Birmingham. The National Liberal Federation, founded in May 1877, was conceived as a means of articulating the voice of Liberal opinion (assumed to be the same as 'public opinion', with the opinions of the Radicals naturally predominating) in a way that would compel the party leaders to listen.[145] What this meant in practice was that this new extra-parliamentary organization, ostensibly the mouthpiece of a Radical consensus on the policies to be pursued by the Liberal party, could be used as a way of buttressing Chamberlain's own activities within parliament. The paramount importance, for Chamberlain, of cultivating and directing 'Liberal opinion' beyond Westminster had already been demonstrated by the failure of an early attempt to build up a small 'party' in the House of Commons, involving about half a dozen MPs, which had effectively broken down by the beginning of 1877 because of the inability of Chamberlain and Cowen to agree on anything.[146]

Even at the time of the National Liberal Federation's inception, however, the Liberal party, and a substantial portion of its Radical element in particular, was already heavily embroiled in the Eastern Question, and the continued preoccupation with this, and the subsequent colonial wars in Afghanistan and Southern Africa, inevitably had the effect of distorting the developments in extra-parliamentary

[143] *Fortnightly Review*, 21, pp. 54–72 and 147–59.
[144] See Jay, *Joseph Chamberlain*, pp. 39, 41.
[145] Hamer, *Liberal Politics*, pp. 46–54. Cf. F. H. Herrick, 'The Origins of the National Liberal Federation', *Journal of Modern History*, 17 (1945), 116–29.
[146] Chamberlain to Collings, 27 July 1876, 8 Feb. 1877, and 16 Feb. 1877, Chamberlain MSS, JC5/16/58, 59, 61.

organization with which Chamberlain was especially concerned. Initially, Chamberlain had been keen to exploit the difficulties posed for the Whig leadership by Gladstone's involvement in the Eastern Question, and during the autumn of 1876, and during the crisis over the five resolutions in May 1877, he had sought to mobilize support for Gladstone in the constituencies in the hope of destroying Hartington.[147] However, this alignment of the Radicals with Gladstone had its own dangers, from Chamberlain's point of view, for not only was Gladstone unlikely to allow himself to be used as a mere 'puppet', in the way Chamberlain wanted, but the obsession of many Radicals with the government's foreign and colonial policies actually tended to draw attention away from domestic matters. Far from being captured by the Radicals in 1876, Gladstone, in an interesting parallel with the events of 1886, succeeded to a considerable extent in capturing the Radicals. His crusade over the Eastern Question was especially important for the way it absorbed into its moral critique of Conservative policies those religious energies that had previously been channelled into the sectarian squabbles of the early 1870s.[148] Indeed, it may be said that, by 1880, Gladstone had made a crucial contribution to the development of a Radical identity based primarily upon an abhorrence of the 'Palmerstonian' style of foreign policy, now that it was being practised by a Conservative government. Disraeli's assumption of Palmerston's 'mantle', in other words, transformed the conduct of foreign policy into a far more distinctively Radical issue than it had ever been in Palmerston's own day.

From the point of view of Radical cohesion, it was probably necessary that attention should be concentrated upon a subject with no direct relevance to questions of domestic reform, as this was the most effective way of transcending their differences in that sphere. It was far easier for all to agree on a purely negative strategy of working for the removal of a government whose policies were considered to be mischievous, if not downright malevolent, as this provided an overriding imperative requiring that sectional differences be put

---

[147] See Chamberlain's letter to Dilke, 10 Oct. 1876, Chamberlain MSS, JC5/24/286, for his view of Gladstone as the Radicals' 'best card'. Cf. Chamberlain to Morley, 10 Oct. 1876, ibid. JC5/54/118, and Chamberlain to Collings, 28 Apr. 1877, ibid. JC5/16/66.

[148] For the importance of the Nonconformist element in 1876, see Shannon, *Bulgarian Agitation*, pp. 147–71.

aside. Such thinking had become firmly entrenched by the end of 1878, when there were at last signs that the government was beginning to falter. Consequently, when James Bryce mooted the idea of a new Labour League, with a programme of domestic reforms, as a means of organizing the working men, he encountered much scepticism and indifference amongst the Radicals. John Morley—not yet an MP but an influential journalist as well as being one of Chamberlain's closest confidants—wrote that he could not see any purpose being served by the proposed organization:

The great object of all public effort at present should be, in my judgment, to drive home to our people the mischievous effects of the foreign policy of the government, both as to its results, and as to its methods . . .

I should have thought that this ought to be for the present the substantive part of a new movement among the workmen. For the moment it seems less important to contribute a new organisation for general objects of Liberalism, than to use and stimulate all the existing organisations—local and national—for the particular object of creating such a vehement hostility to our bad foreign policy as will turn the government out.

If people cannot be aroused by the flagrant misdemeanours of the government in Foreign Affairs, they are not likely to be stirred by the dim hope of the changes so usefully enumerated in the Programme.

We shall make no way until the present Government is displaced. Will they not be more surely (and more justly) displaced on the issues of the hour, than on the prospect of reforms which are for the moment of indisputably secondary interest.[149]

Henry Fawcett was equally doubtful about Bryce's plan, and he gave more specific reasons for thinking it unwise:

If a programme were put forward it would of course have to be a wide one, and a feeling might very probably be encouraged amongst Liberals not to support a candidate unless he was prepared to accept the programme. I feel it to be of such vital importance to displace the present Government that I think it will be the duty of all Liberals at the next election to sink minor differences. However united we may be it will be sufficiently difficult to effect that object, and there will be no chance of doing so, if among any section of Liberals in the Constituencies a feeling should arise against supporting a candidate unless he accepted the articles of a particular programme. I am afraid, however moderate and sensible the promoters of

[149] Morley to Bryce, 14 Dec. 1878, Bryce MSS, UB 31. Morley's interest in disestablishment as a single great unifying issue had waned by 1876–7: Hamer, *John Morley*, pp. 110–11.

the proposed League may be, it would be more likely to create disunion among Liberals, and this is my sole reason for doubting the expediency of attempting to form such a League at present.[150]

When a 'National Labour League' was eventually founded in the summer of 1879, neither Bright nor Chamberlain (who had no wish to see any rival organization set up) would have anything to do with it, and it appears to have made little impact on the elections in 1880.[151]

Chamberlain himself, though anxious after the foundation of the National Liberal Federation to establish a domestic reform programme of his own devising, was also hampered by the Radical preoccupation with foreign policy. His speech at Rochdale in November 1877 shows him to be casting around in the dark for a domestic policy, unsure of what to propose and hopeful that the official party leaders themselves might give a decisive lead. 'For himself he cared little which of the great questions they first attacked. The Church and the land were the Mamelon and Malakoff of privilege, and he knew not which was the key of the position.'[152] Chamberlain's attempt to rectify this situation is of particular interest in view of his activities in the 1880s. In a letter to Bryce, he explained that the National Liberal Federation had set up a publishing committee 'which has resolved to issue a sort of manual of Liberal policy in a series of papers ... These papers will first be published and circulated separately by the agency of the several Associations, and then collected in a volume and published together.' Chamberlain himself was to write on free schools, and others who had agreed to assist were Shaw Lefevre (free trade in land), James

---

[150] Fawcett to Bryce, 29 Dec. 1878, Bryce MSS, UB 31. Cf. the letters from Henry Broadhurst, 10 Jan. 1879, and George Howell, 11 Jan. 1879, ibid., suspecting that it was the intention of the Liberals to secure a return to office without giving any pledges to the working men.

[151] Cf. Chamberlain to Broadhurst, 13 June 1879, and Bright to Broadhurst, 14 June 1879, Broadhurst MSS, vol. 1. A copy of the League's manifesto is enclosed in a letter from Broadhurst to Bryce, 7 Aug. 1879, Bryce MSS, UB 31. This document is itself revealing for its limitations and virtual irrelevance to the interests of the urban working classes. It proposed (i) electoral reform; (ii) land tenure reform (i.e. abolition of entail and primogeniture, and a reform of the system of conveyancy), abolition of the game laws, and compensation for improvements made by tenant farmers; (iii) financial reform (i.e. retrenchment, reduced taxation, and a readjustment of the balance between taxes on property and other types of income); (iv) reform of local government and taxation; (v) a free Church.

[152] *Manchester Guardian*, 8 Nov. 1877, p. 8. The Mamelon height and the Malakoff hill were Russian strongholds during the Crimean war.

Howard (tenant right), John Morley (English Church disestablishment), Dilke (electoral reform), and Cowen (county boards), while Bryce was asked to contribute a piece on Scottish Church disestablishment.[153] This plan bears a striking resemblence to the *Radical Programme* of 1883–5, with Chamberlain trying to stimulate public discussion on a broad range of domestic issues in the hope of creating a favourable climate for a new Radical initiative. However, the projected volume never materialized, for as he explained in a subsequent letter to Bryce, although preliminary arrangements had been made with Macmillan, 'of course all idea of publishing is *for the moment* abandoned. We must get the Eastern Question out of the way before we can hope for a fair hearing for domestic subjects.'[154]

It was not just the vitiating effect of the Eastern Question on domestic reform politics that frustrated Chamberlain, however, for Gladstone had also failed to live up to the expectations held of him. Chamberlain had naturally been dismayed when Gladstone backed down over the five resolutions in May 1877, and Harcourt may have been right in claiming that he regretted having invited Gladstone to the inaugural meeting of the National Liberal Federation.[155] At any rate, it is clear that by the end of 1877, when he first issued an invitation to Hartington to speak at the annual conference of the Federation, Chamberlain's attitude towards the Whigs was undergoing a change. Privately, he declared that he no longer wished to see Hartington displaced from the leadership in the Commons, since Gladstone, the only alternative leader, was 'erratic and cannot be relied on with absolute confidence'.[156] Moreover, after having friendly discussions on the question of county boards, Chamberlain was now convinced that there was scope for co-operation with the Whig leaders, and he had in any case given up all hope of creating a separate party amongst the back-bench Radicals: 'My experience on this question confirms the opinion which I have suggested to you more than once, that our hope, that is the hope of Birmingham

[153] Chamberlain to Bryce, 10 Dec. 1877, Bryce MSS, UB 26.
[154] Chamberlain to Bryce, 11 Jan, 1878, ibid. In fact, between 1879 and 1881 the National Liberal Federation did publish four pamphlets in a 'practical politics series', including those by Howard and Shaw Lefevre, and others on foreign policy and colonial policy by Grant Duff and Wedderburn (ref. Cambridge University Library, xxi. 54. 7.), but the series progressed no further.
[155] Cf. Chamberlain to Collings, 10 May 1877, Chamberlain MSS, JC5/16/67; Harcourt to Granville, 1 June 1877, PRO 30/29/29.
[156] Chamberlain to Collings, 18 Feb. 1878, Chamberlain MSS, JC5/16/77.

politicians, lies rather in a hearty alliance and attempt to influence our present leaders, than in the formation of any new Party. There is no party of Radicals below the gangway; their only point of agreement is the fact that each one differs in some respect or another from the leaders; but their differences among themselves are really greater than those which separate them from the frontbench.'[157]

It was in the context of this more constructive attitude towards the official leaders that, shortly after the Afghan debate in December 1878, Chamberlain renewed his invitation to Hartington to attend the annual conference of the Federation, to be held at Leeds.[158] In spite of the conciliatory tone of Chamberlain's letter of 22 December, in which he expressed a desire to unite with the leadership on the questions on which they were mutually agreed, Hartington, after consultation with several of his colleagues, declined the invitation.[159] But Hartington's refusal to go to Leeds should not be interpreted as an indication of hostility towards the idea of a new form of electoral organization. In fact, as Hartington told his private secretary, 'My reason against going was not so much the fear of frightening or offending old Whigs, as unwillingness to sanction or be supposed to sanction an organisation which may become a very powerful one, but which is altogether independent of and outside the control of the official element of the party.'[160] More specifically, what really rankled with Hartington was the way Chamberlain had tried to deploy the Federation on Gladstone's behalf over the Eastern Question:

Whatever may be the merits of the plan for local purposes, there can be no doubt that a good deal more has been aimed at than the local management of elections, and that an attempt has been made to influence the policy of the party, through the means of a central organisation. Chamberlain may say that this was a mistake and will not be repeated, but he cannot say it at Leeds . . . it is the future which has been most before the public, and I think it would

---

[157] Chamberlain to Collings, 26 Feb. 1878, ibid. JC5/16/79.
[158] Hartington to Chamberlain, 20 Dec. 1878; Chamberlain to Hartington, 22 Dec. 1878; Hartington to Chamberlain, 29 Dec. 1878; Devonshire MSS, 340.781, 782, 784. Extracts of the last two are printed in Holland, *Devonshire*, i. 245–8.
[159] Cf. Harcourt to Hartington, 19 Dec. 1878 (typescript), Harcourt MSS, Box 720, and Adam to Hartington, 27 Dec. 1878, Devonshire MSS, 340.783, favouring acceptance of the invitation; and the letters from Forster and Granville, both 30 Dec. 1878, ibid. 340.785–6, approving of Hartington's decision.
[160] Hartington to Brett, 31 Dec. 1878, Esher MSS, 10/11.

have been a mistake to identify myself with this Association in any way, until they have formally renounced any pretensions of this kind.[161]

Chamberlain was naturally stung by Hartington's decision, but this does not mean, as Dr Rossi has argued, that a breach had therefore occurred between the two.[162] Sir Henry James, who visited Birmingham shortly afterwards, reported to Hartington that Chamberlain was still loyal to the party leaders, and James therefore urged Hartington to make some gesture to show that he was not hostile to Chamberlain's organization as such.[163] What Dr Rossi has failed to note is Hartington's positive response to this request. In his reply to James, he said that he would see Harcourt to discuss possible ways of removing any misconceptions that Chamberlain might have,[164] and the end result was an acknowledgement, in his speech at Liverpool in February, of the importance of the new form of electoral organization, particularly in large constituencies: 'I can conceive nothing more unjust than the abuse which is being lavished upon [the caucus system] on the ground of tyranny and dictation ... Where it is generally adopted and willingly adopted by the bulk of the constituency, as in Birmingham, and as I believe it is also in this place, I conceive that nothing can be more conducive to the interests of the Liberal party.'[165] Chamberlain, for his part, does not appear to have allowed his wounded feelings to overcome his political judgement, and he continued to express, privately, his desire for a compromise with the Whigs over policy.[166]

One further episode involving Hartington and Chamberlain, from which a minor political myth has grown, needs to be dealt with

---

[161] Hartington to Harcourt, 2 Jan. 1879, Harcourt MSS, Box 78.

[162] Rossi, *Liberal Opposition*, p. 97.

[163] James to Hartington, 17 Jan. 1879, Devonshire MSS, 340.792. Cf. Brett's diary, 22 Jan. 1879, Esher MSS, 2/5.

[164] Hartington to James, 19 Jan. 1879, Harcourt MSS, Box 78. Cf. James to Chamberlain, n.d. [19 Jan. 1879], Chamberlain MSS, JC5/46/1, urging him to 'keep the door open for some united action in relation to organisation'. In the event, Hartington observed that the Leeds meeting had been rather 'flat': Hartington to Brett, 23 Jan. 1879, Esher MSS, 10/11.

[165] *Manchester Guardian*, 7 Feb. 1879, p. 8. See also the next morning's leading article, p. 7, and Harcourt's letter of congratulations, 10 Feb. 1879, Devonshire MSS, 340.803.

[166] See e.g. Brett's diary, 20 May 1879, Esher MSS, 2/5. Chamberlain's immediate response to Hartington's refusal had been to summon Dilke to Birmingham to discuss which policies they should press during the forthcoming parliamentary session: Chamberlain to Morley, 7 Feb. 1879, Chamberlain MSS, JC5/54/243.

briefly. This is the row which took place during the parliamentary debate on flogging in the army, in July 1879, when, as the result of a misunderstanding, Hartington's criticism of the obstructionist tactics being pursued by some of the Radicals provoked Chamberlain to repudiate—in an ironic sense—his leadership.[167] Dilke later claimed that this illustrated Hartington's inability to lead a united party, and more recently, scholars like Dr Southgate and Dr Rossi have taken a similar view.[168] And yet it is perfectly clear, from the reaction of the parliamentary party and of the Liberal press, that this was not the case. The Radical *Daily News* joined with the *Manchester Guardian* and the *Leeds Mercury* in condemning Chamberlain's action and praising the unifying quality of Hartington's leadership.[169] It was also noted by the *Leeds Mercury* that, at the time of the incident, 'the feeling unmistakeably manifested on the Liberal benches . . . did much to neutralise the effect', as Hartington enjoyed the unaccustomed privilege of being defended by Radicals like Fawcett, while Chamberlain was left virtually isolated in the division lobby.[170] Furthermore, as James reported to Harcourt, Hartington was given a memorable reception in the House of Commons the following evening: 'on his getting up . . . our people cheered for five minutes louder than you have ever heard them cheer. Below the gangway were as enthusiastic as above. The minority are awfully frightened . . . Hopwood most civil and Rylands came and spoke to Hartington on the level for ten minutes. Everybody on both sides abuse Chamberlain, and he has lost immense way by his conduct.'[171] Hartington's 'failure' lay in the fact that he chose not to press home his advantage over Chamberlain,[172] and subsequently moved an

[167] The *Annual Register* for 1879, pp. 53–65, contains a detailed account of the parliamentary proceedings on the government's Army Regulation Bill.

[168] Cf. Gwynn and Tuckwell, *Dilke*, i. 294; Donald Southgate, *The Passing of the Whigs, 1832–1886* (1962), 361; Rossi, *Liberal Opposition*, pp. 98–9. It should be noted that Dilke's comment was made in his unreliable memoir compiled in 1893 (by which time he was a 'born again' Radical) from diaries which, for the 1870s, have not survived.

[169] *Daily News*, 10 July 1879, pp. 4–5; *Manchester Guardian*, 11 July 1879, p. 5; *Leeds Mercury*, 9 July 1879, p. 4.

[170] *Leeds Mercury*, 9 July 1879, p. 4.

[171] James to Harcourt, 9 July 1879, Harcourt MSS, Box 86. See also the account in the *Leeds Mercury*, 9 July 1879, p. 4.

[172] Chamberlain told Morley that, having spoken to the chief whip, the matter was closed as far as he was concerned: 11 July 1879, Chamberlain MSS, JC5/54/259. See also Chamberlain's letter of 22 July, describing a conversation with Hartington, ibid. JC5/54/265.

amendment himself in favour of the abolition of flogging (after the government had retreated from a compromise arrangement which the opposition leaders had been willing to support), a step which disappointed many moderates and led to a poor Liberal showing in the division—'many Whigs and moderate men not voting'.[173] To have seized the opportunity to 'stamp on' Chamberlain might have been satisfying personally, but Hartington was surely right to put the long-term unity of the party before such feelings.

There were good reasons why the Radicals should have been anxious to assure Hartington of their loyalty. As the *Daily News* pointed out, only a few days before the flogging debate Hartington had shown 'one great additional sign of his capacity as the Liberal leader' by his speech on the reform of the land laws.[174] Gestures of this kind helped to convince the Radicals that Hartington was sufficiently responsive to their views for it to be worth their while to accept his leadership. After all, the party's electoral prospects might have been improving, but no one was thinking in terms of the kind of majority that was actually obtained in April 1880. Indeed, it was doubtful enough whether the Liberals would have a majority at all. Dilke, for instance, was found to be 'not sanguine as to the prospects of the Liberal party—thinks they will lessen the Conservative majority at the elections, but not destroy it'.[175] Consequently, because the Whigs were able to tap vital sources of strength through their hold over moderate Liberal opinion, it was clear to the Radicals that they could not hope to achieve any of their aims unless they were willing to compromise. Thus, a man like Mundella, who had supported Forster's candidacy in 1875 and had been closely associated with Gladstone over the Eastern Question, disapproved of Chamberlain's conduct during the flogging debate and declared that 'I stand by Hartington as a matter of policy and practical sense. If he is weakened so is Radicalism, and Chamberlain can only effect

---

[173] Speaker Brand's diary, 17 July 1879, Hampden MSS. For the dissatisfaction of the moderate Liberals, see W. C. Cartwright's diary, 15, 18 July 1879, Cartwright MSS, 6/14. Hartington's amendment was defeated by 289 votes to 183, with the minority including twenty-five home rulers: 3 Hansard, ccxlviii, cols. 716–19. The decision to oppose flogging altogether had been agreed after it became clear that the government, under pressure from its own supporters, was no longer prepared to confine the punishment to that category of offences otherwise punishable by death: see Childers to Halifax, 28 July 1879, Hickleton MSS, A4/90.

[174] *Daily News*, 10 July 1879, pp. 4–5.

[175] Lord Derby's diary, 8 June 1879, Derby MSS.

anything by Hartington *being strong.*'[176] The paramount need
for Liberal unity, and the folly of unilateral action by the Radical
'faddists', was the central theme, for instance, of an article in the
Nineteenth Century by J. Guinness Rogers, a prominent Nonconformist, who felt confident that Hartington had 'rallied to his side the
strength and earnestness of true Liberalism throughout the
Country'.[177] Similarly, John Morley, writing in the *Fortnightly
Review*, argued that it was necessary for the Radicals to accept in
good faith the 'hopeful signs' emanating from Hartington, and to
co-operate with the Whigs in order to promote at least some of the
measures which they desired: 'nothing can be so indispensable as
that there should be a full and effective harmony among all sections
of the party', and all that was asked in return was 'a recognition on
the part of Liberals, that while the *action* of the party may be
necessarily limited by the timidity of its moderate section, the
discussion, and even the agitation, of more radical schemes of policy
must be allowed to go on with entire freedom'.[178] Hartington had
never offered less.

For ambitious young back-bench Radicals, of course, the inclination to come to terms with the Whigs was inevitably strong
because of the prospect this held for future political advancement.
Trevelyan and Shaw Lefevre are two notable examples of this
tendency, both having had the encouragement of seeing the causes
with which they were particularly associated—county franchise and

---

[176] Mundella to Robert Leader, 25 July 1879, Mundella–Leader MSS, 6P/69.
Dilke wrote in his memoir (Gwynn and Tuckwell, *Dilke*, i. 293–4) about an attempt
by the 'anti-Chamberlain set' to get up a banquet in Hartington's honour, which was
sat on by Adam, Harcourt, and James. What Dilke did not mention was that the
ringleader in this move was Mundella. See Hartington to Adam, 7 Jan. 1880,
Blairadam MSS, 4/427, referring to the proposal made at the end of the 1879 session.
[177] 'The Union of the Liberal Party', *Nineteenth Century*, 6 (Aug. 1879), 361–76.
Even the *Nonconformist*, 20 Aug. 1879, p. 822, while more suspicious of the Whigs,
was prepared to accept the wisdom of securing party unity by playing down specific
issues, provided this was not taken too far.
[178] 'The House of Commons', *Fortnightly Review*, 26 (Aug. 1879), 186–96. A
Radical of the most violent variety, like Edward Jenkins, was also prepared to admit,
in a speech to his constituents at Dundee, that 'Liberals would be forced to forego
some of their zeal and earnestness in pushing forward reforms until they got the
present Government supplanted. He thought the Government which would succeed
the present would be a Whig Ministry, with Lord Hartington, Sir William Harcourt,
and possibly Lord Derby, as members of the Cabinet, and it was hardly possible such a
Ministry would take up such questions as disestablishment or reform of the land laws;
but the Liberal members would take care they should not prove recreant', *Manchester
Guardian*, 5 Nov. 1879, p. 6.

land-law reform respectively—taken up by the party leaders.[179] But the classic example of the promising young Radical eagerly waiting to be absorbed by the official element of the party was Sir Charles Dilke, who, significantly enough, was Chamberlain's closest ally in the House of Commons. By 1879 the reputation which Dilke had been cultivating for several years as a responsible parliamentarian (he had been careful to keep his distance from Chamberlain and Gladstone over the Eastern Question) was flourishing to such an extent that Hartington was prepared to delegate the leading role to him during debates on the Zulu and Greek questions.[180] Meantime, on a social visit to Knowsley, Dilke was full of reassurance about the aims of the Radicals on issues like disestablishment and the land laws.[181] To many political observers, in fact, it was Dilke rather than Chamberlain who seemed to be the 'coming man' among the parliamentary Radicals.[182]

As for Chamberlain, it is clear that, in spite of the friction between himself and Hartington, he had no notion of breaking away from the official Liberal leaders. On the contrary, his letter to Morley in October 1879, enumerating the domestic reforms he wished to see in the party's programme, serves to emphasize once again the point that the Radicals had no clear-cut reform programme that was likely to create any serious difficulties with the Whigs, even on the land question. Chamberlain's primary interest now was in a county franchise measure, which he regarded as a necessary preliminary to a reform of local government in the counties, while, as regards the reform of the land laws, he thought that 'The one thing to keep in view is that for every estate there shall always be someone who has absolute power of sale. If this is secured, I don't care what are the precise means to be adopted.'[183] Early the following month,

---

[179] Trevelyan, as we have seen, backed Hartington over the five resolutions in May 1877, and supported him again during the early stages of the Afghan debate in December 1878: Brett's diary, 10 Dec. 1878, Esher MSS, 2/5. Cf. Shaw Lefevre's ingratiating letter to Hartington, 9 Jan. 1880, Devonshire MSS, 340.872.

[180] See Gwynn and Tuckwell, *Dilke*, i. 272–3, 277–8.

[181] Lord Derby's diary, 8 June 1879, Derby MSS.

[182] Cf. T. Wemyss Reid, *Politicians of Today* (1880), i. 115–28; J. Davidson, *Eminent Radicals In and Out of Parliament* (1880), 38–49.

[183] Chamberlain to Morley, 21 Oct. 1879, Chamberlain MSS, J C5/54/276. When Sir Henry James was commissioned by Hartington to prepare a scheme for reforming the land laws, he took care to seek Chamberlain's views, to the latter's obvious satisfaction: James to Chamberlain, 24 Jan. 1880, ibid. J C5/46/3; Chamberlain to Morley, 25 Jan. 1880, ibid. J C5/54/283.

Chamberlain was inviting Harcourt (who, with James, had adopted the role of mediator between the Whigs and Radicals) to attend a meeting at Birmingham, in these terms: 'though differences do and always will exist . . . they won't prevent cordial union for common objects—and your visit to Radical Birmingham and the welcome you would receive will be a public demonstration of the fact that we are united for all present purposes'.[184]

IV

By the autumn of 1879, the Liberal party was in a better condition than it had been for several years. Paradoxically, the Eastern Question, once it was actually out of the way, appeared to have improved the prospects for Liberal unity, as it had effectively cauterized the wounds inflicted by the sectarian bitterness of the early 1870s—it was a painful treatment at first, but highly beneficial in the long run. This process, acquiring its momentum chiefly from the declining fortunes of the Beaconsfield administration after the Congress of Berlin, led to the development of a penetrating critique of the malignity of Conservative government. The fabric of this critique was woven from three distinct threads. Firstly, the Conservatives continued to be beset by colonial disasters, enabling the Liberals to follow up their debating triumph on the Afghan question, in December 1878, with a highly successful debate and division in both Houses of parliament, in March 1879, after the massacre of a British force by the Zulus in Southern Africa. This latter debate indeed marked the beginning of a process of reattachment to the Liberal party on the part of previously dissident Whig elements,[185] which was to be consolidated, in September, by the news that the British mission imposed upon the Amir of Afghanistan had been massacred

---

[184] Chamberlain to Harcourt, 4 Nov. 1879 (typescript), Harcourt MSS, Box 716.

[185] The Liberal motion in the House of Lords was moved by one of the rising young stars of the Whig section, Lord Lansdowne. Although only sixty-one peers voted for the motion, a further thirty were paired in its favour. The division on an identical motion by Dilke in the Commons on 31 Mar. received support from many of the rebels of the previous year, and was only opposed by four Liberals: Foster and Ripley, who were by now widely regarded as Conservatives and stood as such in 1880, Roebuck, a venomous philosphic Radical who died in Sept. 1879, and Sir Edward Watkin.

in Kabul.[186] Secondly, the budgetary deficit resulting from the high expenditure associated with the government's 'jingoistic' policies, occurring at a time when the British economy was in an acute depression, naturally encouraged the Liberals to draw an equation between the two phenomena. Thus, in a debate on finance raised at the end of April by a Radical MP, Peter Rylands, but supported by the Liberal front bench, great stress was placed on the way that the government's mischievous foreign policy, by raising military expenditure and therefore necessitating high taxation, had (allegedly) brought about the bad state of trade.[187] Thirdly, as Hartington emphasized in a highly acclaimed speech at Newcastle on 19 September, which marked the beginning of an autumn oratorical assault by the opposition leaders,[188] the government's preoccupation with foreign and colonial affairs had led to the neglect of domestic questions, presumably dear to the hearts of all Liberals, such as county franchise, redistribution, local government, and the land laws. Gladstone's vehement denunciations of Beaconsfield's 'system of government', in his Midlothian speeches at the end of the year, may have been more dramatic, but the substance of his charges contained nothing new.

The revival of Liberal fortunes during the course of 1879 seems to have gone hand in hand with a greater willingness on Hartington's part to be assertive in his leadership. His personal triumph in the Afghan debate of December 1878 had undoubtedly boosted his confidence, and he made clear his determination to take a tougher

---

[186] The party also achieved a good division on Trevelyan's franchise motion in Mar. Harcourt's analysis showed that only three Liberals had voted against the motion and only ten of the English and Scottish absentees had deliberately stayed away. More serious was the attitude of the Irish home rulers, twenty-three of whom had been absent. Nevertheless, Harcourt concluded that 'As far as the English and Scottish Liberals go I think the result is very satisfactory and shows the party to be unanimous and earnest . . . the party goes well together', Harcourt to Hartington, 6 Mar. 1879, and accompanying list of absentees (typescripts), Harcourt MSS, Box 720.

[187] This was the theme of speeches by several Liberal MPs, on 24 Apr., including Rylands, Baxter, Laing, Richard, Dodson, and Lubbock. On the second night of the debate, 28 Apr., Gladstone, Goschen, and Childers provided the heavy ammunition. See also the earlier public speeches by Harcourt, at Sheffield, and Chamberlain, at Birmingham, *Manchester Guardian*, 17 Apr. 1879, pp. 5, 8.

[188] See the *Annual Register* for 1879, pp. 105–9, for press reactions to Hartington's speech and for a summary of other Liberal speeches during Sept. and Oct., notably those by Harcourt. Cf. Lord Ripon's diary, 14 Nov. 1879, BL Add. MSS 43642, for the success of a large meeting at Leeds, addressed by Forster, Agyll, Lawson, and himself.

line against the faltering government at a meeting held at Devonshire House in March 1879 to consider the opposition's resolution for the forthcoming Zulu debate. According to Lord Ripon's account, Harcourt, backed by Kimberley, had pressed for the resolution to be strengthened, but Granville and Cardwell were averse to this suggestion and the others were doubtful:

> after some discussion it seemed as if the division would have been in favour of making no change in the Resolution, when Hartington walked up to the writing table, wrote down a few words in Harcourt's sense but in milder language, and came back and read them—The thing was done, they were accepted at once—It is the first real act of leadership I have seen on his part. I am satisfied with the result.[189]

Another significant step taken by Hartington, at the beginning of 1879, was to open up Devonshire House for social gatherings during the parliamentary session. Reginald Brett noted in his diary that 'my Chief is to give Wednesday dinners to be followed by "drums" . . . it is a politic step I am sure'.[190] The first such occasion, early in March, was reckoned to have gone off well.[191] In an age when the sitting of parliament was still intimately related to the London 'season', it would be difficult to exaggerate the value, to the cohesion of the Liberals, of the opening of such a major social venue. One Radical journalist, favoured with an invitation to the Devonshire House 'drum', was suitably impressed: 'It was a brilliant affair; the place is really a palace.'[192]

Hartington's enhanced stature as a popular leader was reflected in his reception at a great Liberal demonstration at the Pomona Gardens, Manchester, on 25 October, where he shared the platform with John Bright.[193] On the great day, the *Manchester Guardian* was lavish in its praise of the noble marquis's virtues:

> as leader of the Opposition during difficult times and in the face of a great reverse of fortune he has succeeded by good judgment, good temper, and an

---

[189] Lord Ripon's diary, 22 Mar. 1879, BL Add. MSS 43641.

[190] Brett's diary, 22 Jan. 1879, Esher MSS, 2/5.

[191] Ibid., 6 Mar. 1879. The opening of Devonshire House became all the more important when a fire seriously damaged the Granville residence at Carlton House Terrace in Mar.

[192] John Morley to his sister, 26 Mar. 1879, in F. W. Hirst (ed.), *Early Life and Letters of John Morley* (1927), ii. 76.

[193] For reports of the proceedings, see the *Manchester Guardian*, 27 Oct. 1879, p. 5, and the *Leeds Mercury*, 27 Oct. 1879, p. 4.

unswerving honesty of purpose in attracting to himself the ungrudging support of every section of the party. No public man has gained so greatly in the estimation of the Country and in the confidence of his party in Parliament during the up-hill work of the last five years as Lord Hartington, and his presence among us at this time will help to bind the party together and to give it unity of purpose and the full consciousness of its strength.[194]

The Radical *Daily News* was equally willing to acknowledge his achievements: 'there is no one who will not readily admit that Lord Hartington has proved still better than the expectations that were formed of him. He must have felt repaid for his patience and his loyalty when he received the address of confidence from so truly representative a body as the Liberal delegations of Manchester [the day before the main meeting], and the Liberal party all over the Country will certainly ratify that expression of confidence.'[195] Significantly, the *Nonconformist* also recognized that Hartington's speech had 'added greatly to his growing reputation', and, taking heart from his criticisms of Conservative foreign policy, it declared that 'for the present we can heartily assent to the principle laid down' of the overriding need for Liberal unity in order to secure the removal of the government.[196]

It was quite on the cards, during the autumn of 1879, that it would be the Whig leaders, rather than Gladstone, who would be the chief beneficiaries of the Liberal revival, no matter how important Gladstone's contribution to this process might have been. Indeed the possibility that, in the event of the Liberals returning to power, Gladstone might accept the post of Chancellor of the Exchequer, in a Whig ministry, was being widely discussed at this time, not only in private but even on the public platform, where this solution commended itself to Radicals such as Sir Wilfrid Lawson and G. O. Trevelyan.[197] Any hope there may have been of such a convenient arrangement was soon to be dashed, however, for on 24 November Gladstone boarded the train for Midlothian.

[194] *Manchester Guardian*, 25 Oct. 1879, p. 7.
[195] *Daily News*, 25 Oct. 1879, p. 4.
[196] *Nonconformist*, 29 Oct. 1879, p. 1069.
[197] Lawson at Newcastle, *Manchester Guardian*, 20 Sept. 1879, p. 8; Trevelyan at Hawick, ibid., 30 Oct. 1879, p. 7. As regards the discussions among the party leaders, Forster seems to have raised the subject with Hartington, who then discussed it with Granville: Hartington to Granville, 28 Oct. and 4 Nov. 1879, PRO 30/29/22A/2; Granville to Hartington, 29 Oct. 1879, Devonshire MSS, 340.844. The letters of 28 and 29 Oct. are printed in Holland, *Devonshire*, i. 255–7.

4

The Resurrection of Gladstonian
Liberalism, 1879–1880

Gladstone's return as Prime Minister, after the Liberal party had secured a decisive majority at the polls in April 1880, was quickly elevated to the realms of Liberal mythology. In retrospect, nothing seemed more obvious than that the series of events marking Gladstone's return to effective political leadership—his opposition to Beaconsfield's foreign policy from 1876, the demonstrations in Midlothian, and the final assault on 'jingoism' at the general election —had been elements of a single, linear process, by which his special sense of affinity with 'the people' was restored and the great electoral victory assured.[1] His resumption of the premiership thus became surrounded by an air of inevitability: the hesitant leadership of the Whigs giving way to that of the man who had inspired the struggle against Beaconsfield's 'system of government', and who alone could command the allegiance of all sections of the great Liberal majority.[2]

Clearly, this traditional interpretation of the way in which 'Gladstonian Liberalism' was re-established is in conflict with the assessment of the Liberal opposition offered in the last chapter. The problem here lies partly with the fact that historians have consistently underestimated the achievements of the Whig leaders, and have allowed themselves to be dazzled by Gladstone's remarkable oratory in Midlothian, but also with their failure to appreciate fully the implications of the continuing uncertainty, in 1879–80, about the Liberal party's electoral prospects. Contrary to the assumptions implicit in the orthodox interpretation of Gladstone's return, few

---

[1] Herbert Paul, *A History of Modern England* (1904–6), iv. 137. According to one recent scholar, the events of 1876–8 had 're-established the Gladstonian style of politics and effectively displaced Hartington', with Gladstone's five resolutions of May 1877 completing 'the resurgence of radical Liberalism that Suez and Bulgaria had begun', Michael Bentley, *Politics without Democracy, 1815–1914* (1984), 227.

[2] Justin McCarthy, *A History of our Own Times* (1905), iii. 115, 145. Sir Robert Ensor wrote of Hartington and Granville that the Midlothian campaigns 'swept their claims away', *England 1870–1914* (Oxford, 1936), 66.

Liberals had anticipated the dramatic reversal of party positions which took place in April 1880. In consequence, as we shall see, the position of the Whig leaders was much stronger, and that of Gladstone correspondingly more tenuous, than is usually supposed. Furthermore, it is only by examining contemporary impressions of the political situation in 1879–80 that we can understand why it was that the question of the Liberal leadership, though revived by Gladstone's first campaign in Scotland (24 November to 6 December 1879), was not finally settled until two weeks after the general election.

I

Throughout the years spent in opposition, the electoral aspirations of the Liberals had been confined within limited boundaries. There was, at this time, no concept of a 'political pendulum' which could be relied upon to swing away from the government, and so restore the Liberal party to the position it had occupied in 1868, and the Whig leaders had always operated, therefore, on the assumption that a considerable length of time would be required before the Conservatives' parliamentary majority could be overturned. Naturally, the difficulties posed by the government's 'patriotic' foreign policy, in the years 1876–8, had done nothing to suggest that the Liberal party had recovered from the trauma of its defeat in 1874, and, as late as October 1879, Hugh Childers could still remark that 'I don't think the majority of 1874 was an accident'.[3]

Nevertheless, it was clear, by the summer of 1879, that the government's popularity was diminishing, and the general feeling was that, when the dissolution came, the Conservatives' majority would definitely be eroded, although the question of to what extent remained in doubt. The limited range of perceived possibilities was indicated, in August, by Hartington's letter to the Liberal chief whip, discussing Speaker Brand's plan to retire at the end of the parliament, in which he contemplated only two scenarios for the next parliament, a majority for the government and a balance of parties.[4] Independent estimates made in June suggested that a majority for the

---

[3] Childers to Sir Andrew Clarke, 30 Oct. 1879, in Spencer Childers, *The Life . . . of the Rt. Hon. Hugh C. E. Childers, 1827–1896* (1901), i. 264.
[4] Hartington to Adam, 22 Aug. 1879, Blairadam MSS, 4/427.

Conservatives over the Liberals of about twenty would be the most likely outcome of the general election.[5]

Only for a brief period, in the autumn of 1879, was the possibility of greater gains for the Liberal party seriously considered. Public opinion seemed at last to be running decidedly against the government, and signs of a revival of Liberal feeling in the towns[6] suggested that the party would be able to recover much of the ground lost in its traditional strongholds in 1874. One of the most optimistic calculations to be made was that by Forster, Harcourt, and Adam, at a meeting towards the end of October. They thought the Liberals might gain a majority over the Conservatives of between thirty and forty-five, a substantial achievement, but still not enough to secure an overall parliamentary majority, because the independent Irish Nationalist party was expected to win up to seventy-five seats.[7]

Hopes for a major Liberal recovery had to be tempered, in any case, by other considerations. Apart from the fact that by no means everyone agreed with the chief whip's confident assessment of the electoral prospects,[8] it was ominous that the prospective Liberal gains were very one-sided, being mostly in the towns. In the counties, the situation was not nearly so promising, as the impact of the agricultural depression meant that the party was having difficulty in finding candidates to contest many of the seats.[9] According to an article in the *Manchester Guardian* early in November, forty-nine county divisions were without a Liberal candidate.[10] Furthermore,

---

[5] Lords Enfield and Kimberley predicted majorities for the government of twenty-two and twenty-three respectively: W. C. Cartwright's diary, 1 June 1879, Cartwright MSS, 6/13. Dilke was also predicting a reduced Conservative majority: Lord Derby's diary, 8 June 1879, Derby MSS.

[6] See e.g. Lord Ripon's diary, 2 Aug., 14 Nov. 1879, BL Add. MSS 43642, for Liberal demonstrations in Yorkshire; also 25 Sept., 25 Oct. 1879, for Hartington's meetings at Newcastle and Manchester.

[7] Cf. Forster's diary, 30 Oct. 1879, in T. Wemyss Reid, *Life of the Right. Hon. W. E. Forster* (1888), ii. 222–3; Harcourt to Chamberlain, 3 Nov. 1879, Chamberlain MSS, JC5/38/3.

[8] Cf. Brett's diary, 27 Oct. 1879, Esher MSS, 2/5, and Childers to Sir Andrew Clarke, 30 Oct. 1879, in Spencer Childers, *Childers*, i. 264, for predictions of defeat.

[9] Cf. Granville to Samuel Morley, 2 Nov. 1879, in E. Hodder, *The Life of Samuel Morley* (1887), 405; W. P. Adam to Edward Heneage, 28 Dec. 1879, Heneage MSS, 2 HEN 5/6, fo. 100.

[10] *Manchester Guardian*, 6 Nov. 1879, p. 5. This report also stated that thirty-five boroughs had no Liberal candidate. The papers of the chief whip include an undated list of twenty-nine English county divisions which either 'might be fought' or 'ought to be fought', Blairadam MSS, 4/426. However, this list consisted mainly of very safe Conservative counties where the Liberals were able to make few gains even in 1880.

no one could be certain that even the gains in the towns envisaged in October 1879 would be translated into actual gains at the general election, for it was considered unlikely that the government would dissolve parliament before the summer or autumn of 1880,[11] and by that time public opinion, which had often seemed inclined to favour Beaconsfield's assertive foreign policy, might easily have shifted away from the Liberals.[12]

The electoral outlook was therefore sufficiently uncertain, at the end of 1879, to ensure that the first Midlothian campaign did not force a settlement of the leadership question. Hartington, it is true, was provoked into threatening 'absolute and irrevocable resignation', because of the humiliating and unconstitutional position in which he, as the official leader in the House of Commons, felt he had been placed by Gladstone's virtual assumption of the leadership of the Liberals in the country.[13] This was not the first time that Hartington had talked of resigning, of course, and it remains unclear whether he seriously intended to do so, or whether he was simply seeking confirmation of his position. At any rate, his colleagues were armed with formidable arguments for why he should not force the issue with Gladstone. It was seriously contended that, far from enhancing the party's prospects, the violence of Gladstone's rhetoric was actually jeopardizing the fragile Liberal recovery by frightening away the moderate voters in England, and that even in Scotland, the influence of his campaign would prove to be ephemeral and make little impression on the eventual outcome of the elections. These points were emphasized by Hartington's private secretary, Reginald Brett:

With regard to the . . . effect of Mr. Gladstone's utterances on public opinion, I should think that there was a great probability of Harcourt's being right when he says that they will lose us very many votes in the South.

It is also doubtful whether their efficacy in the North will not have worn thin before the elections come.

---

[11] Cf. Speaker Brand's diary, 28 Oct. 1879, Hampden MSS; Sir Henry James to Chamberlain, Nov. 1879, Chamberlain MSS, J C5/46/2.
[12] For an earlier comment on the unreliability of public opinion on foreign questions, see Harcourt to Hartington, 7 Nov. 1878 (typescript), Harcourt MSS, Box 720.
[13] Hartington to Granville, 2 Dec. 1879, PRO 30/29/22A/2.

I am curious to see how Adam intends to keep this pot of enthusiasm boiling until perhaps next autumn.[14]

The belief that Liberal unity would not be assisted by Gladstone's resumption of the leadership, at that time, was confirmed by the chief whip himself, at a meeting involving Granville, Hartington, Cardwell, and Harcourt at Devonshire House on 16 December.[15] As a result, Hartington was dissuaded from taking any action, and induced instead, as Brett noted, to 'remain quiet until it is seen how Mr. Gladstone behaves in the next session'.[16]

Hartington's dissatisfaction with his position resurfaced for a time in January 1880, when Mundella revived his proposal for a banquet in Hartington's honour, to be presided over by Gladstone,[17] but he was again persuaded to acquiesce in the strategy urged upon him by Granville of waiting to see how matters developed. Granville's view, as he expressed it to Adam, was that 'a secret engagement [with Gladstone] for the future without regard to alternative contingencies would be dangerous and impolitic',[18] a point that he had earlier made to Hartington by postulating one such 'contingency': a situation where the Liberals gained seats, but Gladstone lost at Midlothian.[19] The argument that probably swayed Hartington, however, was that even if he did try to come to an understanding about the leadership with Gladstone, the latter would make it impossible for him to relinquish the position. As Granville shrewdly predicted, in a letter to Adam, 'I am certain that Gladstone's answer to any overture of Hartington would be—I adhere to my wish to remain apart from the leadership, but I will make any sacrifice which

---

[14] Brett to Hartington, 3 Dec. 1879, Devonshire MSS, 340.855. Cf. Hartington to Adam, 5 Dec. 1879, Blairadam MSS, 4/1096. Robert Lowe ended his letter of congratulations to Gladstone with the observation that 'The worst of it is that [the government] will not be silly enough to give us a dissolution till the effect even of your eloquence has been diminished by time', 11 Dec. 1879, BL Add. MSS 44302, fo. 196.

[15] Wolverton to Gladstone, 17 Dec. 1879, BL Add. MSS 44349, fo. 113. Wolverton had seen Granville after the meeting.

[16] Brett's diary, 31 Dec. 1879, Esher MSS, 2/5.

[17] See Granville and Hartington's letters to the chief whip in the Blairadam MSS, 4/427, and the correspondence in the A. J. Mundella papers, 6P/13.

[18] Granville to Adam, 16 Jan. 1880, Blairadam MSS, 4/427.

[19] Granville to Hartington, 2 Jan. 1880, Devonshire MSS, 340.868. While the dispute over the Liberal leadership centred at this time on Hartington and Gladstone, it should not be forgotten that Granville may still have hoped to obtain the premiership for himself, and his advice against settling the issue before the general election may therefore have been influenced by the recognition that he might then have a role to play as a compromise leader.

Hartington and Granville declare they consider necessary or good for the party"—Could H. and I reply that we think it would be for the good of the Liberal party that the change should be made before the general election[?]'[20]

Dr John P. Rossi, writing about the Devonshire House meeting of 16 December, has argued that the decision not to reopen the leadership question was a 'purely tactical move', calculated to avoid alarming the moderate Liberal voters, and that, in effect, 'The way was . . . prepared for the return of the Liberal Achilles'.[21] There is an obvious inconsistency in this interpretation, of course, because the admission that it was tactically correct for the Whigs not to invite Gladstone to lead the party before the general election must mean that they were justified in their assessment of his effect on the moderate voters, which was a clear indictment of his abilities as a leader.

In fact, the Whig strategy of 'wait and see' was not designed to ease Gladstone's way back to the premiership. On the contrary, it reflected the widely held belief that the continued leadership of Granville and Hartington offered the best guarantee for Liberal unity. Whereas Gladstone was too closely identified with the Radical section of the party for him to be acceptable as leader of the whole, Hartington, as we have seen, had succeeded in broadening his appeal to include the Radicals as well as the moderates. Wemyss Reid, of the *Leeds Mercury*, described Hartington as 'the man who has gained most in personal reputation during the existence of the present Parliament',[22] and it was clear, especially after his platform speeches during the autumn of 1879, that he stood as a formidable rival to Gladstone, offering a style of leadership which appeared better suited to the difficult political conditions of the time. As Lord Selborne observed, in a letter to Granville approving the decision taken at Devonshire House, 'unless the Liberals (and particularly the "left" of the Liberals)' gained 'a much more commanding majority than anybody can expect', the chances of a stable Liberal government being formed by Gladstone would be slim, because 'many moderate Liberals of the class of great landowners . . . and not of the

---

[20] Granville to Adam, 16 Jan. 1880, Blairadam MSS, 4/427: Cf. Granville to Hartington, 2 Jan. 1880, Devonshire MSS, 340.868.

[21] John P. Rossi, 'The Transformation of the British Liberal Party: A Study of the Tactics of the Liberal Opposition, 1874–1880', *Transactions of the American Philosophical Society*, 68 (Dec. 1978), 108–9.

[22] T. Wemyss Reid, *Politicians of Today* (1880), ii. 25–42.

class of great landowners only, would be repelled by Gladstone's *nuance* towards the Bright and Chamberlain section ... to say nothing of their disagreement with their foreign policy'.[23] It therefore appeared certain, to Hartington's private secretary, that if, 'in spite of the Queen and of several of the most powerful among the Liberals in Parliament', Gladstone were to become Prime Minister again, he would 'immediately break up the Liberal party for years, if not altogether'.[24]

Nor was the importance of the cohesive quality of the Whig leadership lost on the Radicals themselves. Granville's confident expectation, expressed in a letter to Spencer, that 'The radicals will now all vote right, the radical leaders are aware now that they require the support of the moderates'[25] was based on the success of Harcourt's visit to Birmingham on 20 January 1880, which had also reinforced Chamberlain's belief in the possibility of a consensus among Radicals and Whigs on a programme consisting of county franchise, local government, and land reform.[26] A letter written by Dilke at a later date in fact states that, around this time, he and Chamberlain had discussed the terms on which they would agree to join a Liberal ministry, and that they had decided to settle for an offer of a Cabinet post for one of them.[27] Furthermore, in his speeches to the conference of the National Liberal Federation at Darlington on 3 February, Chamberlain was to be found stressing the need for a united effort by Liberals of all shades in order to secure the overthrow of the Beaconsfield administration. He even went so far as to praise the attachment of many of the younger members of the aristocracy, like Rosebery, Aberdeen, and Lord Ramsay, to the cause of Liberalism, and declared that the real danger came not from the moderate Liberals, who 'at least ... did not go backwards', but from those self-proclaimed Radicals who distrusted the democratic processes of the 'caucus' system—one of the many shafts directed at the MP for nearby Newcastle, Joseph Cowen.[28] Another Radical who

[23] Selborne to Granville, 27 Dec. 1879, PRO 30/29/22A/4.
[24] Brett to Hartington, 15 Dec. 1879, Devonshire MSS, 340.858.
[25] Granville to Spencer, 23 Jan. 1880, in Peter Gordon (ed.), *The Red Earl: The Papers of the Fifth Earl Spencer, 1835–1910*, i (Northants Record Society, 31; 1981), 139–40.
[26] Chamberlain to John Morley, 25 Jan. 1880, Chamberlain MSS, JC5/54/283.
[27] Dilke to Harcourt, n.d. [6 Apr. 1880] (typescript), Harcourt MSS, Box 720, referring to a conversation with Chamberlain 'two months ago'.
[28] *The Times*, 4 Feb. 1880, p. 11.

was clearly impressed by the advantages of the Granville–Hartington leadership, given the state of the Liberal party, was A. J. Mundella, who had been closely associated with Gladstone during the agitation over the Eastern Question:

Query, is it for the best that there should be any change of leadership before the General Election? Much as I admire Gladstone, *I think not.* Let him . . . be to us as *our Nestor* what Lansdowne was to preceding Liberal Governments, what Bright has been to us of late, and he will give enormous strength to us, and bring the party into perfect cohesion, but a change from H. to G. before the Election would endanger our success. The weak-kneed would grow cold and the timid would fly from us. Gladstone *with* us we shall have all the pronounced Liberals and all the Whigs, but *leading* us we shall have the first alone. This is what I gather from all sides. [Samuel] Morley, who is one of Gladstone's warmest friends takes the same line.[29]

Considerations other than the mutual need for party unity influenced the Radicals in their preference for Granville and Hartington, however. Many, like Chamberlain, had no real emotional attachment to the former leader, and though it was recognized that his considerable political prestige would be a great asset to the Radicals, there was an obvious danger that Gladstone's leadership might have the effect of smothering his closest supporters by taking away their independence.[30] Furthermore, it was assumed that, if Gladstone did become Prime Minister, he would be compelled to 'buy' the support of the Whigs with a large share of ministerial places, at the Radicals' expense, whereas a Granville or Hartington government would have to make more generous concessions in order to accommodate the Radicals. Thus, Frank Hill, the editor of the *Daily News*, was reported to have told Forster's brother-in-law in December 1879 that there were 'many below the gangway . . . by no means anxious that Gladstone should resume the leadership—he named Dilke and Fawcett . . . Lord G. and Lord H. to prove their radicalism must appoint many of the extreme people, and so these men hope something will fall to them'.[31]

The belief that Hartington should retain his position because of his unique ability to lead a united party and form, if necesssary, a strong

---

[29] Mundella to Robert Leader, 17 Jan. 1880, Mundella–Leader MSS, 6P/70.

[30] Chamberlain felt that Gladstone 'would be King Stork and that some of us frogs would have a hard time of it under him', Chamberlain to John Morley, 25 Jan. 1880, Chamberlain MSS, JC5/54/283.

[31] W. T. Arnold to Forster, 15 Dec. 1879 (copy), Devonshire MSS, 340.861, enclosed with Forster to Hartington, 17 Dec. 1879, ibid. 340.860.

government was therefore expressed to him by his colleagues during the consultations in mid-December. On the fifteenth, the day before the meeting at Devonshire House, he had a long talk with Harcourt, whose principal arguments were recorded by Brett:

1. Mr. Gladstone leads only a section of the party—a large and important section no doubt; but not larger or more important that that which is prepared to follow my Chief, and is not prepared to follow Mr. Gladstone. (Note. Mr. Gladstone's section is prepared to follow my Chief.)

2. My Chief, if he leads the party when the elections come, will be easily able to form a Cabinet if necessary. (Note. If he resigns it is not likely that we shall have a majority: and if he formed a Cabinet it would, though perhaps not strong, be stronger than any which Mr. Gladstone could form).[32]

Forster, for his part, had already expressed to Granville his view that it would be 'Better for the Country, [and] safer and more conducive to real progress, that you and H. should lead', while, a few days after the Devonshire House meeting, Lord Ripon confided to his diary that it was clearly the 'true interest of the party to keep Hartington as leader', and that it would be wise to 'let the Scotch excitement calm down'.[33]

Even after Gladstone's campaign in Midlothian, therefore, it was still possible to argue that the future success of the Liberal party depended upon the Whigs exerting themselves as the principal directing influence, so that the party's 'Palmerstonian' credentials might be asserted. In order to become a truly 'national' party again, the Liberal leaders had to cultivate support among that large body of moderate opinion, the 'left-centre', which had been alienated in 1874. This view was exemplified by an article in that traditional organ of Whiggery, the *Edinburgh Review*, which had been encouraged by Hartington. Whig principles, it argued, were 'in the main the principles and opinions of the great mass of intelligence and Liberality in the Country', whose support at the general election was crucial:

It matters little by what name this large and important middle party may be described; call them Whigs, moderate Liberals, or even Liberal Conservatives, if you will. We assert, and we rely upon the fact, that the most

[32] Brett's diary, 15 Dec. 1879, Esher MSS, 2/5.
[33] Forster to Granville, 9, 14 Dec. 1879, PRO 30/29/22A/8, in Lord Edmond Fitzmaurice, *The Life of Granville George Leveson-Gower, Second Earl of Granville, K.G., 1815–1891* (1905), ii. 186–8; Lord Ripon's diary, 27 Dec. 1879, BL Add. MSS 43642.

important and influential portion of English political society at the present consists of men . . . who esteem sobriety of language, dignity of demeanour, and steadfastness in action, as the first qualities of Statesmanship; who distrust alike exuberant powers of eloquence and mysterious artifices of policy . . . who cling to the good old cause of constitutional progress with stability of principles and fixity of purpose. And we affirm that it is in this class of men, who are Liberals without being radicals or democrats, that the true centre of gravity of the Liberal party lies. It rests mainly with them to determine to which side the balance of parties and of power will incline.[34]

This examination of the Whig strategy of keeping in mind 'alternative contingencies' has proceeded on the assumption that their principal concern was to establish the strongest basis for the formation of the next Liberal government, but, while this was undoubtedly the long-term objective, there is much evidence to suggest that the possibility of defeat at the forthcoming general election formed an integral part of the calculations of Granville and others. One of the advantages of failure, in the short term, was obvious. When Granville wrote to Halifax, at the beginning of February 1880, that Gladstone's campaign in Scotland was likely to prove harmful to the Liberal party's prospects elsewhere, and so would 'diminish our chances at a General Election', Halifax observed, in his reply, that a defeat would solve 'the Gladstone difficulty'—'If the Conservatives keep a majority big enough to enable them to go on—it will not arise, and I don't myself see a fair prospect of the majority being turned by the elections.'[35] Such a result would certainly have overcome the embarrassing problem of reconciling the differences between the Whigs and Gladstone, in the field of foreign policy, where the Whigs, though critical of the tone in which the Conservatives had handled matters, generally acknowledged that a dramatic change by a future Liberal government was unrealistic. As Hartington made clear to Northbrook, early in October 1879, Liberal foreign policy would have to be formulated in accordance with the situation as they found it, and it would therefore be most unwise to give specific undertakings, while the party remained in opposition, as to what that

---

[34] 'Plain Whig Principles', *Edinburgh Review*, 151 (Jan. 1880), 257–80. This scarcely concealed attack on Gladstone, by Henry Reeve, went further than Hartington had wanted, presumably in that it expressed the wish that Gladstone might accept the Exchequer in a Whig ministry; see Hartington to Granville, 19 Jan. 1880, PRO 30/29/27B.

[35] Granville to Halifax, 1 Feb. 1880, Hickleton MSS, A4/85; Halifax to Granville, 2 Feb. 1880, PRO 30/29/27B.

policy would be.[36] This view was also emphasized by Granville, later in the month, during a highly significant conversation with the Queen's private secretary, General Ponsonby. Ponsonby approached Granville, at a time when rumours were afloat of a sudden dissolution of parliament, to convey Her Majesty's concern at the prospect of a Liberal administration reversing the policy of the Conservatives, and her objections to certain individuals, notably Gladstone. Granville assured Ponsonby, as he related to Hartington:

> that he might rely upon the desire of you and myself to meet the Queen's wishes as much as we could. That we differed from Harcourt in his sanguine expectations of a majority—that it was probable, though I was not sure that you were of that opinion, that the Government would lose a portion of their numbers—and that it must be remembered that even if the present members lost their majority, their opponents might not be in a position to form a Government.
>
> That in any case particularly with the view of not permanently weakening the moderate section of the Liberals, the most careful consideration must be given to everything that was done after realising the then state of affairs.[37]

In suggesting that, even if the government lost its parliamentary majority, the Liberals 'might not be in a position to form a Government', what Granville probably had in mind was the complication arising from the Irish dimension to the political situation. A brief survey of Liberal–Irish Nationalist relations, from 1874 to 1879, will make it clear why the Irish factor provided the Whigs with another very good reason for not wanting to displace the Conservatives from office.

At the general election of 1874, the Irish MPs connected with Isaac Butt's recently formed Home Rule League had stood independently of the Liberal party, and, in the new parliament, they had elected their own parliamentary committee and appointed their own whips.[38] Hartington's uncompromising attitude towards the Irish party was displayed during the 1874 session, when he delivered a trenchant speech opposing Butt's home-rule amendment, and one of his first acts on succeeding to the Liberal leadership in the Commons was to give full support to the government's new coercive

---

[36] Hartington to Northbrook, 3 Oct. 1879 (typescript), Northbrook MSS, vol. 23.
[37] Granville to Hartington, 14 Oct. 1879, Devonshire MSS, 340.840.
[38] See David Thornley, *Issac Butt and Home Rule* (1964), 138–75, 195–204, 212–19, 252–60.

measures.[39] His position was confirmed in a speech at Bristol, in November 1875, in which he made it clear that, before the Liberals could return to office, they had not only to recover the ground lost in 1874, but also to 'make very considerable fresh gains', as he 'feared they could not and must not expect to reckon upon any support from the great bulk of the Liberal members returned from Ireland'. Any concession to the Irish members on home rule was out of the question, while in the case of denominational education he believed the Nationalists had 'more in common with the Conservative than with the Liberal party; and he could conceive the possibility of the Irish Liberals voting to keep a Conservative government in power for the sake of obtaining denominational education rather than recording their votes in such a way as to place a Liberal Government in power or to retain it in power when it got there'.[40] Hartington had already stated the logical outcome of his position in a letter to Northbrook, several months earlier:

I sincerely trust that [the government] may not for a long time make any . . . mistakes as would turn them out. Our party, though I think now in tolerable good humour, is very far from being united, and nothing but a great change in the opinion of the Country, which would give us a majority without reckoning the Irish members, would bring us back to office with any satisfaction.[41]

Relations between the Liberals and the Irish members continued to deteriorate during subsequent years. This was reflected in the fact that whereas, prior to the 1876 session of parliament, Hartington was still sending out to the Irish members the customary leader's circular requesting their attendance at Westminster,[42] by the beginning of the 1877 session this was clearly no longer the case, as his letter to the Liberal chief whip shows: 'I can't agree with you about the Home Rulers. I wrote to you yesterday that Granville agreed with me. I have no objection to sending them the Whips; but the circular is an assumption of leadership, which may (and did last year) expose

[39] 30 June 1874, 3 Hansard, ccxx, cols. 770–81; 1 Mar. 1875, ibid. ccxxii, cols. 1017–24.
[40] Hartington at Bristol, *Manchester Guardian*, 15 Nov. 1875, p. 6. Cf. Hartington to Harcourt, 21 Nov. 1875, Harcourt MSS, Box 78.
[41] Hartington to Northbrook, 17 May 1875 (typescript), Northbrook MSS, vol. 23.
[42] Hartington to Adam, 14 Jan. 1876, Blairadam MSS, 4/966; 19 Jan. 1876, ibid. 4/1031.

me to snubs from them; and after all it is inconsistent with the fact of the case, to assume that I am their leader.'[43] A similar decision was made before the 1878 session began.[44] Discussions did take place amongst the Liberal leaders during the 1879 session, to consider the possibility of promoting co-operation with the Nationalists—though emphatically not on the question of home rule—and at a meeting on 17 May, 'civilities to Irish M.P.s were agreed upon'.[45] The high hopes entertained by Lord Ripon, a Roman Catholic convert, for joint action in relation to the government's Irish University Bill, were soon to be disappointed, however, as it became apparent that Hartington and most of his colleagues had little enthusiasm for a strategy which they feared would alienate the English Nonconformists.[46] In any case, co-operation between the Liberals and home rulers was being made difficult by the tactics of parliamentary obstruction pursued by some of the more extreme Nationalists since 1877, and, by the autumn of 1879, Hartington felt compelled to use his visit to Newcastle to denounce these methods.[47]

Indeed, by the time of Hartington's Newcastle speech, the 'Irish question' was entering a new and more acute phase, and it is from this point that Ireland may be seen as the most divisive issue in Liberal politics. Following the death of the relatively moderate Butt in July 1879, the initiative fell increasingly to the more extreme elements in the Nationalist party, like Parnell, who were seeking to harness the agrarian discontent in Ireland, caused by bad harvests, to the political movement for home rule. As far as the consequences of these developments for the British parties were concerned, Lord Derby had good grounds for believing that the 'Irish difficulty' would be 'the real rock ahead'.[48] Agrarian crime in Ireland was so serious that, in Kimberley's view, 'A new Coercive bill' would probably become necessary,[49] but this was bound to be made more difficult by the likelihood that, after the general election, the Nationalists would

---

[43]   Hartington to Adam, 3 Jan. 1877, ibid. 4/966.
[44]   Hartington to Adam, 31 Dec. 1877 and 5 Jan. 1878, ibid. 4/966.
[45]   Lord Ripon's diary, 17 May 1879, BL Add. MSS 43641.
[46]   Ibid., 20 May 1879, BL Add. MSS 43641, and 23 June 1879, BL Add. MSS 43642. Cf. Hartington to Brett, 5 June 1879, Esher MSS, 10/11.
[47]   Hartington at Newcastle, *Manchester Guardian*, 20 Sept. 1879, p. 8 Cf. Hartington to Harcourt, 7 Sept. 1879, Harcourt MSS, Box 78.
[48]   Lord Derby's diary, 15 Mar. 1880, Derby MSS.
[49]   Kimberley to J. G. Dodson, 30 Sept. 1879, Monk Bretton MSS.

hold the balance of power in parliament. Thus, the next parliament seemed certain to be torrid and short lived,[50] and if the Liberals came into power, they would have nothing more to look forward to than the 'gloomy prospect' of 'dependence on the ranting roughs'.[51]

It was difficult to imagine how a Liberal government, and particularly one lacking an overall parliamentary majority, could devise a policy for Ireland which would not inevitably rend the Liberal party in two. On the one hand, any hint of concession to the home rulers was certain to alienate many Whig and moderate supporters, while on the other, stern measures to deal with the Irish agitation were bound to be extremely unpopular with the Radical section. The hazards of attempting to conciliate the Irish were fully brought home at the time of the Liverpool by-election, early in 1880.[52] Hartington himself had been opposed to any concessions aimed at capturing the substantial Irish vote in this constituency, but, to his horror, the Liberal candidate, Lord Ramsay, confronted with the threat of a mass abstention, agreed to support a motion of inquiry into the demand for home rule.[53] In spite of this declaration, which provoked an immense row within the Liberal party, Ramsay was defeated on 6 February, thus confirming the view of many Liberals that any public identification with the Nationalists would be electorally disastrous. To Childers, for instance, it appeared that 'this business has alienated as many as Gladstone's violence did in '78'.[54] Not unnaturally, the Conservatives tried to exploit the situation by suddenly announcing resolutions designed to establish a mode of procedure for suspending MPs guilty of obstruction, but the opposition leaders were careful not to be drawn into this trap, and the resolutions were carried with their support on 27 February.

The problem posed by the Radicals mainly arose, unsurprisingly, from the attitude of Chamberlain. Since February 1879, he and Dilke had had a number of secret meetings with Parnell,[55] and, by the

[50] Both Harcourt and Hartington thought the next parliament would be a short one: Brett's diary, 22, 23 Dec. 1879, Esher MSS, 2/5.

[51] Ibid. 31 Dec. 1879.

[52] For a full account, see Rossi, *Liberal Opposition*, pp. 112–15.

[53] Hartington to Granville, 27, 30 Jan. 1880, PRO 30/29/27A. Although Hartington published a letter defending Ramsay's right to make such a declaration, he made it clear that he himself would not have done it: *The Times*, 4 Feb. 1880, p. 6.

[54] Childers to Halifax, 10 Feb. 1880, Hickleton MSS, A4/90. Cf. Brett's diary, 8 Feb. 1880, Esher MSS, 2/5.

[55] J. L. Garvin, *Life of Joseph Chamberlain*, i (1932), 273–4; S. Gwynn and G. M. Tuckwell, *The Life of Sir Charles W. Dilke, Bart M.P.* (1917), i. 281–2.

autumn of that year, Chamberlain was feeling his way towards a scheme for a 'modified form of home rule'—by which he meant giving the Irish control of local business.[56] Evidently, this was intended as a means of cementing an alliance between the Radicals below the gangway and the Nationalists, who had sometimes acted together in parliament, in the hope of gaining an important advantage for himself, *vis-à-vis* the Whigs, in the next Liberal government. Chamberlain's desire for co-operation with the home rulers was a cause of great concern to Hartington, who learned, in January 1880, that he now thought the party should hint at further concessions to the Irish on the land question, if this seemed necessary.[57] Furthermore, early in the parliamentary session, just days after the result of the Liverpool by-election, Chamberlain made a speech, during the debate on Redmond's amendment relating to the distress in Ireland, sympathizing with the Irish grievances and, though rejecting the demand for home rule, endorsing John Bright's policy (declared at Birmingham on 24 January) of land purchase. Chamberlain was one of twenty-nine Liberals who went into the division lobby with the Irish.[58] As yet, Chamberlain's strategy enjoyed the approbation of only a segment of the Radicals, but the potential for future difficulties with a Whig-led government was obvious.

Granville's repeated observation, during late 1879 and early 1880, that the Conservatives still expected to retain a small majority at the general election[59] undoubtedly reflected his desire that the Liberal party should not obtain a parliamentary majority which, as he put it to Halifax, 'in any case would not be sufficient against Tories and Home Rulers'.[60] Of course, one cannot expect to find a great deal of evidence of party leaders, just prior to a general election, openly willing their own defeat, but it is significant that General Ponsonby remained convinced, even after the dissolution, that Granville and

---

[56] Chamberlain to Morley, 21 Oct. 1879, 25 Jan. 1880, Chamberlain MSS, JC5/54/276, 283.

[57] Cf. Chamberlain to Harcourt, 25 Jan. 1880 (typescript), Harcourt MSS, Box 716, enclosed with Harcourt to Hartington, 26 Jan. 1880 (typescript), ibid. Box 720; Hartington to Harcourt, 27 Jan. 1880, ibid., Box 79.

[58] For Chamberlain's speech on 10 Feb., see 3 Hansard, ccl, cols. 388–95. The division list is printed in Ross's *Parliamentary Record* for 1880.

[59] e.g. Lord Derby's diary, 19 Nov. 1879, Derby MSS. Derby's own comment is worthy of note: 'With these numbers they [the government] can go on, but cannot do as they have been doing in the present parliament.'

[60] Granville to Halifax, 1 Feb. 1880, Hickleton MSS, A4/85.

Hartington 'could both do without office',[61] and it is also clear that the feeling that it was preferable for the Liberal party to remain in opposition, rather than come into power tied to the Nationalists, had been widely diffused for some considerable time.[62]

An additional reason for supposing that the Whig leaders were not anxious for an immediate return to office is that it made sense, anyway, for them to bide their time, because of the uncertainty about the future dividing line between the Liberal and Conservative parties. Two senior ministers, Derby and Carnarvon, had already resigned from Beaconsfield's government, and were being cultivated by the Whigs, who hoped eventually to be able to draw them into the Liberal orbit, thus strengthening the moderate section against the Radicals.[63] Furthermore, the fact that Beaconsfield, at 75, was unlikely to lead the Conservatives for much longer, raised the possibility that his departure might be the catalyst for a much larger realignment of political personnel. The following tantalizing note from Ponsonby to Granville, written shortly after their meeting in October 1879, suggests that the question of the Conservative succession may have been touched upon during their conversation: 'Although I thought Lord C[airns] most probable, I am beginning to think Lord S[alisbury] is rising in estimation and that he is ambitious to do so. I had my conversation. I repeated what you had said. H.M. was satisfied as far as it went.'[64]

---

[61] Ponsonby's memorandum, 17 Mar. 1880, in Arthur Ponsonby, *Henry Ponsonby: His Life from his Letters* (1942), 184. Note also the Queen's reaction to the result of the general election, as recorded by one of the outgoing Conservative ministers: 'She discussed the Elections, which had amazed her, as she had assurances from the Liberals that we must succeed', Nancy E. Johnson (ed.), *The Diary of Gathorne Hardy, later Lord Cranbrook, 1866–1892* (Oxford, 1981), 446 (entry for 20 Apr. 1880).

[62] Cf. the speeches by Goschen and Fawcett, *Manchester Guardian*, 27 Aug. 1879, p. 8, and 29 Oct. 1879, p. 8; Childers to Sir Andrew Clarke, 30 Oct. 1879, in Spencer Childers, *Childers*, i. 264; Duke of Somerset to Brinsley Sheridan, 22 Nov. 1879 and 20 Mar. 1880, in W. H. Mallock and Lady Gwendolen Ramsden, *Letters, Remains and Memoirs of Edward Adolphus Seymour, Twelfth Duke of Somerset, K.G.* (1893), 414, 417; W. C. Cartwright's diary, 6 Feb. 1880, Cartwright MSS, 6/14; Lord Morley's diary, Mar. 1880, BL Add. MSS 48291. Kimberley also thought it would be fatal for the Liberal party to be identified with the home rulers: Cartwright's diary, 20 Mar. 1880, Cartwright MSS, 6/14.

[63] Cf. Harcourt to Hartington, 10 Oct. 1879 (typescript), Harcourt MSS, Box 720. Knowsley received visits from several prominent Whigs during the summer and autumn of 1879. For Carnarvon's position, see his diary, 27 Dec. 1879, BL Add. MSS 60914.

[64] Ponsonby to Granville, 23 Oct. 1879, PRO 30/29/22A/4.

In all probability, what Granville wanted to see was a minority Conservative administration after the next general election, buttressed if necessary by a 'patriotic' Whig-led opposition, as the best possible political arrangement for dealing with Ireland and the home rule party, until the Liberals were in a position to establish an alternative government on a firmer parliamentary footing than could be hoped for in the immediate future. This Liberal government might have come into being after another general election, or perhaps following a break-up of the Conservative party. The advantage of the short-term expedient of maintaining the Conservatives in power, clearly, was that it would have the effect of neutralizing the Radicals and home rulers while, at the same time, preserving the existing two-party structure which enabled the Whigs to control the process of reform and forestall the catastrophe of an alignment between the Liberal party and the home rulers. Electoral adversity and the continuation of Conservative rule, it seems, formed the ultimate resource with which the Whigs could hope to maintain their authority over the Liberal party.

Ultimately, of course, the continued credibility of this Whig strategy depended upon the uncertain electoral prospects for the Liberal party, and it is therefore highly significant that those prospects appeared to diminish during the months following the first Midlothian campaign. A series of disappointing by-election results suggested, just as Hartington's advisors had predicted, that the reaction against the government had been a temporary phenomenon, which was now past its peak, and doubts were even raised about the steadfastness of the Liberals' urban base. At Sheffield, in late December, S. D. Waddy held the seat for the Liberals, but with a substantially reduced majority, and in February, Lord Ramsay's defeat at Liverpool was followed within a few days by the loss of a seat at Southwark, which shook the complacency of even the staunchest party newspapers.[65]

These set-backs provided the Conservative press with an easy target, and they were quick to seize the initiative, detecting in the by-election verdicts an emphatic rejection of those 'political doctrines which Mr. Gladstone and some of his friends have lately

---

[65] *Daily News*, 16 Feb. 1880, p. 4; *Leeds Mercury*, 17 Feb. 1880, p. 4. It is perfectly true that the circumstances in all three constituencies were somewhat unusual, and that the results were probably misleading, but we are concerned here with what contemporaries thought, rather than with what historians can see with hindsight.

succeeded in identifying with the name and organisation of Liberalism'.[66] The vociferous campaigning of Gladstone and other Radicals, it was declared, had alienated the more thoughtful classes of voters, who viewed with distaste the erection of a 'platform which substitutes for a policy of its own abuse of the general foreign policy of the present Administration'.[67] Thus it appeared to *The Times* that 'The demand upon the popular credulity has been strained too far, and accumulated charges have collapsed under their own weight', and that the Liberals clearly had 'more to lose than to gain by reviving controversies concerning foreign policy for electioneering objects'.[68] To an ultra-Tory journal like *Blackwood's*, it was evident that 'the opposition has crumbled into ruin', and that there had been a 'complete collapse of Mr. Gladstone's agitation'.[69]

Meantime, a mood of despondency was establishing itself within the Liberal party. Harcourt was found to be 'low about election prospects—very much changed in tone',[70] Childers was predicting a Conservative majority at the general election,[71] and others were beginning to contemplate the necessity of giving the government a 'second innings' before a Liberal victory could be achieved.[72] There was also growing concern in the Liberal press at the signs that a significant portion of the electorate was still 'slightly fascinated by the Jingo policy of the Government',[73] and the fear was expressed that, with the reassertion of Britain's position in Afghanistan and Southern Africa, following the triumphs of Roberts and Wolseley, the 'Jingoes' had 'taken heart again'.[74] As the Liberals' chances of electoral victory appeared to recede, so the speculation grew that the government might, after all, dissolve parliament at any early date.[75] By 6 March, the strongly pro-Gladstonian *Spectator* was predicting a general election before Whitsun:

[66] *The Times*, 16 Feb. 1880, p. 9.
[67] *Daily Telegraph*, 16 Feb. 1880, p. 4.
[68] *The Times*, 9 Feb. 1880, p. 9.
[69] *Blackwood's Edinburgh Magazine*, 127 (Mar. 1880), 400–1; (Apr. 1880), 530.
[70] Lord Ripon's diary, 24 Feb. 1880, BL Add. MSS 43642.
[71] W. C. Cartwright's diary, 6 Feb. 1880, Cartwright MSS, 6/14. This was after the Liverpool result. For a similar view, see Brett's diary, 16 Feb. 1880, Esher MSS, 2/5.
[72] James Stansfeld to Halifax, 24 Feb. 1880, Hickleton MSS, A4/51.
[73] The *Spectator*, 14 Feb. 1880, p. 197. Cf. *Leeds Mercury*, 17 Feb. 1880, p. 4.
[74] The *Spectator*, 21 Feb. 1880, p. 229.
[75] Lord Derby's diary, 14 Feb. 1880, Derby MSS; Lord Ripon's diary, 24 Feb. 1880, BL Add. MSS 43642.

Lord Beaconsfield is one who has noted accurately the curious ebb and flow of party opinion, and doubtless he was well pleased in the autumn to notice that the Liberal wave came too soon for the crisis it was to effect, and had ample time to subside before it could influence the coming election. He will not, if he can help it, make the same mistake. He will not outstay the time when, in his opinion, the Liberal movement is growing less powerful, and the discouragement caused by the late elections is most marked.[76]

Two days later, Beaconsfield announced his intention to dissolve parliament, having first assured the Queen that it was the most favourable moment the government was likely to have.[77] One great advantage of an election at that time was that it enabled the Conservatives to exploit the 'Irish question', which had become highly topical during the short parliamentary session, in the hope of tarring the Liberals with the home-rule brush. Beaconsfield's election address, therefore, took the form of a letter to the Duke of Marl-borough, the Lord Lieutenant of Ireland, in which he emphasized the threat to the union posed by the (alleged) sympathy of the Liberals with the demands of the Nationalists, and then cleverly related this to an unpatriotic design to 'enfeeble our colonies by [a] policy of decomposition'.[78]

Beaconsfield's ploy appeared to have been well judged, and the Conservatives remained hopeful, throughout the election campaign, that they might be returned with a modest majority.[79] The expecta-tions of their opponents, meantime, were equally if not more limited. Speaker Brand noted in his diary on 15 March that 'The general opinion' was that 'the opposition may gain slightly at the general election, but not to an extent to break down altogether the Conserva-tive majority',[80] a view reflected in Lord Aberdare's estimate that the Liberals might 'win several seats in Scotland, Ireland and Wales, and a few in England', but that it was 'very doubtful whether we shall get

[76] The *Spectator*, 6 Mar. 1880, p. 293.
[77] The Queen's diary, 5 Mar. 1880, in G. E. Buckle (ed.), *The Letters of Queen Victoria* 2nd series, 1926–8), iii. 71–2.
[78] Printed in W. F. Monypenny and G. E. Buckle, *The Life of Benjamin Disraeli, Earl of Beaconsfield* (1929 edn.), ii. 1386–8.
[79] Cf. Sir George Russell to Lord Cranbrook, 29 Mar. 1880, in A. E. Gathorne Hardy, *Gathorne Hardy, First Earl of Cranbrook: A Memoir* (1910), ii. 132; Julia Cartwright (ed.), *The Journals of Lady Knightley of Fawsley* (1915), 357 (entry for 9 Mar. 1880); the Queen to Theodore Martin, in Buckle (ed.), *Victoria's Letters*, iii. 73.
[80] Speaker Brand's diary, 15 Mar. 1880, Hampden MSS. Cf. W. C. Cartwright's diary, 8 Mar. 1880, Cartwright MSS, 6/14.

a majority'.[81] Granville told John Morley that he expected a 'Government majority of fifteen or so: short Parliament; dissolution in another year or two at most'.[82] There were still said to be a number of county constituencies without Liberal candidates,[83] and concern was frequently expressed at the continuing reports of internecine rivalry in local Liberal associations which was jeopardizing the party's chances.[84] At Northampton, where two Radical candidates, Bradlaugh and Labouchere, had been put forward, the in-fighting was so serious that Labouchere sought a telegram of support from Gladstone, a request he justified on the grounds that 'the general result of the election seems so doubtful that two seats ought not to be lost, if they can be won'.[85] Liberal hopes did rise slightly, later in the campaign, as it became apparent that candidates were being found to contest seats, even some hitherto regarded as hopeless,[86] and it was also reported that the divisions in most local associations were being overcome.[87] Nevertheless, the London correspondent of the *Manchester Guardian* reported, on the eve of the elections, that even the most sanguine of Liberals only expected a majority over the Conservatives of about fifteen, while most of the party leaders still doubted a Liberal majority at all, so that the real question seemed to be whether or not the government would be able to hold on with a slender majority.[88] As the *Leeds Mercury* conceded, it was 'possible that the election for a single constituency may decide the fate of Lord Beaconsfield's Government and of the Country'.[89] In Birmingham, faced with a concerted attack by the Conservatives, even Joseph Chamberlain was fearful, just days before polling began, that he might lose his seat.[90]

[81] Aberdare to his wife, 14 Mar. 1880, *Letters of the Rt. Hon. Henry Austin Bruce, G.C.B., Lord Aberdare of Duffryn* (privately printed, Oxford, 1902), ii. 85.
[82] John Morley to Chamberlain, 17 Mar. 1880, Chamberlain MSS, JC5/54/293. Cf. Lord Derby's diary, 18 Mar. 1880, Derby MSS.
[83] *Manchester Guardian*, 12 Mar. 1880, p. 5.
[84] *Daily News*, 13 Mar. 1880, pp. 4–5.
[85] Labouchere to Rosébery, Saturday [Mar. 1880], NLS MSS 10041.
[86] *Manchester Guardian*, 31 Mar. 1880, p. 5.
[87] *Daily News*, 30 Mar. 1880, p. 4.
[88] *Manchester Guardian*, 30 Mar. 1880, p. 5.
[89] *Leeds Mercury*, 30 Mar. 1880, p. 5. This bears out the point made by T. O. Lloyd, *The General Election of 1880* (Oxford, 1968), 32–3, that there is no foundation for the belief that the provincial Liberal press had all along predicted a great majority for the Liberal party.
[90] Cf. John Morley to Chamberlain, 29 Mar. 1880; Chamberlain to Morley, 31 Mar. 1880, Chamberlain MSS, JC5/54/297 and 301.

The last thing that almost anyone considered possible was that the Liberals might obtain an overall parliamentary majority, and so it was natural that the dangers of a weak Liberal government should have been driven home repeatedly by the Conservative press. The only Liberal government that could survive for any length of time, it was argued, would necessarily be a sordid alliance of 'Birmingham Radicals and Home Rulers with Whigs and Liberals',[91] which would be forced to make concessions to the Irish contingent while coming under the malign influence of Gladstone in foreign affairs. One leading article in the *Pall Mall Gazette* carried the title 'The Prospect Of A Liberal Government A Prospect Of Confusion And Strife',[92] and the *Daily Telegraph*, with similar sentiments in mind, urged the voters of England and Wales to 'take heed . . . and avoid the immense calamity of a small Liberal majority'.[93] In a situation where a strong government, capable of resisting the forces making for the disintegration of the Empire, was at a premium, the only solution, it was argued, lay in 'the return of a considerable majority of members pledged to support the present Administration', as there was 'no chance at all of such a return for the chiefs of the other party'.[94]

II

If the highly uncertain outlook for the Liberal party lent vital credibility to the strategy of the Whig leadership before the general election, its influence upon the conduct of Gladstone was no less significant. The familiar interpretative problem of how to distinguish between ambition and self-deception is raised again, but what finally emerges is a complex process of interaction, whereby the doubts about the possibility of a Liberal victory were absorbed into Gladstone's peculiar pattern of thinking and made to serve as pillars supporting his own distinctive view of the situation.

There can be little doubt that, albeit unconsciously, Gladstone was ambitious to become Prime Minister again. We have already seen that, in spite of the decision taken in January 1875, he had never really withdrawn from active politics, and even after the Congress of

[91] *Daily Telegraph*, 11 Mar. 1880, p. 6.
[92] *Pall Mall Gazette*, 11 Mar. 1880, p. 1.
[93] *Daily Telegraph*, 30 Mar. 1880, p. 4.
[94] Pall Mall Gazette, 9 Mar. 1880, p. 1. Cf. *Daily Telegraph*, 30 Mar. 1880, p. 4; *Blackwood's Edinburgh Magazine*, 127 (Apr. 1880), 540.

Berlin had settled the Eastern Question, in the summer of 1878, it was clear that Gladstone would pursue his vendetta against Beaconsfield. The Afghan question had quickly provided him with another stick with which to beat the government, and his evident excitement at the first real scent of Conservative blood, and his persistent belief that 'public opinion' was with him, are admirably conveyed in his hyperbolic assertion to Lord Northbrook in November 1878 that 'I have never known so much absorption in foreign policy, and have never known feelings so deeply excited on policy, either home or foreign: even the repeal of the Corn Laws did not, I am inclined to think, equal it, and for its match we must go back to the first Reform Act'.[95] To John Bright, he wrote urging that this was not the time for repose, for although 'You and I have often been in Opposition before', this was 'no common Opposition and no common Government'.[96] Consequently, during the early months of 1879, Gladstone was to be found playing a prominent part in debates on various issues, such as Greece and finance, both in April,[97] while his determination to rally as strong an opposition as possible to the government was reflected in his suggestion to Granville, in January, that there might be scope for a *modus vivendi* with the Irish home rulers on the basis of a local government measure.[98]

Gladstone's decision, at the beginning of 1879, to accept the invitation to contest the Conservative-held constituency of Midlothian, was a clear sign that he intended to carry on his crusade against Beaconsfield's policies to a final issue at the general election. Furthermore, he was anxious that the battle against the Conservatives should be fought squarely on the ground of their previous policies, of which he had been the principal critic, lest the electorate be deceived by a temporary display of moderation on the government's part. He urged on Granville his view that the Conservatives would 'want all past proceedings to be in the main "stale fish"', and would therefore 'very likely commit no new enormity before the Election', making it essential for the Liberals to conduct an autumn campaign in order to 'keep the old alive and warm' and so 'join on

[95] Gladstone to Northbrook, 2 Nov. 1878 (typescript), Northbrook MSS, vol. 7.
[96] Gladstone to Bright, 15 Nov. 1878, BL Add. MSS 43385, fo. 267.
[97] 17 Apr. 1879, 3 Hansard, ccxlv, cols. 540–6; 28 Apr. 1879, ibid., cols. 1270–97.
[98] Gladstone to Granville, 18 Jan. 1879, in Agatha Ramm (ed.), *The Political Correspondence of Mr Gladstone and Lord Granville, 1876–1886* (Oxford, 1962), i. 91–2.

the proceedings of 1876–9 by a continuous process to the Dissolution'.[99] Such a campaign was all the more imperative in the absence, so far as Gladstone could see, of a 'clear and strong programme' as an alternative to 'the retrospective discussion before the constituencies'.[100]

Gladstone's not unnatural desire was that his visit to Midlothian might prove to be the catalyst of an immense upsurge of moral feeling against the government which would ensure its eventual defeat when the general election came. Of course, a massive popular repudiation of Beaconsfield's policies would also have had the effect of securing Gladstone's own political rehabilitation. Lady Frederick Cavendish's description of him, back at Hawarden after the Scottish campaign, is highly suggestive in this respect: 'For the first time, I deliberately believe, in my recollection, he seemed a little personally elated . . . this unheard of enthusiasm for his name . . . after the long time of abuse and loss of influence, has deeply moved him.'[101] This, indeed, went to the heart of the matter, for a successful outcome to a general election, fought on the basis of a retrospective campaign, would have represented to Gladstone the vindication of his past conduct, an acknowledgement that he had been right to speak out against Beaconsfield's foreign policy, when the Liberal 'establishment' had been silent, and right to place his trust in what he once described as the 'unchanging sentiments' of the people.[102] Confirmation of his consciousness of this possibility is provided by the following recollection by his son Herbert: 'for 4 years before the General Election he contemplated the possibility of being recalled to the helm. I think it was in '77 when I was walking with him at Hawarden and asked him direct if he thought he would have to go back to office. He answered then it does not depend upon me, but upon the people.'[103] The difficulty here was that it was important for Gladstone to believe that his conduct was motivated by something more than a base desire for a renewed lease of personal power. This feeling was made all the more acute because a return to the front

[99] Gladstone to Granville, 6 Aug. 1879, ibid. i. 99–100.
[100] Ibid.
[101] J. Bailey (ed.), *The Diary of Lady Frederick Cavendish* (1927), ii. 241 (entry for 8–14. Dec. 1879).
[102] Gladstone to Granville, 19 Nov. 1876, in Ramm (ed.), *Gladstone–Granville Correspondence, 1876–1886*, i. 22–3.
[103] Herbert Gladstone's diary, 30 Jan. 1881, Glynne–Gladstone MSS, printed in his book, *After Thirty Years* (1928), 189–90.

would obviously involve displacing Granville and Hartington, who had led the party so unselfishly in the years after he had 'deserted' it, and was also likely to arouse the personal hostility of the Queen.

Fortunately for Gladstone's peace of mind, he was able to avoid having to face up to this personal dilemma because of the possibility that the people might not, after all, choose to sweep the 'jingoes' from office at the next election. He therefore adopted the position, as he explained to his son Henry shortly before the first Midlothian campaign, that only after 'a very general, a nearly unanimous, call from the Liberals, with the appearance of a sort of national will', would it be possible for him to reconsider his position, and that he could not 'at present see any indication of a state of things which would bring it about'.[104] Nor did Midlothian itself transform the situation, because Gladstone accepted (perhaps rather conveniently) the analysis that many moderate Liberal supporters would be frightened away if he were to assume the leadership at that time.[105] Consequently he took the view, as he explained to Lord Wolverton, that 'the leadership in the new Parliament must, like everything else, be considered in connection with what may appear at the Dissolution to be the sense of the Country'.[106]

Indeed, it was precisely because of the uncertain position of the Liberal party that Gladstone was able to sustain, in his own mind, a coherent explanation for the ambiguous and embarrassing position which he occupied. This was another classic illustration of his ability to synthesize various conflicting impulses. Gladstone convinced himself of his own yearning for retirement from politics, which was ostensibly plausible in view of his age (he was 70 in December 1879), and the inevitable uncertainty about his future health.[107] Then, all the other obstacles to his return to the helm came to occupy his mind in support of the notion of retirement: the enormity of the work to be done if the Liberals returned to office; the particular hostility to

[104] Gladstone to Henry Neville Gladstone, Oct. 1879, in John Morley, *Life of William Ewart Gladstone* (1903), ii. 598.
[105] Wolverton to Gladstone, 20 Dec. 1879, BL Add. MSS 44349, fo. 121, in Morley, *Gladstone*, ii. 602.
[106] Gladstone to Wolverton, 18 Dec. 1879, BL Add. MSS 44349, fo. 119, in Morley, *Gladstone*, ii. 603.
[107] It is interesting to note the depressing effect of his sister's death in Jan. 1880. Harcourt wrote on the 24th, 'I hear Gladstone talks more than ever of retire[ment] and thoughts of the afterworld', Chamberlain MSS, JC5/36/7. A little earlier, on the 10th, Gladstone had lamented to J. G. Dodson his 'growing slowness (clearly related to infirmity) of eyesight', Monk Bretton MSS.

which a government headed by himself would be subjected; his sense of personal loyalty to Granville and Hartington, and the odium of having to impose himself upon the Queen.[108] By this mental path, Gladstone could sincerely believe that the thing he desired of God more than anything else was 'that I may escape into retirement'.[109]

Having thus separated the element of personal ambition from the uphill battle against the government, Gladstone accounted for his involvement in the demonstrations in Scotland by maintaining that he was merely fulfilling his duty, as a loyal subordinate, to 'hold fast by Granville and Hartington, and try to promote the union and efficiency of the party led by them'.[110] His longed-for repose would therefore be the eventual reward for the immediate sacrifice required of him in undertaking the Midlothian contest. In a letter to Henry Broadhurst, which was published in the newspapers, he expressed himself as: 'trusting that the day is near when I may fairly claim to rest from the labours of political contention, but trusting also that I shall deserve my title to retirement from having witnessed, and having to the best of my power assisted in, the overthrow of this dishonouring and disturbing system of government under which the nation at present so gravely suffers'.[111]

Paradoxically, the fact that Gladstone's quest for personal vindication depended upon a popular verdict of such proportions as few thought possible undoubtedly worked to his advantage. It is unlikely that he could have maintained his independent, uncommitted position if a decisive majority for the Liberals had appeared certain all along. In those circumstances, Gladstone would not have enjoyed the luxury of being able to dismiss, out of hand, the suggestion that he might accept a subordinate post in a Whig government,[112] while, at the same time, making no attempt to resolve the question of the

---

[108] Gladstone to Bright, 28 Nov. 1879, BL Add. MSS 43385, fo. 271, in Morley, *Gladstone*, ii. 599–600. Significantly, Gladstone added that he was writing this letter to provide confirmation of his views for the purpose of verification.

[109] Gladstone's diary, 28 Dec. 1879, in Morley, *Gladstone*, ii. 597.

[110] Gladstone to Hayward, 15 Nov. 1879, in Henry E. Carlisle (ed.), *A Selection from the Correspondence of Abraham Hayward, Q.C., from 1834 to 1884* (1886), ii. 308.

[111] Gladstone to Broadhurst, 27 Dec. 1879, Broadhurst MSS, vol. 1. Cf. *Manchester Guardian*, 30 Dec. 1879, p. 5. This letter was in reply to an address from the National Labour League.

[112] In a letter to Hayward, 12 Nov. 1879, Gladstone referred to the 'silly scheme ... for carrying me back over twenty seven years of life, and replacing me in the Finance Department', Carlisle, *Hayward's Letters*, ii. 307–8.

leadership. Instead, he would have been forced either to take the unpleasant step of demanding that he be restored as leader before the general election, in recognition of public opinion, or else to acquiesce in the leadership of Granville and Hartington, which would have made it difficult for him to justify taking the premiership afterwards.

On setting out for Scotland in March 1880, Gladstone remained insistent that he was about to contest 'my *last* General Election', and declared that 'A clear answer from the nation, a clear answer in the highest sense, and a decisive accession of the Liberal party to office without me . . . is what I hope and pray.'[113] But one wonders whether Gladstone would have felt able to say this, had he not been aware of the prevailing opinion about the Liberals' electoral chances.

I think that the experts and the party generally are pretty sanguine. None doubt that the government are to lose [i.e. seats]; a few doubt whether they will be weaker than the Liberals and home rulers; very many whether weaker than Liberals alone. All agree that Scotland will do its duty.[114]

Even in the Midlothian contest, however, Gladstone was being prepared, towards the end, for a slender majority, at which news he 'expressed his bitter disappointment and hinted that in that case the election would be a *coup manqué*'.[115]

III

Within the space of a few days, early in April 1880, the political situation was completely transformed. The early pattern of election results, showing Liberal gains in the boroughs, had seemed only to indicate the small majority, dependent upon the home rulers, which

[113] Gladstone to Lord Acton, 14 Mar. 1880, in Morley, *Gladstone*, ii. 608. It is important to note that Acton conveyed the contents of this letter to Granville, who apparently passed on Acton's letter to Hartington: Acton to Granville, 2 Apr. 1880, Devonshire MSS, 340.922.

[114] Gladstone to Acton, 14 Mar. 1880, in Morley, *Gladstone*, ii. 608.

[115] Rosebery to Granville, 30 Mar. 1880, PRO 30/29/27B. It would be interesting to speculate as to Gladstone's course of action had the Liberals failed to win the general election. In a retrospective entry to his diary, Herbert Gladstone wrote that in January 1880 he had been considering acting as his father's secretary, in private life, if the Conservatives won: 21 Dec. 1880, Glynne–Gladstone MSS. Presumably, Gladstone would have continued to play the independent part he had given himself in 1875. But what would he have done in the event of a hung parliament, with the Nationalists holding the balance of power?

the Whigs feared, prompting Hartington to complain that 'Things are going a great deal too well, and we shall be in before we know where we are.'[116] Fortunately, however, the electors in the counties, as if in response to the anxious pleas of the Liberal press, voted for an overall Liberal majority. Such was the astonishment at the result that one Conservative minister likened it to 'thunder . . . from a clear sky'.[117] On the Liberal side, Harcourt found the 'conquest of the Elections . . . astounding', and Chamberlain had to admit that 'our calculations have been distanced by the vote', while Gladstone was stunned, and rejoiced at 'such a success and such a smash', when only a 'hollow beating' of the government had seemed likely.[118] To the *Leeds Mercury*, it appeared that 'for the moment they [the Liberals] are slightly embarrassed by their own success'.[119]

What remained to be seen was how Gladstone and the Whig leaders would come to terms with this new and unexpected state of affairs, which was further complicated by the absence of the Queen at Baden-Baden, and the knowledge that she would not be back in England until about the seventeenth. It will become apparent that only when they are considered in the context of the pre-election attitudes and assumptions described earlier can the discussions of the 'interregnum' period, and the process by which the leadership question was finally resolved, be fully understood.

The formation of a Gladstone ministry was not regarded as the natural corollary of the general election. On the contrary, it was widely reported 'as matter of fact' that, in spite of the growing Liberal majority and his personal triumph in Midlothian, Gladstone intended to waive all claims to the premiership and favoured Granville, as the senior member of the duumvirate, to assume the responsibility for forming the new government.[120] Such reports were certainly plausible, bearing in mind Gladstone's public expressions of his loyalty to Granville and Hartington and of his desire for retirement, and many of his strongest supporters were evidently in

[116] Hartington to Brett, 2 Apr. 1880, Esher MSS, 10/11. Cf. Lord Derby's diary, 2 Apr. 1880, Derby MSS.

[117] Lord Cranbrook's diary, 4 Apr. 1880, in Johnson (ed.), *Cranbrook Diaries*, p. 443.

[118] Harcourt to Hartington [Apr. 1880], Devonshire MSS, 340.924; Chamberlain to Harcourt, 10 Apr. 1880 (typescript), Harcourt MSS, Box 716; Gladstone to Speaker Brand, 9 Apr. 1880, Hampden MSS.

[119] *Leeds Mercury*, 19 Apr. 1880, p. 4.

[120] *Daily Telegraph*, 7 Apr. 1880, p. 4. Cf. Lord Derby's diary, 5 Apr. 1880, Derby MSS.

the dark as to where he stood.[121] The belief that he would not seek the premiership therefore gained ground even in the Liberal press. As the *Leeds Mercury* noted, on 7 April:

it cannot be forgotten that Mr. Gladstone has most emphatically declared his wish, nay his very firm and deliberate resolve, not to become once more the head of a Ministry, and it is therefore tolerably clear that . . . he is not likely to be the next Prime Minister of England. For all practical purposes the choice may be said to lie between Lord Granville and Lord Hartington.[122]

Similarly, the advanced Liberal *Daily News*, though stressing Gladstone's indubitable claims to the premiership and the clearly expressed opinion of the electorate that he should take the first place in the new government, was forced to admit that:

It is quite possible that that reluctance to take office which he has frequently expressed, will not be overcome. Mr. Gladstone may desire retirement. Sensitiveness as to the relations in which he has stood during the past five years to Lord Granville and Lord Hartington, and an honourable desire not to take from them the opportunity which now comes to them, are sure to act powerfully upon such a mind as his. Mr. Gladstone may be content to have created a great Liberal majority and to have made a powerful Liberal administration possible.[123]

Up to about 12 April, there was a growing consensus in the newspaper world that Gladstone would accept an honorary, advisory position, in a Cabinet formed by Granville.[124] Meantime, in political circles, as the London correspondent of the *Manchester Guardian* put it, 'the hope—I may say too the belief—which generally prevails', was that Gladstone would 'encourage no steps which will result in his assumption of the Premiership'.[125] Spencer wrote to Granville, on the tenth, that 'universal opinion points to you as the right Prime Minister', and Forster, the following day, thought 'the best upshot' would be for either Granville or Hartington to be Prime Minister, with Gladstone 'in the Cabinet without office'.[126] Childers, meantime, was offering to Hartington the advice that:

---

[121] Cf. Malcolm MacColl to Gladstone, 12 Apr. 1880, BL Add. MSS 44243, fo. 311; W. T. Stead to Gladstone, 9 Apr. 1880, BL Add. MSS 44303, fo. 333.

[122] *Leeds Mercury*, 7 Apr. 1880, p. 4.

[123] *Daily News*, 9 Apr. 1880, p. 4.

[124] Cf. *The Times*, 12 Apr. 1880. p. 9; *Daily Telegraph*, 12 Apr. 1880, p. 4; *Leeds Mercury*, 13 Apr. 1880, p. 4.

[125] *Manchester Guardian*, 12 Apr. 1880, p. 5.

[126] Spencer to Granville, 10 Apr. 1880, PRO 30/29/29; Forster to Granville, 11 Apr. 1880, PRO 30/29/28.

as soon as he (Lord Hartington), or Lord Granville is asked to form a government, Gladstone should be requested to join the Cabinet without office . . . and that this should be related promptly, before any outside pressure on the subject can be got up. I said I felt strongly that Gladstone could not refuse this, if put strongly.

But if there is any hesitation on Lord Hartington's or Lord Granville's part in their overtures to him, I fear that Mr. Gladstone . . . may take some step which will end in his becoming Prime Minister again; and I cannot look on this without uneasiness.[127]

There is certainly no reason to suppose that a Whig-led government of the kind being suggested, in the immediate aftermath of the general election, would have had any real difficulty in securing the participation of the Radical section. Chamberlain, it is true, had been eager to exploit the unexpected election gains by raising his own terms for supporting the new government, and he had therefore proposed to Dilke a 'thorough offensive and defensive alliance', with the intention of securing Cabinet rank for them both or else staying out.[128] However, it was clear that Dilke, working on the assumption of a Granville ministry, had no intention of risking his own—almost assured—place in the Cabinet for the sake of Chamberlain.[129] In a letter to Harcourt, whom he had just informed about his and Chamberlain's agreement, two months earlier, to accept one Cabinet post, Dilke declared that 'I shall not bind myself to anything or anybody.'[130] As Reginald Brett commented in his diary, 'Dilke is too sound a politician to make any such compromising arrangement.'[131] Dilke's resolve to accept office clearly rendered Chamberlain's plan unworkable, and, by the eleventh, the latter was already reconciling himself to the possibility of a junior post outside the Cabinet.[132] John Morley agreed with Chamberlain's decision, and was anxious that

---

[127] Childers to Halifax, 12 Apr. 1880, Hickleton MSS, A4/90, recounting a conversation with Hartington the previous day.

[128] Chamberlain to Dilke, 4 Apr. 1880, BL Add MSS 43885, fo. 66.

[129] Dilke to Chamberlain, 5 Apr. 1880, Chamberlain MSS, JC5/24/13.

[130] Dilke to Harcourt, n.d. [6 Apr. 1880] (typescript), Harcourt MSS, Box 720. Harcourt's report to Hartington, after he had seen Dilke on the 5th, conveyed the impression that he had seen both Dilke and Chamberlain, and that both were prepared to acquiesce in an offer of Cabinet rank for one of them: n.d. [5 Apr. 1880], Devonshire MSS, 340.925. Dilke's determination to claim for himself, if necessary, the sole representation of 'young Radicalism' in the Cabinet never altered, as is evidenced by the anxious letters from Chamberlain, 19 Apr. 1880, BL Add. MSS 43885, fo. 70, and Frank Hill, 22 Apr. 1880, BL Add. MSS 43898, fo. 29.

[131] Brett's diary, n.d. [*Apr.* 1880], Esher MSS, 2/5.

[132] Chamberlain to Morley, 11 Apr. 1880, Chamberlain MSS, JC5/54/308.

he should not exclude himself even if another Radical, like Fawcett, was offered Cabinet rank, since the only alternative was to become the 'chief of a group of frondeurs of second rate quality'.[133] Clearly, as Morley recognized, the idea being mooted by Frederic Harrison for the formation of a separate Radical group, in order to maximize their bargaining power with the new government, was out of the question.[134]

The significance of all these discussions is that, even when they were not conducted on the explicit assumption of a Whig-led ministry, hardly any reference was made to the question of Gladstone's position. It is interesting, for example, that Chamberlain's letter of 10 April, arguing that the new government must adopt more Radical policies, should have been addressed to Harcourt—the natural channel for communications with Hartington and Granville, but hardly with Gladstone.[135] Indeed, there is every reason to suppose that, for those who hoped for a substantial Radical accession to high office, the return of Gladstone, whose Cabinet was largely stocked with Whigs, was a great disappointment. In the event, it was Chamberlain who obtained Cabinet rank in April 1880 (he can have had few qualms about overstepping Dilke, given the latter's refusal to co-operate earlier in the month), but, as he subsequently remarked to Collings, 'There is little doubt that if Hartington had been Prime Minister he would have offered the Cabinet to both

---

[133] Morley to Chamberlain, 12 Apr. 1880, ibid. JC5/54/309.

[134] Morley to Chamberlain, 12 Apr. 1880 [no. 2], ibid. JC5/54/311. Harrison had originally made the suggestion to Dilke, on 5 Apr.: BL Add. MSS 43898, fo. 179. Significantly, he had assumed that the new government would be led by the Whigs, and that Gladstone would voluntarily stand aside.

[135] Chamberlain argued that, owing to the improved quality of the parliamentary Liberals, 'The policy which would have been the only one possible in the Parliament we anticipated will not suit the House which is now elected'. Consequently, 'a solid meal must be provided for the Liberal lions—if they are to be kept from rending one another. Redistribution will have to be taken seriously into hand; and land reform will have to be more radical than we thought.' Chamberlain wanted to see two 'omnibus' bills, one covering county franchise, redistribution, and other related matters like registration and hours of polling, the other to include the abolition of primogeniture and entail, the alteration of the game laws, and compensation for improvements: Chamberlain to Harcourt, 10 Apr. 1880 (typescript), Harcourt MSS, Box 716. Jesse Collings also wrote to Harcourt, on 12 Apr., urging the claims of both Dilke and Chamberlain for Cabinet office: ibid., Box 727. Chamberlain's letter to *The Times*, 13 Apr. 1880, p. 10, pointing to the gains made by the Liberal party in those constituencies where the 'caucus' organization existed, was clearly intended to establish his claim for office.

Dilke and myself.'[136] John Morley was more explicit still in stating that he would have preferred to see a Hartington premiership.[137]

It was on 12 April that Gladstone's trusted intermediary, Lord Wolverton, who had spent the evening of the tenth at Hawarden, contacted Granville and Hartington to inform them that Gladstone had discovered, in the result of the general election, circumstances which demanded his return as Prime Minister, and that he would not consider serving in a subordinate post. Wolverton reported to Gladstone, afterwards, that:

> [Granville] has gone to Walmer, and will come up on Friday [the 16th]. He has a good deal to think of in the meantime as to 'the position of the party'. I need not say more than this, as it embraces the whole question, which he *now quite appreciates* . . . Nothing could be more cordial and kind than Granville and Hartington, but I hardly think till today they *quite* realised the *position*, which I confess seems to me as clear as the sun at noon.[138]

Wolverton's reference to 'the position of the party' provides an indication of the way in which Gladstone's mind was working. Naturally, he had been impressed and thrilled by the 'moral influence' of the election results,[139] and the magnitude of the Liberal victory offered the means of reconciling, in his own mind, his eagerness to respond to events by resuming the premiership, with the difficulties involved in depriving Granville and Hartington of their rightful reward and imposing himself upon the Queen. As Gladstone saw it, the justification for doing this lay in the special circumstances arising from the unexpectedly decisive Liberal majority, which called for 'skilled and strong hands' in the task of 'gradual[ly] unravelling . . . the tangled knots of the foreign and Imperial policy'.[140] In other words, he wanted to be invited back, temporarily, by the official leaders of the party, in order to assist in repairing the damage done by six years of 'jingo' government. This is how he explained his position to Wolverton, on the thirteenth:

---

[136] Chamberlain to Collings, 27 Apr. 1880, Chamberlain MSS, JC5/16/94.

[137] W. C. Cartwright's diary, 5 May 1880, Cartwright MSS, 6/14. Leonard Courtney had also favoured a Whig premiership: Morley to Chamberlain, 16 Apr. 1880, Chamberlain MSS, JC5/54/313.

[138] Wolverton to Gladstone, 12 Apr. 1880, BL Add. MSS 44349, fo. 130, in Morley, *Gladstone*, ii. 620, and also p. 621 for Morley's attempt to explain away this letter. For confirmation of the inconclusive outcome of the meeting, see Adam to Granville, 14 Apr. 1880, PRO 30/29/27B. Adam had also been present on the 12th.

[139] Gladstone to Rosebery, 10 Apr. 1880, in Morley, *Gladstone*, ii. 613–15.

[140] Gladstone to Argyll, 12 Apr. 1880, in Morley, *Gladstone*, ii. 615.

My labours as an individual cannot set me up as a pretender . . . if they [Granville and Hartington] should on surveying the situation see fit to apply to me, there is only one form and ground of application, so far as I can see, which could be seriously entertained by me, namely their conviction that on ground of public policy, all things considered it was best in the actual position of affairs, that I should come out.[141]

The decision to invite him back, then, had to be taken by the official leaders, on their own initiative, and solely on the grounds of the public good. Accordingly, as John Bright found, when he visited Gladstone on the sixteenth, 'He remains quietly at Hawarden not to seem to interfere in the discussion in London.'[142]

Of course, there were always others ready to help matters along. A pro-Gladstone campaign was initiated, after the result of the Midlothian election, by a Liberal MP, Samuel Plimsoll, and a London Radical, James Beal, with the object of organizing a great reception for Gladstone on his arrival in London. According to the reports in the *Daily News*, the response to the plan was impressive: several hundred organizations and individuals, including some thirty Liberal MPs and numerous Liberal associations, lent their names to it.[143] Evidently, the impetus for this movement was coming from back-bench Radicals and extra-parliamentary agitators, men who looked to Gladstone as their champion, rather than from those Radicals who aspired to office.[144] There is almost certainly a connection, for example, between the pro-Gladstone campaign and T. B. Potter's letter to Sir Charles Forster, dated 5 April: 'Surely *Gladstone* will be Premier. The Country will not be satisfied if he does not lead the reaction he has created to a successful issue. What can we do? We must be stirring.'[145] Furthermore, the *Daily News* itself began to campaign on Gladstone's behalf, a move that was apparently instigated by Henry Labouchere, a Radical MP, who was one of the paper's proprietors:

---

[141] Gladstone to Wolverton, 13 Apr. 1880, BL Add. MSS 44349, fo. 132, in Morley, *Gladstone*, ii. 621.

[142] Bright's diary, 16 Apr. 1880, in R. A. J. Walling (ed.), *The Diaries of John Bright* (1930), 438.

[143] Lists were published each day, between 6 and 12 Apr.

[144] Although it was reported that Chamberlain had joined the committee organizing the demonstration for Gladstone, this was not true; see Chamberlain to Morley, 11 Apr. 1880, Chamberlain MSS, JC5/54/308.

[145] Potter to Sir Charles Forster, 5 Apr. 1880, BL Add. MSS 44278, fo. 162. It is not clear how this letter found its way into the Gladstone papers.

I have just been talking to the Editor of the *Daily News* about the line that the Newspaper ought to take with respect to the Premiership. We don't want to be out with the 'ins' and we cannot make out whether Mr G. intends himself to be Prime Minister or not. If he throws us over, there is no use in our urging his claims, and to do so, would, from a journalistic point of view, be a mistake. If you have any means of finding out whether he wishes to be Prime Minister, and could let me know we would work for him in the D N, but as it is, we have to trim.[146]

Whether any hint was forthcoming is perhaps doubtful, but there was, nevertheless, a clear change of editorial policy by the *Daily News* on 12 April. Thereafter, the view was expounded that Gladstone must be at the head of the new government because the Liberal majority had been 'almost a national vote of confidence in him', which precluded any other arrangement.[147] The suggestion that Gladstone might stand aside altogether was rejected on the grounds that 'events will bring him to the head of affairs' in any case, as the authentic voice of the new spirit which had invaded the Liberal party, so that it was 'better that the nature of the situation should be recognised and acted upon without delay'.[148]

The pro-Gladstone campaign, together with the general sense of uneasiness created by the sudden transfer of political power, had the desired effect. There was a feeling that the elections had unleashed a force which the Whigs could not control,[149] and if Gladstone was not prepared to accept a subordinate post, then there was no alternative other than that he should be Prime Minister. Any government of which he was not a member would be fatally undermined by its inability to secure the adhesion of the 'left wing' of the party, for whom Gladstone was sure to become the focal point of opposition to the Whigs. As Lord Derby noted, 'danger for danger they [the Whigs] think it better that G. should feel the responsibility and be put under the restraint of office':[150] for, as Lord Ripon observed, towards the end of the crisis, 'Every hour shows more and more that Gladstone is the only man who can make a stable government.'[151]

However, while the leadership question may have been clarified,

---

[146] Labouchere to Rosebery, n.d. [Apr. 1880], NLS MSS 10041.
[147] *Daily News*, 16 Apr. 1880, p. 4.
[148] Ibid., 12 Apr. 1880, p. 4.
[149] Lord Derby's diary, 13 Apr. 1880, Derby MSS.
[150] Ibid., 16 Apr. 1880.
[151] Lord Ripon's diary, 22 Apr. 1880, BL Add. MSS 43643. See also the entries for 13 and 19 Apr., for Forster's change of view.

this did not make the solution of it any simpler. By this stage, attention was centred on Hartington, as it became known that he, rather than Granville, was likely to be summoned by the Queen.[152] His dilemma is illustrated by a letter to his private secretary on 13 April:

I don't think Wolverton's report very satisfactory. He [Gladstone] will take no place except the first—quite decided as to that. Would take the first if proposed; thinks he does not wish to come back, but evidently does. I don't think this is a pleasant prospect for us. Burn this.[153]

Hartington was well aware of the dangers of attempting to form an administration which excluded Gladstone, but he also recognized that his course of action was largely dictated for him by his obligations. Firstly, by agreeing not to resign the previous December, and by jointly leading the Liberal party through the general election, he had incurred an obligation to protect the interests of the many moderate Liberal supporters who had voted on the basis of his and Granville's leadership. For this reason he felt precluded, as a matter of honour and dignity, from asking Gladstone to relieve him of his responsibilities.[154] Secondly, and also arising from his leadership during the elections, Hartington was under a strong obligation to meet, as far as possible, the wishes of the Queen. Her Majesty's feelings about Gladstone were well known to Hartington,[155] and, if he was summoned and the Queen was insistent that he should undertake the formation of the new ministry, then he could not see how the request could be declined. Brett pressed these points forcefully:

all the reasons urged by you in the Autumn [*sic*] for then resigning the lead, or forming a government if asked to do so, bind you irrevocably to this . . .

[152] Granville's relations with the Queen were not what they had once been, but her preference for Hartington was certainly encouraged by Beaconsfield. For the knowledge that Hartington was the prime candidate, see Wolverton to Gladstone, 12 Apr. 1880, BL Add. MSS 44349, fo. 130, in Morley, *Gladstone*, ii. 620.

[153] Hartington to Brett, 13 Apr. 1880, Esher MSS, 10/11. In a letter of the same date, to his father, Hartington observed that, while Gladstone would probably accept the premiership if it was pressed upon him, 'As I don't think it likely to be pressed upon him, it does look a very hopeful prospect for me', Devonshire MSS, 340.932, in Holland, *Devonshire*, i. 271. For the disappointment of the Cavendish family when Hartington did not become Prime Minister, see Bailey (ed.), *Lady Frederick Cavendish Diary*, ii. 248–50 (entry for 19 to 25 Apr. 1880).

[154] Childers to Halifax, 12 Apr. 1880, Hickleton MSS, A4/90. Childers had seen Hartington the previous day.

[155] Ibid.

course . . . the elections have been fought under your leadership, and you are forced to take the consequences however uninviting the prospect before you may be.[156]

Indeed, the matter was not to be settled until the very last moment. When the Prince of Wales met Hartington, on the seventeenth, he was impressed by 'how anxious he is about everything', but informed the Queen that though 'I feel sure [he] is desirous to please you . . . He looked dreadfully worried and careworn, and expressed as much to me.'[157] As late as the nineteenth, Ripon gathered from Brett that, 'if the Queen were to *insist*, Hartington would try to form a Government without Gladstone, but that otherwise he would say that the Queen ought to send for Gladstone'.[158]

On the twenty-second, when he travelled to Windsor in response to the Queen's summons, Hartington recommended that 'it would be best and wisest' if she 'at once sent for Mr Gladstone'.[159] The Queen, however, indicated that she would have difficulty in giving Gladstone her full confidence, and she required Hartington to consult Gladstone to ascertain whether he would be prepared to serve under him.[160] That evening, Hartington called on Gladstone, who confirmed that his position had not altered and explained that though, as an independent member, he would feel duty bound to give all possible support to a Hartington administration, none the less 'Promises of this kind . . . stood on slippery ground, and must always be understood with the limits which might be prescribed by conviction.'[161] The warning was clear. However, according to Gladstone's account, Hartington 'did not indicate, nor did I ask, what he should do if the Queen continued to press him to go on, in

---

[156] Brett to Hartington, 14 Apr. 1880, Devonshire MSS, 340.936. See also Harcourt to Hartington, 18 Apr. 1880, ibid. 340.937, in Holland, *Devonshire*, i. 278.

[157] Prince of Wales to the Queen, 18 Apr. 1880, in Buckle (ed.), *Victoria's Letters*, iii. 79–80.

[158] Lord Ripon's diary, 19 Apr. 1880, BL Add. MSS 43643. Cf. Hartington's undated memorandum, Devonshire MSS, 340.940. For Forster's report of Gladstone's irritation with Hartington, see Ripon's diary, 21 Apr. 1880, BL Add. MSS 43643.

[159] The Queen's diary, 22 Apr. 1880, in Buckle (ed.), *Victoria's Letters*, iii. 80–2. Cf. Hartington's undated memorandum, Devonshire MSS, 340.941, in Holland, *Devonshire*, i. 273–6.

[160] The Queen's diary, 22 Apr. 1880, in Buckle (ed.), *Victoria's Letters*, iii. 80–2.

[161] Gladstone's memorandum, 22 Apr. 1880, BL Add. MSS 44764, fo. 43, in Morley, *Gladstone*, ii. 621–4. The meeting took place at Wolverton's home in Carlton House Terrace.

spite of his advice to her to move in another direction'.[162] Later that evening, at dinner, John Morley found Gladstone 'pale, pre-occupied, forced—not at all like himself'.[163]

The eventual settlement of the question, on the following day, proved to be something of an anticlimax. General Ponsonby records that 'Hartington arrived again and anxious to support his advice that Gladstone should be summoned brought Granville to my house. They asked me if the Queen would see him [i.e. Granville] . . . I said I thought they would find it difficult to persuade the Queen to take Gladstone. Hartington said his interview yesterday showed that. But they must both try.'[164] However, in her separate interviews, first with Hartington then with Granville,[165] the Queen proved to be 'much more amenable', and 'gave way without much difficulty'.[166] When an anxious Ponsonby went to their room afterwards, the relief of the Whig leaders was obvious: 'Granville kissed his hand with a smile like a ballet girl receiving applause. And Hartington threw himself into a chair with "Ha! Ha!" Granville exclaimed—"No difficulty at all—all smooth!"'[167] Later the same day, Gladstone travelled to Windsor and accepted the Queen's commission to form the new government.

IV

The fact that there was a leadership question, in the aftermath of the general election of April 1880, is itself a testimony to the prestige of the Whig leaders, who have been seriously underestimated by historians. As we have seen, the large Liberal majority did not put an end to the possibility of a Whig-led government, for the simple reason that most Liberals had grown accustomed to thinking of Granville and Hartington as men who stood for party unity and sober, responsible leadership, and who themselves deserved a great

[162] Ibid.
[163] Morley to Chamberlain, 23 Apr. 1880, Chamberlain MSS, JC5/54/331.
[164] Ponsonby's memorandum, 23 Apr. 1880, in Ponsonby, *Henry Ponsonby*, p. 188.
[165] The Queen's memorandum, 23 Apr. 1880, in Buckle (ed.), *Victoria's Letters*, iii. 82–4.
[166] Hartington to the Duke of Devonshire, 23 Apr. 1880, Devonshire MSS, 340.943, in Holland, *Devonshire*, i. 278.
[167] Ponsonby's memorandum, 23 Apr. 1880, in Ponsonby, *Henry Ponsonby*, p. 188.

deal of the credit for the remarkable electoral victory.[168] That they would inevitably stand aside and allow Gladstone to take the laurels did not follow. Even in the last days of the crisis, when the press was still uncertain about the outcome,[169] the prevailing view was that, though Gladstone must be Prime Minister if he wished, the Liberals would just as happily accept Granville or Hartington, provided it was clear that Gladstone had voluntarily waived his claim. As the *Leeds Mercury* wrote on the twenty-third, while there was reason to think that Gladstone would now accept the first place, nevertheless: 'We believe that the vast majority of the Liberal party throughout the Country would be well pleased to see his Lordship [Hartington] in the position of Prime Minister, but only on one condition; that is, that it should in the first place have been made quite clear that Mr. Gladstone himself was not disposed to undertake the charge of an Administration.'[170] The previous day, the *Manchester Guardian* had been rather more forthright:

Whatever Mr. Gladstone may decide, we trust he will decide once and for all . . . If he is willing to devote what remains to him of life and strength to the laborious and exhausting duties of high office, the Country will rejoice . . . But if he cannot do this, or if he feels that advancing years have in some degree unfitted him for the task, the difficulty of the position may as well be faced now as later, and those upon whom the burden must ultimately fall may as well undertake it at once.[171]

It may well be that Gladstone was extremely fortunate, in that the outcome of the general election was so unexpected that it was natural for contemporaries, with their highly imperfect understanding of the electorate,[172] to assume that the Liberal victory was attributable primarily to his powerful performance in Scotland. The notion that

[168] The *Manchester Guardian*, 10 Apr. 1880, pp. 6–7, and 19 Apr. 1880, p. 5, perhaps motivated by a certain amount of Lancastrian chauvinism, claimed that Hartington, who had successfully challenged the Conservatives in North East Lancashire, had made a greater contribution to the Liberal victory than even Gladstone. In fact, it was calculated that Hartington had made by far the greatest number of major speeches during the election campaign, twenty-four, to Gladstone's fifteen, compared with six each by Harcourt and Bright: *Annual Register* for 1880, p. 51.
[169] Cf. *The Times*, 19 Apr. 1880, p. 9; *Manchester Guardian*, 20 Apr. 1880, p. 5. From the 16th, the *Daily Telegraph* had been advocating a Hartington premiership, no doubt for purely mischievous reasons.
[170] *Leeds Mercury*, 23 Apr. 1880, p. 4.
[171] *Manchester Guardian*, 22 Apr. 1880, p. 4.
[172] 'I am inclined to think that these great alterations are what we must expect under our extended suffrage and secret ballot. The older system was the steadier; but I do not doubt that we shall get on well enough with the new one, when we get fully to understand its working', Ripon to Halifax, 2 Apr. 1880, Hickleton MSS, A4/89.

Gladstone had succeeded in harnessing some hitherto unsuspected popular force undoubtedly had a decisive influence upon the Whigs, who, as Derby noted, were 'a little frightened at their own success —or rather they feel that they have been rather pushed on than acted themselves as the motive force—and the sensation is not wholly agreeable'.[173] To what extent Gladstone really was responsible for the Liberal victory is impossible to judge, but there are strong grounds for supposing that the economic depression, and the way this was associated in the popular mind with the government's financial policies, accounted for many of the Liberal gains,[174] and while the débâcles in Afghanistan and Southern Africa undoubtedly worked in the Liberals' favour, it is questionable whether this represented the culmination of a sustained public concern with Beaconsfield's 'jingo' policies dating from 1876. Leonard Courtney, himself a 'Little Englander', suspected that, in his own Cornish constituency, 'The voters that swayed around did not object to the immorality of [Beaconsfield's] policy, but that it did not work out smoothly.'[175] After all, there were signs, early in 1879, that the public had grown tired of the Eastern Question *per se*,[176] and it may have been purely a matter of chance that Gladstone's personally motivated efforts to rekindle an old issue were caught up in the rising flames of another fire, enabling him to interpret a secular reaction against the government in terms of his own moral crusade against the iniquities of Beaconsfield's 'system of government'. Ultimately, the question must remain open: it is conceivable that Gladstone's activities made virtually no difference to the result of the general election; while the most that can be said for the alternative view is that Gladstone's strength lay in his ability to provide a moral critique of 'Beaconsfieldism' which offered a more satisfying emotional framework for what were essentially materialistic feelings of discontent.[177]

---

[173] Lord Derby's diary, 23 Apr. 1880, Derby MSS.

[174] See Helen C. Colman, *Jeremiah James Colman: A Memoir* (privately printed, 1905), 295, for the case of Norwich.

[175] Courtney to Richard Oliver, 4 May 1880, in G. P. Gooch, *Life of Lord Courtney* (1920), 152.

[176] Cf. James Bryce to Edward Freeman, 23 Mar. 1879, Bryce MSS, vol. 9, fo. 207; Edward Heneage to Thomas Wintringham, 19 Feb. 1879, Heneage MSS, 2 HEN, 5/6, fo. 12.

[177] Cf. Lloyd, *Election of 1880*, pp. 157–60. The mythological Gladstone created in a rash of popular biographies, after 1880, has been examined in an interesting article by D. A. Hamer, 'Gladstone: The Making of a Political Myth', *Victorian Studies*, 22 (1978–9), 29–50.

Whatever the case, it is clear that while the unexpected election results created an impression—possibly misleading—that Gladstone had been the principal architect of the Liberal victory, there was not seen to be an inevitable link between this and his acceptance of the premiership. Consequently, when he sought to convert the impression of power into actual power, he found it necessary to resort to the ultimate threat that he might be driven into opposition to a Liberal administration of which he was not the head. Gladstone wanted to be recalled to the helm, so that he might be the one to steer the ship of state back into calm waters, but he had first to convince the crew that, if they did not let him, he might well sink the ship.

5
Whiggery and the Second Gladstone Ministry, 1880–1885

Introduction

It was beyond all reasonable contemporary doubt that the Liberal party's electoral triumph in April 1880 had also been very much a personal one for Gladstone. The strength of what was taken to be 'Liberal feeling' in the country had been seriously underestimated by the official leadership before the election, and the manifestation of its true force naturally encouraged the assumption that it was to Gladstone alone that its allegiance was owed. His command of Liberal opinion appeared such that no stable government could be formed without him. As in 1868, an inspired act of leadership had established Gladstone's claim to be the personal embodiment of 'Liberalism'.

The supersession of 'Whiggery' by 'Gladstonianism', as the prevailing influence upon the Liberal identity, had serious implications for the subsequent position of the Whigs within the party. At the ministerial level, their numerical preponderance could not conceal the fact that they were almost powerless to resist the authority of the Premier. And yet, though the Whigs were no longer the sole exponents of 'official' Liberalism, their executive mentality remained so deep-rooted that it was inconceivable that they should act together as a group, and merely represent the interests of one section of the party, or that they should attempt to organize the moderates within the parliamentary party.[1] What Dr Matthew has written recently

---

[1] Contrary to Herbert Gladstone's later assertion (*After Thirty Years* (1928), 170, 178), Hartington did not act as the leader of an organized Whig section, nor did he give instructions for Whig action. Albert Grey's letter to Lord Halifax, 28 Jan. 1884, Hickleton MSS, A4/84, indicates the lack of communication between Hartington and the Whig back-benchers: 'he complains that the moderate Liberals do not speak so loud and so often as some of the others. This is entirely his fault. Hartington's hounds would hunt as well as Chamberlain's if he would only lift them on now and then . . . when we are standing with our heads up he never thinks of making a charge and Chamberlain does not hesitate . . . we are in the end whipped on by Hartington himself at the end of Chamberlain's pack.'

about the first Gladstone administration holds true for the second, at least so far as the Whig ministers are concerned: 'Cabinet members do not seem to have thought in terms of a Party structure of electoral management. The Cabinet continued to act chiefly as an executive body, distanced and often estranged from the political structure which had placed it in power.'[2] In fact, the picture of Cabinet proceedings that emerges from the diary kept by Lord Derby, who joined the government in December 1882, is one in which the majority of ministers were usually silent, except on matters affecting their own departments, or unless specifically appealed to for an opinion.[3] Consequently, Hartington, who tried to act as a brake upon the Radical tendencies of the government, often found himself isolated inside a predominantly Whig Cabinet.

Hartington's unwillingness to cultivate a following in the parliamentary party did not mean, however, that the potential for a counterbalancing force to the Radicals did not exist. On the contrary, the composition of the Liberal party in the House of Commons reflected the fact that the support of the landowning class continued to be indispensable for electoral success, and that in 1880, thanks to the Hartington-Granville leadership, 'the upper stratum' had been 'all for the cause'.[4] As Professor Hanham has observed, 'It is difficult to overstress the contribution of Whig landowners to the Liberal cause in the Counties even as late as the eighties. There were few agricultural Counties in which they could not sometimes win one seat and occasionally two', and their individual influence was all the greater because 'The typical Whig was not a small County squire but a County magnate enjoying considerable influence.'[5] It is difficult to

---

[2] H. C. G. Matthew (ed.), *The Gladstone Diaries*, vii (Oxford, 1982), p. lxviii. Chamberlain's attitude was quite different, as one might expect: Lord Derby noted that he 'has an odd, peculiar manner, of referring everything to the judgment of friends outside, rather than giving an opinion of his own: as though he considered himself in Cabinet less as an advisor, than as the representative of a party or section: which indeed is the case', diary, 24 Feb. 1883, Derby MSS.

[3] Lord Derby's diary, 24 Feb. 1883 and 27 Nov. 1884, Derby MSS. The latter entry shows that the Radicals were again an exception to the rule: 'Chamberlain and Dilke both assert themselves a good deal and the former is apt to threaten resignation, though indirectly. He "will find it impossible to support" this that or the other. He is not much liked: Dilke on the contrary is popular.'

[4] Northbrook to Halifax, 25 Mar. 1880, Hickleton MSS, A4/54a. Lord Fitzwilliam claimed credit for the election of six Liberal MPs: Fitzwilliam to Granville, 18 Apr. 1880, PRO 30/29/22A/8.

[5] H. J. Hanham, *Elections and Party Management: Politics in the Time of Disraeli and Gladstone* (1978 edn., Hassocks), 25.

obtain the detailed knowledge of local situations necessary to quantify, in any precise way, the contribution made by the Whigs to the Liberal victory, and there are, in any case, other factors to be taken into account like the agitation by the Farmers' Alliance.[6] However, it might be noted that, without the net gain of thirty-eight seats made in the English and Scottish counties, the party would have fallen a long way short of an overall parliamentary majority.[7] Even predominantly industrial county divisions such as North East Lancashire, South Northumberland, and South Durham returned members of Whig families with local interests,[8] and the Whigs similarly supplied representatives for many boroughs, especially in southern England. The most conspicuous demonstration of Whig power, of course, was to be found in those constituencies where a controlling influence was still held, which was worth between twenty and twenty-five seats to the Liberal party.[9] In 1880, as before, the scions of Whig houses were entering the House of Commons at a very early age.[10]

An examination of the composition of the parliamentary Liberal party after the 1880 general election reveals that of the 346 members

[6] Ibid. 30–2. Nevertheless, as Hanham notes, the Farmers' Alliance deliberately moderated its tone in order to avoid alienating the Whigs.

[7] See the *Pall Mall Gazette*, 19 Apr. 1880, p. 4, for a comparison between the 1874 and 1880 county election results. The crucial importance of Whig landlords in North Northamptonshire, where Lord Spencer's half-brother was elected, is shown in the correspondence edited by Peter Gordon, *The Red Earl: The Papers of the Fifth Earl Spencer, 1835–1910*, i (Northants Record Society, 31; 1981), 137–51. Even in Wales, where few Whigs were returned, the support given by landowners to Liberal candidates was by no means inconsiderable: K. O. Morgan, *Wales in British Politics, 1868–1922* (3rd edn., Cardiff, 1980), 56.

[8] For the continued influence of Whig families in the northern counties of England, see Alfred E. Pease, *Elections and Recollections* (1932), 40.

[9] This is based on the appendix by Hanham, *Elections and Party Management*, pp. 405–12. The situation was never static, but Hanham identifies eighteen seats which were definitely controlled by a Liberal patron in 1880, and four others where there is some doubt, and he also mentions three seats where Liberals held a predominant interest. Chester and Macclesfield are not included, as they had their writs suspended because of corruption during the 1880 election.

[10] The following were elected in 1880 for the first time (age attained in 1880 in parentheses): Lord Moreton (23), Hon. C. R. Spencer (23), Hon. F. W. Lambton (25), Hon. R. Carrington (28), Albert Grey (29), Hon. R. P. Bruce (29), Hon. G. Leigh (29), Lord Baring (30). Lord Ebrington was elected in 1881 at the age of 27. An interesting measure of the Whig commitment to the Liberal cause during the opposition years 1874–80 is provided by the following list of by-election victors (with age attained in the year they were elected): Lord Tavistock (23), Lord Lymington (24), Lord Douglas Gordon (25), Lord Colin Campbell (25), Hon. W. J. Fitzwilliam (26). All were still under the age of 30 when re-elected in 1880, as was Lord Stafford, who had sat throughout the 1874 parliament.

remaining, after allowance has been made for election petitions,[11] forty-one were members of the nobility, that is to say, they were the heirs, sons, or brothers of peers, twenty-eight were baronets (eighteen of these being listed in John Bateman's *Great Landowners of Great Britain and Ireland*), and eleven were the sons of baronets, making a total of eighty members of the 'aristocracy'. In addition to these, fifty-three Liberal MPs were listed as 'great landowners' by Bateman, and a further eighteen were included in *Burke's Landed Gentry*.[12] This produces a total of 151 MPs for the 'aristocratic-landowning' section of the party, or 43.6 per cent, a fractional increase on the figure for 1874. It is interesting to note, in comparison, that the proportion of 'industrialists and merchants' (as defined by their entries in *Dod's Parliamentary Companion*) actually fell slightly, with a total of 114 MPs, or 32.6 per cent of the parliamentary party,[13] and so it was at their expense, at this stage, that the growth in the legal element, which now consisted of ninety-three MPs, or 26.9 per cent of the party, occurred.[14] The paradox of the situation after 1880, it would seem, was that the threat to the political power of the landed élite posed by the agricultural depression and the Radical demands for land reform which this encouraged occurred at just the time when the Whigs' commitment to the Liberal cause had reached a level not seen since the days of Palmerston.[15]

It is hardly surprising that, with such a large representation in the House of Commons, the aristocratic and landowning class was liable to be provoked into defending its interests, when the policies of the new government were thought to be leaning too heavily in favour of the Radicals. The determination of the 'Whigs' to make their voice

[11] Hanham, *Elections and Party Management*, p. 232, gives the figure as 353. *Dod's Parliamentary Companion*, for 1880, lists 350 Liberals (including Arnold Morley, who was returned in place of J. S. Wright, who died immediately after being elected and so never took his seat), but this omits Lowe and Hugessen, who were elevated to the peerage, and also Harcourt, a minister who had lost his seat when seeking re-election but who quickly found a new one. On the other hand, Dod lists twelve MPs who were subsequently unseated on petition, and omits five new MPs elected in their place.

[12] Thirty-two of the 'great landowners' were also listed by Burke.

[13] In 1874 the figure had been 35.2 per cent. The overlap between the aristocratic and business sections was twenty-two MPs, or 19.3 per cent of the latter group.

[14] In 1874 the figure had been 23.2 per cent. The total for 1880 comprised twenty-four Queen's Counsel, fifty-nine other barristers, and ten solicitors, but thirty of these 'lawyers' (32.3 per cent) overlapped with the 'aristocratic-landowning' section.

[15] Cf. Hanham, *Elections and Party Management*, pp. 25–9.

heard was stated plainly by one of the newly elected MPs, in a letter to the editor of a local newspaper in November 1880, at a time when the uncertainty surrounding the government's Irish policy was causing some speculation about the future conduct of the Whigs. In Arthur Elliot's opinion, it was essential that the Liberal party should act as a united body in the pursuit of agreed reforms, but this could only happen if the government was prepared to take into account the views of its moderate as well as its Radical supporters: 'The successes of the last election were chiefly won in the Counties, where in many cases success would have been hopeless but for energetic Whig support. As regards Roxburghshire you must know as well as I do, that were the Liberal party broken up by half a dozen leading Whigs joining for the time the Conservative ranks, a Liberal candidate might as well stand for the moon as endeavour to come in for that County. And leading Whigs in Roxburghshire and elsewhere can hardly be expected cordially to help the party unless their views as well as those of other sections of it, are treated with respect.'[16]

This attitude was to result in a number of Whig revolts during the lifetime of the second Gladstone administration, notably with regard to Irish policy, and these have customarily been regarded as symptoms of the last phase of a long-term Whig decline, leading inexorably to secession.[17] It will become apparent from a study of the back-bench Whigs, however, that they did not form a solid, easily organized bloc, willing to rebel against their own government at any moment, and that in the case of the small hard core of activists which did exist, their Whiggery proved to be a viable strategy for political advancement within the Gladstonian Liberal party. Furthermore, it will be seen that the Whigs were not opposed to special ameliorative legislation to deal with the problems of Ireland, but that they were concerned lest the policies adopted by the government under Gladstone's auspices should pave the way for future domination of the Liberal party by Chamberlainite Radicalism, in alliance with the Irish Nationalists. The fact that Gladstone remained leader of the Liberal party until 1894 has tended to obscure the point that, in April 1880, his resumption of this position was supposed to be a provisional arrangement, which would probably not last for more

---

[16] Elliot to T. Craig (editor of the *Kelso Chronicle*), 23 Nov. 1880 (copy), Elliot MSS.

[17] e.g. Donald Southgate, *The Passing of the Whigs, 1832–1886* (1962), 372–6.

than a couple of years. Similarly, although the Duke of Devonshire lived until 1891, the possibility that Hartington might succeed him at any moment created a permanent air of uncertainty around the long-term leadership of the Liberal party in the House of Commons. And yet, recognition of these crucial points has an important bearing on the way we conceive of Liberal politics during the early 1880s. The rivalry that has appeared to historians to be indicative of the chronically divided state of the Liberals was primarily the result of the competition for influence over the destiny of the party in the post-Gladstonian era.

1. *The Whigs in Parliament*

The activities of a small group of 'young Whigs' in the House of Commons, during the early 1880s, provided an ideal subject for the pen of a well-known parliamentary journalist of the day, Henry Lucy. In Lucy's view, the young Whig, as exemplified by H. R. Brand, the son of the Speaker, was distinguished by his 'serious introspective air . . . He feels the responsibility which rests upon him.' Unlike the Radical and the Tory, the Whig had 'thought only for his Country. A sort of Atlas, he laboriously picks his way through life, bearing on his shoulders the weight of his native land.' The manner of these Whigs was 'serious, argumentative, unemotional, prophetic', something that was 'in the blood at birth'.[18] Inevitably, as Lucy observed on a later occasion, their premature air of gravity added a 'decidedly middle aged flavour' to their youth. Brand, though 'still young in years', was 'one of the most middle aged young men of the present epoch', while in the case of Edward Heneage, the member for Great Grimsby, though 'far removed from the period of life called middle age . . . none would think of regarding Mr. Heneage as a young man, or of speaking disrespectfully of the Constitution within his hearing'.[19] Their political conduct was conspicuously independent:

When critical divisions are at hand there is a diligent counting up of Whigs, and much speculation indulged in as to how they will vote. When the division bell rings the House beholds ten or a dozen grave and essentially

---

[18] 'A Young Whig' (17 June 1881), in Henry Lucy, *A Diary of Two Parliaments, 1874–1885* (1885–6), ii. 176.
[19] 'The Whigs' (26 May 1882), ibid. ii. 251–2.

middle aged men file out, and instinctively knows that these are the Whigs, more especially if they are assisted to the conclusion by finding them walking out before the division.[20]

In fact, the group of young Whigs identified by Henry Lucy formed the nucleus of a much larger body which consisted, according to newspaper estimates, of up to seventy-five Liberal M Ps.[21] This figure somewhat exaggerated the active membership of the 'Whig oligarchy',[22] but, nevertheless, their activities were sufficiently serious to provoke criticism from the advanced Liberal press. The *Pall Mall Gazette* commented severely on those Liberal M Ps who in no way represented the 'forces which gave Mr. Gladstone the enormous majority of last year'.[23] It was impossible to discern the 'true will of the Country . . . from the vote of Mr. Lambton, Lord Stafford and so forth', and yet, the *Pall Mall Gazette* complained, 'it comes to this, that the majority of the House of Lords, *plus* Mr. Heneage, Sir E. Colebrooke, Mr. Albert Grey and Lord Edmond Fitzmaurice, ought to be free to set aside the judgment and will of the majority of the House of Commons'.[24] It was enough to make the *Daily News* hint darkly that 'a reform in our electoral system is necessary in order to make a nominally and partially Liberal majority really and wholly Liberal'.[25]

The origins of the Whig group are obscure. Several of its more prominent members, like Fitzmaurice, Brand, and Heneage, in spite of their relative youth, had parliamentary experience stretching back to the 1860s. Some may have belonged to the 'Whig committee'[26] organized, in the months preceding the general election of 1880, by Albert Grey, the charismatic nephew and heir of Earl Grey and Liberal candidate for South Northumberland. Unfortunately, very little is known about the composition of this committee, but one of its members was Richard Burdon Haldane, the future Lord Chancellor, who was sent to Liverpool to speak on behalf of the by-

---

[20] Ibid.
[21] Cf. *Pall Mall Gazette*, 29 July 1881, p. 1; *Manchester Guardian*, 30 July 1881, p. 7.
[22] A term used by the *Daily News*, 4 July 1881, p. 5. For an estimate of the numerical strength of this Whig group, based on parliamentary division lists, see Appendix II.
[23] *Pall Mall Gazette*, 28 July 1881, pp. 1–2.
[24] Ibid., 29 July 1881, p. 1.
[25] *Daily News*, 27 July 1881, p. 4.
[26] R. B. Haldane to his mother, 22–3 Jan. 1880, NLS MSS 5930, fo. 3.

election candidate, Lord Ramsay.[27] By mid-February, according to Haldane, 'Albert Grey's political committee' was 'in full swing. Lord Northbrook has asked us to go to his house to be coached up in Indian politics, and we have got a good many M.P.s among our numbers.'[28] To what extent the members of Grey's committee acted together, after the general election, is impossible to tell, and all that is known is that in March 1881 the committee was reconstituted, broadening its membership among Liberal MPs and becoming known as the Eighty Club.[29] Perhaps it was a reflection on the change in the tone of Liberal politics brought about by the general election that within a year this Whig committee was being recast on more official lines, with the chief whip as its President.

It is possible, however, to trace in some detail the emergence of an organized Whig group in the House of Commons during the first two sessions of the 1880 parliament. The new government quickly revealed its susceptibility to pressure for legislation in matters relating to land, when it introduced, in June 1880, the Hares and Rabbits Bill. This measure, which later became known as the Ground Game Bill, was a response to the demands of the Farmers' Alliance, which had been very active during the election campaign, and gave to tenant farmers absolute power over the destruction of ground game on their holdings. In this instance, the response from the representatives of the landed class was mixed, and no attempt at organized resistance is apparent. Brand was the most prominent Whig critic, deploring interference by the State in contracts between landlords and tenants and fearing that the bill would provoke friction in relations which had hitherto been cordial,[30] but others welcomed it as a sensible settlement of a difficult question.[31] The bill eventually received its second reading in the Commons without a division,

[27] R. B. Haldane to his mother, 22–3 Jan. 1880, NLS MSS 5930, fo. 3.

[28] Haldane to his sister, 19 Feb. 1880, NLS MSS 6010, fo. 9.

[29] See Haldane's letters to his mother, Jan. to Mar. 1881, in NLS MSS 5931. These reveal several inaccuracies in the account given by Haldane in his *Autobiography* (1929), 79–81, where he states that the reconstruction took place before the 1880 general election, and claims that it was carried out 'independently' of Albert Grey, when in fact Grey was elected Vice-President of the new Eighty Club. One suspects that Haldane's memory was distorted by the fact that, in the later 1880s, the Eighty Club was dominated by the 'new Radicals' of whom, by then, he was one.

[30] Brand (29 July 1880), 3 Hansard, ccliv, cols. 1681–92.

[31] Ibid., cols. 1692–5 (Lymington); 1723–5 (Heneage); 1799–80 (Lord E. Cavendish).

and, following the advice of Lord Beaconsfield, it was also passed by the Conservative-dominated Upper House.

A simultaneous and much more serious threat to the landed interest in Britain came indirectly, through the land question in Ireland. The Gladstone administration responded to the agitation of the Land League by bringing in a Compensation for Disturbance Bill, which attempted to stem the rising tide of evictions in Ireland, resulting from bad harvests and the (alleged) inability of many tenants to pay their rents, by the provision that, until 1 January 1882, tenants evicted for non-payment of rent would be entitled to take the landlord to court and claim compensation for disturbance. This was widely regarded as a hasty, ill-conceived measure (most Whig ministers regretted it in private), and it provided the occasion for the first demonstration of the power of the Whig section to make life difficult for a Liberal ministry. The bill was subjected to fierce criticism from the Whigs in the House of Commons, and, on the second reading division, twenty-one Liberal MPs voted against it and a further seventy (by no means all of whom would normally be regarded as Whigs) were absent unpaired. Sir John Ramsden was probably justified in maintaining that the division reflected a widespread dissatisfaction with the government's bill within the parliamentary party, which extended to many of those who had voted for it.[32] The strength of this opposition undoubtedly emboldened the peers in their determination to reject the bill, and this was done, on 3 August, by an overwhelming margin (282 : 51), with even a majority of the Liberal peers present voting against their own government.[33]

It is clear from the debates that, in their opposition to the Compensation for Disturbance Bill, the Whigs were thinking about its wider implications. There was no questioning the shortcomings of the system of land tenure in a country so poor and overpopulated as Ireland, and it was generally acknowledged that major changes were unavoidable. Indeed, a number of Whig speakers were already hinting at the desirability of a land purchase scheme.[34] What caused the greatest concern was the hesitant, hand-to-mouth manner in

[32] See the copies of Ramsden's letters to H. J. Morton and J. Lupton, both dated 29 July 1880, Ramsden MSS, 71/11, and Ramsden to James Kitson (copy), 5 Aug. 1880, ibid. 42/10.

[33] For the division list, see 3 Hansard, cclv, cols. 110–13.

[34] Cf. Brand (14 July 1880), 3 Hansard, ccliv, cols. 450–2; Lansdowne (2 Aug. 1880), ibid., cols. 1870–87; Duke of Somerset (3 Aug. 1880), cclv, cols. 63–7.

which the government was dealing with the Irish land problem, which had led it into a highly dubious and potentially dangerous temporary expedient. Whereas the Whigs would have preferred to see an emergency relief bill, to enable the Irish tenant farmers to fulfil their contractual obligations while consideration was being given to a more permanent settlement,[35] the government appeared to have been panicked into an imprudent attempt to prop up the existing system by further interference in the contractual relations between landlords and tenants, which threw the entire financial burden onto the landlords rather than it being shared by the community as a whole.[36] As Brand observed, the Compensation for Disturbance Bill was establishing a precedent for the eventual settlement of the question of Irish land tenure,[37] and, because it was believed that the government's inept handling of the situation was simply storing up problems for the future, with tenants accumulating arrears of rent and being evicted in large numbers when the government's measure expired,[38] many feared that the government would be compelled to make even greater incursions into the principle of free contract. This was the case put by Ramsden:

If the position of the Irish tenant was such that it required special intervention now, what would it be in 1882 when he had to face these accumulated arears of rent, when the protection given to him by this Bill would have ceased . . . [the Irish chief secretary says] he proposed this Bill as a temporary remedy for a temporary emergency, and, no doubt, he would be true to his word, and eighteen months hence he would be precluded from prolonging this measure; but he would have to face a far greater emergency, and how was he to meet it? He must either turn a deaf ear to an outcry to which the present complaints would be as nothing, or else propose some larger measure of relief, far greater than if the case were thus dealt with at the present moment.[39]

In fact, the Whigs were sure that the government's willingness to abrogate the settlement of 1870 would encourage further agitation by the Irish tenantry, and that, as Lord Zetland predicted, 'the

---

[35] Brand (14 July 1880), 3 Hansard, ccliv, cols. 450–2; Hon. C. Fitzwilliam and Ramsden (26 July 1880), ibid., cols. 1383–4, 1409–13.

[36] Hon. C. Fitzwilliam and Ramsden (26 July 1880), ibid., cols. 1383–4, 1409–13.

[37] Brand (14 July 1880), ibid., cols. 450–2.

[38] Cartwright and Kingscote (5 July 1880), ibid. ccliii, cols. 1683–4, 1695–7.

[39] Ramsden (26 July 1880), ibid., ccliv, cols. 1409–13.

measure would not die a natural death . . . there was certain to be a clamour, not only for its continuance, but for its extension'.[40]

The underlying consideration here, which was stated most explicitly in the powerful speech by Lord Lansdowne, who had resigned from the government in June because of this bill, was the likelihood that any settlement of the Irish land question would have important implications for future legislation affecting land tenure in Britain. With the Radical demand for 'free trade' in land particularly in mind, Lansdowne argued that 'If it is once admitted that contracts affecting land are liable to revision by the Legislature in the spirit of this Bill', the consequences for the English land market would be disastrous as no one would want to buy land and no one would be able to sell it: 'No settlements, no legal ingenuity, will fetter the possession of land with such disabilities as a course of legislation of the kind which the House is invited to approach.'[41]

Undoubtedly, the rejection of the Compensation for Disturbance Bill was a severe rebuff for the Gladstone government, but it is important to emphasize that, at this stage, there was little evidence to suggest that the Whigs were operating as members of an organized 'cave', or that there was any widespread desire that they should do so. The initiative in the Commons appears to have come largely from two members, Albert Grey and Colonel Kingscote. Grey had been very outspoken on the Irish land question early in June, before the government's intentions were known, in the determination that ministers should be made aware 'that they have got another party of their supporters to reckon with besides the tail'.[42] Naturally, he regarded the division on the second reading as a great success,[43] but he was to discover, only a couple of days later, how difficult it was to induce members who had rebelled once to repeat the act: 'Nigel Kingscote and I were both very anxious to vote against the Speaker leaving the Chair, but on finding that about 15 of the 21 who voted with us on Monday had *run away*, we thought it better to abstain

[40] Marquis of Zetland (3 Aug. 1880), 3 Hansard, cclv, cols. 66–7; also Earl Grey and the Marquis of Lansdowne (2 Aug. 1880), ccliv, cols. 1851–64, 1870–87. Cf. Ramsden to S. Oddy, 8 July 1880, Ramsden MSS, 71/11.

[41] Lansdowne (2 Aug. 1880), 3 Hansard, ccliv, cols. 1870–87. The *Daily News*, 4 Aug. 1880, p. 4, thought the peers were actuated by the 'feeling that land questions are likely to be prominent in the immediate future'. Cf. *Manchester Guardian*, 5 Aug. 1880, p. 5.

[42] Albert Grey to Earl Grey, 8 June 1880, Grey MSS, Box 89.

[43] Albert Grey to Earl Grey, 6 July 1880, ibid.

also.'[44] Similarly, when it came to the third reading, Grey reported to Lord Halifax that there had been a number of 'war losses' which could not be replaced, while others including Brand were wavering, and that although Kingscote had 'been working very hard trying to persuade men to stay away . . . he cannot tell me how many will do so'.[45] The only evidence of attempts to organize meetings of dissentient Liberals is to be found during the committee stage and before the third reading, that is, after the main revolt had taken place. Who arranged the meetings, which were reported to have been held on 15 and 23 July, is not known, nor is it clear how many MPs actually attended them, but in any case these meetings were evidently confined to discussing the situation rather than taking tactical decisions.[46] Certainly, they had no noticeable effect on the final stages of the proceedings in the House of Commons.

The confidence of the Whigs in the Gladstone ministry was to be strained further, however, during the winter of 1880, as the government procrastinated over whether it should apply the coercive remedy (something it had eschewed on taking office, allowing the legislation of 1875 to lapse) to the deteriorating state of social order in Ireland. This naturally encouraged hopes on the Conservative side that the Whigs might break away from Gladstone and join in a new middle party,[47] and concern was clearly felt in the Whig ranks at the way the government seemed to be allowing the Birmingham Radicals to dictate policy.[48] Nevertheless, it is equally clear that the general view among the Whigs was that the point had not yet been reached where a secession from the Liberal party was necessary. As Sir John Ramsden advised one Whig constituent in the West Riding, Gladstone was so 'all powerful' that 'a break up now would only

[44] Albert Grey to Earl Grey, 9 July 1880, ibid.

[45] Albert Grey to Lord Halifax, 24 July 1880, Hickleton MSS, A4/84. Cf. Albert Grey to Arthur Elliot, 24 July 1880, Elliot MSS, urging his attendance for the division. Elliot did not come.

[46] These meetings were reported by the special correspondent of the *Leeds Mercury*, 16 July 1880, p. 8, and 24 July 1880, p. 10. On the former occasion, it was stated that 'Lord E. Cavendish, Mr. Grey, Mr. Brand, Mr. Walter, and other gentlemen were present'. It was also stated, ibid., 20 July 1880, p. 4, that there had been no intention of getting up a 'cave'.

[47] The possibility of a Liberal split was played down at this time by the advanced Liberal dailies; cf. *Pall Mall Gazette*, 22 Nov. 1880, p. 1; *Daily News*, 23 Nov. 1880, p. 4.

[48] Lord Fitzwilliam to Hartington, 4 Dec. 1880, Devonshire MSS, 340.1036; F. Foljambe to Hartington, 20 Dec. 1880, ibid. 340.1046.

play into the hands of the extreme party'. The best way for the moderates to bring influence to bear on Gladstone was by 'working with him [rather] than by an open rupture', and, for this reason, Ramsden felt that the Whig ministers were justified in remaining in office. Furthermore, 'so long as they who are our most trusted leaders remain I believe our wisest course will be to support them as far as we honestly can, even in measures we don't like'.[49] Similar considerations no doubt influenced the decision taken by a group of Whig peers, just before Christmas, not to withdraw their confidence from the government and sit on the cross-benches. They were evidently inclined to wait, instead, for an eventual reconstruction of the ministry, on more satisfactory terms, when Gladstone was gone. As Lord Fitzwilliam remarked, 'I can't help thinking that Gladstone (without our secession) will get such heavy shakes that his official life will not be long. When that time comes it will not fall to the lot of Messrs Bright and Chamberlain to rule the roost.'[50] The Duke of Bedford also remained convinced that, while 'Ingratitude surrounds the Whigs at this time ... they are the party of common sense in politics ... The Radicals have much to learn before they can govern wisely', and he expressed his confidence in the capacities of Hartington, whose 'perfect temper, sound sense and power of speaking become more apparent with every fresh difficulty'.[51]

Nevertheless, after the experiences of the 1880 session and the winter recess, Whiggery, as an organized force in the House of Commons, proved to be better co-ordinated and more effective during the session of 1881, in which the government, after finally pushing through coercive legislation, sought to pass a new and far-reaching Land Bill. This improved organization may be attributed to the participation of two relatively experienced MPs who had not been involved in the opposition to the Compensation for Disturbance Bill. One was Edward Heneage, an 'agricultural' member, who preferred to think of himself as a man of the 'centre' rather than as a 'Whig': his rather absurd conceitedness makes it more difficult to assess the value of his contribution, but it was almost

---

[49] Ramsden to Ayscough Fawkes, 1 Jan. 1881 (copy), Ramsden MSS, 42/10.

[50] Fitzwilliam to Earl Fortescue, 19 Dec. 1880, Fortescue MSS, FC 135. This letter also mentions the opinion of Lord Minto. A further letter from Fitzwilliam, on the 20th, ibid., refers to the opinion of the Duke of Somerset.

[51] Duke of Bedford to Lord Cowper, 27 Jan. 1881, in Countess Cowper (ed.), *Earl Cowper, K.G.: A Memoir* (privately printed, 1913), 470–1.

certainly smaller than he himself believed.[52] Of far greater significance was the role of Lord Edmond Fitzmaurice, brother of the
Marquis of Lansdowne, who had been absent from Westminster
during the 1880 session because of his duties as Her Majesty's
Commissioner for the organization of Eastern Roumelia under the
treaty of Berlin. It is probable, however, that he had spent some time
in Ireland, during November, inspecting the state of the country,[53]
and he had certainly been highly critical of the government's failure
to grasp the nettle of coercion.[54]

Fitzmaurice appears to have been in contact with Grey, Brand, and
Arthur Elliot almost immediately after the government's announcement of its Irish Land Bill on 7 April,[55] and, during the course of the
debates on the second reading (25 April to 19 May), a regular series
of meetings took place at his rooms in St James's Place. The numbers
attending the early meetings were small, W. C. Cartwright's diary
lists six and eight names respectively for the meetings on 3 and 7
May,[56] but these were mostly the more active Whigs, men like Grey,
Brand, Dundas, Heneage, Blennerhassett, and Ramsden, and as the
object was to discuss possible amendments to the Land Bill, the
potential significance of these gatherings far exceeded its numerical
strength. Indeed, the zealous Grey was hopeful that, 'if we do our
business well', the group might 'become eventually a party . . . which
will form a counterbalancing weight to the Radicals below the

---

[52] Heneage liked to present himself as a mediator between the government and the
Whigs. He claimed that ministers were 'rather glad that . . . circumstances . . . have
placed me for the moment at the head of the moderate Liberal section instead of the
weak kneed Whigs fighting under the lead of one of themselves', Heneage to Thomas
Wintringham, 25 June 1881, Heneage MSS, 2 HEN 5/8, fo. 42. See also his letter of
22 June, ibid., fo. 39: 'I venture to say that Grimsby has not had for 30 years a
representative who held the same position in the House as myself and who is on more
confidential terms with the Party leaders, but I am an Educative member and not an
ignorant and paid delegate of a Society.'

[53] Fitzmaurice stated his intention of making such a trip in letters to W. C.
Cartwright, 12 Oct., 1 Nov. 1880, Cartwright MSS, Box 20, fos. 591, 598.

[54] 'I totally disagree with the Bright–Chamberlain line . . . An Arrears Act ought to
have been passed two months ago and then there would have been no necessity to be
talking about the Habeas Corpus Act now. If the English democracy is going in for a
policy of mawkish sentiment about Ireland . . . by talking weak twaddle and [doing]
everything its *enemies* wish it to do, we shall in a short time have civil war in Ireland.
English Democracy must show it can *coerce*, justly of course, but wisely and firmly',
Fitzmaurice to Ashton Dilke, 22 Nov. [1880], Dilke MSS (Churchill College,
Cambridge), 6/10.

[55] Albert Grey to Earl Grey, 9 Apr. 1881, Grey MSS, Box 89.

[56] W. C. Cartwright's diary, 3, 7 May 1881, Cartwright MSS, 6/15.

gangway'.[57] The 'moderates', as Grey never tired of complaining, were by their nature unassertive and did not understand that 'if they are ever to have power they must be feared not loved'. Fitzmaurice and he were therefore trying, 'quietly and in such a manner as will not alarm their timid natures', to 'gradually get them into some organisation—we have meetings now twice a week and at each meeting a new member turns up—the object of the meeting is only to discuss amendments to the Land Bill but still I hope that something useful may come out of them when Gladstone goes'.[58] In Grey's view, which he expressed to another uncle, Lord Halifax, it was necessary to 'organise ourselves into some shape and prepare for the day when the battle between the radicals and *moderate Liberals* takes place', for although Hartington was 'radical enough to keep the party together', there seemed little likelihood of Gladstone retiring in the immediate future, and if, by the time he did retire, Hartington had gone to the House of Lords, there would clearly be a great struggle for supremacy in the Commons.[59] Halifax took a similar view:

As to the position and conduct of the Whigs I quite agree with you. Either there will be a Liberal government in which the Whigs ought to take the lead[,] and in order to do so effectively they ought to draw together, not in an ostentatious anti-radical [*sic*] but so as not to be scattered by internal dissension—if on the other hand the radical section goes so far that joint action is impossible, so that the Whigs are compelled to act with the Conservatives[,] their power and influence will essentially depend in like manner on their acting together.

Whichever way the cat jumps they *should* act in concert with each other and be *prepared to do so* and not caught unawares.[60]

The Whig group enjoyed a certain amount of success in extracting concessions from the government. It was decided, at an early stage, that the Land Bill was unavoidable, given the social condition of Ireland, and that it should be supported when the division on the second reading was taken.[61] However, while admitting the

[57] Albert Grey to Earl Grey, 12 May 1881, Grey MSS, Box 89.
[58] Albert Grey to Earl Grey, 20 May 1881, ibid.
[59] Albert Grey to Halifax, 23 June 1881, Hickleton MSS, A4/84.
[60] Halifax to Albert Grey, 24 June 1881, Grey MSS, 211/6.
[61] Albert Grey to Earl Grey, 7 May 1881, Grey MSS, Box 89. It was also generally accepted, by the Whig peers, that the Land Bill was necessary: for the views of Bedford, Argyll, and Lansdowne, see the entries in Lord Derby's diary, 16 May, 25 May, 17 June 1881, Derby MSS; for the views of Fitzwilliam and other Irish landowners, see W. C. Cartwright's diary, 23, 26 May 1881, Cartwright MSS, 6/15.

applicability of the so called '3 f's' (fair rent, fixity of tenure, and free sale) in the Irish case, the Whigs were intent on pressing for a number of amendments, when the committee stage was reached, which were designed partly to ensure equal treatment for the Irish landlords, but more especially to emphasize the extraordinary nature of the land question in Ireland and thus reduce the risk of any precedents being established for the extension of the '3 f's' to Britain. These amendments sought to secure access to the land court for landlords as well as tenants, a redefinition of fair rent (with the aim of striking out all reference to the tenant's 'interest' as one of the elements to be taken into account in the calculation of the rent),[62] the exclusion of holdings worth over £50 per annum from the fair rent provisions (this figure was later changed to £100), and the exclusion of estates managed on the 'English' principle (that is, where the landlord rather than the tenant paid for improvements to the farm) from the free sale clauses.[63]

At a conference of Whig members on 15 June, it was decided that the first demonstration of their strength should be made the following day, on an amendment in Heneage's name relating to the exclusion of 'English' estates, and a whipping up operation was accordingly got under way.[64] The debate on this amendment provided Heneage with a perfect opportunity to articulate Whig fears about the wider implications of the government's legislation:

It was not only this Bill that must be looked at, but if the Committee once began by saying that free sale was to be imported into estates managed on the English principle, where were they to stop? Mischievous people who had nothing to do with land, but who were always ready to interfere with other people's property, would be found, in a few years, using the Act to introduce free sale into holdings in England.[65]

In the subsequent division, the government's majority was reduced to twenty-five, a result which the Whigs regarded as a great success.

---

[62] Both Lansdowne and Derby regarded this as the most important point: Lord Derby's diary, 17 June 1881, Derby MSS.

[63] Albert Grey to Earl Grey, 12 May 1881, Grey MSS, Box 89. See also the *Daily News*, 30 May 1881, p. 5, for a note about the concerted Whig amendments.

[64] W. C. Cartwright's diary, 15 June 1881, Cartwright MSS, 6/15. Cf. Cartwright to M. J. Guest, 'Weds night' [15 June 1881], BL Add. MSS 57935, fo. 115.

[65] Heneage (16 June 1881), 3 Hansard, cclxii, cols. 681–4. Cf. ibid., cols. 688 (Dundas); 693–7 (Fitzmaurice); 708–10 (Hon. C. Fitzwilliam).

Thirty-four Liberals had voted for the amendment, and, allowing for abstentions, the full scale of the revolt was reckoned at about fifty.[66] Gladstone was obviously shaken into a conciliatory mood, for he made a statement the following day indicating his willingness to concede two of the other Whig demands, landlord access to the land court and the removal of the reference to the tenant's 'interest' in the definition of fair rent.[67] These concessions, bitterly resented by the advanced Liberal press,[68] were hailed by Grey as a triumph for the 'carefully refined programme' of 'Fitzmaurice and Company',[69] and as proof of the enhanced status of the Whig section: 'Before, the Whigs were despised. Now they are beginning to get feared and everyone is accordingly civil.'[70]

In spite of the impact of the Heneage amendment, however, it was not easy for the Whigs to find a suitable means of following up their success. The feeling against acting as an organized group, apart from the main body of the Liberal party, was always very strong, and when Fitzmaurice proposed to raise the one remaining item in the Whig programme, the exclusion of holdings worth over £100 per annum from the fair-rent clause, it was found to be difficult to raise support for it. As Grey complained, the Whig rebels were 'frightened at their own audacity and were afraid to repeat a hostile vote against the government',[71] and the amendment was consequently postponed, for fear that a bad division would damage the position which had been gained by the earlier vote.[72] The difficulty of securing a good turn-out of moderates is further illustrated by the complications arising from Ramsden's proposed land purchase amendment, which did not command widespread moderate support and which, it was feared, would 'disintegrate our force and paralyse our

---

[66] Cartwright's diary, 17 June 1881, Cartwright MSS, 6/15, states that about fifteen members paired for dinner did not return. It was also reported that Granville and other Whig ministers had sympathized with the amendment: Albert Grey to Halifax, 20 June 1881, Hickleton MSS, A4/84.

[67] Gladstone (17 June 1881), 3 Hansard, cclxii, cols. 764–5. For the significance of his concessions, cf. Lord Derby's diary, 20 June 1881, Derby MSS; Halifax to Ripon, 30 June 1881, BL Add. MSS 44529, fo. 193.

[68] *Daily News*, 18 June 1881, p. 5, 23 June 1881, p. 7; *Pall Mall Gazette*, 18 June 1881, p. 1.

[69] Albert Grey to Halifax, 24 June 1881, Hickleton MSS, A4/84.

[70] Albert Grey to Halifax, 20 June 1881, ibid.

[71] Albert Grey to Earl Grey, 23 June 1881, Grey MSS, Box 89.

[72] Ibid. See also W. C. Cartwright's diary, 22 June 1881, Cartwright MSS, 6/15.

power to make an effective effort on the Report',[73] when Fitzmaurice now intended to move his amendment. It was therefore necessary to persuade Ramsden to drop his amendment so that the Whig effort could be concentrated on the report stage.[74]

The debate on Fitzmaurice's amendment was a recapitulation of the evils arising from unrestricted government legislation in an age when the mentality of State interference seemed to be pervasive. Fitzmaurice welcomed the Land Bill as necessary for the interests of small tenants, but the larger ones, he argued, were capable of looking after themselves, and the government ought not to interfere in their contracts. Parliament had therefore to ask itself whether, 'considering that the whole of the Bill was by the confession of the Government exceptional legislation, it was desirable to make the field of that exceptional legislation one inch broader than was absolutely necessary'.[75] For, as Brand emphasized, it was only on the ground of exceptional circumstances that State intervention could be justified, because otherwise 'there was no reason why the provisions of the Bill should not be applied to every tenancy in England and Scotland, as well as in Ireland'.[76] On this occasion twenty-five Liberals voted for the amendment, and the government's majority was reduced to thirty-six, which was regarded as only a moderate success by the whigs,[77] but evidently came as a relief to the government.[78] It may well be true, as Ostrogorski claimed, that some MPs had been intimidated by the pressure being applied by the National Liberal Federation, following the Heneage division.[79] Certainly, the Fitzmaurice amendment was noteworthy less for the scale of the Whig revolt than for the way it provoked the wrath of other Liberal members and the Liberal press. The amendment was denounced as being hostile to the principles of the Land Bill, and the Whigs were

[73] Cartwright's diary, 13 July 1881, Cartwright MSS, 6/15. Ramsden's amendment was considered to be unacceptable because of the enormous financial liability to which it would have exposed the treasury.

[74] Ibid., 14, 15 July 1881.

[75] Fitzmaurice (26 July 1881), 3 Hansard, cclxiii, cols. 1936–40.

[76] Brand, ibid., cols. 1945–50; see also Cartwright, ibid., cols. 1953–4.

[77] Cartwright's diary, 26 July 1881, Cartwright MSS, 6/15.

[78] 'Thought we were beaten, but got majority of 36', Herbert Gladstone's diary, 26 July 1881, Glynne–Gladstone MSS.

[79] On 29 June, the executive committee of the NLF had urged its member associations to apply pressure to the Whig rebels of 16 June, and the Birmingham 800 had gone so far as to declare that they should be removed from their seats: M. Ostrogorski, *Democracy and the Organisation of Political Parties* (1902), i. 209.

accused of inciting the House of Lords to seek a conflict with the government.[80] This latter assertion was not quite accurate, but what the Whigs were hoping was that members of the Upper House could be found to take up their amendments and insert them into the bill. Indeed, a great deal of effort had been expended by the young Whigs in the Commons in an attempt to co-ordinate their activities with the peers.

Three peers figured prominently in this respect. Lansdowne could naturally be looked to for assistance, as the brother of Fitzmaurice, as an Irish landowner, and as a powerful critic, in his own right, of the government's policies. However, in spite of his growing reputation, Lansdowne was still lacking a little in weight. This was amply compensated for by the Duke of Argyll, who had resigned from the government in April 1881, because of his fears about the implications of the Irish Land Bill for the land question in Britain (and presumably the Scottish highlands in particular),[81] and when he was approached by the young Whigs he gave his blessing to their planned series of amendments.[82] A special significance was attached, however, to the position of the fifteenth Earl of Derby, whose independent stance following his resignation from Beaconsfield's government in March 1878 had contributed towards a reputation which was, if anything, exaggerated by his contemporaries, and as yet undiminished by failings in office. Derby had for some time been identified as a potential leader of a reconstructed moderate Liberal ministry, perhaps drawing in moderate Conservatives as well, once Gladstone followed Beaconsfield to the grave.[83] The greatest constraint here was to be Derby's own habitual caution and reserve, but he was clearly aware of the opportunity that lay in front of him, and

[80] For the reaction of the press, cf. *Daily News*, 27 July 1881, p. 4; *Leeds Mercury*, 28 July 1881, p. 4; *Pall Mall Gazette*, 28 July 1881, p. 1. For the reaction in the House of Commons, cf. Cartwright's diary, 28 July 1881, Cartwright MSS, 6/15, and the London correspondent of the *Manchester Guardian*, 28 July 1881, p. 5.

[81] Argyll told Lord Dufferin on 7 Apr. 1881 that one of his reasons for resigning was 'that being a party to this Bill as a Minister would fatally embarrass me in questions still before us', *George Douglas, 8th Duke of Argyll (1823–1900): Autobiography and Memoirs*, ed. the Dowager Duchess (1906), ii. 370. He accepted the necessity for the Irish Land Bill, however, though objecting to the principle of free sale and the definition of fair rent, and preferring land purchase: Lord Derby's diary, 25 May 1881, Derby MSS.

[82] Albert Grey to Halifax, 4 June 1881, Hickleton MSS, A4/84.

[83] Albert Grey to Halifax, 10 June 1881, ibid. For an earlier comment, see the *Pall Mall Gazette*, 22 Nov. 1880, p. 1.

his conduct since April 1880 had been tactically astute. He had kept his distance from the new Liberal ministry, which he thought might eventually break up,[84] and his alarm at the return of Gladstone, whom he regarded as dangerous and dictatorial, probably convinced him that his own standing would be far higher if he retained his independence.[85] In the meantime, as a friendly critic of the government, he had been careful to avoid acrimony with his prospective political partners, and had actually supported the Compensation for Disturbance Bill.

It was characteristic of Derby's timidity that the first approach to the young Whigs should have been made on his behalf by Lady Galloway, his stepdaughter,[86] who indicated to Albert Grey that Derby would be willing to assist them with their amendments.[87] This hint was taken up by Fitzmaurice, who wrote to Derby on 8 June, arguing that, as the government was so dependent upon the support of moderate Liberals, there was a great opportunity for the moderates to influence the course of the Land Bill, provided the ground was well chosen. He also urged the importance of co-ordination between the moderates in both Houses, as it was essential that 'whatever amendments it may be intended to propose from the Liberal side', in the Upper House, 'should be first proposed in the House of Commons, in order to strengthen the position of the moderate peers'.[88]

Derby's reply to Fitzmaurice, indicating his approval of the young Whigs' programme of amendments,[89] cleared the way for future co-operation, and after the division on Heneage's amendment and Gladstone's concessions, Fitzmaurice saw Derby and was apparently encouraged to move the other amendment relating to £100 holdings.[90] This had to be postponed, as we have already seen, but when it was decided to raise the question at the report stage, Fitzmaurice again saw Derby, who clearly approved of the amendment and gave the Whigs the impression that he would take it up in

---

[84] Lord Derby's diary, 23 Apr. 1880, Derby MSS.

[85] Ibid., 24 Apr. 1880, also 12 Sept. 1880.

[86] No doubt this was Lady Derby's doing: Halifax to Albert Grey, 6 June 1881, Grey MSS, 211/6.

[87] Albert Grey to Halifax, 4 June 1881, Hickleton MSS, A4/84.

[88] Fitzmaurice to Derby, 8 June 1881, Derby MSS.

[89] Lord Derby's diary, 11 June 1881, Derby MSS.

[90] Ibid., 18 June 1881. Cartwright recorded in his diary on 19 June that Derby was willing to raise the amendment: Cartwright MSS, 6/15. Cf. Fitzmaurice to Derby, 21 June 1881, Derby MSS, stating that he would be moving the amendment.

the Lords.[91] What caused Derby to change his mind and draw back is not certain, though it may have been that the hostile reaction to the Whigs, for pressing their amendment, persuaded him that it would be damaging for him to be associated with it. At any rate, in spite of pressure from Fitzmaurice and Lansdowne,[92] Derby not only did not take up the amendment but decided not to speak during the debate on the second reading in the Lords, because, as he confided to his diary, no effectual protest against the government's policy seemed possible.[93]

The failure of Derby to come forward openly as the champion of the young Whigs was no doubt a disappointment, though probably not entirely unexpected.[94] There was some compensation in the fact that Argyll did take up Heneage's amendment, which was then accepted by the government, but there is nothing to suggest that the duke would ever have thought of setting himself up as the inspirational head of an organized Whig group in the Commons.[95] The most significant point for the long term, however, was the emergence, during the later stages of the Land Bill debates in the Commons, of G. J. Goschen as a potential focus for the moderate Liberals. Goschen's doctrinaire opposition to the reform of the county franchise had prevented him from taking office in 1880, but for a year the post of Ambassador Extraordinary to the Sultan of Turkey had kept

---

[91] Derby wrote in his diary on 22 July: 'This I approve of and he agrees to give notice of it', Derby MSS. Cf. Cartwright's diary, 22 July 1881, recording a meeting at Fitzmaurice's rooms where the amendment was agreed upon: 'Lord Derby will then move the same in Lords', Cartwright MSS, 6/15.

[92] Fitzmaurice to Derby, 29 July 1881, Lansdowne to Derby, 29 July 1881, Derby MSS.

[93] Lord Derby's diary, 2 Aug. 1881, Derby MSS. It may be said, in Derby's defence, that neither Lansdowne nor Argyll touched the amendment.

[94] See Halifax to Albert Grey, 12, 24 June 1881, Grey MSS, 211/6, for doubts about Derby's ability to lead.

[95] Argyll's view of the future, expressed just after the Phoenix Park murders in May 1882, is nevertheless worth quoting: 'You ask a difficult question about politics. On the one hand, I see no possibility of a Conservative Government being formed just now, nor do I believe that a Liberal Government could be formed on purely Whig lines. On the other hand, I have the deepest conviction of the mischievous tendencies of Gladstone's leadership, and of the utter instability he is imparting to all the fundamental principles of government as hitherto understood in all civilised Countries. I can only advise that the truth in this matter should be spoken freely, in the hope that when Gladstone disappears from the stage, there may be some return to sounder principles of legislation. I do not wish to see a change of Government just now', Argyll to Henry Reeve, 8 May 1882, in J. K. Laughton, *Memoirs of the Life and Correspondence of Henry Reeve* (1898), ii. 305.

him away from Westminster. It is quite probable that, like Derby, Goschen was cognizant of the advantages of remaining apart from a ministry, and a first minister, whose tendencies he in any case distrusted. His position, as he described it to Lord Acton early in 1881, was this: 'I consider that I have a clear if modest duty before me. I firmly believe that I render service to the Country by the course I am pursuing, and that indeed I can render greater service, if I do not allow myself to lose my individuality so as to be engulfed in a stream which may carry me heaven knows where.'[96]

After his return to the House of Commons early in June 1881, Goschen's position was naturally rather delicate, and any outright action against the government's Land Bill would have been thought inappropriate. However, he had privately expressed his support for the Heneage amendment,[97] and, after consulting with Fitzmaurice and Heneage,[98] he had finally decided to vote for Fitzmaurice's amendment at the report stage—a step that was recognized as being of the greatest significance.[99] Indeed, the Duke of Argyll was quick to urge him to assume the leadership of the moderate section of the Liberal party:

> I wish I could impress on you my own sense of the great importance of men of moderate opinions in the Commons and men of independent position showing that they will not slip down the inclined plane on which we are now all standing;—to the letting go of all that has hitherto been understood as sound Liberal principles. Depend upon it the effect on the Cabinet would be great if a good body of independent Liberals were *to set up their backs a little.* You are the only man in a position to give such a party some coherence just now.[100]

Goschen's emergence, publicly, as a leader of moderate Liberal opinion, during the autumn of 1881, certainly came at a critical time for the landowning class, who feared an imminent assault upon their interests. Yet another bad harvest, the fifth in succession, was fuelling Radical hopes of early action by the government on the question of 'tenant right' in Britain, and there was nothing to discourage them in Gladstone's ominously vague speech at Leeds in

---

[96] Goschen to Lord Acton, 12 Feb. 1881, Acton MSS.
[97] Albert Grey to Earl Grey, 17 June 1881, Grey MSS, Box 89.
[98] Cartwright's diary, 9 July 1881, Cartwright MSS, 6/15.
[99] Ibid., 26 July 1881.
[100] Argyll to Goschen, 31 July 1881, in Hon. A. D. Elliot, *Life of . . . Viscount Goschen, 1831–1907* (1911), i. 253. Halifax had apparently written in a similar vein two days earlier, ibid.

October.[101] The widespread sense of unease amongst Whig land-owners about Gladstone's possible intentions[102] was manifest at the time of the North Riding by-election in January 1882, although the circumstances here were exceptional. This vast constituency had usually been divided between the Liberals and Conservatives with-out a contest (there had not been one since 1868), and the vacancy that occured in 1882 was the 'Conservative seat'. The Conservatives' candidate was not only popular personally, but held fairly advanced political opinions. Furthermore, the Whig landowners had been upset by the selection of a member of the Farmers' Alliance to contest the seat for the Liberal party. As a result, the Marquis of Zetland seceded from the party, and Earl Grey (in his eightieth year) and the Duke of Cleveland (in his seventy-ninth year) declared their support for the Conservative candidate, who narrowly won the seat.[103] It would be an exaggeration to describe this as 'the first great secession of the Whigs' (as did Sir Alfred Pease, writing fifty years after the event),[104] for most of the landowners merely seem to have abstained. A more accurate assessment of the situation was made at the time by Lord Halifax, who reported that 'the Liberal gentlemen stood neuter generally'.[105]

In his speeches at Watford and Rugby in November 1881, Goschen began the work of developing 'moderate Liberalism' as a force which could exert influence over the present government while establishing its claim to power when the time came to construct the next Liberal government. At Watford, he took care to express his loyalty to the Prime Minister, whose continued presence Goschen declared to be of 'imperative national necessity', and he further emphasized his orthodox Liberal credentials with an attack on the

[101] For Gladstone's speech, see the *Manchester Guardian*, 8 Oct. 1881, p. 7. For the hopes of the Radicals, see the *Daily News*, 24 Aug. 1881, p. 5. For the condition of agriculture, see Halifax to Ripon, 29 Sept. 1881, BL Add. MSS 44529, fo. 228.

[102] Cf. Argyll to Derby, 17 Oct. 1881, Derby MSS; Argyll to Halifax, 14 Nov. 1881, Hickleton MSS, A4/82; Duke of Somerset to Brinsley Sheridan, 9 Oct. 1881, 3 Jan. 1882, in W. H. Mallock and Lady Gwendolen Ramsden, *Letters, Remains and Memoirs of Edward Adolphus Seymour, Twelfth Duke of Somerset, K.G.* (1893), 523–4.

[103] See the reports in the *Leeds Mercury*, 24 Jan. 1882, p. 4, 26 Jan. 1882, p. 4. Cf. the *Annual Register* for 1882, pp. 5–6.

[104] Pease, *Elections and Recollections*, pp. 58–61. Cf. Southgate, *Passing of Whigs*, pp. 369–70. It should be remembered that Pease was trying to depict himself as 'the last of the Whigs'.

[105] Halifax to Ripon, 10 Feb. 1882, BL Add. MSS 44530, fo. 11. This view is confirmed by the reports in *The Times*, 19 Jan. 1882, p. 9, 26 Jan. 1882, p. 9.

advocates of 'fair trade'.[106] A fortnight later, in his speech at Rugby, Goschen outlined a set of policies to counter the Radical demands for a reform of the county franchise and an attack on landed property. This moderate Liberal response took the form of a vision of a revivified community life in the counties, brought about by the creation of local authorities based on a wide franchise to encourage popular participation. He argued that this would be 'for the sake of the immense political and social advantage of the increasing local interests . . . He yielded to none in his desire to enlarge their interest in order to educate them as town ratepayers, and so as to educate them for national work. He trusted that his zeal for local government reform in the most Liberal sense might be taken as proof that he was not behind his party in his desire for a progressive development of public life amongst all classes of the State.' Parochial councils and a reform of the rating system were to be other aspects of the new order. And, as for the land laws, Goschen was prepared to contemplate reforms to 'strik[e] the shackles of limited ownership' and so increase the amount of capital available for improvements. He remained opposed to the importation of 'free sale' from Ireland, but he was willing to support a bill, like that of Sir Thomas Dyke Acland's, to give tenant farmers compensation for certain improvements. Even the creation of peasant proprietors, if a suitable scheme could be devised, would be welcomed, as 'he should measure their advantages not by the scale of productiveness but by social advantages'.[107]

English land reform, it appeared, was going to be the politics of the future, and Goschen, in order to place himself at the forefront of moderate Liberalism, was duly getting up the subject. As he wrote to Acland, shortly after the Rugby speech, 'I am giving all the attention I possibly can to all the Literature on the land question: and I am being initiated more or less here in Sussex [in] practical farming as I see something of my neighbours and have just enough land to be able to learn on a very small scale what many of the technical points really are . . . I know you will warn me off any dangerous ground on the land question if you see me on it but I think you will admit that I have been quite prudent thus far.'[108] But it is important to emphasize here

[106] Goschen at Watford, *Manchester Guardian*, 16 Nov. 1881, p. 8.

[107] Goschen at Rugby, ibid. 30 Nov. 1881, p. 8.

[108] Goschen to Sir Thomas Dyke Acland, 4 Dec. [1881], Bodleian MS Eng. Lett. d. 81, fo. 61.

that Goschen's strategy, as his public speeches indicate, was aimed far more at establishing himself as the leader of moderate Liberal opinion in the country as a whole, than at setting himself up as the leader of an organized group of MPs at Westminster. The reserved and cautious nature of his relationship with the 'young Whig party' is indeed illustrated by events during the 1882 session of parliament, in which Irish problems again predominated.

In spite of the Land Act, the autumn and winter of 1881 had witnessed a further deterioration of law and order in Ireland, forcing the government to take the step of arresting Parnell and a number of other Nationalist MPs. Whig confidence in the government's resolve to adhere to its rigorous policy of coercion—the Peace Preservation Act was due in any case to expire at the end of September 1882, unless renewed—was not great, however.[109] Concerted action by the moderate Liberals, to prevent the government from caving in to Radical pressure, seemed to be essential, particularly after the beginning of April, when what was assumed to be a Birmingham-inspired campaign was got under way in John Morley's *Pall Mall Gazette*, calling for an overhaul of the Dublin Castle administration (involving the removal of Forster as chief secretary), the concession of an arrears bill, and the release of Parnell and his colleagues.[110]

By the second week of April, therefore, Fitzmaurice was pressing Goschen to enter into consultation with the moderates in preparation for taking action if the government wavered under the pressure which, it was thought, was being orchestrated by Chamberlain's faction.[111] Heneage, too, was clear about the need

[109] 'The landed Whig gentry do not trust them and are very much afraid of what they may do if the extreme radicals complain of the coercion in Ireland', Halifax to Ripon, 2 Feb. 1882, BL Add. MSS 44530, fo. 7.

[110] 'A New Policy For Ireland', *Pall Mall Gazette*, 3 Apr. 1882, and subsequent articles. See also F. W. Hirst, *Early Life and Letters of John Morley* (1927), ii. 121–3. In fact, Chamberlain was not responsible for initiating these articles, and he considered Morley's action premature. Nevertheless, from the middle of Apr., he was definitely involved in communications designed to bring about an arrangement between the government and Parnell: J. L. Garvin, *Life of Joseph Chamberlain*, i. (1932), 348–63.

[111] Fitzmaurice to Cartwright, 8 Apr. 1882, Cartwright MSS, Box 16, bundle 5. Cartwright recorded in his diary, on 12 Apr., that Fitzmaurice had seen Goschen: ibid. 6/15. Fitzmaurice apparently told Goschen that fifty Liberal MPs would oppose the government if the law was not strengthened, and up to fifty more would absent themselves: Elliot, *Goschen*, i. 263.

for organization: 'as regards consultation amongst "Liberals (or Whigs)" which we are as distinct from "Radicals", I am all for keeping up our organising power, as a protest against the Birmingham Caucus and with a view of letting the Government know that they have a compact party behind them ready to support them against the Ultra-Radicals at any time when the Caucus is produced'.[112] Goschen, for his part, was naturally anxious to see the government kept up to the mark, and, though he doubted that ministers would cave in to the 'Birmingham School', he agreed that the moderates must be prepared to speak out in defence of Forster and against any tendency to show leniency towards the 'Irish rebels'.[113] However, he did not always find it easy to restrain his more zealous young associates, who were disinclined to adopt a 'wait and see' approach and wanted to make a demonstration in the House of Commons.[114] This problem arose when it was feared that the government might give way on Tim Healy's Irish Land Act Amendment Bill: Fitzmaurice took counsel with Lansdowne, Heneage, Lord Listowel (Heneage's brother-in-law), Albert Grey, and W. C. Cartwright,[115] and though Goschen, who clearly had inside information, was aware that ministers had no intention of accepting the bill,[116] Fitzmaurice went ahead and delivered a strong speech particularly critical of the Radicals.[117]

The pressure on Goschen to speak out became more intense at the end of April, as rumours began to spread of an imminent change in the personnel of the Irish administration and a new departure in policy.[118] For a time, indeed, after the announcement of Forster's resignation and the subsequent rumours that Chamberlain was to be appointed in his place, Goschen did show a clear determination to act, as Cartwright discovered when he saw him on the morning of 3 May: 'He feels strongly and is prepared to go far . . . He thinks authority and order are seriously shaken in the Country, and that if

[112] Heneage to Cartwright, 18 Apr. 1882, Cartwright MSS, Box 16, bundle 5.
[113] Goschen to Cartwright, 14 Apr. 1882, ibid. See also Cartwright's diary, 13 Apr. 1882, ibid. 6/15, recording a conversation with Goschen.
[114] Cf. Cartwright's diary, 21 Apr. 1882, ibid. 6/15, for Fitzmaurice's view.
[115] Ibid., 25 Apr. 1882.
[116] Ibid.
[117] Fitzmaurice (26 Apr. 1882), 3 Hansard, cclxviii, cols. 1512–22. Cf. Cartwright's diary, 26 Apr. 1882, Cartwright MSS, 6/15, for Goschen's disapproval.
[118] Cf. Cartwright's diary, 28, 30 Apr. 1882, Cartwright MSS, 6/15; Albert Grey to Earl Grey, 29 Apr. 1882, Grey MSS, Box 89.

public opinion will reconcile itself to Chamberlains being invested with the administration of Ireland, then there is no longer a moderate Liberal party in the Country of any real force.'[119] However, when it became known, the following day, that Lord Frederick Cavendish, rather than Chamberlain, was to be the new Irish chief secretary, Goschen resumed his more usual pose of extreme caution and remained aloof from the anxiety of the young Whigs to force the government to show its hand. They arranged that Lord Lymington should move a resolution, drafted by Fitzmaurice,[120] urging the government to announce at once its intentions with regard to coercion, and at a gathering of about fifteen Whigs at St James's Place, on Saturday 6 May, there was a 'General agreement that the Government were not to be allowed without vigorous remonstrance to postpone indefinitely their measures for preserving peace and maintaining law in Ireland, or to drift into another autumn and winter without saying how they meant to perform their primary duty in that Country'.[121] Accordingly, it was decided that as many of them as possible would speak out on the following Monday, when the government's Arrears Bill—a further concession to the Irish —was due to come on.[122]

Of course, the tragic news, that same night, of the murders in Phoenix Park transformed the situation from the young Whigs' point of view, as it now became clear that the government was resolved to press forward with new and more rigorous coercive legislation, which meant there was no need for any demonstration of the kind that had been planned. Attention was consequently focused on the details of the Prevention of Crimes Bill, and the efforts of the Whigs, during the protracted debate at the committee stage, were devoted to ensuring that sufficient pressure was kept up to prevent the government from making any concessions to the Nationalists. Reports were circulating, after the division on the second reading, that ministers

---

[119] Cartwright's diary, 3 May 1882, Cartwright MSS, 6/15.
[120] Ibid., 5 May 1882.
[121] Arthur Elliot's diary, 6 May 1882, Elliot MSS. Fitzmaurice wrote to Hartington afterwards informing him of the Whigs' concern and of Lymington's resolution: Fitzmaurice to Hartington, 6 May 1882, Devonshire MSS, 340.1146.
[122] Elliot's diary, 6 May 1882, Elliot MSS. According to this account, 'Cartwright, Heneage, J. C. Dundas, Albert Grey, Kingscote, Foljambe, Creyke, Sir J. Ramsden, Ebrington, Lymington, Sir R. Blennerhassett, and one or two more' were present at Fitzmaurice's.

were still in communication with Parnell,[123] and Goschen was reported as being 'very desirous that there should be a heavy muster of moderates' when the committee stage began, 'with the view of voting against Government on the first move of conceding to Irish clamour against the stringency of the Crime Act'.[124]

On the whole, the Whigs were successful in achieving their aims, although it was not always possible to secure fully united action. For instance, a Radical amendment to except treason and treason felony from the provision for trial without jury, which Goschen, Brand, Cartwright, and Francis Buxton all encouraged the government to resist, was nevertheless supported by Fitzmaurice, Heneage, and Grey.[125] This, understandably, 'made Goschen very angry'.[126] There was virtually united support, on the other hand, for an amendment to clause 12, by Morgan Lloyd, which proposed that the Aliens Act of 1848 should be re-enacted in its original form, thus applying to the whole of the United Kingdom rather than just to Ireland as the government intended. Cartwright noted that, on this occasion, 'The support from the moderate Liberals was overwhelming, the Radicals were nowhere and Government had to accept the amendment.'[127] An even more notable victory was scored at the report stage on 7 July (famous for Gladstone's loss of temper and threat of resignation), when twenty-four Liberals helped to defeat an amendment proposed by the government itself, which would have restricted the powers of inspectors to enter dwelling-houses at night in search of arms and illegal documents.[128] As a gloomy Herbert Gladstone recorded in his diary afterwards, 'It seems that [the Whigs] have been planning this for some days and the Tories take

[123] Goschen mentioned this in a conversation recorded in Cartwright's diary, 19 May 1882, Cartwright MSS, 6/15. In fact, Harcourt was fighting hard in Cabinet, against Gladstone and Chamberlain, to prevent any deal with Parnell—Lewis Harcourt's diary, 16, 18 May 1882, Harcourt MSS—which suggests that Harcourt may well have been Goschen's Cabinet informant. Whig distrust of Gladstone was well justified, for in June he was still encouraging Chamberlain's efforts to secure an arrangement with Parnell: Gladstone to Chamberlain, 8 June 1882, Chamberlain MSS, JC5/34/12.

[124] Cartwright's diary, 20 May 1882, Cartwright MSS, 6/15.

[125] The amendment was easily defeated, 277:70.

[126] Cartwright's diary, 1 June 1882, Cartwright MSS, 6/15.

[127] Ibid., 22 June 1882. The amendment was carried, 328:51.

[128] 3 Hansard, cclxxi, cols. 1797–8 (Cartwright); 1808–11 (Goschen); 1825 (Lambton). The government's amendment was defeated, 207:194. Ibid., cols. 1799–803, for Gladstone's outburst.

advantage of it ... the Government Whips were in a state of complete ignorance of the danger ... Cartwright declared that 70 or 80 men had promised to vote for him, but the Prime Minister's declaration turned about 50 votes. This is the worst day we have had in this parliament.'[129]

The passing of the Prevention of Crimes (Ireland) Act, which was designed to last for three years, marked a significant turning-point in the relations between the Gladstone ministry and its Whig supporters. Goschen considered the 'Gladstone–Parnell alliance' to have been 'shattered',[130] and as the situation in Ireland improved, under the new regime of Spencer and Trevelyan, so Whig confidence in the government grew.[131] Thus, Goschen, in public speeches during 1883, promised full support to the Irish administration and recommended that patience be shown until the fruits of recent concessions became clear.[132] Even an alarmist like Albert Grey was content to believe that 'all that is wanted is to strengthen the hands of Lord Spencer and Trevelyan and to allow them quietly to continue their vigorous administration which is already beginning to show good results, and abstain as far as possible from any action which is likely to excite ill feeling between England and Ireland and make the task of the Government of Ireland more difficult—If we wish to avoid being obliged to face the odious alternative of Separation or the Disfranchisement of Irish electors'.[133] In the meantime, the government had further enhanced its reputation by the firm action it had taken in Egypt in July 1882,[134] and it was in the context of this transformation in ministerial fortunes that three key figures from the moderate Liberal section were absorbed into the government in December. Whereas only a few months earlier the moderates had been content to keep their distance from Gladstone, and leave it to

[129] Herbert Gladstone's diary, 9 July 1882, Glynne–Gladstone MSS.

[130] Goschen to Lord Dufferin, n.d., cited by T. J. Spinner, *George Joachim Goschen* (Cambridge, 1973), 88.

[131] Cf. Halifax to Ripon, 19 Oct. 1882, 29 Nov. 1882, BL Add. MSS 44530, fos. 101, 121; Sir Rowland Blennerhassett to Cartwright, 5 Dec. 1882, Cartwright MSS, Box 16, bundle 1.

[132] Goschen at Ripon, *Manchester Guardian*, 23 Jan. 1883, p. 8, and at Edinburgh, ibid., 1 Nov. 1883, p. 5.

[133] Albert Grey to Earl Grey, 28 Feb. 1883, Grey MSS, Box 89, and a similar letter on 7 Mar.

[134] Heneage to Wintringham, 15 July 1882, Heneage MSS, 2 HEN 5/9, fo. 18. Goschen wrote to Granville on 15 Sept., congratulating him on the government's action, PRO 30/29/150.

him to extricate the country from the 'mess' for which he was held responsible,[135] Derby and Goschen both declining offers of Cabinet posts,[136] by the winter of 1882 the government seemed to be in an impregnable position.[137] Derby was at last persuaded to accept the Colonial Office, and two of the principal figures in the House of Commons group, Fitzmaurice and Brand, were given the posts of Foreign Under-secretary and Surveyor-General of the Ordnance, respectively.[138] This ministerial reconstruction demonstrates clearly that, far from being a secessionist mentality, 'Whiggery', in the early 1880s, was still a viable route to personal advancement for ambitious politicians.[139] As Stuart Rendel observed, rather sourly, there appeared to be 'a premium on caves'.[140]

It would be a mistake, in any case, to depict the Whigs as simply a group of inflexible and unimaginative gentlemen wedded to freedom of contract and other unchanging principles of political economy. On the contrary, it was generally accepted that Ireland had to be treated as a special case, and it was in this spirit that most of the Whigs supported the Arrears Bill, which accompanied the coercive legislation of 1882, for this was seen as a necessary measure to enable tenants to take advantage of the 1881 Land Act.[141] The Arrears Bill in fact serves to show just how isolated a doctrinaire politician with rigid principles, like Albert Grey, could find himself, as only two other Liberals joined him in voting against the second and third

---

[135] Sir John Ramsden to Ayscough Fawkes, 6 May 1882, Ramsden MSS, 41/4.

[136] Cf. Goschen to Gladstone, 2 June 1882, BL Add. MSS 44161, fo. 284, declining the War Office; Derby to Gladstone, 17 May 1882, BL Add. MSS 44141, fo. 55, declining an offer which, according to Derby's diary, 15 May 1882, was of either the India Office or the Lord Presidency of the Council.

[137] Lord Derby's diary, 30 Nov. 1882, Derby MSS.

[138] Lansdowne was also removed from the scene, soon afterwards, when he accepted the post of Governor-General of Canada in May 1883.

[139] Fitzmaurice was apparently 'cross' at being left out of the new government in April 1880: Dilke's memoir, BL Add. MSS 43934, fo. 161. Cartwright had aspired, at this time, to the Foreign Under-secretaryship; see his diary, 11 Apr., 22 May 1880, Cartwright MSS, 6/14. Heneage was later reported by Chamberlain as being ambitious for office: Lewis Harcourt's diary, 5 Dec. 1884, Harcourt MSS.

[140] Rendel to Grant Duff, 21 Jan. 1883, in F. E. Hamer (ed.), *The Personal Papers of Lord Rendel* (1931), 221.

[141] Cartwright's diary, 22 May 1882, Cartwright MSS, 6/15. Fitzmaurice, in an earlier assessment of the needs of Ireland, had argued that 'it is the question of arrears which is at the root of the row', to Ashton Dilke, 23 [Dec.?] 1881, Dilke MSS (Churchill College, Cambridge), 6/10.

readings, on 23 May and 21 July.[142] Brand, by contrast, was
prepared to accept that 'when we come to deal with Irish land we had
to throw political economy to the winds . . . He thought, if they were
going in for generous legislation, the sooner they set about it the
better', and Lymington similarly urged that 'at a critical time like the
present they ought to endeavour to look at Irish legislation not so
much from a theoretical as from a practical point of view'.[143] These
and other speakers saw the need for a substantial increase in the
amount of money made available by the government to assist those
who wished to emigrate.[144] Furthermore, most of the Whigs seem to
have been prepared to countenance some form of State intervention
for the purpose of reorganizing the system of land tenure in Ireland.
Fitzmaurice, characteristically, had his own plan for solving the
problem, which involved the creation of a two-tier system: 'small
cottier tenants should be made into something like copyholders;
subject to a just rent fixed once for all by authority; with facilities
given through land banks or otherwise (as was done in Germany) for
the redemption by the occupier of the rent. Real agricultural tenants
who came in as a matter of fact *by bargain* to be left to deal by free
contract as in England and Scotland.'[145] Others, meanwhile, were
inclined to favour a State financed system of land purchase, and
Albert Grey noted in March 1882 that there was now a general
opinion in the House of Commons in favour of 'increasing the
number of Proprietors which the security of the very institution of
landownership seems to require'.[146] Indeed, the growing interest
displayed by both the Liberal and Conservative parties in land

---

[142] Grey, M. J. Guest, and Richard Fort (a landowner) voted against the second
reading: see 3 Hansard, cclxix, cols. 1445–8, for the division list. Grey, Guest, and Sir
John Ennis (an Irish landowner) voted against the third reading: ibid. cclxxii, cols.
1319–23. The only hostile move against the bill in which a few Whigs were involved
was Sir John Lubbock's amendment, which aimed to tighten up the wording of the
clause giving the Land Act commissioners the power to regard the tenant's 'interest' as
an asset, where this was considered reasonable. Eight Liberal MPs, including
Goschen, voted for this amendment on 13 July, with Lubbock and Grey acting
as tellers, but it was opposed by other Whigs like Brand, Fitzmaurice, Heneage,
Lymington, and Ramsden. Ibid. cclxxii, cols. 372–4, for the division list.

[143] Brand (2 May 1882), ibid. cclxix, cols. 1320–2; Lymington (6 July 1882), ibid.
cclxxi, cols. 1649–52.

[144] Francis Buxton and John Ramsay (20 July 1882), ibid. cclxxii, cols. 1157,
1159. Cf. Lansdowne (27 July 1882), ibid., cols. 1932–8.

[145] Arthur Elliot's diary, 3 June 1882, Elliot MSS.

[146] Albert Grey to Earl Grey, 4 Mar. 1882, Grey MSS, Box 89. In a subsequent
letter of 10 Mar., Grey took comfort in the thought that it would thus be possible to
'establish the reign of Economic law', ibid.

purchase, as a solution for the problems of Ireland, is of the utmost significance, for the implications of such a measure were not perceived as posing the same threat to the English landowning class as the government's earlier legislation. If the Irish question was going to provoke a split in the Liberal party simply along 'class' lines, it would have happened in 1881.

Gladstone may have succeeded in 'buying off' some of his more dangerous Whig critics in December 1882, but this did not mean that the back-bench Whigs ceased to pose problems for his administration during subsequent parliamentary sessions. The Whig rebels of 1880–2 figured prominently, for instance, in two divisions during the committee stage of the Agricultural Holdings Bill in 1883. This measure, which sought to establish a compulsory system of compensation to outgoing tenant farmers for certain categories of improvements made by them, was supported by all parties at the second reading stage on 29 May. However, twelve Liberals voted for an amendment, proposed by Arthur Balfour, on 17 July, limiting the compensation to be given for that class of improvements which did not require the landlord's consent, and this was carried against the government by a majority of eight.[147] Less than a week later, sixteen Liberals voted for an unsuccessful amendment, by Hicks Beach, which would have allowed landlords and tenants to contract out of the bill's provisions where a satisfactory agreement had been reached.[148]

A more impressive and more broadly based demonstration had taken place earlier in July in support of a Conservative resolution calling for the Privy Council to be given powers to prohibit the importation of cattle from countries affected by foot-and-mouth disease. This resolution was carried by a majority of eight, with twenty-seven Liberals (including the representatives of the Farmers' Alliance) voting in the majority, and Kingscote acting as one of the tellers.[149] Similarly, when the government introduced a Contagious Diseases (Animals) Bill, during the 1884 session, consultations took place amongst the 'Agricultural Liberals', notably Heneage,

[147] The division list is printed in 3 Hansard, cclxxxi, cols. 1793–5. Nine of the twelve Liberals appear in the list produced in Appendix II. This vote was subsequently rescinded at the report stage.

[148] 23 July 1883. The division list was published by the *Pall Mall Gazette*, 24 July 1883, p. 9. Ten of the sixteen Liberals appear on the list produced in Appendix II.

[149] 10 July 1883. The division list is printed in 3 Hansard, cclxxxi, cols. 1083–6. Cf. W. C. Cartwright's diary, 10 July 1883, Cartwright MSS, Box 101.

Kingscote, and Cartwright,[150] who feared that ministers might yield to pressure from the free trade lobby. Consequently, when the bill reached the House of Commons—it had originated in the Lords, where the Conservatives had used their majority to stiffen its provisions—and the government proposed an amendment restricting the prohibitory powers of the Privy Council, twenty-seven Liberals (and Heneage acting as a teller) joined the Conservatives to defeat the government by a majority of twenty-four.[151] On this occasion, ministers gave way and a new amendment was proposed by the government, which, according to Cartwright, consisted of 'words drafted by Heneage with our concurrence', to the effect of the original Lords' amendment.[152]

Clearly, the materials still existed, after December 1882, for the organization of a moderate Liberal group in the House of Commons. What was lacking was an individual with real political weight prepared to give the necessary lead. Goschen took no part in the revolts over the agricultural legislation of 1883–4, and his disinclination to put himself forward as the head of an organized political group was even apparent on an issue with which he had a particular interest, that of Egypt. At the beginning of 1884, for example, Michael Biddulph, the hitherto inconspicuous member for Herefordshire, fearing among other things that the government was contemplating an early evacuation of Egypt, wrote to Cartwright to suggest that 'the time is come when the Liberal County Members should combine' to strengthen Hartington's hand in the Cabinet.[153] Cartwright, very sensibly, replied that care had to be taken to avoid any 'precipitate demonstration', and he advised that 'Goschen should be consulted'.[154] Whether Goschen was actually approached is not known, but in February it was Biddulph and John Pender, the MP for Wick, who were attempting to organize a memorial to Gladstone urging the government to take rigorous action in

---

[150] Cartwright's diary, 5 Mar. 1884, Cartwright MSS, Box 101. Cf. Heneage to Cartwright, 15, 18 Mar. 1884, ibid., Box 20, fos. 660–1.

[151] 22 Apr. 1884. The division list is printed in 3 Hansard, cclxxxvii, cols. 346–9. In all, forty-three Liberals voted against the government on one or both of the divisions on the cattle diseases issue, and seventeen of these appear in Appendix II. Most of the others were also landowners.

[152] Cartwright's diary, 25 Apr. 1884, Cartwright MSS, Box 101. See also the entry for 24 Apr., for the informal communications between ministers and back-benchers.

[153] Biddulph to Cartwright, 8 Jan. 1884, Cartwright MSS, Box 16, bundle 6.

[154] Cartwright's diary, 16 Jan. 1884, ibid., Box 101.

Egypt.[155] More striking evidence of Goschen's lack of leadership is provided by Lord Stafford's letter to Albert Grey on 29 June, just the day before a Conservative motion of censure was due to come on, in which he urged: 'Do let us make a party to stop this dreadful Egyptian policy . . . Could you not talk to Mr. Goschen about this—you and he would have no difficulty in getting support from our side.'[156] As Cartwright's diary makes clear, however, in spite of his dissatisfaction with the government's vacillating policy, Goschen was reluctant to take any step which might hamper ministers in their negotiations with the other European Powers and perhaps even bring the government down.[157]

Goschen's position in 1883–4, it must be appreciated, was one of considerable difficulty. At the root of the problem lay the fact that he was still committed to opposing the extension of the borough household franchise to the counties, at a time when the resilience of Gladstone's ministry made just such a measure appear inevitable, and, indeed, when Chamberlain was embarking upon a public campaign to promote franchise reform as a necessary prelude to other, far-reaching social reforms, particularly with regard to the land question.[158] The increased likelihood of a new franchise bill naturally had the effect of undermining the alternative, pre-county franchise programme which Goschen had produced in the autumn of 1881, and which he had reiterated in a speech to his constituents at Ripon in January 1883.[159] Privately, he was becoming pessimistic about the prospects for owners of property,[160] and doubted the ability of the moderate Liberals to resist the Radicals, who appeared to be on firmer ground. As Lord Halifax noted, 'He is not . . . very sanguine as to the future and thinks the democratic wave advancing very fast.'[161] It is significant that Goschen's 'Address to the Philosophical Institution at Edinburgh on Laissez Faire and Government Interference' (November 1883) consisted mainly of an analysis of the

---

[155] Ibid., 8, 11 Feb. 1884.

[156] Stafford to Albert Grey, 29 June 1884, Grey MSS, 213/5.

[157] Cartwright's diary, 4 July 1884, Cartwright MSS, Box 101. See also the earlier entry for 6 May 1884.

[158] For Chamberlain's campaign in 1883, see Garvin, *Chamberlain*, i. 384–407.

[159] Goschen at Ripon, *Manchester Guardian*, 23 Jan. 1883, p. 8.

[160] Cf. W. C. Cartwright's diary, 31 Oct. 1882, Cartwright MSS, Box 101: 'Goschen hazarded the prediction that compulsory division of property would be the law in the Country five and twenty years hence.'

[161] Halifax to Ripon, 25 Jan. 1883, BL Add. MSS 44530, fo. 151.

reasons why a democratically organized society would tend to favour increased regulation by the State, and contained no suggestion that this trend could in any way be resisted—though he thought its effects might be mitigated by delegating powers to local bodies. His despondency about the future undoubtedly explains why he was seriously tempted by Gladstone's offer, in November 1883, of the Speakership of the House of Commons, which he was apparently only prevented from accepting by the advice of his oculist.[162] Furthermore, Goschen's fatalistic attitude provides the only plausible explanation for his failure, during the 1884 session of parliament, to provide the moderates with badly needed leadership on the questions of franchise and redistribution. He had himself demonstrated that, even after the inevitability of a county franchise measure was accepted, there remained ample scope for a stand on the issue of minority representation, which had a particular relevance to Ireland, whose parliamentary representation was going to be disproportionately high if, as Gladstone had indicated in his opening speech, the government's future Redistribution Bill was based on the principle of not reducing the number of Irish seats in accordance with the decline in the population since the famine.[163] He might have attempted, as Albert Grey sought to do, to promote minority (or proportional) representation as the best means of securing the return of moderate Liberal candidates, and as a way of imposing some restraint upon the rule of numbers.[164] But, in the end, Goschen remained aloof from the proportional representation society— which, in spite of its broadly based support amongst Whig, Radical, and Conservative MPs, was seriously handicapped by the absence of a substantial political figure willing to lead it[165]—and allowed himself instead the distinction of being the only Liberal to vote

---

[162] For the correspondence between Goschen and Gladstone on the question of the Speakership, see BL Add. MSS 44161, fos. 268–94.

[163] Goschen at Ripon, *Manchester Guardian*, 31 Jan. 1884, p. 6. Cf. W. C. Cartwright's diary, 1 Mar. 1884, Cartwright MSS, Box 101; Goschen in the House of Commons, 3 Mar. 1884, 3 Hansard, cclxxxv, cols. 416–30. Lord Ebrington reported to his father on 28 Mar. that Goschen favoured proportional representation but was still 'not very hopeful about the future', Fortescue MSS, FC 55.

[164] Cf. Albert Grey to Lord Melgund, 21 Jan. 1885, NLS MSS 12424; Grey to Lubbock, 8 Oct. 1884, BL Add. MSS 49647, fo. 88.

[165] For the activities of the proportionalists, and their shortcomings, see Andrew Jones, *The Politics of Reform 1884* (Cambridge, 1972), 95–104. Both Fawcett and Forster declined to lead the society when it was formed in Jan. 1884.

against the second reading of the Franchise Bill.[166] As some of his sympathizers recognized, Goschen's chance to re-establish himself in the front rank of the Liberal party would not come until a settlement of the franchise question had liberated him from his self-imposed political exile.[167]

2. *Hartington and the Liberal Succession*

The longevity of Gladstone's second administration placed Hartington in an increasingly perplexed and frustrating position. While there was little doubt that the leadership would revert to him when Gladstone retired, so long as he remained in the House of Commons at least, the logic of the temporary arrangement which had brought Gladstone back to power in April 1880 dictated that Hartington should act, in the meantime, as the representative—both in the Cabinet and the country—of that body of 'moderate' opinion which the Whig duumvirate had supposedly harnessed on the Liberals' behalf at the general election. This was a reflection of the sense in which 'Whiggery' had been reduced to the status of a mere section of the Liberal party as a result of Gladstone's coup. Hartington thus found himself combining the role of heir apparent with that of the guarantor of the interests of the moderates, although these responsibilities frequently conflicted with one another, and each imposed serious limitations upon his ability to fulfil the other. Whereas, on the one hand, his efforts to resist certain measures tended to diminish his credibility as a leader capable of uniting the whole party (which in turn helped to persuade Gladstone that he must delay his retirement), on the other, Hartington's ultimate inability to counter many of the 'Radical' trends in governmental policy had the effect of damaging his reputation among those moderate Liberals whose interests he was supposed to be protecting. In this way, Gladstone's continued leadership served to weaken Hartington's footholds on both sides of the Liberal divide.

Hartington's sense of obligation to the moderate Liberals, coupled

---

[166] For Goschen's speech during the second-reading debate, 7 Apr. 1884, see 3 Hansard, cclxxxvi, cols. 1867–80. Cf. Halifax to Ripon, 10 Apr., 30 May 1884, BL Add. MSS 44531, fos. 126, 144, regretting the damage done to Goschen's position by his vote.

[167] e.g. Arthur Elliot to Lord Melgund, 13 Apr. 1884, Elliot MSS. Cf. Cartwright's diary, 22 Nov. 1884, Cartwright MSS, Box 101.

with a natural desire to ensure that his political inheritance, when it finally came to him, was not seriously depleted, led him to resist as far as possible the Prime Minister's strong inclination towards the views of the Radicals. This frequently involved behaving as an obstructionist in Cabinet. For instance, one entry in Dilke's diary for April 1883, when Hartington was Secretary of State for war, reads: 'Cabinet . . . A tremendous row over Contagious Disease. The Cabinet sat very late, because Hartington never knows when he is beat.'[168] Similarly, in May 1884, we find that 'Hartington obstructed as to the "5 years"'—a reference to the proposed period of the British occupation of Egypt, which he considered to be too short.[169] In the case of the Agricultural Holdings Bill in 1883, Hartington found himself completely isolated, as Dilke noted: 'all my Lords very Radical indeed today except our Marquis, who was ferocious to the highest point, being thoroughly at bay'.[170] Hartington seems to have practised his art so systematically that it almost became a matter of principle for him to obstruct, as though this were his primary function, and his private secretary observed how unfortunate it was that 'being so violent as he is in the Cabinet he forgets from time to time what his opinions are on particular subjects: e.g. County Franchise and Clôture'.[171] On one occasion in January 1885, he threatened to resign, along with Northbrook, in order to force Gladstone to reject the French proposal for an international 'enquête' on the question of Egyptian finance.[172] Perhaps it was understandable that Gladstone should have regarded Hartington as a 'difficult colleague'.[173]

Hartington enjoyed a notable success early in 1883, when he was able to veto the idea, favoured by the Prime Minister, of a local government bill for Ireland. This was the culmination of a battle that had gone on ever since the Phoenix Park murders of May 1882, with Hartington resisting Gladstone's inclination towards the strategy, favoured by Chamberlain, of promoting co-operation between the

---

[168] Dilke's diary, 28 Apr. 1883, BL Add. MSS 43925.

[169] Ibid., 27 May 1884.

[170] Ibid., 21 Apr. 1883.

[171] Ibid., 6 Nov. 1882, recording Brett's conversation.

[172] A. B. Cooke and John Vincent (eds.), *Lord Carlingford's Journal: Reflections of a Cabinet Minister, 1885* (Oxford, 1971), 53–9 (entries for 20, 21, 27 Jan. 1885). This would have been a formidable secession, as Childers, certainly, and Carlingford, possibly, would have resigned as well.

[173] D. W. R. Bahlman (ed.), *The Diary of Sir Edward Walter Hamilton, 1880–1885* (Oxford, 1972), ii. 839 (entry for 15 Apr. 1885).

government and the Parnellite home-rule party. Hartington had the advantage, throughout, of the powerful support of the Home Secretary, Harcourt, who fought furiously to thwart Gladstone's attempts—using Chamberlain, via Labouchere, as an intermediary—to negotiate a deal with the home rulers by offering to amend the Prevention of Crimes Bill.[174] During the autumn of 1882, Gladstone showed an interest in a fresh initiative to establish relations with the Nationalists by conceding further land legislation and setting up an Irish Grand Committee,[175] but Hartington and Harcourt stood firm in their opposition to any deal with Parnell.[176] Gladstone remained undeterred in his wish for a *rapprochement* with the Irishmen, however, and by mid-January 1883, when he left for a convalescent holiday at Cannes, he was urging upon Harcourt, at Charing Cross station, the need for an Irish local government bill.[177] Ominously, this idea was followed up in speeches by Chamberlain at Birmingham, and by Herbert Gladstone at Leeds.[178]

Hartington responded immediately to the danger in a speech, at Bacup, in which he ruled out the possibility of any local government measure so long as there remained a danger that the Nationalists might use such institutions for the purpose of further agitation.[179] As

[174] See Dilke's diary, 15, 17 May 1882, for Harcourt's fury at this negotiation, and 22 May 1882 for Hartington and Harcourt's opposition to any amendments to the crimes bill, BL Add. MSS 43924. The strength of their opposition is indicated by the following intriguing letter from Harcourt to Hartington: 'I have been thinking over the subject of our conversation yesterday and there seems to me no safety except in getting G. to stay where he is at least till the end of the Session. The jealousies and difficulties to which the gap will give rise are so serious that I see no way at present of abating them. I hope therefore you will consider what I said yesterday as *non avenue* at least until we can resume the conversation', 19 May 1882 (typescript), Harcourt MSS, Box 720. The negotiation with the Irish continued, however: cf. Gladstone to Chamberlain, 8 June 1882, Chamberlain MSS, JC5/34/12, but Harcourt made a triumphant stand at the Cabinet on 10 June: Lewis Harcourt's diary, 10 June 1882, Harcourt MSS.

[175] This followed an approach from Parnell: Gladstone to Granville, 7 Oct. 1882, in A. Ramm (ed.), *The Political Correspondence of Mr Gladstone and Lord Granville, 1876–1886* (Oxford, 1962), i. 443.

[176] Hartington to Gladstone, 14 Oct. 1882, BL Add. MSS 44146, fo. 87. For Hartington and Harcourt's opposition to the Grand Committee, see Dilke's diary, 21 Nov. 1882, BL Add. MSS 43925.

[177] Harcourt to Granville, 17 Jan. 1883 (typescript), Harcourt MSS, Box 721. Spencer had previously informed Hartington that Gladstone was prepared to go as far as a provincial councils scheme for Ireland: 13 Jan. 1883, Devonshire MSS, 340.1310.

[178] See *The Times*, 17 Jan. 1883, p. 6, 20 Jan. 1883, p. 6, for reports.

[179] Ibid., 20 Jan. 1883, p. 6. Cf. Harcourt to Hartington, 22 Jan. 1883, 1 Feb. 1883 (typescripts), Harcourt MSS, Box 720, congratulating him for speaking out.

he explained afterwards to Granville, 'My reason for forestalling the discussions in the Cabinet was that other members of the Government . . . had spoken very strongly in the sense of advocating a large change in the local government of Ireland, and that it appeared to me that the Cabinet might, to a certain extent, become committed to a policy which it had never discussed, and to which I felt the strongest objection.'[180] The arguments of the outraged Prime Minister in favour of a local government bill were dismissed as 'dreams'.[181] To make matters worse for Gladstone, it then emerged that even Chamberlain had changed his mind about Irish local government, after being advised by Francis Schnadhorst, the secretary of the National Liberal Federation, that it would be imprudent to pursue the subject because of the need to devote the forthcoming parliamentary session to English legislation.[182] Of the other ministers, only Granville was willing to support the Premier in his 'wish to hand over the Government of Ireland to the Fenians',[183] and, after a Cabinet meeting on 3 February, Gladstone had to be informed that there was no desire for action on the subject in the 1883 session.[184] Furthermore, in a letter to Gladstone a few days later, Hartington made it clear that it would be impossible for him to lead the government, during the debate on the Address, without expressing an opinion 'so far at least as I am personally concerned whether it is or is not within the intentions of the Government to attempt to deal with Irish Local Government in the next Session', and on 22 February he duly repeated to the House of Commons what he had said at Bacup.[185]

In this instance, Hartington was able to ensure that the government did not drift into Gladstone's Irish plans, partly because of the latter's geographical remoteness from events, but also because Chamberlain proved to be no more interested in an Irish local

[180] Hartington to Granville, 25 Jan. 1883, PRO 30/29/27A, in Bernard Holland, *Life of Spencer Compton, Eighth Duke of Devonshire, 1833–1908* (1911), i. 388–9.
[181] Hartington to Granville, 30 Jan. 1883, Devonshire MSS, 340.1316, in Holland, *Devonshire*, i. 390. For Gladstone's complaint, see his letter to Granville, 22 Jan. 1883, in Ramm (ed.), *Gladstone–Granville Correspondence, 1876–1886*, ii. 9–11.
[182] Schnadhorst to Chamberlain, 29 Jan. 1883, Chamberlain MSS, JC5/63/5. Cf. Chamberlain to Dilke, 4 Feb. 1883, ibid. JC5/24/352. See also Harcourt to Hartington, 1, 2 Feb. 1883 (typescripts), Harcourt MSS, Box 720, conveying this intelligence.
[183] Hartington to Harcourt, 3 Feb. 1883, Harcourt MSS, Box 79.
[184] Granville to Gladstone, 6 Feb. 1883, in Ramm (ed.), *Gladstone–Granville Correspondence, 1876–1886*, ii. 19.
[185] Hartington to Gladstone, 9 Feb. 1883, BL Add. MSS 44146, fo. 169; Hartington (22 Feb. 1883), 3 Hansard, cclxxvi, cols. 666–85.

government bill than Hartington. Such a combination of circumstances was fortuitous, however, and it was more often the case that
Hartington found himself up against a united front of Gladstone and
the Radicals which exposed the weakness of his position.

The early efforts of the Gladstone ministry to formulate a policy
for Ireland illustrate Hartington's difficulties. He had opposed the
decision, taken at the outset, not to renew the coercive legislation of
1875, and, along with many other ministers, he had regretted the
hastily conceived Compensation for Disturbance Bill, which aimed
at countering the agitation of the Land League by appeasing the Irish
tenant farmers.[186] Finally, in November 1880, the continued deterioration of social order in Ireland provoked a crisis in the Cabinet,
with Hartington, Spencer, and Argyll backing Forster, the Irish chief
secretary, in his request that parliament be recalled immediately to
pass a new coercion bill. Gladstone, however, took the side of Bright
and Chamberlain in opposing any such precipitate action, and
preferred, instead, to delay the decision until the government was at
least in a position to announce its plans for ameliorative
legislation.[187] It was probably a considerable relief to Hartington
that, in the event, Forster backed down and settled for making the
fullest use of the existing law, for, as he observed to Ripon during the
midst of the crisis, 'the refusal of Gladstone to agree to coercion and
the resignation of Forster etc and myself on this question would
practically break up not only the government but the party'.[188] If a
split had occurred, it would have been with Gladstone on the side of
the Radicals,[189] which would of course have strengthened their
claim to be his natural heirs and thus weakened the position of the
Whigs. The conclusion to be drawn from the crisis of November
1880 was therefore clear. As Hartington's private secretary noted,

[186] For Hartington's complaints about the drift of the government's Irish policy,
and his warning about the future, see his letter to Gladstone of 19 Dec. 1880, BL Add.
MSS 44145, fo. 160. For his view of the Compensation Bill, see his letter to Lord
Ripon, 9 July 1880, BL Add. MSS 43565, fo. 67. Cf. Granville to Ripon, 21 July
1880, BL Add. MSS 43521, fo. 132, and Childers to Halifax, 16 July 1880, Hickleton
MSS, A4/90.
[187] Cf. Reginald Brett's diary, 19 Dec. 1880, Esher MSS, 2/5; Hartington to
Ripon, 19 Nov. 1880, 17 Dec. 1880, BL Add. MSS 43565, fo. 200, and 43566, fo. 25.
For letters of support to the Lord Lieutenant, Cowper, from Argyll (26 Nov.), Spencer
(28 Nov.), and Hartington (8 Dec.), see Countess Cowper, *Earl Cowper*, pp. 436,
438–9, 444.
[188] Hartington to Ripon, 19 Nov. 1880, BL Add. MSS 43565, fo. 200.
[189] Brett to Lord William Compton, 20 Nov. 1880, Esher MSS, 2/5.

there was 'no chance of doing anything without Mr. Gladstone. If he holds up his finger the Country will go to him, and if the Whigs secede they will cease to be a factor in politics.'[190]

This perception of the Whig predicament followed logically from Hartington's acknowledgement, in declining the premiership in April 1880, that it was impossible for him to construct a viable alternative government because of the strength of Gladstone's attraction for the Radicals. Thereafter, Gladstone's position rested upon the notion that he performed a unique service as a balancing force between the Whig and Radical sections of the Liberal party, and whenever Hartington or any other Whig minister contemplated resigning, they were usually susceptible to the argument that, in doing this, they would be tipping the scales in the Radicals' favour and correspondingly weakening the power of the Liberal aristocracy.[191] The weight of this consideration was apparent, for example, during the Cabinet crisis over the renewal of the Prevention of Crimes Act in May 1885, when Hartington, Granville, Derby, Northbrook, Kimberley, Rosebery, and Carlingford met at Devonshire House to decide whether to accept a compromise. According to Carlingford's account, 'the one thing that turned the scale in favour of acceptance . . . and against resignation was the great mischief (if the Govt broke up upon this) of having Chamberlain, Dilke etc with P[arnell] & Co., under Gladstone's aegis, arrayed against Hartington and the moderate Liberals'.[192] Indeed, Gladstone himself was ready to use this argument as a timely reminder of the consequences of any attempt to undermine his government. When Hartington threatened to resign over the franchise question in December 1883, Gladstone reacted by suggesting that if, as he thought probable, the government fell as a result of this secession, he would have to consider 'put[ting] upon H. the duty of accepting the Govt. with Liberal colleagues and [with] Reform postponed . . . we supporting his Govt'.[193] The threat was clear: if the government was wrecked, Gladstone would be driven into the hands of the Radicals while Hartington was left with the near impossible task of putting together

---

[190] Brett to William Cory, 25 Nov. 1880, ibid.

[191] See Granville's letters to the Dukes of Argyll and Bedford, in Jan. 1881, in Lord Edmond Fitzmaurice, *Life of Granville George Leveson-Gower, second Earl of Granville, K.G. 1815–1891* (1905), ii. 296.

[192] Cooke and Vincent (eds.), *Carlingford's Journal* (15 May 1885), 102–3.

[193] Gladstone to Granville, 18 Dec. 1883, in Ramm (ed.), *Gladstone–Granville Correspondence, 1876–1886*, ii. 130.

an alternative Liberal administration which, even if it could be done, would lead in all likelihood to 'The great[est] disaster of all—a Dissolution, with the Liberals in two camps'.[194]

It was clear that the only way in which Hartington and the Whigs could hope to exercise an influence upon the future direction of the Liberal party, and prevent it from falling into the hands of the Radicals, was by accepting Gladstone's leadership and waiting for him to relinquish it voluntarily. Any attempt to remove him prematurely would lead to the deployment of his immense political authority against them, to the advantage of the Radicals. In the meantime, all that could be done was to make the most of the compensatory fact that the Radicals were faced with a similar problem, and were equally anxious lest an imprudent step should play into the hands of their rivals.[195] Gladstone's authority was of such an independent character that he could compel the Radicals to swallow unpalatable measures in the same way that he force-fed the Whigs. Thus, by supporting Gladstone, the Whigs had at least a guarantee of Radical acquiescence in certain essential measures, even if it meant accepting the necessity for other, less desirable ones. In 1881, for example, this enabled Hartington and all but one of the other Whig ministers to justify their support for an Irish Land Bill which they viewed with pessimism and distaste, on the grounds that only Gladstone could induce the Radicals to accept new coercive legislation as a quid pro quo.[196]

These considerations no doubt account for the growing disposition, on Hartington's part, not only to avoid any step which might cause Gladstone to resign the Liberal leadership, but actually to encourage him to retain it. In the light of his experience in April 1880, Hartington can have had few illusions that, when it came to the point, Gladstone would stand down for the purely altruistic reason of allowing the Whig leader to have his turn; and it would

---

[194] Ibid. See also 23 Dec. 1883, ibid. ii. 135. Cf. Granville to Hartington, 23 Dec. 1883, PRO 30/29/28, conveying Gladstone's threat, and Hartington to Granville, 25 Dec. 1883, PRO 30/29/22A/3, for Hartington's protest.

[195] Frank Hill, the editor of the *Daily News*, warned Dilke that, by resigning over the franchise question, 'You would leave the Gladstone tradition with the Whig and aristocratic section; and it will be an immense power long after he has departed', 5 Oct. 1884, BL Add. MSS 43898, fo. 74.

[196] Hartington to Granville, n.d. [probably Apr. 1881], PRO 30/29/22A/3. For other Whig views of the Land Bill, cf. Kimberley to Ripon, 12 Apr. 1881, BL Add. MSS 43522, fo. 263; Selborne to Lord Wolmer, 9 May 1881, 2nd Earl of Selborne MSS, 91, fo. 91; Northbrook to Halifax, 30 July 1881, Hickleton MSS, A4/54a.

have been equally clear that, even if Gladstone did retire, his restlessness was sure to bring him back into the field, where he would fatally undermine a Hartington administration. In the circumstances, Hartington evidently thought it better that Gladstone should be kept in his place, where he could continue to exercise a restraining influence over the Radicals, until compelling reasons for retirement arose. Reginald Brett noted of his chief, in November 1882, that he 'has never believed that Mr. Gladstone would be allowed to retire, whatever he might desire to do'.[197] This was at a time when the Prime Minister was indulging in his periodic contemplation of retirement, and Hartington had already written a letter warning him, in forceful terms, of the disastrous consequences which his departure would have:

as to the effect of your retirement upon the party, I feel bound to state my own clear and distinct opinion. I think the leadership of the House of Commons in its present temper an impossibility for anyone but yourself. The advanced section, which forms the strength, if not the majority of the party, would require stronger measures from any successor than it would from you—measures in which I should certainly not be prepared to lead them. And if any other leader should attempt to lead, I do not think that the tie—already strained—which unites the moderate section with the party would hold for a moment.

He then directed his argument onto the question of parliamentary procedure, which was of special concern to the Prime Minister at that time, as proof of 'how unfit and how indisposed I am to take charge of legislation—especially in regard to Ireland as I conceive you anticipate as necessary, and which certainly the advanced party have been led to expect, and I more than doubt whether I should be justified in attempting to resume the leadership in the House of Commons under such circumstances'. This was a clear warning that if Gladstone wished to see particular measures passed, they would have to be done under his own auspices, for Hartington would not tackle them and would make it impossible for any other Liberal leader to do so:

It would be no sacrifice to me to see it [the leadership] placed in the hands of others who would not feel the same difficulties, but I cannot pretend to think that such an arrangement would have any prospect of permanence . . . I cannot feel a doubt in my own mind that your retirement would lead to the

---

[197] Political Memorandum, 21 Nov. 1882, Esher MSS, 10/5.

speedy if not the immediate dissolution of the government and of the present Liberal majority.[198]

His anxiety that Gladstone should continue was demonstrated in more practical terms a month later, during a ministerial reshuffle, when Hartington went out of his way to facilitate Dilke's admission to the Cabinet by persuading J. G. Dodson to relinquish the Local Government Board.[199]

The crisis over the franchise question in December 1883 illustrates the way in which Hartington intentionally exploited Gladstone's authority in order to 'muzzle' the Radicals. During the autumn, Gladstone, unwilling as usual to commit himself to a lengthy extension of his time in office, had inclined towards a mode of procedure whereby a County Franchise Bill for the whole of the United Kingdom would be introduced alone, with the Redistribution Bill being delayed until after his retirement.[200] Hartington objected to this proposal on two grounds. Firstly, he disliked the prospect of proceeding by means of a 'single-barrelled Reform Bill', which he regarded as 'a rather lazy electioneering trick'.[201] The separation of franchise from redistribution, Hartington believed, was 'almost certain to postpone the latter to another Parliament', and he evidently feared that, after a general election, the Radicals would be in a stronger position to demand an extensive redistribution measure: 'if that Parliament should happen to be elected by the new voters in the old constituencies, I do not see how it is possible to form any estimate of the probable result'.[202] Secondly, and of at least equal concern, Hartington was apprehensive about the likely consequences of a county franchise measure in Ireland, given the prevailing social conditions in that country.[203]

Hartington's fear, almost certainly, was that a simple Franchise Bill for the United Kingdom, being so advantageous from the point of view of the Radicals and the Parnellites, was likely to encourage these

[198] Hartington to Gladstone, 12 Nov. 1882, BL Add. MSS 44146, fo. 101, in Holland, *Devonshire*, i. 377–8.

[199] Hartington to Gladstone, 18 Dec., 20 Dec. (copy, telegram), 20 Dec., 22 Dec. 1882, BL Add. MSS 44146, fos. 132, 136, 137, 140.

[200] Granville to Hartington, n.d. [Sept. 1883?], Devonshire MSS, 340.1372.

[201] Hartington to Spencer, 18 Oct. 1883, in Gordon, *Spencer Papers*, pp. 252–3.

[202] Hartington to Gladstone, 24 Oct. 1883, BL Add. MSS 44146, fo. 222, in Holland, *Devonshire*, i. 395–6.

[203] Ibid. See also his letter of 6 Nov., ibid., fo. 228, asking Gladstone for further information.

two groups to co-operate in a common cause which would have the effect of considerably weakening the power of the Whigs to resist them in a future parliament.[204] Clearly, it was essential for Hartington to induce the Prime Minister to agree to a more definite commitment which would effectively tie the Radicals' hands. However, at the Cabinet on 22 November, he had been isolated in his opposition to procedure by means of a separate Franchise Bill for the whole of the United Kingdom (Spencer, the Lord Lieutenant, favoured the inclusion of Ireland in the bill), and he could only state afterwards that he needed more time in which to consider the matter.[205]

Fortunately, a catalyst was provided by Chamberlain's speech to the annual meeting of the National Liberal Federation at Bristol, on 26 November, which, in its forceful advocacy of the separation of franchise from redistribution and the inclusion of Ireland within the franchise arrangements (matters on which the Cabinet had made no final decision), fully confirmed the fear that the Radicals were angling for Nationalist support. Hartington, who was speaking at Manchester the same day, learned of Chamberlain's utterances just beforehand, and responded by emphasizing the difficulties posed by Ireland and redistribution to any settlement of the franchise question.[206]

With this public advertisement of the differing views of the Whig and Radical leaders, there followed a political drama acted out at the highest level without the knowledge of the general public. It leaves the distinct impression of a heavily contrived performance, at least as far as the two principal actors, who might have been reading from scripts, were concerned. Hartington opened with a letter to the Prime Minister, several days after the Manchester speech, regretting that his differences with his colleagues had been disclosed prematurely as a result of Chamberlain's utterances, but emphasising, at the same time, that he had no intention of retreating from his position as the public now understood it:

[204] In fact, Dilke was approached by the Irish with an offer of support for the Franchise Bill, in return for permission to hold public meetings, and he conveyed this offer to Gladstone: Dilke's diary, 7, 9 Nov. 1883, BL Add. MSS 43925.

[205] For the Cabinet meeting, see Granville to Spencer, 23 Nov. 1883, in Gordon, *Spencer Papers*, p. 255. Cf. Hartington to Gladstone, 23 Nov. 1883, BL Add. MSS 44146, fo. 233.

[206] See *The Times*, 27 Nov. 1883, pp. 7, 10, for reports of these speeches.

There seems to be now no alternative for me, between abandoning the position which I have publicly, perhaps prematurely, taken up, and sooner or later separating myself from the Government.

I do not think it is possible for me to take the former course without so weakening my position in the Country as to prevent my being of any further service to the Government . . .

I will not in this letter discuss the other alternative, although it seems to me to be the inevitable one. I would rather wait to hear your opinion on what I have already written . . . [I hope] you will be inclined to agree with me that after what has taken place, it would not be for the credit of the Government, or for my own, that I should now, even if it were possible, recede from the position which I have taken up.[207]

In effect, Hartington was inviting Gladstone to devise some arrangement which would allow the crown prince to save face and avoid banishment from the kingdom. The process of establishing exactly what Hartington was prepared to accept would prove to be a lengthy one, however, as ministers were dispersing for the Christmas holiday. Gladstone initially delegated to Granville the task of communicating personally with Hartington in London,[208] but with the latter 'talk[ing] rather freely to Harcourt and other colleagues',[209] a conciliation bandwagon was soon on the road: Harcourt and Lord Richard Grosvenor, the chief whip, spent the evening of the eighteenth and morning of the nineteenth of December at Chatsworth, where Hartington had retreated, and then, joining up with Childers at Crewe station, they went on to Hawarden where, on the morning of the twentieth, Gladstone was at last 'got . . . thoroughly to feel the great seriousness of the situation'.[210] Harcourt and Grosvenor informed Gladstone that, in their assessment, Hartington's difficulty amounted to a 'disinclination to· have the chief responsibility for dealing with redistribution after franchise has been disposed of', and, accordingly, that if the Premier was prepared to extend his personal commitment to the government for a period sufficient to deal with redistribution as well as franchise, Hartington 'might not object to the severance of the two'.[211]

[207] Hartington to Gladstone, 2 Dec. 1883, BL Add. MSS 44146, fo. 235, in Holland, *Devonshire*, i. 396–7.

[208] Granville had two meetings with Hartington, on 12, 13 Dec.: Granville to Gladstone, 12, 14 Dec. 1883, in Ramm (ed.) *Gladstone–Granville Correspondence, 1876–1886*, ii. 124, 127–8.

[209] Granville to Gladstone, 14 Dec. 1883, ibid. ii. 127–8.

[210] Harcourt to his wife, 19, 20 Dec. 1883 (typescripts), Harcourt MSS, Box 741.

[211] Gladstone to Granville, 20 Dec. 1883, in Ramm (ed.), *Gladstone–Granville Correspondence, 1876–1886*, ii. 133–4.

With signs that Gladstone was prepared to meet Hartington's wishes by giving a pledge to stay on and settle the redistribution measure, Granville argued that a great point had been gained.[212] But Hartington, now staying at Kimbolton with the Duchess of Manchester, was not yet ready to settle, as he indicated to Harcourt on the twenty-fourth:

Of course I am grateful to Mr. Gladstone for being willing to consider the possibility of remaining to deal with the redistribution Bill. But that can hardly be expected to remove all my difficulties, till I know on what principles he intends to deal with it. Nor does it remove the Irish difficulty. However, no doubt it offers the possibility of an arrangement, if there is any real agreement amongst us, as to what is to follow the Franchise Bill.[213]

Hartington's position, as stated in a memorandum written on Christmas Day and sent to Gladstone on the twenty-seventh with an accompanying letter, was that if there could not be a comprehensive franchise and redistribution measure at once, then the very least that he required was 'that the Cabinet should agree in the principles of the Redistribution Bill which they will introduce in the next Session, and that these should be stated by Mr. Gladstone in such a way as to bind every member of the Cabinet'.[214] On this point, Hartington was hopeful of an agreement, but there remained the question of Ireland, where he saw no means of reconciling his views with those of the rest of his colleagues, believing as he did that the inclusion of Ireland in the Franchise Bill, without some provision for minority representation, would 'have the effect of strengthening the party of rebellion, and of discouraging if not crushing the remaining supporters of order in Ireland'.[215]

Gladstone, in his reply, stated that he was willing to consider some personal guarantee as to the extent of the redistribution of seats, but gave no sign of being prepared to enter into any specific commitment on the question of minority representation for Ireland.[216] There then

[212] Granville to Hartington, 23 Dec. 1883, PRO 30/29/28.
[213] Hartington to Harcourt, 24 Dec. 1883, Harcourt MSS, Box 79.
[214] Hartington's memorandum, 25 Dec. 1883, BL Add. MSS 44146, fo. 258.
[215] Hartington to Gladstone, 27 Dec. 1883, ibid., fo. 254.
[216] Gladstone to Hartington, 29 Dec. 1883 (copy), ibid., fo. 267. It might be noted here that, had Irish redistribution been planned on anything like a population basis, then Ireland would have lost about half of her 103 seats because of the depopulation that had occurred since the famine of the 1840s. The government's unwillingness to even consider such a measure was doubtless due to fear of obstruction from the home-rule party in parliament, and perhaps also of civil disorder in Ireland. It was presumably for this reason that Hartington made his stand on the question of minority representation, rather than on a proposal for reducing the number of Irish seats.

followed an 'indifferent' meeting between Hartington and the Prime Minister in Downing Street on New Year's Eve,[217] after which Hartington evidently came to the conclusion that he had extracted all the concessions he could realistically hope for. On 2 January, he wrote accepting Gladstone's offer to make a statement of his own views on redistribution, when the Franchise Bill was introduced in the House of Commons, which would leave minority representation as an open question.[218]

On the whole, Hartington professed himself to be satisfied with what he had achieved. Having 'persuaded' Gladstone to accept the responsibility for the redistribution scheme as well as the Franchise Bill, he had then secured the promise of a parliamentary statement of the Premier's own very moderate views on redistribution (he was opposed to equal electoral districts and to large-scale disfranchisement)[219] which, though not committing the Cabinet, nevertheless committed him—'and I am not much afraid of what Chamberlain and company could do in opposition to him'.[220] Allowing that a Franchise Bill was unavoidable, Hartington had at least ensured that Chamberlain's hands were tied as to redistribution, so that there was no danger of a sweeping measure being carried after a general election on the new franchise; and though Ireland was to be included in the Franchise Bill, the idea of minority representation had, at any rate, been kept alive. In the circumstances, he felt justified in thinking that he 'could [not] have refused to accept what I have got'.[221] But it is most unlikely, in spite of the fears of mediators like Granville and Harcourt, that he ever seriously intended to resign on this occasion. Hartington's gruff and indifferent manner easily led people into supposing that he was incapable of deception, and perhaps only Gladstone recognized the astute game of bluff that was being played.

However shrewd and realistic Hartington's tactics may have been, there can be no doubt that he felt frustrated with his position. Lord Derby's survey of his Cabinet colleagues in November 1884 noted of Hartington that his 'observations are frequent, but generally mere

---

[217] Edward Hamilton to Horace Seymour, 31 Dec. 1883, Glynne–Gladstone MSS.
[218] Hartington to Gladstone, 2 Jan. 1884, BL Add. MSS 44147, fo. 1.
[219] Hartington to the Duke of Devonshire, 14 Jan. 1884, Devonshire MSS, 340.1401, in Holland, *Devonshire*, i. 402–4.
[220] Hartington to Brett, 4 Jan. 1884, Esher MSS, 10/12.
[221] Ibid.

growls of dissent. He does not like his situation, and makes the fact evident.'[222] Hartington felt, acutely, the charge that he had failed to protect the interests of the Whigs, and had merely allowed them to be dragged at the Radicals' heels,[223] and he seems increasingly to have welcomed the prospect of being released from the ties of office.[224] Indeed, he had consoled himself, at the time of his acquiescence in the Franchise Bill, with the thought that the government was unlikely to survive for long, and might well fall before the Franchise and Redistribution Bills could be carried.[225]

All this would suggest that the prospects for Liberal unity after Gladstone's retirement were bleak, and in moments of exasperation, such as those caused by the Cabinet crises over Irish coercion in the winter of 1880–1, Hartington was to be found expressing the belief that a split must come, and that when it did he would be willing to take responsibility only for the leadership of the Whigs.[226] However, against such sentiments must be balanced the fact that Hartington's sense of duty was exceptionally strong, and that, against his own better judgement, he ultimately acquiesced in such measures as the Irish Land Act of 1881 and the decision to evacuate the Sudan in 1885. Furthermore, he had already proved—and was to prove again—his ability to rise to the occasion. It is interesting to note, for instance, the success of Hartington's performance during the last part of the 1880 parliamentary session, when he acted again as leader while Gladstone was absent through illness. According to the *Annual Register*, 'The opinion was universally expressed . . . that he had established a reputation as a first-rate Parliamentary leader', by the determination with which he pushed through the government's legislative programme in the face of Irish Nationalist and Fourth Party obstructionism.[227] Speaker Brand also noted, in his summary of that session, that 'Hartington gained much credit and popularity in his leadership of the House . . . He is more at home and animated; and his position is much strengthened on both sides of the House.'[228]

---

[222] Lord Derby's diary, 27 Nov. 1884, Derby MSS.
[223] Lewis Harcourt's diary, 14 May 1885, Harcourt MSS.
[224] e.g. Cooke and Vincent, (eds.), *Carlingford's Journal*, p. 94 (25 Apr. 1885).
[225] Hartington to the Duke of Devonshire, 14 Jan. 1884, Devonshire MSS, 340.1401, in Holland, *Devonshire*, i. 402–4.
[226] See Brett's diary, 24 Nov. 1880, Esher MSS, 2/5; also 2 Jan. 1881, ibid. 2/6.
[227] *Annual Register* for 1880, pp. 101–2.
[228] Speaker Brand's diary, Sept. 1880, Hampden MSS.

The arrangement that would probably have best suited Hartington was one where he succeeded Gladstone as leader of the Liberal
party in opposition. Given that Ireland and its MPs continued to
pose the greatest threat to the maintenance of a stable Liberal
administration, it would have been to the Whigs' advantage to assist
in the implementation of a bi-partisan policy by offering a Conservative government the support necessary to carry the appropriate
measures to deal with obstructionism in parliament and lawlessness
in Ireland. Hartington's strategy in relation to the Irish Nationalists,
in other words, would have been similar to that which was apparently being contemplated before the general election of 1880.
Evidently he was thinking along these lines in the summer of 1883,
before it became clear that county franchise was going to be the
immediate issue confronting the Liberal ministry. According to his
private secretary's account of a conversation with him, Hartington
expressed great dissatisfaction with his position and indicated that
he might not be able to remain in the government for very much
longer. He complained about the manner in which the Liberals had
expedited their legislative business 'by an arrangement with Parnell'
which he could not tolerate again. Gladstone, he was aware, had
'views about Ireland—so have Chamberlain and Dilke—which I do
not share', and he 'could not agree to any further compromises with
the disloyal party'. Hartington suspected that it was Gladstone's
intention to introduce an Irish local government bill, which he would
find impossible to support:

BRETT. Your idea is a Coalition between the moderate parties on both sides
against the Irish?

HARTINGTON. Yes. There is no serious *opposition by one English party to
the other*. If I were leader of the opposition in a new Parliament to a Tory
Government, I should be inclined to give them a general support on
Foreign questions and a cordial support against the Irish. The Irish
Nationalist Party are our enemies nowadays.[229]

With the Liberals out of office, and Hartington once again in
possession of the authority of the official leader, the Whigs might

[229] Brett's diary, 1 Sept. 1883, Esher MSS, 2/6, recording a conversation in
London on 25 Aug. The accusation about a secret deal between the government and
the home rulers was repeated by Cotes, a junior whip: W. C. Cartwright's diary, 21
Sept. 1883, Cartwright MSS, Box 101. According to Jones, *The Politics of Reform*,
p. 43, such complaints arose from the government's decision to withdraw its
Irish Constabulary Bill.

also have been more strongly placed to resist the Radicals. As in the late 1870s, Chamberlain and other Radicals would have found it much more difficult to pursue schismatic tactics in the face of a respected Whig leadership representing the 'official' Liberal party, rather than just a section of it in a Cabinet supposedly held together by Gladstone. The opportunity to force Hartington's hand, by aligning with Gladstone, would have disappeared, and the Radicals would have had no alternative between coming to terms with the Whigs and risking their own political ruin by trying to destroy them.[230]

Further doubts about the inevitability of a Liberal schism, after Gladstone's retirement, arise when we consider the nature of the threat posed to the authority of Hartington and the Whigs by 'Radicalism' during the early 1880s. Contrary to the view of one American scholar,[231] the threat to the Whigs cannot be understood simply in terms of the existence of a dynamic and numerically powerful group of back-bench Radicals determined to sweep away the Whigs and take control of the Liberal party. In practice, the complexity both of major political issues and of the Liberal party itself make it impossible to use parliamentary division lists as a means of isolating a large group of 'Radical' MPs with a distinct and coherent identity of their own over a range of issues.[232] Of course, the difficulty in quantifying parliamentary Radicalism in any meaningful way should not lead us to underestimate the significance, or at least the nuisance value, of a body of back-bench opinion characterized by its dislike of social privilege and its distrust of the Executive, but the libertarian attitudes that might, for example, provoke protests from below the gangway against the foreign and

---

[230] Frank Hill saw the danger that the Liberals might be 'split up into an official or moderate Liberal party, and a critical and semi-hostile radical wing', Hill to Dilke, 5 Oct. 1884, BL Add. MSS 43898, fo. 74.

[231] T. W. Heyck, *The Dimensions of British Radicalism: The Case of Ireland, 1874–1895* (Illinois, 1974), 3–21, 237–42.

[232] For a detailed critique of Dr Heyck's methodology, see my thesis, 'Gladstone and Whiggery: A Study in Liberal Leadership and Politics, 1874–1886' (Cambridge Ph.D., 1984), 194–204. In many cases, there were considerable differences of opinion as to what MPs were voting for when they supported various motions. It is interesting to note that of the forty-nine 'Whigs' whom I have listed in Appendix II, twelve voted for Willis's motion (21 Mar. 1884) to remove the bishops from the House of Lords, and twenty-four voted for Lawson's resolution (15 June 1881) on 'local option'—two divisions which figure prominently on Heyck's shortlist.

colonial policy of the Gladstone ministry[233] were not of the kind best suited to producing constructive solutions to problems nearer to home. Indeed, what is most striking about the parliamentary 'Radicalism' of the early 1880s is its inability to evolve a positive programme even in relation to such crucial issues as English land and Ireland.[234]

If there was a challenge to Hartington and the Whigs from the 'left' in the early 1880s, this was to be found in the endeavours on the part of a small coterie of Radicals, dominated by Joseph Chamberlain, to impose their own particular version of 'Radicalism' upon the Liberal party as a whole. Chamberlain's principal allies in parliament were Dilke, who was appointed Foreign Under-secretary in April 1880 and entered the Cabinet as President of the Local Government Board in December 1882, and Jesse Collings, a fellow Birmingham politician who had succeeded Chamberlain as the President of the National Liberal Federation; while Trevelyan, Shaw Lefevre, and Courtney, all of whom were appointed to junior office on or soon after the formation of the Gladstone ministry, were less intimately connected. Of equal importance were Chamberlain's journalist friends John Morley, who edited the *Fortnightly Review* and the *Pall Mall Gazette* before entering the Commons in February 1883, and Morley's successor at the *Fortnightly*, T. H. S. Escott, who was going through a Radical phase but later reverted to his original Conservatism.

In no sense could the Chamberlain group be regarded as repre-

---

[233] Henry Richard's resolution (29 Apr. 1881) alerting the House of Commons to the danger of the power of British representatives abroad, which secured fifty-two Liberal votes, was an implicit criticism of Gladstone's failure to reverse the policies of Beaconsfield. The largest revolt of all took place on John Morley's amendment (27 Feb. 1885) criticising the military intervention in the Sudan. Sixty-seven Liberals voted for this amendment.

[234] It is instructive to note that in the age of Henry George and A. R. Wallace, the only significant Liberal initiative on the English land question during the parliament of 1880–5 was Broadhurst's Leaseholders Enfranchisement Bill (19 Mar. 1884), which proposed that leaseholders who had held a house or cottage with no more than three acres of land for a continuous period of twenty years should be allowed to acquire the freehold through compulsory purchase. The bill's supporters included a dozen Conservatives, in addition to the seventy-seven Liberals. With regard to Ireland, the number of Liberal MPs who regularly entered the division lobby with the home rulers was extremely small in the early 1880s, no more than fifteen or twenty. Only the infringement of civil liberties resulting from the government's coercive legislation occasionally led to more significant Radical protests, as is reflected in the forty-six votes for Stansfeld's amendment (15 Feb. 1881) requiring that warrants covering crimes other than treason should be specific as to time and place. Generally speaking, it seems fair to say that it was not until 1886 that most Radicals discovered Ireland as an appropriate object for their empathy.

sentative of 'mainstream' Radicalism, which, in so far as it can be
defined, was more likely to be identified with the older tradition
embodied in John Bright.[235] It was to be primarily by harnessing new
sources of extra-parliamentary opinion, rather than by acting as the
leaders of a substantial Radical 'wing' of the existing parliamentary
party, that Chamberlain and his friends sought to consolidate their
position within the Liberal hierarchy. Morley, for instance, in conversation with Lord Derby after the 1880 general election, maintained that the 'extreme or radical party', with which he identified
himself, was 'some 25 in number' in the new House of Commons,[236]
and his close friend Frederic Harrison, the positivist, seems to have
had a similar idea, for he urged Dilke to assume the leadership of a
group of 'thirty or forty' Radicals, 'such men as [Ashton Dilke],
Bryce, Rogers, Davey . . . practically radicals of a very different type
from the Lusk or Peter Rylands type of old stick-in-the-mud
radicals'.[237] There was no belief that the 'crotchet-mongers' below
the gangway could form the basis of an organized Radical party,[238]
and the self-appointed function of the Chamberlainites, as indicated
by Escott's article in the *Fortnightly Review* for July 1883, was to
provide the discipline necessary to extract the essence of Radicalism
from the anarchic mass of individual Radical opinions, and so turn it
into a credible political force:

Radicalism is not so much represented as it is burlesqued by politicians of the
stamp of Sir Wilfrid Lawson, Mr Cowen, Mr Storey, and Mr Henry
Labouchere. The tendency of each of these gentlemen, and others who could
be mentioned, is to identify it with some hobby or craze of their own, and by
so doing frequently to discredit it . . . We might perhaps say that Radicalism
is the *general* opinion of the most advanced section of the Liberal party for
the time being. The epithet italicised is of importance. The mere circum-
stance that a man holds extreme views on some single or group of subjects,
gives him no claim to be considered a Radical. Nor is it necessary for a
Radical to hold every extreme view which might be put forward by any

---

[235] It is indicative of the superior personal influence of Bright, who was a member
of the Cabinet until July 1882, when he resigned because of the government's
interventionist policy in Egypt, that on the occasions when Chamberlain and Dilke
contemplated resignation, e.g. over the question of coercion in Ireland and over the
government's policy towards the Transvaal, they were anxious to align themselves
with Bright and not have to go out alone. See Dilke's diary, 15 Nov. 1880, 2, 15 Mar.
1881, BL Add. MSS 43924.
[236] Lord Derby's diary, 7 Apr. 1880, Derby MSS.
[237] Harrison to Dilke, 5 Apr. 1880, BL Add. MSS 43898, fo. 179.
[238] Cf. Morley to Chamberlain, 12 Apr. 1880, Chamberlain MSS, JC5/54/311.

clique of Utopian Progressivists or speculative reformers. Above all things, Radicalism is a body of practical doctrines ready for immediate expression in legislation, seeking first and most earnestly the reforms which are nearest at hand and easiest to conclude. It is not the creed of mere theorists, but is practical alike in its objects and its methods.[239]

Like all good Radicals, the Chamberlain set reserved their greatest contempt for others of their kind, and in particular those 'windbags', like Fawcett and Mundella, whose aspirations to high office threatened their own speedy advancement.[240] It followed that the Chamberlainites were interested not in filling the Cabinet with as many Radicals as they possibly could, but in concentrating the representation of Radicalism, at the higher levels of the government, in their own hands. Thus, when the possibility of a Cabinet reshuffle was in the air, in the winter of 1882, from which Dilke hoped to be admitted at last to the Cabinet, Reginald Brett found that 'he objects to any other possible *radical* in the Cabinet. He would prefer Goschen.' The reasoning was simple: 'It is obvious that Dilke and Chamberlain *acting together* would be more influential than they could hope to be with a radical colleague fighting for his own hand.'[241]

Whatever the limitations of the Whigs, then, it was recognized that the traditional, aristocratic section of the party remained an indispensable source of human material for the Liberal front bench. Dilke, in noting the paucity of first-rate men of administrative potential below the gangway, had posed the unavoidable question, during the Cabinet crisis of November 1880: 'Where is the material for the next Liberal Cabinet[?] If we extinguish the present Whigs, and become the next Whigs ourselves—where are our men[?]'[242]

---

[239] 'The Future of the Radical Party', *Fortnightly Review*, 34 (July 1883), 1–11. This important article was the prelude to the *Radical Programme*, which is discussed in ch. 6.

[240] Dilke's diary, 23 Nov. 1880, BL Add. MSS 43924. For Chamberlain's gall at the possibility of being passed over for Cabinet rank by Fawcett or Mundella in Apr. 1880, see his letter to Morley, 11 Apr. 1880, Chamberlain MSS, JC5/54/308.

[241] Political memorandum, 20 Nov. 1882, Esher MSS, 10/5. Dilke's admission to the Cabinet caused great dismay to Trevelyan, however: 'As far as I can judge from the papers . . . it is understood that Chamberlain and Dilke are in some way accepted as the representatives of pronounced Liberalism, and that they have a claim to a position in the party entirely different from that which I have earned. My own view is that I have claims, both of seniority, in party services, and in the estimation of the party and the House, to stand with them . . . I will venture to say that [Gladstone's] taking Dilke without me, as a representative of the ideas embodied in Household Suffrage, has perhaps done my business as far as an influential position in the party is concerned', Trevelyan to Harcourt, 31 Dec. 1882 (typescript), Harcourt MSS, Box 725.

[242] Dilke's diary, 23 Nov. 1880, BL Add. MSS 43924.

The answer had to be to compromise with the 'present Whigs', and whenever the possibility arose that Hartington might take Gladstone's place, as in July 1882 and January 1885, the Chamberlain group were willing enough to consider the terms on which they might come to an arrangement with him.[243] The essential pragmatism of Chamberlain's strategy is illustrated by a letter to Henry Labouchere, a prominent back-bench Radical who wished to see the Whigs driven out of the party and into the arms of the Conservatives, where they truly belonged:

you must remember that the only chance for the sheep is getting the wolves to attack the foxes and vice versa. If you set all the 'ferae naturae' against you at one time, they will make common cause and the sheep will have a good deal to suffer.

Therefore I am for step by step reform and not for showing more of your hand than is necessary to gain the confidence of those whom we want to serve.[244]

Chamberlain seems to have accepted that the Whigs had a legitimate role to play which was necessary for the success of the Liberal party—at least, the party could not do without them—but he was anxious that Hartington should offer a positive style of leadership. This view was expressed in a revealing conversation with Granville, also at the time of the franchise crisis in December 1883, which Granville related to Hartington: ' "What moderate Liberals want of Hartington is that he should be a guarantee and not a drag". This phrase he repeated several times . . . I understand it to mean that you were to save them from extreme measures but to help them to get those which were generally desired by the party.'[245] In fact, Chamberlain's main complaint about Hartington was not the moderation of his views, or the likelihood of his being the next Prime Minister, but his tendency to adopt the role of the obstructionist, on behalf of the moderates, rather than behaving as the future leader of the whole party.[246]

Chamberlain's pragmatism was allied, however, to a strong element of opportunism, and it was clear that, so long as Gladstone

[243] Cf. Dilke's diary, 7, 10 July 1882, BL Add. MSS 43925; Dilke to Chamberlain, 1 Jan. 1885, Chamberlain MSS, JC5/24/90; Chamberlain to Dilke, 5 Jan. 1885, ibid. JC5/24/397; Lewis Harcourt's diary, 4, 5 Jan. 1885, Harcourt MSS; Brett to Wolseley, 9 Jan. 1885, Esher MSS, 2/7.

[244] Chamberlain to Labouchere, 28 Dec. 1883, Chamberlain MSS, JC5/50/22.

[245] Granville to Hartington, 20 Dec. 1883, PRO 30/29/28.

[246] Cf. Chamberlain to Dilke, 29 Nov. 1883, Chamberlain MSS, JC5/24/360.

remained in political life, there would always be possibilities for outmanœuvring Hartington and the Whigs. One such possibility, which Chamberlain toyed with in February 1885, after the death of General Gordon at Khartoum, was that Hartington might be left in charge of a 'patriotic' government committed to the continued occupation of the Sudan, while Chamberlain and his friends withdrew along with Gladstone and offered the government an 'independent' support.[247] Similarly, in July 1882, when it seemed that Gladstone might resign because of his distaste for the impending military intervention in Egypt, Chamberlain and Dilke had been alarmed by the prospect of belonging to a government which was all too likely to be undermined by an unmuzzled ex-Premier. Dilke's account of a discussion with Chamberlain at this time provides an admirable summing-up of the Radicals' position: 'we agreed that we could not join a new government if Mr. Gladstone were outside it in the House of Commons, but that the case might be different if he quitted political life, or went to the Lords—and if we were satisfied with the new bill of fare'.[248] Clearly, while Gladstone remained an active force in politics, there could be no question of Hartington forming a stable Liberal government. Whether, on Gladstone's departure, Hartington and Chamberlain could have established a reasonable working relationship, is one of the great imponderables of late nineteenth-century politics. It is possible to detect certain areas of policy, notably concerning foreign and imperial matters, where there was a great deal of common ground between Hartington and the younger school of Radicals, and this might have provided the basis for an accommodation along 'Liberal Imperialist' lines. There were indeed occasions during Gladstone's second ministry when Hartington co-operated with Chamberlain and Dilke, as, for example, when they tried to stir the Cabinet into action over Egypt in June 1882, and later, when they wanted a military demonstration at Suakim in support of General Gordon.[249] On the other hand, given

[247] Chamberlain to Dilke, 25 Feb. 1885, ibid. JC5/24/412.
[248] Dilke's diary, 7 July 1882, BL Add. MSS 43925.
[249] See Dilke's diary, 15, 21 June 1882, BL Add. MSS 43924, and 7, 8, 12 Feb. 1884, BL Add. MSS 43926. For examples of Chamberlain and Dilke's support for colonial annexations in Africa and the Pacific, see Dilke's diary, 25 Mar. 1884, 6 Aug. 1884, 22 Sept. 1884, ibid. For Chamberlain's bellicose attitude towards France and Germany, see Lewis Harcourt's diary, 3, 20, 22 Jan. 1885, Harcourt MSS. Of course, Chamberlain and Dilke's attitude represented a potentially fundamental point of division between themselves and Radical associates with a 'Little Englander' mentality, like Morley and Courtney.

Chamberlain's habit of overestimating his own strength, and with our retrospective knowledge of his dismal record as a promoter of harmony and unity, it must be doubted whether serious conflict could have been avoided entirely. The history of 'Hartingtonian Liberalism' would surely have been characterized by the perpetual tension between Whigs and Radicals, punctuated by occasional periods of disruption followed by reconciliation.

6

The Crisis of 1885

At the beginning of 1885, it appeared that politics in Britain was about to enter a new phase. The Gladstone ministry, contrary to many expectations, had survived the 1884 session of parliament, and, in so doing, it had ensured the passage of both its Franchise and Redistribution Bills, thanks to a closet agreement with the Conservative leaders.[1] An entirely new and unpredictable electoral dispensation was thus created. The inevitable extension of the borough household franchise to the counties (an arrangement in which Ireland was included) added at least two million adult males to the electorate, and this was accompanied, at the Conservatives' insistence, by a sweeping redistribution measure which rendered worthless the guarantees Hartington had extracted from Gladstone during the winter of 1883–4. In all, some 142 seats were to be redistributed, but worse still, the new system was to involve the widespread creation of single-member constituencies, which T. H. S. Escott, in an article entitled 'The Revolution of 1884', predicted would put an end to the electoral co-operation between Whigs and Radicals and result in the extinction of the former.[2] It was certainly true that the Whigs themselves feared the new arrangements would work heavily to the Radicals' advantage: 'Goschen . . . and other moderate Liberals' were reported as regarding the Redistribution Bill with 'the strongest aversion . . . forsee[ing] the most fatal results from it',[3] and Hartington expressed the opinion that the composition of the next House of Commons would be *very* Radical'.[4] To Lord Derby, it was clear that after the next general election, which seemed likely to take place before the end of the year, there would be 'a new world, an unknown world, possibly a world which some of us will not care to explore', and that the intervening period would be 'a very critical interval'.[5]

[1] See Andrew Jones, *The Politics of Reform 1884* (Cambridge, 1972), 196–222.
[2] 'The Revolution of 1884', *Fortnightly Review*, 37 (Jan. 1885), 1–10.
[3] Albert Grey to Lord Halifax, 8 Dec. 1884, Hickleton MSS, A4/84.
[4] Arthur Elliot's diary, 14 Dec. 1884, Elliot MSS.
[5] Derby to Granville, 5 Jan. 1885, PRO 30/29/22A/5.

The crucial question, during 1885, was whether Chamberlain would succeed in pulling off a coup at the Whigs' expense in the way Gladstone had in 1880. With opportunism at a premium, Chamberlain was not slow to assert his position within the new political system, making three speeches in January in which, while taking care to avoid specific commitments, he elaborated on the kind of policies which he believed the new electorate would require. His agenda included manhood suffrage, the abolition of plural voting, the payment of MPs, the extension of local government to the counties, powers for local authorities to purchase land compulsorily in order to create smallholdings and improve working-class housing, and also graduated taxation—which introduced the notion that the owners of property must pay a 'ransom' for the security of their possessions.[6] In private political circles, meantime, he was predicting 'a large majority at the election', with great gains in the major cities and the possibility of inroads into the counties where, he claimed, 'the Tories are just beginning to find that they are not sure of the support of the labourers'.[7] Similarly, at a dinner shortly after the first Birmingham speech, Chamberlain was reported as having 'talked in a rather swaggering style about what the new electors would do: assuming that an enormous majority of them will return candidates of the ultra-democratic type'.[8]

If Goschen was going to assert himself again, as a constructive leader of moderate Liberal opinion, he had an opportunity to reply to Chamberlain in a speech planned for Edinburgh—where he hoped to be selected as the Liberal candidate—at the end of January. In this speech, Goschen condemned Radical attempts to arouse class feelings and provoke a war against capital, and sought instead to 'plead the cause of freedom against State interference'. His own programme of social reforms was, in essence, an adaptation of the earlier pre-county franchise version, designed for the specific purpose of countering Chamberlain's bid: the enfranchisement of the rural labourers had, of course, to be accepted, but he continued to advocate the creation of new local authorities as a way of instilling a sense of civic responsibility in the counties, and favoured handing

---

[6] See J. L. Garvin, *Life of Joseph Chamberlain*, i (1932), 545–58. Two of the speeches were made at Birmingham, on 5 and 29 Jan., and the other at Ipswich, on the 14th.

[7] Lewis Harcourt's diary, 5 Dec. 1884, Harcourt MSS.

[8] Lord Derby's diary, 7 Jan. 1885, Derby MSS.

over to these authorities as many duties as possible, so that things like sanitation were paid for by ratepayers rather than by taxpayers. 'It was wiser in these days of what was called State Socialism to strengthen their local authorities, and then, through them, to deal with some of those questions which in the hands of the State were so much more dangerous.' As regards the working men, Goschen looked to (undefined) forms of voluntaryism or co-operation as preferable means of betterment to interference by public officials. Finally, with regard to the land question, he favoured 'free sale' but rejected the demand for 'fair rents', and while professing a desire to see a larger number of agricultural holdings, he did not feel that this should be brought about through artificial means by local authorities.[9]

The Edinburgh speech was generally cautious, and in some re-spects rather vague, but it nevertheless served a purpose. As Goschen explained to Arthur Elliot shortly afterwards, he had been 'anxious . . . to run one reforming policy against another and not to be only negative and critical'.[10] Arguably, Goschen's 'reforming policy' did not amount to a great deal, and if implemented would probably have generated very little reforming activity at the local level, but the essential point was that he had at least asserted the existence of an avowedly Liberal alternative to the picture of the future being painted by Chamberlain, and had thus prevented the President of the Board of Trade from appearing to be the spokesman of the Liberal party as a whole.[11]

Goschen, it therefore seems, had no intention, at this stage, of breaking away from the Liberal party, and his immediate concern was rather to stake a claim for moderate Liberalism in the new political territory opened up by the franchise and redistribution measures. In a letter around this time to Sir Henry James, who had just made a speech in defence of moderate Liberalism at Bury, he maintained that 'There is nothing I should like better than that the Liberal party, as distinguished from the Radicals should show its strength, which I really believe to be very considerable: and if it does

[9] Goschen at Edinburgh (31 Jan.), Manchester Guardian, 2 Feb. 1885, p. 6.
[10] Goschen to Elliot, 6 Feb. 1885, Elliot MSS. For favourable comments on the speech, cf. Albert Grey to Halifax, 31 Jan. 1885, Hickleton MSS, A4/84, and, from a middle-of-the-road Liberal, T. R. Buchanan to Elliot, 4 Feb. 1885, Elliot MSS.
[11] Goschen's private secretary, Alfred Milner, had urged the importance of doing this in letters of 8–9 Jan., 25 Jan. 1885, Milner MSS, Box 6.

show its strength and assert itself, I think there is less risk of party distintegration than if they allow themselves always to be over-shadowed or ignored.'[12] Goschen and his young Whig friends still sometimes spoke as if they anticipated an eventual split between moderate and Radical Liberals: Albert Grey, for example, always one of the more idealistically minded of the young Whigs, looked forward to the emergence, once Gladstone was gone, of a 'counter-balancing weight . . . supplied by a crossbench party led by some man like Goschen', which would attract both Liberals and Conservatives repelled by the 'tendency of leaders of both parties to outbid each other in attempts to win favour with Demos . . . If we can only get together in the next parliament a small nucleus of men who will act together in pursuance of some Hard principles, men will quickly rally round it.'[13] Whatever the future might bring, however, the immediate problem was one of survival and consolidation within the existing party structure. This was how Lord Ebrington sought to justify to his father his wish to seek re-election to the next parlia-ment: 'moderate men will never have so good a chance as they have now with the new constituencies, whose character will be affected for some time to come by their new members'. Furthermore, 'Unless I stand for the next parliament I do not think I should be likely to be asked to stand for the next after—unless by the Tories, nor do I see what chance there is of a moderate or coalition party coming to the front, unless there is a foundation for it in the coming parliament.'[14]

In any case, the Whigs were naturally reluctant to contemplate a schism while Gladstone remained at the helm, and after his govern-ment had fallen in June, it appeared increasingly likely that he would lead the Liberal party into the forthcoming general election.[15] Their strategy, therefore, as Goschen advised Arthur Elliot in a conver-sation on 14 June, had to be based on the danger that the Liberal party would 'obtain another "Gladstonian" majority', after which

[12] Goschen to James, n.d. [but after 21 Jan. 1885], Hereford and Worcester Record Office, M45/1571. For James's speech, see *The Times*, 22 Jan. 1885, p. 7.

[13] Albert Grey to Halifax, 19 May 1885, Hickleton MSS, A4/84.

[14] Ebrington to Earl Fortescue, two letters dated 15 Feb. 1885, Fortescue MSS, FC 55. Cf. Hartington's letter to Colonel Kingscote, 21 Jan. 1885, urging him to reconsider his decision to retire: 'I cannot help saying that if you and others like you, who I am afraid may under any circumstances be fewer in the next Parliament, decline to come forward, it will be a bad prospect for those who like myself are not prepared to go every length in conciliating the new democracy', Kingscote MSS.

[15] Albert Grey to Earl Grey, 9 June 1885, Grey MSS, Box 89.

'Gladstone would retire, Chamberlain becoming his successor through the idleness or carelessness of Hartington'. It was therefore essential, in Goschen's view, to 'put [. . .] Hartington forward during this Parliament as the destined successor to Gladstone'.[16] The situation was made all the more complicated by the obvious fact that the longer Gladstone remained leader, the greater was the danger that Hartington might be summoned to the House of Lords,[17] creating a power vacuum in the Lower House which, if filled by Chamberlain, might well render Hartington's leadership untenable. For Goschen, however, the possibility of securing the reversion to the leadership in the Commons provided a powerful inducement for him to work from within the party, promoting himself as Hartington's loyal lieutenant.

Chamberlain's speeches in January were the opening shots in a battle for 'Liberal opinion' which was resumed in earnest with an intensive campaign of speeches, beginning in August and continuing through the autumn, accompanied by the *Radical Programme*—which was published early in September, not in July, as is usually stated.[18] The *Radical Programme* consisted of articles by various politicians and journalists, collected from the *Fortnightly Review*, where they had been published over a period of two years. Clearly, the idea of preparing such a 'programme' was by no means new, for it was shown in Chapter 3 that Chamberlain had planned a similar venture during the winter of 1877–8. Nor were most of the ideas outlined in 1885 particularly impressive or original. 'The main features of the programme', as Escott observed in his first article, were 'those enumerated by Mr. Chamberlain several years ago [1873] . . . under the heads of "Free Church", "Free Schools", "Free Land" and "Free Labour"'.[19] The old bones of the Radical faith were being exhumed, and occasionally reconstructed in accordance

[16] Arthur Elliot's diary, 14 June 1885, Elliot MSS.
[17] For a gloomy view of the problems Hartington's elevation was likely to cause, see Elliot to Lord Melgund, 4 Jan. 1885, Elliot MSS.
[18] C. H. D. Howard, 'Joseph Chamberlain and the Unauthorised Programme', *English Historical Review*, 65 (1950), 483–4, states that the *Radical Programme* was published in late July; Richard Jay, *Joseph Chamberlain: A Political Study* (Oxford, 1981), 112, puts it even earlier, in mid-July. D. A. Hamer, who has edited a recent reprint of *The Radical Programme 1885* (Hassocks, 1971), gives no date for its appearance. For evidence of the true date of publication, see the *Pall Mall Gazette*, 10 Sept. 1885, p. 10. Chamberlain also referred to it in his speech at Warrington, *The Times*, 9 Sept. 1885, p. 6.
[19] *Radical Programme* (ed. Hamer), p. 20.

with new ideas (such as allotments for agricultural labourers), while others which had acquired a topical interest (such as working-class housing) were grafted on.[20] Even though the principle of State intervention was frequently asserted, the details were usually left vague, and, as Howard rightly notes, the 'socialism' that was espoused tended to be of the municipal variety.[21] In the case of land policy, the issue on which, as Chamberlain had been aware for some time, Radical thinking had advanced most rapidly since 1880,[22] it emerges from his correspondence with Escott during the winter of 1883 that a projected 'article on landlords' had had to be dropped,[23] its place eventually being taken by Jesse Collings's less ambitious piece on 'The Agricultural Labourer', arguing the case for improved cottages and allotments *after* free-education and county-government reform had been enacted. Another projected article, on foreign policy, to have been written by Escott, did not materialize at all.[24] The *Radical Programme* which did emerge was a rather hurriedly improvised affair, with articles on federal government (reflecting Chamberlain's renewed interest in the Irish question) and taxation being added at the last moment,[25] and Escott's piece from January, on 'The Revolution of 1884', being used as an introduction.

[20] Cf. Jay, *Joseph Chamberlain*, pp. 112–13.

[21] Howard, *English Historical Review* (1950), 489.

[22] 'I am strongly inclined to believe that something much more drastic than Free Trade in land is looming in the near future, and I am told that the London working men are buying George and Wallace's books on land nationalisation by thousands', Chamberlain to Dilke, 31 Dec. 1882, Chamberlain MSS, JC5/24/343.

[23] Chamberlain's letter of 2 Nov. 1883 shows that Archibald Forbes had been asked to write an 'article on Landlords'. Evidently, the draft supplied by Forbes was unsatisfactory, for on 16 Nov. Chamberlain dismissed it as 'idiotic'—'it is clear you cannot rely on him and you have had a narrow escape'. A second article, presumably relating to landed property in London, had been planned as well, for Chamberlain went on in his letter of 16 Nov. to advise that 'I would certainly drop all idea of dealing with the Country property and would not touch even the London article unless you can absolutely depend on the accuracy of your informant. D. is all sensational writing say I! On the whole I am inclined to give up the idea altogether—its realisation is too risky under the circumstances.' BL Add. MSS 58777.

[24] Chamberlain wrote, on 3 Dec. 1883, urging Escott not to be in a hurry to write the article on foreign policy: 'It really is a matter of considerable difficulty to lay down anything in the nature of distinctive principles and to say how they can be applied to the varying circumstances of our Foreign relations and yet without this the article will want force and importance and can hardly be accepted as part of the programme of a party. As far as he has gone in the notes you showed me Dilke has really not at present formulated any principles. Both he and I are as you know a little Jingo', ibid.

[25] Chamberlain to Escott, 2 Nov. 1883, ibid., shows that James Stansfeld had originally been approached to write an article on finance. In the event, it was written by Francis Adams, better known as a campaigner for free, secular education.

It is hardly surprising, in the circumstances, that the articles were poorly co-ordinated and that, in his introduction to a recent reprint of the *Radical Programme*, Professor Hamer should have thought it helpful to provide an index to the whereabouts, in the articles, of particular aspects of the 'programme'.[26] But the crucial point which needs to be emphasized is that the *Radical Programme* was not an election manifesto, and that, as C. H. D. Howard has shown, Chamberlain's campaign speeches differed from it in many important respects.[27]

A closer examination of the circumstances in which the *Radical Programme* was conceived in 1883 will show why this was the case. After the Liberal victory in 1880, Chamberlain had looked forward to a rapid consolidation of the party's position through comprehensive legislation on the questions of land and the franchise, believing that these measures would 'arouse much enthusiasm—or at least . . . keep the present fire alive and if it be necessary to dissolve again after a Reform Bill we should go to the Country under the best conditions and before the present wave has spent its force'.[28] In reality, by the beginning of 1883, Chamberlain's brand of Radicalism appeared to be in a rut, as the government's uninspiring Irish and foreign policies were commanding public attention, and little interest was being shown in domestic questions.[29] Clearly, it was in Chamberlain's interest to attempt to rekindle popular enthusiasm for social reform, as a means of retrieving the government's electoral position which would, at the same time, enable him to gain the initiative in domestic politics.[30] However, as he had confessed to Morley in May, he remained perplexed as to precisely what form the new departure should take: 'I do not see my way very definitely out of the present difficulties and am consequently much disinclined to make speeches. The time is come when our Party (of 3 or 4) must have a programme and know exactly what it is aiming at. Anyone who has anything definite to propose will be sure of a hearing and has a good chance to

[26] *Radical Programme* (ed. Hamer), pp. xv–xvi.
[27] Howard, *English Historical Review* (1950), 477–91. Church disestablishment, for example, was not part of Chamberlain's election platform.
[28] Chamberlain to Harcourt, 10 Apr. 1880 (typescript), Harcourt MSS, Box 716.
[29] For the political quiescence of the time, cf. Lord Derby's diary, 24 Nov. 1882, Derby MSS; John Bright to Goldwin Smith, 7 Jan. 1883, in A. Haultain (ed.), *A Selection from Goldwin Smith's Correspondence* (1913), 142; John Morley at Newcastle, Feb. 1883, in F. Hirst (ed.), *Early Life and Letters of John Morley* (1927), ii. 160.
[30] Cf. Chamberlain to Dilke, 20 Jan. 1883, Chamberlain MSS, JC5/24/349.

be hailed as a saviour. But have we a gospel?' Chamberlain could see no use in 'trying to elevate Bankruptcy and Patents into a new dispensation', and the government's foreign and colonial policies could hardly provide a 'satisfactory text', still less so its Irish policy: 'These reflections "make for the melancholies" . . . The moral is that half policies never succeed and unfortunately in the present state of things whole policies are absolutely impracticable.'[31] The *Radical Programme*, which began to appear in the *Fortnightly* in August 1883, was obviously intended to help remedy this situation, and Chamberlain's speech to the National Liberal Federation at Bristol on 26 November, highlighted many of the subjects being dealt with in the articles.[32] But these domestic reforms were being discussed not as measures for immediate implementation, but as matters which, in Chamberlain's own opinion, would have to be dealt with once a reform of the system of parliamentary representation had been carried out. This rendered the status of the *Radical Programme* even more inferior, for it was unlikely that franchise reform could be separated from the problem of obstructionism by the Conservative-dominated House of Lords, and, in any case, it is doubtful whether Chamberlain had any wish to separate them. In fact, he had argued strongly against the idea of an early general election, to be fought on the promise of a franchise bill, when this was discussed in Cabinet in May 1883, because he believed 'it would probably end in defeat, the position he thought thoroughly unsatisfactory'.[33] During a dinner conversation with Harcourt, James, and Cotes (a junior whip) in mid-November, however, while Chamberlain still agreed with the general view that an immediate dissolution on the franchise question would lead to defeat, he was now hinting that 'if we could get up a good cry . . . we shall get in'.[34] The precise 'cry' which Chamberlain had in mind was indicated to another diarist, who dined with him a few days later, and it was then stated publicly, in a threatening speech at Wolverhampton on 4 December, in which he urged that the Liberals should adhere to their Reform Bill even if it meant a collision with the House of Lords.[35]

[31] Chamberlain to Morley, 19 May 1883, ibid. JC5/54/505.
[32] *The Times*, 27 Nov. 1883, p. 7.
[33] Lord Derby's diary, 26 May 1883, Derby MSS.
[34] Lewis Harcourt's diary, 16 Nov. 1883, Harcourt MSS.
[35] *The Times*, 5 Dec. 1883, p. 6. Cf. Arthur Elliot's diary, 22 Nov. 1883: 'should say he *wants* the Lords to throw out the [Franchise] Bill, that he may work a democratic cry against that House', Elliot MSS.

At the time of its conception, then, the *Radical Programme* was intended to play a subordinate role to the reform of the franchise, which was, in its turn, to be subordinate in the short term to that agitation against the House of Lords which alone, Chamberlain believed, could win the next general election for the Liberals. An interesting point emerges from this about Chamberlain's political methods. Professor Hamer has argued that Liberal leaders could unite the party either by devising a programme of reforms appealing to a wide range of interests, or by concentrating on a single, unifying issue into which all the other sectional interests could be submerged, and that of these two strategies Chamberlain preferred the former.[36] Franchise reform (and the agitation against the Lords to which it was related), however, provides a clear example of Chamberlain using the single issue approach, as it was presented as an essential precondition for various other reforms: 'I believe that all Liberal measures will gain by pushing forward the change in the machinery which has now become an urgent necessity.'[37] But a popular agitation on the question of franchise reform, based on the cry that the obstructionist methods of the peers were delaying other reforms which must inevitably follow, could only be credible if there was a clear idea in the public mind that there really was a traffic jam of 'Liberal measures' waiting impatiently for the green light. Chamberlain, it therefore seems, in promoting a single, unifying issue, had to accompany it with what Professor Hamer regards as its antithesis, a programme: in reality, the two could be inextricably linked.

Moreover, during the spring of 1885, by which time Chamberlain's original calculations had obviously been rendered obsolete, it seemed that the reform of local government, with special reference to Ireland, might provide an alternative single, unifying issue for the forthcoming election campaign. On a number of occasions since the late 1870s, Chamberlain had been keen to promote himself as an intermediary between the Liberal party and the Irish Nationalists,[38] in the belief that it was natural and logical for the Irishmen to work in conjunction with the 'leaders of the English democracy'.[39] In May

[36] D. A. Hamer, *Liberal Politics in the Age of Gladstone and Rosebery* (Oxford, 1972), 45–6.
[37] Chamberlain to James Beal, 15 Oct. 1883, Greater London Record Office, F/BL/3.
[38] Most notably with the so-called Kilmainham treaty in the spring of 1882: Garvin, *Chamberlain*, i. 348–63.
[39] Chamberlain to Morley, 21 Jan. 1885, Chamberlain MSS, JC5/54/598.

1885, therefore, he tried to persuade the Cabinet to agree to a new departure in Irish policy, on the basis of a plan for a Central Board in Dublin to administer local affairs, which he believed was acceptable to Parnell.[40] This proposal had to be dropped because of opposition from Hartington and a majority of the other Cabinet ministers, but in public speeches immediately after the fall of the government in June, Chamberlain continued to promote the Central Board plan as part of a programme of local government for the whole of the United Kingdom, which he presented as a necessary preliminary to other social reforms.[41] As Edward Hamilton discovered, during a dinner conversation with Chamberlain on 14 June, 'He places Local Government throughout the United Kingdom in the foreground and social questions must and will follow.'[42]

Chamberlain's attempt to establish an alliance with the Irish Nationalists, which would help to provide the impetus for the Radicalization of the Liberal party's social policies, was to end in failure by mid-July, owing to Parnell's unwillingness to co-operate. In consequence, Chamberlain was forced to change his strategy again, focusing this time on social policy itself. The content of the new 'programme' was to remain fluid for some time, however, and it is not quite accurate to see Chamberlain's speeches at Hull and Warrington in the way Howard does, as the promulgation of what came to be known as the 'unauthorized programme'—land reform, free education, and graduated taxation.[43] Chamberlain's original intention, as he informed Hartington during a conversation early in August, was to 'devote himself chiefly to land questions',[44] and this emphasis was very clear in his speech at Hull on the fifth. Free education was mentioned as an issue which he hoped would be dealt with in the next parliament, and he also advocated some form of graduated taxation, but an extensive list of land reforms was presented as the 'most important' of the issues to which he wished to

[40] For the background to the Central Board plan, see C. H. D. Howard, 'Joseph Chamberlain, Parnell and the Irish "Central Board" Scheme, 1884–5', *Irish Historical Studies*, 8 (1952–3), 324–61.

[41] Chamberlain at Islington, *The Times*, 18 June 1885, p. 7. See also his speech to the Cobden Club, *Pall Mall Gazette*, 15 June 1885, p. 6.

[42] D. W. R. Bahlman (ed.), *The Diary of Sir Edward Walter Hamilton, 1880–1885* (Oxford, 1972), ii. 884 (entry for 14 June 1885).

[43] Howard, *English Historical Review* (1950), 484–5.

[44] Hartington to Granville, 5 Aug. 1885, PRO 30/29/22A/3, in Bernard Holland, *Life of Spencer Compton, Eighth Duke of Devonshire, 1833–1908* (1911), ii. 71–2.

draw his audience's attention. In addition to 'free trade' in land, Chamberlain wished to import from Ireland two of the '3 f's', fair rents and free sale, and in cases where landlords failed to provide allotments and decent cottages for their labourers, local authorities (not yet in existence of course) were to be given powers to compulsorily purchase land for these purposes, and would only be required to pay the fair market price, regardless of the prospective value of the land.[45]

It was over a month before Chamberlain returned to the public platform, and, during the interval, Hartington delivered a speech at Waterfoot effectively (though without naming Chamberlain) throwing cold water on the entire land programme.[46] Chamberlain's retort at Warrington on 8 September was relatively mild, dismissing the moderates as 'armchair politicians' and implicitly likening Hartington to 'Rip van Winkle', but he nevertheless urged the need for Liberal unity in order to obtain a parliamentary majority independent of the Nationalists. Referring to the *Radical Programme*, which had just been published, Chamberlain asserted again that land reform was the 'most important of these proposals', but, significantly, he now moderated his position, dropping all mention of fair rents and free sale, and confining himself to the need for compulsory powers of land purchase with which to create smallholdings and allotments, and to improve the agricultural labourers' dwellings. He again expressed the hope that the next parliament would provide for free education, and then went on to mention briefly several other issues discussed in the *Radical Programme*, such as graduated taxation, the abolition of the game laws, and an inquiry into illegal appropriations of land and endowments, but added that 'I do not say that every one of these points is necessarily an article of the Liberal programme; but I do say that any attempt to exclude them from a fair and full and impartial consideration will be fatal to unity'.[47] In fact – and we shall return to this later—it was only after the publication of Gladstone's election manifesto on 18 September, which was prompted by Hartington's speech at Waterfoot, and which sided mainly with the Whig leader in terms of policy, that Chamberlain was provoked into issuing a rather rash ultimatum that he would not join

---

[45] Chamberlain at Hull, *The Times*, 6 Aug. 1885, p. 6.
[46] Hartington at Waterfoot, ibid., 31 Aug. 1885, p. 8. His speech made no mention of free education or graduated taxation.
[47] Chamberlain at Warrington, ibid., 9 Sept. 1885, p. 6.

any government which did not accept land reform, free education, and graduated taxation as part of its programme. There was an essential truth, I would suggest, in Chamberlain's later remark to Henry Labouchere that his original intention had been merely to give 'a "friendly lead" to candidates in the new constituencies', and that it was the 'idiotic opposition of the Whigs' which had turned his 'gentle hint into a great national policy'.[48]

The object of this summary of the background to the *Radical Programme* and Chamberlain's election campaign is not to belittle the significance of the political impact made at the time, but to throw light on the precise functions they were intended to serve, and thus to define the nature of the threat posed to Hartington and the Whigs. The *Radical Programme* was conceived not as a platform for the general election, but as an attempt to evoke an atmosphere of impending change, at a time of great political uncertainty, by airing various aspects of Radical thinking. In this way, Chamberlain sought to become identified with the politics of the future, as the one prominent Liberal with a clear perception of what those politics would be. His election speeches were designed to set a tone which other Liberal candidates, intimidated into sharing his assumptions about the political disposition of the new electors, would feel compelled to adopt. He boasted to Escott, for example, after Hartington's speech at Waterfoot, that his programme of land reforms was on the verge of being 'universally accepted by the party. At this moment two-thirds at least of Liberal county candidates are more or less pledged to [it] . . . After the election they will all have to swallow it.'[49] Indeed, Goschen observed that while 'No one can say to what extent [Chamberlain] is gaining ground' with the electorate, it was alarming to 'see multitudes of candidates going in for his views and very few moderate speeches'.[50] Chamberlain's strategy, it therefore seems, was to Radicalize the Liberal candidates themselves, rather than to drive out the Whigs, in the confident expectation that

[48] Chamberlain to Labouchere, 20 Oct. 1885, in A. L. Thorold, *Life of Henry Labouchere* (1913), 239–40.

[49] Chamberlain to Escott, 3 Sept. 1885, BL Add. MSS 58777. A letter of the same date, to Harcourt, confirms that, when he referred to his 'programme', Chamberlain meant the land reforms outlined at Hull: Chamberlain to Harcourt, 3 Sept. 1885 (typescript), Harcourt MSS, Box 716.

[50] Goschen to W. C. Cartwright, 11 Sept. 1885, Cartwright MSS, Box 16, bundle 3.

his version of Radicalism would take hold so far as to establish
himself as the arbiter of the domestic policies pursued by a future
Liberal government. Hartington, he assumed, would eventually
'yield, grumbling as usual, but still yielding',[51] and Chamberlain
sought to make Goschen the Radicals' 'whipping boy', in the hope of
making him impossible for the next Liberal Cabinet, and in this way
avoiding direct personal attacks on Hartington.[52] For Hartington
and the Whigs, apparently, the prospect ahead was one not of
imminent political destruction, but of subjugation within a Liberal
party in which 'Chamberlainite Radicalism' was acknowledged to be
the principal inspiring force.

The perception of a serious Radical challenge to Whig control of
the post-Gladstonian Liberal party made it real enough to contemporaries, of course, but there are reasons, quite apart from the
improvised nature of Chamberlain's election platform, for regarding
his bid to become the directing power behind Liberal policy as a bold
gamble taken from what was in some ways a defensive position.
Firstly, as both Andrew Jones and Richard Jay have shown, Chamberlain had been surprised by the agreement between Gladstone and
Salisbury over franchise and redistribution in November 1884,[53]
and in spite of his confident predictions about the consequences of
this settlement, he and many other Radicals were as fearful of
the implications of single-member constituencies as the Whigs. The
reason why redistribution was 'generally unpopular among the
politicians of the towns', as Forster (no lover of the caucus system)
explained to Derby, was that 'it disturbs the arrangements of the
wire-pullers and lessens their influence'.[54] Chamberlain himself had
to admit that 'I hate single member districts', and though he tried to
argue that the new system would benefit the Radicals, A. J. Mundella

[51] Chamberlain to Labouchere, 20 Oct. 1885, in Thorold, *Labouchere*,
pp. 239–40.
[52] Chamberlain to Dilke, 13 Oct. 1885, Chamberlain MSS, JC5/24/437. In his
speech at Trowbridge the following day, Chamberlain likened Goschen to 'the
skeleton at Egyptian feasts. He is there to repress our enthusiasm and moderate our
joy', *The Times*, 15 Oct. 1885, p. 6. Later in the month, the campaign of vilification
intensified: ibid., 29 Oct. 1885, p. 9; but in a letter to Dilke of 31 Oct., Chamberlain
seemed to assume that Goschen would be in the next Cabinet: Chamberlain MSS,
JC5/24/445.
[53] Jones, *Politics of Reform*, pp. 31, 217; Jay, *Joseph Chamberlain*, pp. 79–80.
[54] Lord Derby's diary, 5 Dec. 1884, Derby MSS.

was certainly not convinced.[55] Similarly, John Bright told the Harcourts that single-member seats were 'much disliked in the large towns and . . . likely to tell against us',[56] while W. C. Cartwright recorded that 'Both Henry Fowler and John Morley have expressed to me their profound dislike of single member constituencies', and some days later he found Jacob Bright and William Rathbone voicing similar sentiments.[57]

Secondly, it is clear that at no time during 1885 was Chamberlain able to rely upon the fidelity of his Radical associates. His weakness in this respect was brought home, early in the year, when he contemplated resigning from the government because of his suspicion that a prime ministerial rebuke for his provocative speeches at Birmingham and Ipswich was part of a Whig-inspired plot against him.[58] In spite of Schnadhorst's assurance that the Liberal associations were firmly behind him,[59] Chamberlain received little support from his own coterie. John Morley was reported to have been 'colloguing' with Hartington and Harcourt, and was 'evidently under the impression that W[higger]y is the stronger section, and is likely to be unduly wakened',[60] Shaw Lefevre was also said to be taking a 'Whig' line,[61] and Trevelyan was suspected by Chamberlain of being ready to desert.[62] Any idea of a general Radical secession was therefore out of the question, and Dilke advised Chamberlain that it would be a mistake to resign, as he would be playing into the Whigs' hands.[63]

Throughout the critical months ahead, Chamberlain's Radical colleagues displayed a marked inclination towards the central ground in Liberal politics, tempered only by the fear of what a breach with Chamberlain might bring. Trevelyan, in particular, became

[55] Chamberlain to Mundella, 7 Dec. 1884, Mundella MSS, 6P/17; Mundella to Robert Leader, 8, 11, 13 Dec. 1884, Mundella–Leader MSS, 6P/74. Sheffield provided a classic illustration of the way that the system of single-member seats created Conservative strongholds in the suburban and business districts of the big cities.
[56] Lewis Harcourt's diary, 5 Dec. 1884, Harcourt MSS.
[57] Cartwright's diary, 20 Nov., 2 Dec. 1884, Cartwright MSS, Box 101. Cf. Fowler to Morley, 6 Feb. 1885, in Edith H. Fowler, *The Life of Henry Hartley Fowler, First Viscount Wolverhampton, C.C.S.I.* (1912), 184–5.
[58] See Garvin, *Chamberlain*, i. 558–9.
[59] Chamberlain to Morley, 2 Feb. 1885, Chamberlain MSS, JC5/54/602.
[60] Dilke to Chamberlain, 31 Jan. 1885, ibid. JC5/24/108.
[61] Ibid.
[62] Chamberlain to Dilke, 1, 2 Feb. 1885, ibid. JC5/24/406–7.
[63] Dilke to Chamberlain, 3 Feb. 1885, ibid. JC5/24/109.

notoriously Hartingtonian,[64] and Lord Derby found him full of
reassurance about the future: '[he] thinks that the next House of
Commons will not differ so much as is supposed by many: that
candidates of a good class socially will come forward nearly everywhere, and have the best chance of being returned . . . he thought that
the party as a whole would accept the leadership of Hartington, even
Chamberlain not objecting'.[65] A few days later, Derby added that
'He evidently distrusts and dislikes Chamberlain, to whose half-
socialist talk he referred as being dangerous, both to the party and
the Country.'[66] Nevertheless, in May and June, his evident fear of the
Radical leader forced Trevelyan, along with Shaw Lefevre, to side
with Chamberlain in Cabinet over the question of the Irish Central
Board,[67] although in private Trevelyan was urging him not to break
up the party.[68] Morley was placed in a similar dilemma. He, too,
seems to have favoured the Hartingtonian succession,[69] and, after a
row with Chamberlain over the question of the Sudan in February,
there appears to have been a breach between the two, lasting until the
end of August, during which time Morley agonized as to whether he
should support Chamberlain's 'socialist' programme.[70] Even during
the autumn campagn itself, Chamberlain was obviously angered by
the lukewarmness of some of the members of what J. L. Garvin
described as a 'Radical Junta', which, Dr Barker acknowledges,
never acted as such.[71]

[64] Cf. Bahlman (ed.), *Hamilton Diary*, ii. 754 (entry for 14 Dec. 1884); A. B.
Cooke and John Vincent (eds.), *Lord Carlingford's Journal: Reflections of a Cabinet
Minister, 1885* (Oxford, 1971), 76–7 (entry for 7 Mar. 1885).

[65] Lord Derby's diary, 25 Jan. 1885, Derby MSS.

[66] Ibid., 28 Jan. 1885. Later in the year, Trevelyan wrote of Chamberlain that 'I
hope and think that he is beginning to see that we must keep together to win',
Trevelyan to Elliot, 10 Sept. 1885, Elliot MSS. See also the expressions of loyalty in
Trevelyan's letter to Hartington, 28 Nov. 1885, Devonshire MSS, 340.1837.

[67] Cf. Bahlman (ed.), *Hamilton Diary*, ii. 857 (5 May 1885); Cooke and Vincent
(eds.), *Carlingford's Journal*, pp. 112–13 (8 June 1885).

[68] Trevelyan to Chamberlain, 6 May 1885, Chamberlain MSS, JC5/70/10.

[69] Morley to his sister, Nov. 1884, in Hirst, *Early Life of Morley*, ii. 206.

[70] The normally very full correspondence in the Chamberlain papers ceases after
15 Feb. until June, and only a handful of letters exist for the period June to Aug. For
Morley's dilemma, see Kate Courtney's diary, 2 Aug. 1885, Courtney MSS. Leonard
Courtney, who shared Morley's Little Englandism and dislike of 'socialism', was by
this time almost totally estranged from Chamberlain. Chamberlain's letter to Morley
of 30 Aug., Chamberlain MSS, JC5/54/621, seems to mark their reconciliation.

[71] Michael Barker, *Gladstone and Radicalism: The Reconstruction of Liberal
Policy in Britain, 1885–94* (Hassocks, 1975), 10. Cf. Chamberlain to Dilke, 28 Sept.,
17 Oct. 1885, Chamberlain MSS, JC5/24/432, 439, for complaints about Shaw
Lefevre and Morley.

Already, the ground was being prepared for the Radical desertions from Chamberlain which were to follow the general election. In the meantime, however, the precise outcome of the elections would be crucial in determining the strength of 'Chamberlainite Radicalism', and until this was clear, no prediction could be made as to the terms on which the Liberal party might act in the future. As Granville recognized, Chamberlain was an 'opportunist', whose 'attitude after the elections [would] depend much upon their result'.[72] In a situation where the limits to his future influence might be prescribed only by the extent of the Liberal majority, it was a natural part of Chamberlain's 'game' to intimidate his rivals and his colleagues into fearing that he might well sweep the board. This was why his favourite topics of conversation at the dinner table were of such things as a 'complete social revolution', or a 'dictatorship'.[73] It is highly unlikely that Chamberlain thought he could destroy the authority of Hartington and the Whigs, but by the nature of things, he was bound to take his challenge as far as the power of the forces he was summoning up would take him, and at the height of Liberal optimism about their electoral prospects, Schnadhorst was encouraging Chamberlain to believe that the party was heading for a landslide victory.[74] Such a result would clearly have been a set-back for the Whigs.

Whether Hartington was seriously alarmed by the challenge from the 'left' is open to question, but it was clear that the interests of the moderate Liberals would be best served if he continued his strategy of encouraging Gladstone's leadership of the party, as this afforded the most effective way of 'muzzling' the Radicals. During the summer, there had remained some doubt as to Gladstone's intentions, for he had not announced that he would definitely lead the Liberal party into the general election, and there is a strong suspicion that Hartington's speech at Waterfoot on 29 August, shortly after Gladstone's return from a sailing holiday to Norway, was in fact a deliberate attempt to provoke a row with Chamberlain in order to force an early settlement of the leadership question. Earlier in the month, Hartington and Chamberlain had met to discuss their respective strategies, and at that time the former had seemed resigned to the

[72] Granville to Derby, 9 Aug. 1885, Derby MSS.
[73] Lord Derby's diary, 2 June 1885, Derby MSS.
[74] Schnadhorst was confident of victory in 366 seats, and thought the prospects favourable in a further 26: Chamberlain to Dilke, 1 Nov. 1885, Chamberlain MSS, JC5/24/446.

Radical experiments.[75] At Waterfoot, however, Hartington, who must have felt obliged to do something to encourage the moderates, made a blatantly provocative speech, lumping together Chamberlain's land proposals with other more extreme demands, like the compulsory division of property, and dismissing all such schemes for artificially redistributing the land.[76] This provoked bitter complaints from the Radicals: Dilke felt that Hartington had 'not behaved fairly' towards Chamberlain, and that, as a result, 'the general agreement' between the two 'no longer holds'.[77] Hartington may have allowed Morley to soothe Chamberlain's wounded feelings with the explanation that it was all a misunderstanding, resulting from the clumsiness of his arrangement of the speech and the inaccurate reporting of it by the press,[78] but a letter to his father, written immediately after the speech, shows that he knew exactly what he was doing: 'I should not be surprised if it produced a protest from the Radicals and perhaps a regular split in the Party.'[79]

Gladstone's reaction to this situation must have been exactly what Hartington had hoped. On 3 September, he wrote a discreet, probing letter regarding his own position, dwelling mainly on the problem of Irish policy, but Hartington was able to take the opportunity, in his reply, to relate Chamberlain's anger at the Waterfoot speech and the likelihood of some form of retaliation, and to urge upon Gladstone that it was 'of the utmost importance that your decision as to the part which you intend to take in the approaching election should be formed and announced as soon as possible'.[80] Gladstone had already begun working on an election address, and when this was issued on

[75] Hartington to Granville, 5 Aug. 1885, PRO 30/29/22A/3, in Holland, *Devonshire*, ii. 71–2.
[76] Hartington to Waterfoot, *The Times*, 31 Aug. 1885, p. 8. Hartington's own programme dwelt upon the need for a reform of local government, and for measures to facilitate the transfer of land. Significantly, the *Annual Register* for 1885, p. 147, noted that the speech was very well received by the provincial Liberal press and even by the advanced *Daily News*.
[77] Dilke to James, 1 Sept. 1885 (typescript), BL Add. MSS 43892, fo. 54; Dilke to Rosebery, 31 Aug. 1885, NLS MSS 10083, fo. 244.
[78] Morley to Chamberlain, 3 Sept. 1885, Chamberlain to Morley, 4 Sept. 1885, Chamberlain MSS, JC5/54/622, 624.
[79] Hartington to the Duke of Devonshire, 29 Aug. 1885, Devonshire MSS, 340.1799.
[80] Gladstone to Hartington, 3 Sept. 1885 (copy), Hartington to Gladstone, 6 Sept. 1885, BL Add. MSS 44148, fos. 114, 120, in Holland, *Devonshire*, ii. 78–81.

18 September, it brought dismay to the Radicals and undoubted satisfaction to Hartington, for none of Chamberlain's policy suggestions were included, and on the crucial question of land reform an avowedly Hartingtonian line was taken.[81] Dilke's complaint that 'If it had not been for Hartington's unlucky speech this would not have been necessary'[82] was rather disingenuous, though, as Gladstone was surely only looking for a suitable pretext with which to justify extending his leadership, and the differences between moderates and Radicals provided the most obvious point for him to seize upon. But it had, at the same time, served Hartington's purposes admirably, as he indicated in a letter to Goschen on 20 September: 'I think that the prospects of the moderate section of the party are improving; at all events after your and my speeches, and Mr. Gladstone's address, the moderate men cannot reasonably complain, as they were inclined to do, that they were being abandoned to the leadership of the most extreme members of the Party.'[83]

Considered in this light, Hartington's cautious attitude towards 'Chamberlainism' during the general election campaign of 1885 becomes readily intelligible. Once Gladstone's commitment to lead the Liberal party had been secured, no purpose could be served by forcing an immediate showdown with the Radicals over the question of future policy. As it was, Hartington had to do no more than endorse the proposals included in Gladstone's manifesto, while treating the other issues highlighted by Chamberlain as open questions requiring further discussion. He therefore contented himself with expressions of doubt as to the practical feasibility of certain projects, and of concern at the possibility that expectations might be raised which could not be satisfied.[84] What is really striking, in the circumstances, is the great care taken by Hartington not to commit himself irrevocably against any of the various Radical nostrums. He refused, for example, to 'raise a howl of terror about plunder and confiscation and all the rest of it', recognizing that parliament had previously granted powers of compulsory purchase when this was deemed to be in the public interest, and he merely refused to pledge

---

[81] *The Times*, 19 Sept. 1885, p. 8. The main items in Gladstone's programme were the reform of parliamentary procedure, local government, the land laws, and the registration system.

[82] Dilke to James, 14 Sept. 1885 (typescript), BL Add. MSS 43892, fo. 65.

[83] Hartington to Goschen, 20 Sept. 1885, in Holland, *Devonshire*, ii. 73.

[84] Hartington at Rawtenstall, *The Times*, 12 Oct. 1885, p. 8.

himself to further applications of the principle of expropriation 'for objects which are not yet clearly defined' and which had not been sufficiently discussed.[85] Free education, too, though Hartington had serious reservations about its practicability, he admitted to be a 'question of expediency',[86] and while he was opposed, at the time, to disestablishment, he declined to state that this would always be his position regardless of the circumstances.[87] For immediate purposes, Hartington argued that there were no differences between moderate and advanced Liberals, and he dismissed as impracticable and undesirable the call, from Conservative quarters, for the moderates to form a third party, on the traditional Whig grounds that it was necessary for the Liberal party to embrace all classes of society and all shades of opinion in order to ensure that future political changes were carried out by peaceful means. All that he asked was that there should be mutual toleration, and a free and full discussion of various opinions, and only if one section tried to force on policies for which the party, as a whole, was not ready would he feel compelled to leave the party.[88]

During the autumn of 1885, then, Hartington reconciled himself to another deferment of his succession to the Liberal leadership. With Gladstone still present, and obviously not yet ready to retire, it was both futile and dangerous for Hartington to consider obstructing him, a point that had been made clear on several occasions in the past, but it was at least possible to extract some advantage from Gladstone's power to curb the Radicals on matters of domestic policy. Hartington's use of this tactic is apparent again in his letter of 8 November, shortly before Gladstone commenced his campaign in Midlothian, in which he complained about the damaging effect of Chamberlain's speeches on the confidence of moderate Liberals in himself, and therefore urged upon the Liberal leader that 'the only

---

[85] Hartington at Darwen, ibid., 26 Oct. 1885, p. 7.

[86] Hartington at Nelson, ibid., 2 Nov. 1885, p. 8.

[87] Hartington at Accrington, ibid., 31 Oct. 1885, p. 10.

[88] Hartington at Nelson, ibid., 2 Nov. 1885, p. 8. Even in reply to a communication from the Queen, urging him to dissociate himself from the Radicals, Hartington would go no further, explaining that 'I do not think . . . any of the proposals which have actually been put forward by the Radical leaders, can be described as revolutionary. I think that some of them are open to question on the ground of expediency, and I have already expressed my opinion to that effect', Hartington to General Ponsonby, 6 Oct. 1885, in reply to Ponsonby's letter of 3 Oct., in G. E. Buckle (ed.), *The Letters of Queen Victoria*, 2nd series (1926–8), iii. 698, 696.

possibility of keeping the moderate men in the party seems to lie in your taking a strong and decided line against the Radicals'.[89]

The Whig leader's strategy was undoubtedly effective. Chamberlain may have regarded Gladstone's manifesto as a 'slap in the face' for the Radicals,[90] but he was very quickly forced to retreat from the rash ultimatum, delivered at the Victoria Hall, Lambeth, on 24 September, that he would not join a government which did not adopt his programme of graduated taxation, free education, and powers for the compulsory purchase of land. Within a week, at Bradford on 1 October, this demand had been diluted to a statement that he could not join a government which specifically excluded these policies,[91] and by the time of his speech at Birmingham, accepting his candidature there, early in November, Chamberlain had backtracked even further. Not only did he now accept that the items in Gladstone's manifesto were an essential precondition for further reforms, but he no longer pressed specifically for graduated taxation, merely wishing to see a fairer distribution of the tax burden, and being 'perfectly satisfied to leave in the hands of him whom I recognise as my master or teacher in this science the method and the details and the plans by which it may be accomplished'. As for free education, while Chamberlain considered the issue to be ripe for settlement, he noted that Hartington and other moderates felt more discussion was needed, and argued that the Radicals ought not to object to a bona fide inquiry in order to satisfy them. Similarly, with regard to the land question, Chamberlain urged that 'Lord Hartington is entitled to the fullest and the most respectful consideration for anything he may have to say . . . he asks us for more information, for fuller discussion. I think that we who know, who recognise, the value of his past

---

[89] Hartington to Gladstone, 8 Nov. 1885, BL Add. MSS 44148 fo. 142, in Holland, *Devonshire*, ii. 90–1. At Birmingham, the previous day, Chamberlain had made a rather provocative speech, indicating the form which he thought the disestablishment question might take at a future general election: *The Times*, 9 Nov. 1885, p. 10.

[90] Chamberlain to Dilke, 20 Sept. 1885, Chamberlain MSS, JC5/24/428.

[91] Chamberlain at Lambeth, *The Times*, 25 Sept. 1885, p. 7, and at Bradford, ibid., 3 Oct. 1885, p. 12. J. L. Garvin, *Chamberlain*, ii. 71, by inaccurately describing the content of Chamberlain's Lambeth speech, managed to avoid the inconvenient fact that he was backing down. D. A. Hamer's failure to appreciate that the 'ultimatum' speech of 24 Sept. did not represent Chamberlain's strategy throughout the election campaign flaws his account: *Liberal Politics*, p. 100. Richard Jay, *Joseph Chamberlain*, p. 116, does recognize this point, but he mistakenly states that the climb-down took place at Lambeth.

services, and who appreciate his character and work, are bound to do all in our power to meet his wishes, and, if possible, to overcome his objections.'[92]

Hartington's view that there was no need to risk splitting the Liberal party, while Gladstone remained, naturally precluded Goschen and the young Whigs from pursuing a divisive strategy. Following the publication of Gladstone's manifesto, therefore, Goschen's immediate objective had to be to re-establish himself within the Liberal hierarchy (he had not sat in Cabinet since 1874), so that he might be in a position to influence events when the time finally came to find a new leader. As he explained to Albert Grey, on 20 September, it was now his intention to 'join a Cabinet formed by Gladstone', if the offer was made, in order to 'keep Hartington up to the mark in resisting the Radicals in the Cabinet, to keep them strictly to the accepted programme put forward by Gladstone, and then when the latter retires, either to assist toward making Hartington the first power or to split off'. By ensuring that the voice of the moderate Liberals was heard, he hoped that 'the split, which must come, might find the moderates in a stronger position than now: at any rate personally I should be able to come forward in defence of moderate Liberalism, as one of the joint heirs of Gladstone and of his "sound economic school" instead of as a malcontent and outsider" '.[93] This reinforces the point that, once Gladstone was gone, the Whigs would have been better placed to break with the Radicals, if necessary, without sacrificing their claims to Liberal orthodoxy. In the mean time, it was easy for Goschen to take shelter, along with everyone else, beneath the 'Gladstonian umbrella', endorsing the contents of the venerable leader's manifesto while dubbing those additional items propounded by Chamberlain and Dilke as an 'unauthorised programme' which remained a matter for debate.[94] His own moderate Liberal campaign, setting himself up as the chief antagonist of Chamberlainite Radicalism, contained a series of entirely unexceptionable proposals, including reform of parliamentary procedure, reform of local government and taxation, reforms to facilitate the transfer of land, the possibility of a reform of the composition of the House of Lords, the possibility of Church disestablishment in

[92] Chamberlain at Birmingham, *The Times*, 4 Nov. 1885, p. 7.
[93] Goschen to Albert Grey, 20 Sept. 1885, Grey MSS, 211/3.
[94] G. J. Goschen, *Political Speeches Delivered during the General Election 1885* (Edinburgh, 1886), 71 (at Glasgow, 14 Oct. 1885).

Scotland, and a foreign policy conducted on the basis of the 'three C's'—'continuity, clean-handedness and courage'. Only one item of the programme, the encouragement of co-operative farming, which Goschen related to the growth of smallholdings, represented a potentially innovative policy, although it was severely qualified by an insistence that smallholdings ought not to be created artificially, through the compulsory purchase of land by local authorities, as Chamberlain proposed.[95] Nevertheless, there was undoubtedly a genuine interest in this subject among some of the young Whigs, like Albert Grey and Ebrington, who were anxious to promote small-holdings as a means of reconciling the desire for the extension of property ownership with the preservation of free-market principles.[96] In terms of practical policies, Goschen's moderate Liberalism may well have amounted to very little, but the essential point remained that he had succeeded in showing that there was more than one path for the Liberal party to follow: 'The question now is, will the moderate Liberals stand firm? or will they drift towards Chamberlain in the next Parliament? The next three months must decide a great deal.'[97] An enthusiastic Albert Grey declared that Goschen had 'by his Scotch performances spoken himself into the saddle of leader of the moderates . . . I think we ought to push emphasise and maintain Goschen's claim upon the future leadership of the party in the House of Commons when Gladstone and Hartington go.'[98]

An interesting report by the central news agency, which had collected information from its correspondents in all the constituencies, provides an indication of the balance of forces within the Liberal party by the end of October. It suggested that the avowed

[95] Ibid. 95 (at Hendon, 21 Oct. 1885).

[96] Ebrington wrote to his father that is was desirable to extend the number of landholdings, and that 'if it was not so much trouble to buy land the working classes would by means of "*people's banks*" and "*Friendly societies*" and the like be glad to invest their large (aggregate) savings in that way', Ebrington to Earl Fortescue, 7 Aug. [1885], Fortescue MSS, FC 55. Albert Grey, along with the Duke of Westminster, had been involved in the meeting at Willis's rooms on 24 Apr. 1885 to promote the Small Farm and Labourers Holding Company, which aimed to provide capital to create smallholdings, operating on the lines of a building society: S. H. Harris, *Auberon Herbert: Crusader for Liberty* (1943), 273–4. For other examples of the many schemes floating around at this time, see Donald Southgate, *The Passing of the Whigs, 1832–1886* (1962), 388 n. 2.

[97] Goschen to W. C. Cartwright, 29 Oct. 1885, Cartwright MSS, Box 16, bundle 3.

[98] Albert Grey to Cartwright, 18 Oct. 1885, ibid., Box 16, unmarked bundle.

supporters of Hartington and of Chamberlain were roughly even:
'232 of those [Liberal] candidates have declared themselves in favour
of the principles and platform enunciated by Mr. Chamberlain,
while the utterances and addresses of 238 candidates show that they
are more inclined to follow the guidance of Lord Hartington.' The
report is even more revealing, though, as to the obvious perplexity of
many Liberal candidates at a time of tremendous political uncertainty: 'One candidate is described as "holding with Hartington, but
running with Chamberlain"; another says he knows no leader but
Gladstone; a third says he will go with Chamberlain if he sees the
electors actually want it; while many who decline to give distinct
pledges say they will support the leader of the party "whoever he may
be".'[99]

Of course, the strategies pursued by Hartington, Goschen, and
other Whig or moderate Liberals throughout the first half of the
1880s would have mattered little if they had been devised in the
context of a general movement away from the Liberal party by
the aristocratic and landowning classes. The conventional view is
that this had indeed been happening,[100] but, in fact, there is little evidence to suggest that Whig losses to the Conservatives had reached
significant proportions by 1885. As late as July 1884, for example, it
was still possible for ministers to secure a substantial turn-out of
peers for a crucial division, Cairns's amendment to the Franchise Bill.
On this occasion, as Edward Hamilton observed, 'Everybody almost
(with the exception of that contemptible man, Lord Brabourne) of
any pretensions to be a Liberal voted straight.'[101] Excluding the
spiritual peers, 133 voted against the Conservative amendment, and
a further sixteen were paired against it.[102] In normal circumstances,
a Liberal turnout of 90 or 100 would have been considered good.

Regrettably, in the absence of a study of the general election of
1885, and with few local studies covering this period, it is impossible
to make a systematic assessment of the level of Whig participation in
the constituencies. However, it is noticeable that in many of the rural
counties where the Liberal party performed well, aristocrats and
local landowners figured prominently among the successful candidates, suggesting that considerable Whig influence was still being

[99] *Manchester Guardian*, 30 Oct. 1885, p. 8.
[100] Cf. Southgate, *Passing of Whigs*, pp. 409–18.
[101] Bahlman (ed.), *Hamilton diary*, ii. 650 (9 July 1884).
[102] 8 July 1884, 3 Hansard, ccxc, cols. 477–9, for the division list.

exerted for the Liberal cause. In Buckinghamshire, for example, the party won two of the three seats, with representatives from the Rothschild and Verney families, and in Dorset, where three of the four victorious candidates were Liberals, two of these were the sons of peers. Liberal gains in Devon, Somerset, and Wiltshire similarly owed a great deal to the participation of Whig families. In Lincolnshire, the level of landlord activity on the Liberal side was, if anything, greater than at the previous general election.[103]

It would appear that the problem for the Liberal party was not that Whig landowners were seceding *en masse*, but that concern aroused by Chamberlain's 'unauthorized programme' was causing some of them to abstain, especially when the alternative was to endorse a candidate who subscribed to Chamberlain's policies. Thus, in Cheshire, the Duke of Westminster found himself in 'the difficult position of a moderate Liberal', unable to support the Radical candidate for the Eddisbury division, but unwilling for that reason to support the Conservative,[104] while in the Crewe division, the largest landowner, the Marquis of Crewe, felt unable to support 'such a Radical' as G. W. Latham.[105] Meantime, in the Howdenshire division of Yorkshire, Lord Wenlock, though still a Liberal, was cold-shouldering the Liberal candidate.[106] He had expressed his perplexity at the political situation in a letter to Lord Ripon, declining an invitation to attend a Liberal meeting at York:

I have been much exercised in my mind lately by certain of Mr. Chamberlain's speeches, and I cannot help being alarmed at the manner in which the new constituencies are being wooed. I am so disgusted with the way in which the Tories are behaving in Ireland, that I think just now politics are to be avoided. The Tories are scrambling up and seizing our platform, and our own party are, in their anxiety to keep ahead, proposing measures which in my opinion are unwise in their effect and unjust in principle.[107]

[103] R. J. Olney, *Lincolnshire Politics, 1832–1885* (Oxford, 1973), 218–22. The Hexham division of Northumberland was characterized in 1885 by 'a number of large estates, the owners of which threw their weight into the Liberal scale', and defections only took place in 1886: Anna G. MacInnes, *Recollections of the Life of Miles MacInnes* (1911), 189–91.

[104] *Pall Mall Gazette*, 11 Nov. 1885, p. 8, citing a letter from the duke to the Conservative candidate. The 'advanced Radical' candidate, Laurence Irwell, was shunned by almost the entire Cheshire squirearchy: *Daily News*, 28 Nov. 1885, p. 6.

[105] *Manchester Guardian*, 2 Dec. 1885, p. 5, referring to a letter from the marquis to the Conservative agent in the constituency.

[106] *Leeds Mercury*, 21 Nov. 1885, p. 10.

[107] Wenlock to Ripon, 24 Oct. 1885, BL Add. MSS 43565, fo. 170.

There were a few instances where Whig parliamentary candidates
took an independent Liberal stance, most notably the Fitzwilliam
brothers. At Peterborough, where the two sitting Liberal MPs both
contested the one seat remaining after redistribution, the Hon. John
Fitzwilliam defeated Sydney Buxton with the assistance of the powerful Fitzwilliam influence and the Conservative vote.[108] The Hon.
Henry Fitzwilliam offered himself as a candidate for the Rotherham
division of the West Riding, on the basis that 'If elected, he would
give an independent and general support to the Liberal party, and
should any question involving the well-being of his Country arise he
should vote according to his conscience.'[109] He, too, would have had
the advantage of the Conservative vote, but, in the event, he withdrew his candidature, on grounds of health.[110] In the case of the
Hon. John Dundas, an invitation from the Howdenshire Liberal
delegates to contest that constituency was originally accepted,[111] but
he subsequently withdrew, partly for personal reasons (his brother,
the Marquis of Zetland, would not support him), but also because he
saw little hope for future co-operation between the sections of the
Liberal party.[112] However, he denied, in a letter to *The Times*, that
he had therefore seceded from the Liberals,[113] and he explained his
position more fully to Arthur Elliot:

Possibly my views may be coloured by my wish to be out of Parliament for
the present, but I own that I should hardly feel justified in accepting the
support of Radicals without a very plain understanding of our points of
difference, and I fancy I should not be an acceptable candidate after I had
told them my mind plainly.

If the Tories intend carrying out what they say, their programme seems to
be sufficient for the present . . . If the late Government had not made such an
awful mess of it, and Gladstone had not shewn his want of power or will to
keep his Cabinet in order, I should have been more ready to place confidence
in him so far as carrying out his immediate programme is concerned.

[108] See *The Times*, 27 Oct. 1885, p. 6, also 27 Nov. 1885, p. 6, 28 Nov. 1885, p. 6.
The previous year, Fitzwilliam had informed the local Liberal association that he
would not submit to a selection procedure: ibid., 28 June 1884, p. 12.
[109] *Leeds Mercury*, 28 Sept. 1885, p. 8. He had previously represented the old
southern division of the West Riding, but had decided to retire because of his poor
relations with the local Liberal association: Charles Milnes Gaskell to Halifax, 8 Aug.
1884, Hickleton MSS, A4/169.
[110] *Leeds Mercury*, 9 Oct. 1885, p. 8. It was only afterwards that the Conservatives
put up a candidate: ibid., 12 Oct. 1885, p. 8.
[111] *The Times*, 31 July 1885, p. 9.
[112] *Leeds Mercury*, 30 Sept. 1885, p. 8.
[113] *The Times*, 3 Oct. 1885, p. 7.

I admire the frankness of Hartington's and Goschen's speeches . . . but they seem to me to have very little in common with the spirit which animates the Radicals who if I mistake not will form the overpowering majority of the Liberal party in the next House of Commons.

I look forward to a considerable shindy within the ranks of the party, after which I shall know better where I am.[114]

The determination of most Whigs to preserve their Liberal identity is confirmed by the publication in *The Times*, on 4 November, of a manifesto exhorting the defenders of the Church of England to organize themselves in order to counter the pressure being placed on election candidates by the Liberation Society.[115] This manifesto was an almost exclusively Whig affair, bearing the signatures of the Dukes of Westminster, Somerset, Bedford, and Devonshire, the Marquis of Crewe, Earls Grey, Fitzwilliam, Ducie, and Selborne, the second Viscount Halifax and Lord Mount Temple, among others, as well as several commoners including Dundas and E. P. Bouverie.[116] It had been provoked by a challenge from Lord Salisbury, whose own party was making great political capital out of the anti-disestablishment cry,[117] and was thus a clear sign that the Whigs still regarded themselves as being distinct from the Conservatives. Indeed, some publicly repudiated suggestions that they had defected: the Duke of Westminster was reported as having 'expressed a cordial adhesion to the programme of Mr. Gladstone's manifesto',[118] and Lord Mount Temple emphasized that 'I rejoice in being ranked amongst [Gladstone's] followers. It is as a consistent and zealous Liberal that I am opposed to the Liberationists.'[119]

Nevertheless, there remains some truth in Dr Southgate's argument that the combined effect of the Franchise and Redistribution Acts, and the curbs on electoral expenditure imposed by the Corrupt Practices Act of 1883, was to impair the political influence of the

[114] Dundas to Elliot, 12 Oct. 1885, Elliot MSS.

[115] A survey had found that of the 579 Liberal candidates in Britain, 403 had expressed themselves as being favourable to the principle of disestablishment: *Pall Mall Gazette*, 11 Sept. 1885, pp. 1, 11. Of course, as the *PMG* noted, in many cases such a commitment would have been purely abstract, as the issue was not considered to be one of immediate practical politics.

[116] *The Times*, 4 Nov. 1885, p. 9. A supplementary list of signatories was published on 9 Nov., p. 9.

[117] See Alan Simon, 'Church Disestablishment as a Factor in the General Election of 1885', *Historical Journal*, 18, (1975), 791–820.

[118] *Pall Mall Gazette*, 9 Nov. 1885, p. 7.

[119] *Leeds Mercury*, 28 Nov. 1885, p. 10.

Whig, landowning class in the constituencies.[120] It is questionable whether very much emphasis should be placed on the enfranchisement of the agricultural labourers, for there was no obvious reason why this should have undermined the position of landed families who took the Liberal side, and some Whiggish candidates were clearly very successful in attracting the support of the new voters.[121] One also wonders whether the restrictions on election spending were so unwelcome to landowners experiencing a decline in their rent rolls. Of the impact of the Redistribution Act, however, there can be no doubt. The new electoral dispensation registered the relative decline of agriculture, transferring on a large scale seats from southern England to London and the industrial north, and virtually eliminating the old nomination seats.[122] Furthermore, the redrawing of constituency boundaries resulting from the general introduction of single-member seats inevitably exacerbated the tension between Whig houses and the 'new' men of the local Liberal associations, creating opportunities for tests of political strength which the former could not always hope to win. The Earl of Durham, for example, evidently had problems exerting the traditional Lambton influence in county Durham, where he was hoping to find a seat for his friend Reginald Brett: 'I don't like the political outlook here. The local manufacturing and coalowning plutocrats mean to divide the County amongst them. But I shall oppose their designs in one respect at least.' Brett did not get the seat, however.[123] Charles Milnes

---

[120] Southgate, *Passing of Whigs*, p. 381.

[121] Perhaps the best example is Sir Frederick Milbank, who, against the odds, won the predominantly rural Richmond division of the North Riding; see the *Leeds Mercury*, 19 Nov. 1885, p. 7. Some unsuccessful candidates in rural constituencies had run the Conservatives very close, thanks to the support of the agricultural labourers, as was the case with Sir Maurice FitzGerald (South Northamptonshire) and Lord Esme Gordon (Huntingdonshire, Ramsey): *Daily News*, 28 Nov. 1885, p. 6, 3 Dec. 1885, p. 3.

[122] See Michael Kinnear, *The British Voter: An Atlas and Survey since 1885* (1968), 13–16, and Barker, *Gladstone and Radicalism*, Appendix A, pp. 257–8. Another result of the Redistribution Act was that many small boroughs, especially in southern England, were absorbed into the county constituencies. Over a million borough voters were thus transferred to the counties: Jones, *Politics of Reform*, p. 206.

[123] Durham to Brett, 11 Jan. 1885, Esher MSS, 10/7. It is not clear whether these difficulties had any bearing on the position of the earl's brother, the Hon. F. W. Lambton, who had announced his intention of retiring from the representation of South Durham several months earlier, before the redistribution settlement: *The Times*, 26 July 1884, p. 11. In Bedfordshire, at about the same time, the Duke of

Gaskell, the chairman of the Liberal association in the old southern division of the West Riding, devoted much effort, in the early months of 1885, to keeping control of the selection of candidates for the eight new single-member constituencies, but found that 'There is a great jealousy of all the old leaders and the new men are determined to have everything their own way and to dictate also the candidates' views.' It was therefore difficult, he complained, for 'those who have been accustomed to the old ways to come forward before these new Yorkshire constituencies. If I come forward it will be very grudgingly.'[124] Perhaps the most painful cases of all were those of sitting MPs unable to find a new constituency to contest. W. C. Cartwright, for example, felt that his political career in Oxfordshire had been destroyed by 'the animus of middle class Radicals',[125] and M. J. Guest found himself isolated when he unilaterally announced his candidature for the Eastern division of Dorset, and eventually he had to withdraw.[126]

After the general election of 1885, the representation of 'noblemen' on the Liberal side stood at twenty-three, with twenty-four baronets (eighteen of whom were listed by John Bateman as great landowners), and eight baronets' sons, making a total of fifty-five members of the 'aristocracy'. In addition to these, thirty MPs had an entry in Bateman's *Great Landowners of Great Britain and Ireland*, and twenty more were listed in *Burke's Landed Gentry*.[127] Altogether, then, 105 Liberals, or 31.4 per cent of the parliamentary party, may be categorized as belonging to the 'aristocratic-

Bedford had forbidden Lord Tavistock to stand again for the county because 'he will not stand the dictatorial temper of the Luton Radicals', W. C. Cartwright's diary, 15 June 1884, Cartwright MSS, Box 101. However, according to the wife of Cyril Flower, the Liberal candidate for the Luton division in 1885, the duke was still on the Liberal side at that time, as was the other major landowner, Earl Cowper. Again, the defections did not take place until 1886: Lady Battersea, *Reminiscences* (1922), p. 193.

[124] Milnes Gaskell to Halifax, 14 Apr. 1885, Hickleton MSS, A4/169. See also the earlier letters of 29, 30 Jan. 1885, ibid.

[125] Cartwright's diary, 3 July 1885, Cartwright MSS, 6/16. Cartwright had issued an address to the electors of the Woodstock division, but was repudiated by the Liberal association, ibid., 9, 20 Apr. 1885.

[126] Lord Richard Grosvenor to Guest, 17 Apr. 1885, Guest to Grosvenor (copy), 19 Apr. 1885, Grosvenor to Guest, 20 Apr., 15 May 1885, BL Add. MSS 57937, fos. 78, 80, 84, 87. Guest felt that he was being punished by the party managers for his rebellion against the Liberal government's Egyptian policy.

[127] Twenty of the thirty 'great landowners' were also entered in Burke.

landowning' section. This was clearly a significant decline from the figure of around 43 per cent for the parliaments of 1874 and 1880, but a social group which constituted almost one-third of Liberal MPs was still a considerable force to be reckoned with. The notion of a flood of Whig defections is rendered even more doubtful when we remember the Whig members from the 1880 parliament who stood again without success in 1885, such as the Hon. Rupert Carrington, Cowper, Ashley, Francis Foljambe, Francis Buxton, Lord Baring, and Ffolkes, all of whom were defeated in straight contests with Conservatives in county divisions or smaller boroughs where probably only a Whig-Liberal would have had any chance of winning.[128] There are also several instances where the continued support of a Whig family for the Liberal party was affirmed by the fact that a replacement candidate was provided for a retiring one: the Duke of Argyll's influence in Argyllshire may have been undermined, and Lord Colin Campbell did not stand for parliament again, but Lord Lorne was the unsuccessful Liberal candidate in Hampstead; Sir Tollemache Sinclair retired from the representation of Caithness-shire, but his son was persuaded to stand as a Liberal, against the Crofters' candidate, after receiving a requisition from Liberals in Thurso,[129] and though Lord Douglas Gordon, the Marquis of Huntly's son, decided not to seek re-election in Huntingdonshire,[130] his brother Lord Esme Gordon contested the Ramsey division of that county. Interestingly enough, the decline in the representation of the

---

[128] The importance to the Liberal cause of having local landowners willing to come forward is illustrated by the case of Gloucestershire. It had been hoped that the two sitting Whig MPs from the old western division, Colonel Kingscote and Lord Moreton, would contest two of the new divisions in which the Conservative influence was strong: 'I am sure in my own mind that if you fought Thornbury Division and he [Moreton] Tewkesbury, both seats would be won for the party. *Nobody but you could win that South seat*', A. B. Winterbotham to Kingscote, 10 Jan. 1885, Kingscote MSS. See also Sir William Guise to Kingscote, 24 Jan. 1885, ibid. In the event, however, Kingscote retired from parliament in Feb. 1885, accepting a Crown appointment, and Moreton later decided not to stand again, giving health reasons: *The Times*, 4 May 1885, p. 7. Whether Moreton's reasons were genuine is not clear, for his father Lord Ducie had earlier discussed which seat Moreton should contest, as well as offering to pay Kingscote's election expenses: Ducie to Kingscote, 9, 16 Dec. 1884, 19 Jan. 1885, Kingscote MSS. The Ducie influence was exerted on the Liberals' behalf at the general election: Henry Pelling, *Social Geography of British Elections 1885–1910* (1967), 155, but Lord Ducie subsequently became a Liberal Unionist. The Tewkesbury division became a Conservative stronghold after 1886 as the Liberals lost the support of Lords Fitzhardinge and Sudeley. Ibid.

[129] *The Times*, 26 Aug. 1885, p. 9.

[130] Ibid., 23 May 1885, p. 12.

'aristocratic-landowning' section in the new parliament was made up not by any real increase in the numbers of 'industrialists and merchants', who, at 116, or 34.7 per cent of the parliamentary party, only recovered to their 1874 level,[131] nor by any further growth in the size of the 'lawyers' group, who, at ninety-one, or 27.2 per cent, showed little change from 1880,[132] but by an increasing diversity of professions and backgrounds, with small but cumulatively significant numbers from, among others, journalism, science, and medicine, along with twelve working-mens' representatives.[133]

However, what mattered at least as much as the numerical strength of the 'Whiggish' MPs, from a political point of view, was the fact that the general election was interpreted as a major setback for Chamberlainite Radicalism. The Liberal party did, it is true, make considerable gains in the counties, though it has been questioned whether Chamberlain's land policies made any real impact here,[134] but the surprisingly strong Conservative performance in Lancashire, London, and the English boroughs generally was attributed by many politicians to the alarm caused by Chamberlain's campaign.[135] As one of the survivors in Lancashire wrote to another, 'I get letters daily from politicians of various degrees of Radicalism, attributing their difficulties or disasters to our friend Chamberlain

---

[131] It should be noted, however, that there was a smaller overlap between the members of this group and the 'aristocratic-landowning' group—only sixteen, or 13.8 per cent of the 'industrialists and merchants'. Previously, the figure had been around 20 per cent.

[132] This group consisted of twenty Queen's Counsel, sixty other barristers, ten solicitors, and one other MP who, according to *Dod's Parliamentary Companion*, was 'formerly in the legal profession'. The overlap with the 'aristocratic-landowning' group was only slightly less than before, accounting for twenty-four (26.3 per cent) of the 'lawyers'.

[133] One of the most interesting features of the general election was the very high turnover of MPs: 321 members of the old House of Commons did not sit in the new one, and 168 of these were Liberals. Eighty-three of these Liberals had retired, while eighty-five were defeated. For a full list, see *The Times*, 11 Dec. 1885, p. 7.

[134] Henry Pelling, *Popular Politics and Society in Late Victorian Britain* (2nd ed., 1979), 6–7, suggests that fears about the effect of tariffs on living standards may have been the main reason for the Liberal gains. On the other hand, Alan Simon, *Historical Journal* (1975), 818–19, points to the resentment felt by the agricultural labourers towards the parsons.

[135] 'What a smash in London! I expected that the "Radical Programme" would lose us many votes, but the result goes far beyond my expectations', Kimberley to Monk Bretton, 28 Nov. 1885, Monk Bretton MSS. Lyulph Stanley reported that hostility to Chamberlain had played a part in the Liberal carnage in Lancashire: Stanley to Elliot, 28 Nov. 1885, Elliot MSS. For criticism, by a Radical, of Chamberlain's 'want of statesmanship which has been very gross', see William Rathbone's letter to James Bryce, 27 Nov. 1885, Bryce MSS, UB 26..

and his programme, and the spirit in which he has thrust it forward.'[136] His call for free education had backfired in a particularly disastrous fashion, demonstrating the risks Chamberlain had taken in promoting ill-thought out policies. The Church of England had naturally been frightened by Chamberlain's suggestion that free education should ultimately be financed from the proceeds of disendowment, but because he had been anxious to play down the question of disestablishment, which he argued was not ripe for settlement, Chamberlain had proposed, to the anger of the more extreme Nonconformists, that the exchequer grants needed in the meantime to pay for free education should be separated from the long-term question of public control of the voluntary schools. In this way, Chamberlain managed to hand the Conservatives a valuable rallying cry while, at the same time, alienating many Nonconformists by not going far enough. Free education proved to be a serious electoral liability to the Liberal party, and Chamberlain himself virtually dropped the issue during the last part of his campaign.[137] The Conservatives were also very successful in exploiting the related cry of 'the Church in danger', tarring the Liberal party with the disestablishment brush in spite of Gladstone's and Chamberlain's efforts to shelve the question.[138] 'Fair trade', the demand for retaliatory tariffs against Britain's industrial competitors, proved to be another vote winner for the Conservatives in the boroughs.[139] Furthermore, they benefited from Parnell's manifesto of 21 November, instructing the Irish voters in British constituencies to oppose Liberal candidates, although, as C. H. D. Howard has pointed out, many would probably have done so in any case because of the influence of the Catholic priests, who were alarmed by Chamber-

---

[136] Sir Ughtred Kay Shuttleworth to Rylands, 28 Nov. 1885, L. G. Rylands, *Correspondence and Speeches of Mr. Peter Rylands, M.P.: With a Sketch of his Life* (Manchester, 1890), i. 352—3.

[137] See Alan Simon, 'Joseph Chamberlain and Free Education in the Election of 1885', *History of Education*, 2 (1973), 56—78. For the damage done to Chamberlain's standing with the Nonconformists, see Edward Hamilton's diary, 8 Dec. 1885, BL Add. MSS 48642.

[138] Simon, *Historical Journal* (1975), 791—820. Shaw Lefevre (Reading) and Childers (Pontefract) both blamed the Church question for their defeats: Shaw Lefevre to Chamberlain, 28 Nov. 1885, Chamberlain MSS, JC5/52/7; Childers to Mundella, 11, 28 Nov. 1885, Mundella MSS, 6P/18.

[139] Reginald Brett and Alfred Milner attributed their defeats, at Plymouth and Hendon respectively, to this cause: Brett to Chamberlain, 9 Dec. 1885, Chamberlain MSS, JC5/6/3; Milner to Bryce, 8 Dec. 1885, Bryce MSS, UB 26.

lain's free-education proposals.[140] According to one contemporary estimate, there was a powerful Irish vote in twenty-four English and Scottish constituencies, and in a further sixteen constituencies the Irish were considered strong enough to turn the election.[141] Even when the Irish vote was not decisive, however, it was frequently one of several contributory factors in the defeat of Liberal candidates.[142]

At the end of the day, then, Chamberlain failed to sweep the board in the new constituencies in the way many had feared, and the Liberal party narrowly failed to secure an overall parliamentary majority, winning 334 of the 670 seats, with this total including several independents. For the moderates, such a result could be regarded as a triumph for themselves. Goschen was relieved to find that 'On the whole, the advance of democracy has not been so great as I anticipated it would be',[143] and he declared the electorate's verdict to be a 'crushing defeat' for the Radicals and 'a complete justification of moderate Liberalism'.[144] Indeed, the Liberal chief whip estimated that only 101 members of the new parliament were 'Radicals'.[145] One sure sign of the way the wind was now blowing was John Morley's denunciation of 'the baffled trickster, JOE', and his acceptance that the elections had shown that the Radicals could not do without the moderates.[146] Early in December 1885, it seemed that if only the forces of moderation within the Liberal party were prepared to assert themselves, their prospects were more favourable than they had been for some time.[147]

[140] C. H. D. Howard, 'The Parnell Manifesto of 21 November 1885, and the Schools Question', *English Historical Review*, 62 (1947), 42–51.

[141] *Manchester Guardian*, 30 Oct. 1885, p. 8. Even at this stage, three weeks before Parnell issued his manifesto, it was thought that the Irish vote would go to the Conservatives.

[142] Sir Robert Cunliffe attributed his defeat, in the Denbigh district of boroughs, to the loss of the Irish vote, the activities of the parsons, and the fair-trade cry: Cunliffe to Elliot, 12 Dec. 1885, Elliot MSS; while Sir Wilfrid Lawson, who was narrowly defeated at Cockermouth, thought that the Irish vote and fair trade had both counted against him: G. W. E. Russell (ed.), *Sir Wilfrid Lawson: A Memoir* (1909), 179. R. T. Reid, on the other hand, had no hesitation in ascribing his defeat in Dunbartonshire to the Irish: Reid to Broadhurst, 7 Dec. 1885, Broadhurst MSS, vol. 2.

[143] Goschen to Lady Blennerhassett, n.d. [Dec. 1885], Cambridge University Library Add. 7486, E.52.

[144] Goschen to Albert Grey, 1 Dec. 1885, Grey MSS, 211/3.

[145] Lord Richard Grosvenor to Gladstone, 12 Dec. 1885, BL Add. MSS 44316, fo. 148.

[146] Morley to his sister, 2 Dec. 1885, in Hirst, *Early Life of Morley*, ii. 274; Lewis Harcourt's diary, 7 Dec. 1885, Harcourt MSS.

[147] Cf. Albert Grey to Cartwright, 7 Dec. 1885, Cartwright MSS, Box 5, fo. 533; Cartwright's diary, 4 Dec. 1885, ibid. 6/16.

7

Glastone and the Liberal Party
The Road to Irish Home Rule

It has been seen how the peculiar circumstances surrounding the general election of 1880, and the scale of the Liberal victory, led Gladstone to invent a justificatory theory of his conduct which explained his resumption of the premiership on the grounds of the extraordinary difficulties involved in putting right the damage done by the Beaconsfield administration. The purpose of this chapter is to demonstrate that this rationalization in fact set the tone for Gladstone's subsequent leadership, exerting an enduring influence upon his own perception of his position in Liberal politics, and reacting with his experiences as the head of a divided Cabinet in such a way as to create a new mental synthesis. This synthesis, it is suggested, provides the key to an understanding not only of the motives behind Gladstone's adoption of the cause of home rule for Ireland in 1885–6, but also of the particular manner in which he attempted to carry through his new-found commitment.

The character of Gladstone's leadership from 1880 to 1885 was governed by a persistent assumption of his own imminent retirement, which derived from his subjective interpretation of the events leading up to his return to office. Gladstone had come out of retirement for a special purpose, and as this meant that the claims of Granville and Hartington to the premiership were placed only in temporary abeyance, further compelling excuses were required on each occasion when his repeated assertion of his desire for retirement at the earliest possible moment failed to issue in the act of retirement itself. The pattern was established in the autumn of 1881, after the long second session of the new parliament, and followed lengthy communications with his colleagues, family, and friends. In a letter to John Bright, at the end of September, Gladstone explained that he had accepted office in April 1880 as 'a special and temporary mission', which he had 'never hoped to get over . . . sooner than in the autumn of the present year'. However, while he acknowledged that great progress had been made in most aspects of the mission, such as 'India, the Eastern Question, and perhaps finance', unfortunately 'Ireland . . . came upon us unawares, looming very large':

This question, and the question of the Transvaal, still hang in the balance. From neither of them can I run away. I must, health and strength continuing, remain chained to the oar until each of them has reached what, in our own way of speech, we call a settlement. But when it pleases God that that point is arrived at, then I think will be the suitable and becoming time for me to retire.[1]

Thus, the impression was given that his long-desired retirement would be deferred for no more than another year, an arrangement which had an additional advantage in that it would allow his most likely successors in the House of Commons, Hartington and then Dilke, the opportunity to acquire more experience.[2] He remained clear in his own mind, as he wrote to Lord Acton at the end of the year, that 'when the great specialities are disposed of I am outwardly free and inwardly bound to ask for my dismissal'.[3] But, in the autumn of the following year, Gladstone was still to be found in Downing Street, claiming that the reform of parliamentary procedure was 'the last of those [subjects] which I am bound to try to work in the House of Commons',[4] and indicating that he would resign in December.[5] With a little encouragement from his colleagues, this deadline was put back until Easter 1883,[6] and at Easter 1883 was delayed further until the autumn.[7] By December of that year, he was preparing to 'mortgage another piece of my small residue of life', in order to assist the passage of the Franchise and Redistribution Bills,[8] and a year later, with the progress of these bills assured, following an agreement with the Conservatives, Gladstone planned to retire at

---

[1] Gladstone to Bright, 29 Sept. 1881, BL Add. MSS 44113, fo. 158.

[2] Gladstone to Granville, 15 Nov. 1881, in Agatha Ramm (ed.), *The Political Correspondence of Mr Gladstone and Lord Granville, 1876–1886* (Oxford, 1962), i. 311. Cf. Lucy Masterman (ed.), *Mary Gladstone—Mrs Drew: Her Diaries and Letters* (1930), 235–6 (entry for 15 Nov. 1881).

[3] Gladstone to Lord Acton, 26 Dec. 1881, Acton MSS.

[4] Gladstone to Granville, 20 Nov. 1882, in Ramm (ed.), *Gladstone–Granville Correspondence, 1876–1886*, i. 437.

[5] Mary Gladstone to Lord Acton, 7 Oct. 1882, Acton MSS.

[6] D. W. R. Bahlman (ed.), *The Diary of Sir Edward Walter Hamilton, 1880–1885* (Oxford, 1972), i. 367 (entry for 27 Nov. 1882).

[7] Lord Derby's diary, 30 Apr. 1883, Derby MSS.

[8] Gladstone to Harcourt, 26 Dec. 1883 (copy), BL Add. MSS 44198, fo. 169.

Easter 1885.[9] By May of that year, he hoped to be able to go at the end of the parliamentary session, discerning the possibility of 'a wind-up better than I could at any time have hoped', once the two outstanding matters of Russia and Ireland had been settled.[10]

The annual emergence of new 'specialities' for Gladstone to stay on and deal with was evidently a necessary psychological device for a man who, while temperamentally incapable of a permanent, voluntary withdrawal from political life, was yet unable to overcome certain qualms about retaining his position for so long. The uncomfortable feeling that he was depriving Granville and Hartington of the position due to one of them[11] demanded that some special justification be produced for his failure to restore the leadership to its rightful owner. Lord Frederick Cavendish was probably right in thinking that Gladstone's talk of retirement 'was not so much prompted by the personal longing for it ... as by conscientious scruples with regard to Lord Granville and Lord Hartington', and that the prospect of it was in reality 'a vision which refreshes and cheers him to turn to'.[12] The idea of retiring from politics into a private world of study and preparation for the afterlife was a helpful mental crutch, easing his feelings of guilt but, at the same time, fortifying him for the immediate task in hand, in the assurance that he would then be able to go 'at Easter', or 'in the autumn', or whenever it might be. This habit of thought was undoubtedly reinforced by the genuine problems of age and health: Gladstone was in his seventy-first year when he took office, and the following five years were to be punctuated by periods of serious ill health. Even in the first session of the new parliament, he suffered a severe illness which threatened to bring his premiership to an abrupt and early end, and he was similarly incapacitated in the spring of 1884; he spent two months convalescing at Cannes early in 1883, and in January 1885 it appeared for a time as if that trip would have to be repeated. It should not be difficult to see from this why Gladstone was able to convince himself that he must soon retire, and there is no

[9] Gladstone to Sir Arthur Hamilton-Gordon, 5 Dec. 1884, BL Add. MSS 44321, fo. 222; Mary Gladstone to Lord Acton, 19 Jan. 1885, Acton MSS.
[10] Gladstone to his wife, 1 May 1885, also 2 May 1885, in A. Tilney Bassett (ed.), *Gladstone to his Wife* (1936), 246–7. Cf. Dilke's diary, 20 May 1885, BL Add. MSS 43927.
[11] Mary Gladstone to Lord Acton, 12 Nov. 1881, Acton MSS.
[12] J. Bailey (ed.), *The Diary of Lady Frederick Cavendish* (1927), ii. 295 (entry for 4 Nov. 1881).

reason to doubt his sincerity when he 'set up' his contention that ' "when the hurly burly's done" I shall be entitled if it pleases God to set up my fifty years of service as reason why I should run, or walk, out to grass, instead of being driven on until I am fit only for the Knacker'.[13]

Dr Andrew Jones, however, has argued that Gladstone's constant talk of retirement was, in fact, a deliberate and subtle tactic designed to keep his ambitious and argumentative Cabinet colleagues in line.[14] Such a convenient and tidy interpretation is certainly very tempting, but it is more likely that talking of retirement was part of a subconscious process, so common with Gladstone, by which his actions created the most favourable conditions for himself. This may be illustrated by the way he sometimes spoke of relinquishing the premiership and adopting an independent position in the House of Commons, similar to that taken by Sir Robert Peel after 1846, a notion that undoubtedly had a genuine appeal to Gladstone but which infallibly prompted his colleagues to press him to remain at his post.[15] Indeed, there is a paradox to be found in the fact that Gladstone's talk of resignation was so indiscriminate—'he has spoken of it quite casually to various people, and always takes it for granted that they will take it for granted'[16]—that it had a serious effect on the way he handled the Cabinet, and served to undermine his position within it.

Gladstone's habit of thinking of himself as being on the point of retiring tended to encourage the evasion of difficult or uncongenial policy decisions, with the result that his government too often lacked a clear overall direction in its policy making. The session of 1883, in particular, proved to be a shambles from the point of view of legislative achievement, because of Gladstone's unwillingness to look more than a few months ahead and his plea that he was not able to cope with major issues.[17] Even Herbert Gladstone was struck by

---

[13] Gladstone to Lord Acton, 14 Dec. 1881, Acton MSS.
[14] *Historical Journal*, 16 (1973), 215–18, reviewing Bahlman's edition of the Hamilton diaries.
[15] Cf. Bahlman (ed.), *Hamilton Diary*, i. 348 (22 Oct. 1882); Harcourt to Chamberlain, 10 Dec. 1882 (typescript), Harcourt MSS, Box 716.
[16] Mary Gladstone to Lord Acton, 12 Nov. 1881, Acton MSS. Cf. Lord Derby's diary, 7 Nov. 1881, Derby MSS.
[17] For the problems this caused, see e.g. Harcourt to Hartington, 2 Feb. 1883 (typescript), Harcourt MSS, Box 720. For Dilke's complaint in May, see Lord Crewe, *Lord Rosebery* (1931), i. 170. Cf. Lewis Harcourt's diary, 16 Nov. 1883, Harcourt MSS, and Lord Derby's diary, 9 Dec. 1883, Derby MSS.

the fact that his father seemed 'rather disinclined to work and go *at* the difficult questions of the day'.[18] Similarly, at the beginning of 1885, when the government's difficulties in the Sudan were placing Gladstone in an unpleasant position, his tendency to shirk questions was apparent. Lord Derby noted the Premier's liking for long, casual conversations when he paid business visits, and was told by Gladstone on one of these occasions that 'he found his great pleasure in reading . . . at his age he found much work impossible. Three hours were his usual limit, in case of necessity he could go up to five hours, but anything more exhausted him. Thus he had of necessity a good deal of leisure.'[19]

The most serious problem of all was that so long as the uncertainty about the leadership persisted, Gladstone's political heirs were themselves disinclined to allow major, long-term policy decisions to be settled. In consequence, Gladstone was confronted with what seemed to him to be disunity amongst his colleagues, and he responded by assuming the role of peacemaker in Cabinet instead of being the director. As Lord Derby noted, after two years in Gladstone's Cabinet, 'The Premier listens with more patience, and speaks less, than anywhere else. He is far from being dictatorial.'[20] This conciliatory function was by no means congenial to him, however, and Derby was informed by Granville that 'there was nothing which the Premier disliked so much as a Cabinet . . . his extreme gentleness and readiness to submit to contradiction, were not natural to him, but imposed by an effort of will, and . . . he made no secret of its being a painful one'.[21] Indeed, as time went on, Gladstone became more and more averse to summoning Cabinets at all, as the complaints of his colleagues testify,[22] and the inability of the Cabinet to agree on policy when it did meet meant that important executive decisions were often taken outside of it. According to Lord Derby's assessment, in December 1884:

---

[18] Herbert Gladstone's diary, 22 Apr. 1883, Glynne–Gladstone MSS. Cf. Lord Derby's diary, 12 Apr. 1883, Derby MSS.

[19] Lord Derby's diary, 14 Feb. 1885. But Gladstone was obviously not counting his hours of attendance in the House of Commons.

[20] Ibid., 27 Nov. 1884.

[21] Ibid., 10 Aug. 1883.

[22] Ibid., 26 June 1884, for complaints by Granville and Kimberley. See also Granville to Derby, 3 June 1885, Derby MSS. Those Cabinets that were held were often summoned at very short notice, see e.g. Derby's diary, 7 Mar. 1884, Derby MSS.

Our chief administrative danger . . . lies in the careless, slipshod way in which Cabinet business is done: questions taken up, talked about, dropped with no decision taken, and then after some weeks one finds that they have been settled by the sole authority of some one department, perhaps with, perhaps without, the sanction of the Prime Minister . . . I can scarcely think that in his best days he would have let things slide as he does now. To this hour I do not know who was responsible for the sending of Gordon to Khartoum: nor when the expedition for his relief was finally settled.[23]

Unofficial committees of the Cabinet—Reginald Brett apparently called them 'Cabals'—were occasionally summoned by Gladstone,[24] but a number concerned with foreign policy decisions were convened by the Foreign Secretary and did not include the Prime Minister,[25] and in one case, in May 1883, Harcourt was responsible for calling a meeting of all the Cabinet ministers in the House of Commons (plus Kimberley) except Gladstone, which took the decision to press forward with the whole of the government's legislative programme for that session.[26]

On the surface, the Liberal government of 1880 to 1885, confronted with perhaps intractable problems in Ireland, Egypt, and elsewhere, gives the appearance of being hopelessly divided and also tempestuous in its deliberations. Indeed, it has been suggested by some historians, with the Cabinets of May 1885 particularly in mind, that argumentativeness was second nature to Liberal ministries.[27] But this view is greatly exaggerated. The Cabinet, according to Derby, though unbusinesslike, was remarkably harmonious, for instance: 'Our discussion [on the relief expedition for General Gordon] was long, and as usual in such cases, rather desultory: quite amicable, no sign of temper on the part of anyone, but much perplexity, and no agreement as to what should be done.'[28] In fact, Derby thought it a pity that Cabinet ministers did not quarrel more, as they might at least have reached agreement in this way.[29]

---

[23] Ibid., 7 Dec. 1884.
[24] Dilke's diary, 15 Nov. 1882, BL. Add. MSS 43925.
[25] Ibid., 6 Nov. 1882, 18 Jan. 1884, 27 Feb. 1884.
[26] Ibid., 24 May 1883.
[27] See Andrew Jones in *Parliamentary Affairs*, 25 (autumn 1972), 351–4, reviewing Hamer's *Liberal Politics in the Age of Gladstone and Rosebery*. The chapter in A. B. Cooke and John Vincent's *The Governing Passion: Cabinet Government and Party Politics in Britain, 1885–86* (Hassocks, 1974) dealing with the last six months of the second Gladstone ministry is entitled 'Government by Dispute'.
[28] Lord Derby's diary, 21 Apr. 1884, Derby MSS.
[29] Ibid. 13 Mar. 1884.

Even the disputes over Irish policy in May 1885 were apparently conducted in good temper.[30] Nor is there much evidence that personal relations between ministers were bad.[31] The inability to agree on major issues of policy reflected not an intrinsic love of 'Government by Dispute', but the fact that, in the climate of uncertainty created by Gladstone's talk of retirement, rival ministers were reluctant to be committed to anything at all. Gladstone's problems of leadership, it is therefore suggested, were largely—though of course unconsciously—of his own making. The situation was summed up by Derby in January 1885, at a time when the Cabinet was in hopeless disagreement on the question of Egypt: 'The peculiar position of the Premier, who is always declaring himself to be on the point of retiring, increases the difficulty, for he is very unwilling to do anything that may bind him to stay longer in office, and we cannot act without him.'[32]

The crucial point which follows from this is that, while Gladstone's hand-to-mouth style of leadership virtually ensured that there would be lack of unity amongst his colleagues, it had the effect, for that very reason, of convincing him that he must continue to lead in order to save the Liberal party from disintegration. This process is illustrated well by the crisis of December 1883. Throughout that year, Gladstone had protested his inability to grapple with large measures, and when, towards the end of the summer, he began to show signs of willingness to contemplate a further extension of his leadership, he would speak only in terms of a simple Franchise Bill without redistribution, so that he might avoid the responsibility for bringing on a dissolution of parliament.[33] Furthermore, he remained insistent, even after the plan had been discussed in Cabinet, that it was nothing more than a tentative suggestion, as he reminded Hartington on 7 November: 'I have as you will remember *proposed* nothing to the Cabinet; but have merely stated hypothetically a course of main business, which would enable me—in my 75th year—at least to begin the session with my colleagues . . . Certainly at present no one is committed.'[34] Of course, the result of this unwillingness to look far ahead was to provoke a public disagreement between Hartington and Chamberlain, who, assuming after

---

[30] Ibid., 15 May 1885.
[31] Ibid., 27 Nov. 1884.
[32] Ibid., 8 Jan. 1885.
[33] Granville to Hartington, n.d. [Sept. 1883?], Devonshire MSS, 340.1372.
[34] Gladstone to Hartington, 7 Nov. 1883 (copy), BL Add. MSS 44146, fo. 231.

the Cabinet on 22 November that the government was to proceed
with a simple Franchise Bill, were both determined to speak out on
the related issues of the Irish representation and redistribution.
Gladstone still maintained that 'the Cabinet has decided nothing as
to the measures it will proceed with except that *if* it proceeds with the
franchise, it will be the franchise alone',[35] but this method of
procedure had almost guaranteed that the differences between
Hartington and Chamberlain would be brought to the surface. In the
end, Gladstone had to be persuaded that Hartington could only
accept the separation of franchise from redistribution provided he
agreed to remain long enough to supervise the passage of the latter:
'This casts the political difficulty now before us into a personal form
and makes a demand on me which is formidable, and which requires
to be carefully weighed.'[36] After carefully weighing the situation,
Gladstone agreed to the prolongation of his leadership.

Gladstone's growing conception of his own indispensability was
encouraged, above all else, by the recalcitrance of the Whig ministers
on the question of policy towards Ireland. Hartington, in particular,
demonstrated a marked proclivity towards strong coercive measures, while resisting Gladstone's attempts to balance these with
concessions on Irish local government. As we have already seen, such
resistance proved successful, early in 1883, when Hartington was
able to block the plan for provincial councils in Ireland favoured by
the Premier, who was 'convalescing' at Cannes. This episode merits a
little closer attention, as there is a strong suspicion that Gladstone's
holiday was prolonged deliberately, as a result of the obstructionism
of his colleagues, with the intention of proving how badly they
needed him. The original plan, in mid-January, when Gladstone
announced that he was going to Cannes, was that he would return on
3 February.[37] This date was later put back until 12 February, still in
time for the opening of parliament,[38] but, as the opposition amongst
Liberal ministers to any further concessions to the Irish became
plain, Gladstone altered his schedule again and announced that he

[35] Gladstone to Hartington, 3 Dec. 1883 (copy), ibid. fo. 239.
[36] Gladstone to Granville, 20 Dec. 1883, in Ramm (ed.), *Gladstone–Granville Correspondence, 1876–1886*, ii. 133.
[37] Gladstone to Granville, 13 Jan. 1883, ibid. ii. 8. Cf. Edward Hamilton to Horace Seymour, 12 Jan. 1883, Glynne–Gladstone MSS.
[38] Gladstone to Granville, 31 Jan. 1883, in Ramm (ed.), *Gladstone–Granville Correspondence, 1876–1886*, ii. 13. See also his letter of 22 Jan., ibid. ii. 9–11, wishing to defer the decision on Irish local government until Easter.

would remain in Cannes until Easter.[39] It is unlikely that this decision had anything to do with the dictates of health, as Gladstone was reported by one of his private secretaries as having recovered considerably soon after his arrival in France.[40] Furthermore, his doctor had indicated, as Gladstone informed Granville, that he might return to England at any time, 'for public reasons',[41] and it is noticeable that his letters to Granville were spiced with allusions to unforeseen contingencies, arising when parliament met, which might necessitate an early return. On 15 February, for instance, Gladstone wrote: 'The first few days in the House of Commons may I think probably throw light on the question of my future movements: but my part will be simply to remain as agreed upon, unless I hear from you to the contrary.'[42] His wish was granted. Granville had to telegraph on 19 February asking him to return because of the complications to the debate on the address, arising from the opposition's determination to discuss the 'Kilmainham treaty' of the previous spring.[43] Gladstone replied on the twenty-first, expressing his willingness to comply with his colleagues' request, although he subsequently made it clear that he would prefer to delay his return until the Kilmainham debate itself was over.[44] There is a hint in his letter of the twenty-fifth of the way Gladstone must have been relishing the situation: 'I am ... glad to think I shall somewhat lighten the burden on your's and Hartington's shoulders.'[45] Lord Acton, who was with the Gladstone entourage, drew the obvious conclusion: 'It of course escapes nobody that there can be no pretence of retirement in summer if he is sent for after two days of the new session.'[46] Once back in England, as Dilke noted in his diary, Gladstone seemed to have forgotten all about his retirement.[47]

[39] Gladstone to Granville, 7, 8 Feb. 1883 no. 2, ibid. ii. 20–2. Cf. Hamilton to Brett, 8 Feb. 1883, Esher MSS, 5/2, expressing surprise at Gladstone's decision.

[40] George Leveson Gower to Seymour, 25 Jan. 1883, Glynne–Gladstone MSS.

[41] Gladstone to Granville, 8 Feb. 1883 no. 2, in Ramm (ed.), *Gladstone–Granville Correspondence, 1876–1886*, ii. 21–2.

[42] Gladstone to Granville, 15 Feb. 1883, ibid. ii. 25. It was characteristic of Gladstone that, at the same time, he was engrossing himself in Homer and theology: Spencer Lyttelton to Seymour, 19 Feb. 1883, Glynne–Gladstone MSS.

[43] Granville also wrote a letter to follow the telegram: Granville to Gladstone, 19 Feb. 1883, in Ramm (ed.), *Gladstone–Granville Correspondence*, ii. 29.

[44] Gladstone to Granville, 21, 25, 27 Feb. 1883, ibid. ii. 29–30, 32–3, 33.

[45] Ibid. ii. 32–3.

[46] Acton to Granville, '6 pm Tuesday', [20 Feb. 1883], PRO 30/29/29.

[47] Dilke's diary, 29 Mar. 1883, BL Add. MSS 43925.

The function, then, of such episodes as the trip to Cannes and the franchise crisis of December 1883 was to contribute to the gradual emergence of a new Gladstonian mental synthesis which regarded his continued leadership as essential for the preservation of Liberal unity. His belief that the Whigs were proving their inability to assume the responsibilities of leadership was finally demonstrated, to Gladstone's satisfaction, by the failure of the Cabinet, in May–June 1885, to agree on an Irish policy for the future. Gladstone himself was in favour of a 'declaration of policy' by the Cabinet, even though there was no time to legislate before the dissolution of parliament,[48] and he approved of Chamberlain's plan for the creation of a Central Board in Dublin to administer local affairs, which he saw as a means of forestalling the more extreme demand for 'home rule'.[49] However, much to the Prime Minister's displeasure, Chamberlain withdrew his scheme because of the opposition to it from Spencer, Hartington, and a majority of their Cabinet colleagues on 9 May,[50] although he then retaliated by resisting Spencer's request for a renewal of the crimes act, for two years, and a Land Purchase Bill. An impasse was thus reached, and no escape had been found by the time of the Whitsun recess.[51]

In fact, this situation was another instance of the way in which the continuing uncertainty about Gladstone's position prevented any agreement being reached by Liberal ministers, whose only objective, in the short term in which everyone was dealing, was simply to prevent the government from being committed to anyone else's policy.[52] On several occasions, from 6 May, Gladstone threatened to resign immediately, because he felt unable to agree to the renewal of the crimes act,[53] and if this was not enough to ensure instability in the Cabinet, he persistently stated that he was due to retire at Whitsun in

[48] Lord Derby's diary, 29 Apr. 1885, Derby MSS.
[49] Ibid., 10, 14 May 1885. Granville told Derby that Gladstone 'believes good administration will satisfy them [the Irish] without Home Rule', ibid., 14 May 1885.
[50] See Lewis Harcourt's diary, 10, 11 May 1885, Harcourt MSS.
[51] For a record of the events of May 1885, see Cooke and Vincent, *The Governing Passion*, pp. 225–44. Spencer's memoranda are printed in Peter Gordon (ed.), *The Red Earl: The Papers of the Fifth Earl Spencer, 1835–1910*, i: *1835–1885* (Northants Record Society, 31; 1981), 300–5.
[52] Harcourt was convinced that Hartington and Chamberlain were being deliberately obstructive, in order to prevent any agreement from being reached: Lewis Harcourt's diary, 15 May 1885, Harcourt MSS.
[53] Ibid., 6, 9 May 1885. Cf. Bahlman (ed.), *Hamilton Diary*, ii. 859–60 (10 May 1885).

any case.[54] It was not until 20 May that Harcourt managed to extract a pledge from him to remain at the helm until the end of the parliamentary session.[55] The effect of the Cabinet crisis, nevertheless, was to convince Gladstone that there remained an urgent need for his conciliatory style of leadership in order to assist the party through the critical months ahead. His commitment to his colleagues still did not extend, at this point, to leading the party through the general election,[56] but, during the Whitsun holiday, the first signs began to appear that he was contemplating a further extension of his time in harness. While at Hawarden, according to an entry in his diary, he 'opened rather a new view as to my retirement' with his old confidant Lord Wolverton,[57] and when he returned to Downing Street, early in June, his private secretary noticed a marked change in his attitude, finding him 'extraordinarily well, and . . . much more settled in mind. He does not refuse to talk of doing things some weeks or months hence, as he did a short time back.'[58]

On 8 June, however, the government was suddenly defeated in the House of Commons on a detail of the budget quite unrelated to the Irish question. The precise circumstances surrounding this vote remain a mystery: Gladstone was evidently aware of the danger of defeat earlier in the day, and yet the whipping was said to have been extraordinarily lax;[59] nor is it clear why he and Dilke, having declared during the debate that the vote would be regarded as one of life or death for the government, did not simply move for an adjournment.[60] There was undoubtedly a death-wish among many members of the Cabinet, who had actually discussed taking a 'dive' a month earlier, on the Registration Bill,[61] and there must be a strong suspicion, though there is no direct evidence to support it, that Gladstone took the opportunity provided to escape from office

[54] Lewis Harcourt's diary, 19 May 1885, Harcourt MSS.
[55] Ibid., 20 May 1885.
[56] Dilke's diary, 20 May 1885, BL Add. MSS 43927.
[57] Gladstone's diary, n.d., in John Morley, *Life of William Ewart Gladstone* (1903), iii. 196.
[58] Bahlman (ed.), *Hamilton Diary*, ii. 876 (6 June 1885).
[59] Cf. A. B. Cooke and John Vincent (eds.), *Lord Carlingford's Journal: Reflections of a Cabinet Minister, 1885* (Oxford, 1971), 112–13 (8 June 1885); Albert Grey to Lord Halifax, 9 June 1885, Hickleton MSS, A4/84.
[60] Cf. Lord Cowper to Lady Florence Herbert, 17 June 1885, in S. H. Harris, *Auberon Herbert: Crusader for Liberty* (1943), 276.
[61] Lord Derby's diary, 7 May 1885, Derby MSS. Harcourt and Chamberlain were the main advocates of this course.

before a decision had to be taken on the crimes act. Whatever the case
may have been, his reaction to the situation at the subsequent
Cabinet meeting was significant. As Lord Rosebery's diary for 9 June
has it: 'Cabinet at noon. All in high spirits except Mr G. who was
depressed. He began by saying anxiously that he would like to have
announced that the Cabinet had come to agreement about Ireland,
but unless he is now told there is such agreement, he must take the
reverse for granted. No one speaking, he proceeded to the result of
the division.'[62] In other words, the ministry had fallen before
Gladstone could round off the last session of the 1880 parliament by
settling, as he had told his wife at the beginning of May that he still
hoped to,[63] the one outstanding question for which he felt a special
responsibility—the government of Ireland.

The way was now open for Gladstone to justify staying on as party
leader for a little longer in order to prepare the Liberals with a policy
to deal with Ireland after the general election.[64] A reply to Gladstone
from Lord Wolverton, dated 18 June, indicates the drift of the
former's thinking, and also throws light on the conversation at
Hawarden at Whitsun:

The 'secret draft' which I enclose is indeed in accord with all you have said to
me in confidence. I feel the greatest delicacy in alluding to the great step
which you contemplate, for *personal* and *party* considerations seem so
antagonistic. The Irish question, the solidity, and the existence of the party
as a *united* Liberal party, and the success at the elections can only be assured
if you are leader. I would hope and trust on the grounds of party that those
who read your memorandum will feel that your proposed Irish policy should
produce the 'state of facts' which would at least give you some grounds for
the further consideration, before the close of the Parliament, of the position,
and perhaps that it may give you a 'stand point of finality' without creating a
'new departure' for an *indefinite period* or with an *undefined future*. I almost
venture to hope that reading between the lines of your memorandum, I see
your patriotic inclination upon a defined and great policy to forego for the
sake of all, your strong claim for immediate release.[65]

---

[62] Crewe, *Rosebery*, i. 241.
[63] Tilney Bassett (ed.), *Gladstone to his Wife*, pp. 246–7 (1 May 1885).
[64] There was for a time a possibility that Salisbury might be unable to form a
government, and it is interesting to note that Gladstone seemed inclined, if recalled, to
reconstruct his ministry without Hartington and Spencer: Bahlman (ed.), *Hamilton
Diary*, ii. 894 (22 June 1885).
[65] Wolverton to Gladstone, 18 June 1885, BL Add. MSS 44349, fo. 182. I have
found no trace of Gladstone's 'secret draft'.

This suggests that while Gladstone was willing to lead the Liberals into the general election, on a platform of local government for Ireland, it remained important for him to be able to present this decision as a temporary expedient with a specific object in mind, which should not appear to be in conflict with his recent professions of wanting to retire. Thus the established pattern of Gladstone's relationship with the Liberal party since 1880 was repeated again. He would continue, but there had to be a 'standpoint of finality' and no 'new departure': the continuity between the late Liberal ministry and the next one had to be absolutely clear. Moreover, as he explained to Dilke, he could only justify his position if the policy to be pursued was the Central Board and not some lesser measure, for which work 'others would suffice'.[66] Two essential pre-conditions were also stipulated: one, as Edward Hamilton discovered, in a conversation on 26 June, was that the Liberal party had to be united on a 'definite programme', as he 'declines to fight merely the battle of the Whigs and Radicals for the purpose of determining the political "ins" and "outs"';[67] the other, as Dilke learned, was 'Parnell's acquiescence' in this programme: 'If Parnell, having got more from the Tories, was going to oppose, he, Mr. Gladstone, could not go on.'[68]

Until July 1885, then, Gladstone was thinking in terms of a limited concession of autonomy for Ireland, which he hoped would unite the Liberal party and secure the co-operation of Parnell. This position was undermined, however, when it became clear that the new Conservative administration was bidding for Nationalist support by dropping coercion, offering a land-purchase measure, and attacking the regime of Lord Spencer.[69] The 'perfidy' of the Conservatives appeared to have destroyed the basis for a moderate settlement of the Irish question, for the time being at any rate, but whereas most Liberals concluded (as we shall see in the next chapter) that the

---

[66] Dilke's diary, 6 July 1885, BL Add. MSS 43927. Gladstone wrote to Spencer on 30 June that 'Nothing can withhold my retirement except the presentation of some great and critical problem in the national life, and the hope, *if* such a hope shall be, of making some special contribution towards a solution of it', Gordon (ed.), *Spencer Papers*, p. 311.

[67] Bahlman (ed.), *Hamilton Diary*, ii. 899 (26 June 1885).

[68] Dilke's diary, 6 July 1885, BL Add. MSS 43927.

[69] In fact the new Lord Lieutenant, Carnarvon, had a secret meeting with Parnell on 1 Aug. (with the knowledge of Salisbury, but not of the rest of the Cabinet), to discuss the question of home rule: Sir Arthur Hardinge, *The Life of Henry Howard Molyneux Herbert: Fourth Earl of Carnarvon, 1831–1890* (1925), iii. 174–81. Of course, Gladstone and the Liberals were also unaware of this meeting.

higher terms which Parnell was being encouraged to demand were politically impracticable, Gladstone was drawn to the opposite view, that the concession of 'home rule', which he had tried for so long to forestall, could be delayed no longer. The detached tone of a letter to Derby, on 17 July, was ominous: Gladstone wrote of the 'important changes' in the 'facts of the situation' during the previous few weeks, and after speculating as to the precise form which Parnell's new demand might take, he merely observed that any such scheme would 'constitute an entirely new point of departure and raise questions of an order totally different to any that are involved in a Central Board appointed for local purposes'.[70] Communications with Parnell, via Mrs O'Shea, early in August confirmed Gladstone's opinion that the Central Board plan was now obsolete,[71] and when Hartington met him, on 7 August, he found Gladstone's 'state of mind about Ireland . . . extremely alarming. He seems to consider the Central Board the minimum which might have sufficed; but that, as that plan appears to have collapsed, a separate legislature in some form or other will have to be considered. Resistance to any further demands for separation . . . he does not seem to consider a practical policy.'[72]

Gladstone's main problem, from this point, was how to square the political circle and secure united Liberal action on a more extensive concession of Irish self-government which could be accepted by Parnell. In other words, the two conditions laid down earlier for his continued leadership remained essential. Gladstone could only justify staying on if there was a 'speciality' before him which he felt peculiarly equipped to deal with, and consequently the position he maintained in private, during the autumn of 1885, was that he was leading the Liberal party through the elections 'with a view of being, by a bare possibility, of use afterwards in the Irish question, if it should take a favourable turn'.[73] But how was the Liberal party, which had not been able to agree on the Central Board scheme in May, to be persuaded now to accept the need for full-blooded home rule?

[70] Gladstone to Derby, 17 July 1885 (copy), BL Add. MSS 44142, fo. 137.
[71] Gladstone to Mrs O'Shea, 4 Aug. 1885 (copy); Mrs O'Shea to Gladstone, 5 Aug. 1885, BL Add. MSS 56446.
[72] Hartington to Granville, 8 Aug. 1885, PRO 30/29/22A/3, in Bernard Holland, *Life of Spencer Compton, Eighth Duke of Devonshire, 1833–1908* (1911), ii. 77–8. Cf. Spencer to Granville, 8 Aug. 1885, PRO 30/29/22A/5.
[73] Gladstone to Granville, 5 Oct. 1885, in Ramm (ed.), *Gladstone–Granville Correspondence*, ii. 401.

A solution to this dilemma was offered by the confident antici-
pations of a large majority in the next House of Commons which
were being transmitted to the Liberal leadership by the party managers. In September, the chief whip, Lord Richard Grosvenor, was
predicting that the Conservatives would be reduced to 210 seats after
the general election which, allowing for between 80 and 90 Irish
nationalists, put the Liberal total at between 370 and 380—a result
of almost 1906 'landslide' proportions.[74] Gladstone's reaction to
this report was significant: 'All the accounts are most sanguine. This
makes the prospect formidable—on account of Ireland, and on that
account alone.'[75] Even in the middle of November, by which time the
Liberal campaign had lost some of its momentum, a comfortable
overall majority of about forty was still expected,[76] and this, as
Gladstone observed to Grosvenor, 'though reduced will do well
enough'.[77] In the expectation of an independent Liberal majority,
which could turn out the Conservatives without committing itself in
any way as regards Ireland, Gladstone felt free to state publicly that
such a majority was a prerequisite for any action on the Irish
question by a Liberal government.[78]

The implication is that Gladstone probably did not anticipate
bringing on his home-rule policy immediately after taking office, and
assumed instead that he would have time in which to convert his
party. Viewed in this way, Gladstone's conduct during the autumn of
1885 becomes readily intelligible, as it reflected that concept of his
function as leader which was described in Chapter 1. Gladstone saw
his role in terms of helping the Liberal party to educate itself, and his
aim, in late 1885, was to prepare the ground from which an internal,
'spontaneous' conviction might grow that the concession of home
rule to Ireland was both necessary and just. He did not wish to be
seen to be openly pushing the party along a path on which it had no

---

[74] Hamilton's diary, 10 Sept. 1885, BL Add. MSS 48641.
[75] Gladstone to Rosebery, 17 Sept. 1885, NLS MSS 10023, fo. 95.
[76] Lord Richard Grosvenor to Alfred Lyttelton, 17 Nov. 1885, BL Add. MSS
44316, fo. 107, estimated 358 Liberals. Cf. Hamilton's diary, 22 Nov. 1885, BL Add.
MSS 48642, for a similar estimate by Schnadhorst, the secretary of the National
Liberal Federation.
[77] Gladstone to Grosvenor, 18 Nov. 1885, BL Add. MSS 44316, fo. 110.
[78] See Morley, *Gladstone*, iii. 237–8, for Gladstone's campaign statements. Cf.
Gladstone to Herbert Gladstone, 18 Oct. 1885, in J. L. Hammond, *Gladstone and the
Irish Nation* (1964 ed.), 447. It was Gladstone's public declarations, of course, that
prompted Parnell's manifesto of 21 Nov., instructing Irish voters in British constituencies not to vote for Liberal candidates.

wish to travel,[79] and he was therefore anxious to avoid committing himself, or anyone else, to a specific policy until the Liberals, and indeed the country, were ready for it. Thus, when he formally agreed to lead the party through the general election in September, he declined Hartington's request for a meeting of the ex-Cabinet to decide party policy, one of his reasons being 'The effect it would have in binding you and the party to such opinions as I might afterwards emit'. Instead, he urged Hartington to 'give the Irish case a really historical consideration'.[80] Some time later, Gladstone confided to him his view that, while 'At present things look as if at first Ireland would dominate the situation', and though he personally favoured 'action at a stroke', nevertheless he had 'no intention, as at present advised, of signifying it'.[81] Chamberlain was another recipient of hints about 'an Imperial question that seems at present possible to be brought into immediate view'.[82] Gladstone described his strategy very fully in the following letter to Rosebery of 13 November:

the production at this time of a plan by me would not only be injurious, but would destroy all reasonable hope of its adoption. Such a plan, proposed by the heads of the Liberal party, is so certain to have the opposition of the tories en bloc, that every computation must be founded on this anticipation. This opposition, and the appeals with which it will be accompanied, will render the carrying of the measure difficult even by a united Liberal party; hopeless or most difficult, should there be serious defection . . . The idea of constituting a legislature for Ireland, whenever seriously and responsibly proposed, will cause a mighty heave in the body politic. It will be as difficult to carry the Liberal party and two British nations in favour of a legislature for Ireland, as it was easy to carry them in the case of Irish disestablishment. I

[79] Of course, this did not preclude Gladstone from urging Knowles, the editor of the *Nineteenth Century*, to publish articles on the question of Irish administration: Gladstone to Knowles, 5 Aug. 1885, in Hammond, *Gladstone and the Irish Nation*, p. 410. It appears that Knowles approached Barry O'Brien to write on the subject: R. B. O'Brien, *Life of C. S. Parnell* (1899), ii. 101–3. The Nov. issue of the *Nineteenth Century* contained an article by O'Brien on 'Irish Wrongs and English Remedies', and in Jan. 1886 another article appeared on 'Federal Union with Ireland'.

[80] Gladstone to Hartington, 8 Sept. 1885 (copy), BL Add. MSS 44148, fo. 127, in Holland, *Devonshire*, ii. 81–3.

[81] Gladstone to Hartington, 10 Nov. 1885 (copy), BL Add. MSS 44148, fo. 146, in Holland, *Devonshire*, ii. 91–3. A few days later, Gladstone also expressed his preference for 'one decisive measure for Ireland', rather than 'another long series of Parliamentary operations', implying that he would not assume the responsibility if the latter course were taken: 18 Nov. 1885, BL Add. MSS 44148, fo. 154, in Holland, *Devonshire*, ii. 94–5.

[82] Gladstone to Chamberlain, 22 Sept. 1885, Chamberlain MSS, JC5/34/41, also 6 Nov. 1885, ibid., fo. 44.

think that it may possibly be done; but only by the full use of a great leverage. That leverage can only be found in their equitable and mature consideration of what is due to the fixed desire of a nation, clearly and constitutionally expressed. Their prepossessions will not be altogether favourable; and they cannot in this matter be bullied. I have therefore endeavoured to lay the ground by stating largely the possibility and the gravity, even the solemnity, of that demand. I am convinced that this is the only path which can lead to success.[83]

This important document presents a picture of Gladstone's intentions with regard to Ireland which is seriously at odds with the view, put forward by Cooke and Vincent, that he became committed to home rule only in March 1886, as a short-term tactical expedient.[84] The conflict is even more remarkable when the notes on Irish home rule dated 14 November 1885, the day after the letter to Rosebery, in a collection of Gladstone's papers rediscovered in 1969, are taken into consideration. Of course, we need hardly be surprised that these outlines of a home-rule measure differed in several important respects from the bill which Gladstone introduced in April 1886, but they do nevertheless indicate a detailed consideration of the subject, and reveal the extent to which he had travelled in the direction of setting up an Irish legislature. These notes are printed and discussed in Appendix III.

In conclusion, there seems little doubt that the discreet tactics adopted by Gladstone in the autumn of 1885 were founded upon the assumption that the Liberal party would obtain a parliamentary majority sufficiently large to allow him time in which to foster an appropriate moral climate for the reception of a home-rule measure. He appears to have been confident that, once confronted with the strength of Irish Nationalist feeling as demonstrated by the election of 80 or 90 Parnellite MPs, British public opinion, the political parties, and even the House of Lords, would be compelled to recognize the need for this concession.[85]

The crucial point, once again, relates to Gladstone's sense of 'timing'. There is no doubt that he had a long-term perspective on

[83] Gladstone to Rosebery, 13 Nov. 1885, NLS MSS 10023, fo. 112, in Morley, *Gladstone*, iii. 239–40.

[84] Cooke and Vincent, *The Governing Passion*, pp. 55–6.

[85] See Gladstone to Rosebery, 13 Nov. 1885, NLS MSS 10023, fo. 112, in Morley, *Gladstone*, iii. 239–40. The precedent of the franchise and redistribution settlement in 1884 may well have encouraged Gladstone's optimism about the attitude of the Conservatives and the House of Lords.

the Irish question, and, although he had hoped that alternative measures, like local government, might make it possible to forestall home rule,[86] he had also recognized that it might eventually become necessary to concede the larger measure.[87] He had always been careful, therefore, to adopt a cautious ambiguity about the subject, as Lord Derby discovered when Gladstone visited Knowsley in October 1883:

I tried to induce him (being alone) to give his real views as to the prospects of Home Rule: he went readily into the question but perhaps by my own fault, I could not follow him: he talked about the prejudice and timidity of the English mind where Ireland was concerned, said that he would never agree to anything that would destroy the supremacy of the Imperial Parliament: but did not seem absolutely to reject the notion of a subordinate Irish Parliament, but as to this he was very vague, and I think did not wish to be otherwise.[88]

Two scholars have recently suggested different reasons why the home-rule option may have been attractive to Gladstone: he may have seen it as a preferable alternative to a major land-purchase scheme (something he was never more than lukewarm about), in the belief that, once given the responsibility for administering their own affairs, the Irish would soon come to their senses on economic matters such as contractual relations between landlords and tenants; equally, it may be that home rule appealed to Gladstone, the High Churchman, as a way of defending the principle of the separation of the civil and religious powers in the State.[89] Possibly for a number of reasons, then, Gladstone experienced relatively little difficulty in making the intellectual leap from a policy of local government for Ireland to one involving the creation of an Irish legislative assembly. However, while this may explain *how* Gladstone was able to come to terms with the demand for home rule, there remains the question of why he accepted it when he did, and this can only be explained in

[86] e.g. Bahlman (ed.), *Hamilton Diary*, i. 392 (24 Jan. 1883). Cf. John Vincent, 'Gladstone and Ireland', *Proceedings of the British Academy*, 63 (1977), 193–238.

[87] Cf. Bahlman (ed.), *Hamilton Diary*, ii. 620 (20 May 1884); Sir Algernon West, *Recollections, 1832 to 1886* (1899), ii. 206–7 (diary entry for 7 Oct. 1884).

[88] Lord Derby's diary, 8 Oct. 1883, Derby MSS.

[89] Allen Warren, 'Gladstone, Land and Social Reconstruction in Ireland, 1881–1887', *Parliamentary History*, 2 (1983), 153–73; J. P. Parry, 'Religion and the Collapse of Gladstone's First Government, 1870–1874', *Historical Journal*, 25 (1982), 100.

terms of his need for a new 'speciality' which would enable him to justify retaining the leadership of the Liberal party.

Thus, while broadly endorsing J. L. Hammond's account of Gladstone's conversion to Irish 'home rule', which clearly took place some months before the general election of 1885,[90] it seems unnecessary to deny that this was dictated by his personal ambition, which took the form of a desire to be called upon one more time to solve a great 'national' problem. But it is important to recognize that the process by which this impulse was refined in his own mind led to the creation of an entirely independent rationale, which was able, in its turn, to react with and against its own creator: the circumstances which brought Gladstone back to office in 1880 required a justificatory theory which exerted a profound influence upon his subsequent style of leadership, and this style of leadership, in its turn, helped to create the political conditions that enabled him to justify the abnegation of his obligations as defined by the original theory. A self-perpetuating cycle was thus established—the manifestations of Gladstone's failure of leadership became the 'cause' of his need to carry on.

This analysis of Gladstone's leadership also helps to explain why his position with regard to Ireland in 1885–6 does not fit in neatly with the tempting interpretation propagated in later years by Joseph Chamberlain, that Gladstone adopted home rule as a way of diverting attention away from the social programme of the Radicals, thereby reasserting his own authority over the Liberal party.[91] Of course, Chamberlain conveniently overlooked the point that the result of the general election was by no means a great success for the Radicals, but quite apart from this, his claim cannot be squared with the fact that, as early as June 1885, Gladstone's mind had settled on Irish policy as the basis for an extension of his leadership. What is even more significant is that the plan Gladstone intended to adopt at that time was Chamberlain's own Central Board proposal. This chronological consideration also raises doubts about the validity of the more subtle interpretation, put forward by Professor Hamer, that Gladstone conceived of Irish home rule primarily as a single great unifying issue, transcending the deep divisions between the Whig and Radical sections which were exhibited during the autumn election

---

[90] Hammond, *Gladstone and the Irish Nation*, pp. 390–426.
[91] C. H. D. Howard (ed.), *A Political Memoir 1880–92, by Joseph Chamberlain* (1953), 179–80.

campaign.[92] It is true that, in September, Gladstone exploited the public differences between Hartington and Chamberlain in order to justify carrying on as leader of the Liberal party for the duration of the general election, but this step was taken with a preconceived strategy relating to Ireland foremost in his mind. No doubt the potential of home rule as a means of pushing into the background troublesome sectional issues like disestablishment reinforced Gladstone's strategy, but this was not the original reason for it.

It was after the failure of the Cabinet to agree on a new policy in May 1885 that the Irish question acquired, in Gladstone's mind, an existence of its own as a symbol of Liberal disunity and a proof of the paramount need for him to stay on as leader for a little longer in order to help his party tide over the impending crisis. In other words, the Irish cause came to be identified inseparably with Gladstone's leadership. It was another great 'speciality' which only he had the political expertise to deal with. Once this idea was fixed in his mind, the formation of the Conservative–Parnellite 'alliance' in July, and the consequent raising of the Nationalist leader's terms, simply confirmed Gladstone's belief that only he could handle the situation; and a discreet strategy of gently guiding the Liberal party into support for home rule was accordingly evolved. What had originally been a question of local government expanded, during the summer and autumn of 1885, into the heroic proportions of a great imperial question which, in his later years, Gladstone would look back upon as one of the instances where his special gift of 'insight' had been deployed.

Gladstone, it is therefore argued, was motivated by a highly subjective analysis of the Irish question, in relation to his leadership of the Liberal party, which led him to adopt whatever policy seemed to be dictated by the prevailing circumstances. The tragedy for the Liberal party was that Gladstone, perhaps after all an 'old man in a hurry', drew a conclusion about the need for Irish home rule which many others did not share.

[92] D. A. Hamer, *Liberal Politics in the Age of Gladstone and Rosebery* (Oxford, 1972), 104–12. Professor Hamer places particular emphasis upon Gladstone's concern with the disestablishment question, which emerged as a major issue during the later stages of the election campaign.

8

The Irish Question in Liberal Politics
June 1885 to February 1886

The ultimate object of the preceding chapters has been to establish a broader chronological context within which to examine the schism in the Liberal party provoked by Gladstone's Irish home rule bill. By restoring the Whigs to their rightful place in the mainstream of Liberal politics, it has become clear that the traditional interpretation of the secession of the 'Liberal Unionists' is no longer tenable. Our knowledge of the Granville–Hartington leadership in the 1870s, and the subsequent position of the Whigs during the second Gladstone ministry does not accord with the view that the split was simply the culmination of a long-term movement away from the Liberal party, resulting from the growing Radical threat to the propertied rights and political power of the landed class, with Irish home rule providing a convenient pretext for a breach made inevitable by deeper, underlying forces.[1]

It is equally clear, however, that the emphasis which I have placed on the Irish question as a threat to the stability of the Liberal party, from the late 1870s onwards, is in conflict with a more recent interpretation of the events of 1885–6 put forward by Cooke and Vincent. According to these scholars, the Whigs, at both ministerial and back-bench level, were merely cynical opportunists, interested in the Irish question only in so far as it created new possibilities for personal advancement. Thus, they argue that Goschen devised his political strategy in the autumn of 1885 'without reference to Ireland', that Hartington's eventual opposition to home rule was dictated entirely by tactical considerations, and that there was little

---

[1] Cf. Donald Southgate, *The Passing of the Whigs, 1832–1886* (1962), 355–416; Gordon L. Goodman, 'Liberal Unionism: The Revolt of the Whigs', *Victorian Studies*, 3 (1959–60), 173–89; J. L. Hammond, *Gladstone and the Irish Nation* (1964 edn.), 473–4; Michael Barker, *Gladstone and Radicalism: The Reconstruction of Liberal Policy in Britain, 1885–94* (Hassocks, 1975), 11–24.

evidence of principled resolve among the Whigs when Gladstone came to form his third ministry in January 1886.[2]

The purpose of this chapter, therefore, is to expose the weaknesses in Cooke and Vincent's interpretation by focusing, in the first instance, on the period in which the Liberals were in opposition, from June 1885 to January 1886. It will be shown that Cooke and Vincent's preoccupation with Cabinet government, and their consequent neglect of the Liberals in opposition, has led them to overlook the crucial fact that the attitude of the Whigs towards the Irish question was conditioned, at this time, by the emergence of a consensus among Liberals of all shades which held out the hope that it might yet be possible to contain the threat from Parnellite Irish Nationalism within the existing framework of political parties. Once this point has been established, it will then be necessary to examine, in detail, the background to the formation of Gladstone's third ministry, in order to clarify the objectives of both Hartington and the Whigs, and of Gladstone himself.

I

The conditions for a Liberal consensus on Ireland developed after the collapse, early in the summer of 1885, of Chamberlain's Central Board initiative. As we have already seen, Chamberlain had proposed this scheme to his Cabinet colleagues in May, believing it to be acceptable to Parnell, in a clear attempt to forge a new alliance between the Liberals and the Irish Nationalists, as he had tried to do in 1882. However, the plan was rejected by Hartington and a majority of the Cabinet, as they were unwilling to be committed, in the way Gladstone and Chamberlain wanted, to a policy for a future parliament.[3] After the fall of the government in June, it soon became evident that Parnell was now intent on playing off the two British parties in order to raise the terms for his support. Chamberlain himself became the object of attacks in the Nationalist press, forcing him to cancel a planned tour of Ireland with Dilke, and provoking him to retort that 'If [Parnell] throws us over, I do not believe that we

---

[2] A. B. Cooke and John Vincent, *The Governing Passion: Cabinet Government and Party Politics in Britain, 1885–86* (Hassocks, 1974), 101, 87–97, 119–33.

[3] Cf. Hartington to Gladstone, 29 May 1885, BL Add. MSS 44148, fo. 75.

can go further at present'.[4] By the middle of July, it was clear that the Conservatives and the Nationalists were operating as allies, and Chamberlain consequently dropped the Central Board plan altogether and devoted his energies exclusively to domestic issues. In the mean time, the Parnellites were to be allowed to '"stew in their juice" until they find out their mistake . . . I am not unwilling to keep silence for a time and await the course of events . . . Sooner or later, the Parnellites will find that they have been sold.'[5] Parnell's demand for 'Legislative Independence'[6] had rendered any immediate settlement of the question of Irish self-government impossible (and it was clearly not in his interests to compromise before the general election), and Chamberlain therefore denounced the Nationalist leader in a speech at Warrington, on 8 September.[7] This explains why it was that Chamberlain seemed unconcerned, during the months ahead, by Gladstone's evident desire for a *modus vivendi* with the Nationalists, for he considered a compromise to be unattainable. Thus, after receiving information from Labouchere that Gladstone was angling for Irish support, Chamberlain wrote to Dilke, on 26 October, that Gladstone was 'trying to get Parnell's ideas in detail etc etc', but added his opinion that 'it is no use'.[8] Similarly, on 4 November, following a report from O'Shea, Chamberlain told Dilke that he was 'convinced that Mr. G. has been trying to make a treaty all to himself', but thought 'it must fail'.[9] The prevailing orthodoxy within the Chamberlain camp, during the election campaign, was that 'The Irish business is not the first just now':[10] Harcourt, for instance, who had infiltrated the Chamberlainites in the hope of strengthening his position as a future mediator between them and the Liberal leadership, considered the party's Irish policy to have been 'practically

[4] Chamberlain to Dilke, 29 June 1885, Chamberlain MSS, JC5/24/422. Cf. J. L. Garvin, *Life of Joseph Chamberlain*, ii (1933), 16–27.
[5] Chamberlain to Labouchere, 18 July 1885, in A. L. Thorold, *Life of Henry Labouchere* (1913), 230.
[6] In a speech at Dublin, *The Times*, 25 Aug. 1885, p. 4.
[7] Ibid. 9 Sept. 1885, p. 6.
[8] Chamberlain to Dilke, 26 Oct. 1885, Chamberlain MSS, JC5/24/442. Cf. Labouchere to Chamberlain, 18 Oct. 1885, in Thorold, *Labouchere*, pp. 237–41. Chamberlain had reported to Dilke, after a visit to Hawarden earlier in the month, that Gladstone still seemed interested in the Central Board plan: 9 Oct. 1885, Chamberlain MSS, JC5/24/434.
[9] Chamberlain to Dilke, 4 Nov. 1885, ibid. JC5/24/447. Cf. O'Shea to Chamberlain, 2 Nov. 1885 (copy), BL Add. MSS 62114A.
[10] Chamberlain to Dilke, 17 Oct. 1885, ibid. JC5/24/439.

settled by the course of events', and even John Morley, who was sympathetic to home rule, conceded that 'the hour for it has not yet struck'.[11]

With the breach between Chamberlain and Parnell, and the demise of the Central Board plan, the short-term prospects for Liberal unity were greatly enhanced. There was little likelihood of a Whig secession while the most divisive issue between themselves and Chamberlain lay dormant, and Hartington was aware, after a meeting early in August, that Chamberlain was 'inclined to drop the Irish proposals altogether for the present' and devote himself to other matters.[12] His neutral stance with regard to Chamberlain's domestic policies, which was discussed in Chapter 6, must therefore be understood in the context of the removal of a far more serious obstacle to co-operation between the Whig and Radical sections. Consequently, after Chamberlain's speech at Warrington on 8 September, Hartington advised Goschen that he thought the Radical leader had no wish to split the Liberal party, and suggested instead that 'It would be most useful to support the position I have taken up by arguments; not to advance the position and attack Chamberlain more than can be avoided; but to show up some of the fallacies, and also to argue out some of the consequences of Home Rule, or separation, as now explained by Parnell.'[13]

The possibility of a Liberal consensus on Ireland depended ultimately, of course, upon the position taken up by Gladstone, given his presumed intention to lead the party through the general election and his obvious preference for a policy of conciliation. An exploratory correspondence between Hartington and Gladstone served to clarify the situation in this respect, and, as on earlier occasions, their letters provide us with an interesting anatomy of the political relations between them.

Hartington's opportunity arose shortly after his speech at Waterfoot on 29 August, in which he had attacked Parnell and hinted at the possibility of a coalition between the British political parties in order to resist Irish pressure for home rule.[14] On 3 September, he received a

---

[11] Harcourt to Chamberlain, 30 Sept. 1885, ibid. J C5/38/36; Morley to Chamberlain, 19 Sept. 1885, ibid. J C5/54/627.
[12] Hartington to Granville, 5 Aug. 1885, P R O 30/29/22A/3, in Bernard Holland, *Life of Spencer Compton, Eighth Duke of Devonshire, 1833–1908* (1911), ii. 71–2.
[13] Hartington to Goschen 13 Sept. 1885, in Hon. A. D. Elliot, *Life of George Joachim Goschen, First Viscount Goschen, 1831–1907* (1911), i. 308–10.
[14] Hartington at Waterfoot, *The Times*, 31 Aug. 1885, p. 8.

letter from Gladstone, who had just returned from Norway, indicating his willingness to assume the leadership for the duration of the elections, but, at the same time, conveying the ominous advice that the Liberals should be circumspect in their language, regarding Ireland, until the elections had clarified the situation: 'Every object is, I think, gained for the present, by declaring substantively our view as to the unity of the Empire.'[15] Hartington responded in the most trenchant terms, arguing that, since the Central Board plan was no longer acceptable to any section of the Liberal party, and since no alternative policy of conciliation was available, 'there seems to be no course open to that portion of the Liberal party with which I am especially connected but to disclose as early as possible an uncompromising resistance to the present [Irish] demands'. He acknowledged that Gladstone's leadership was an essential pre-condition for Liberal unity during the elections, but warned that 'I feel . . . I do not know enough of your ideas with regard to Ireland to say whether it would be possible for me to accept them', and ended by suggesting an early meeting of some leading Liberals to discuss the question of party policy.[16]

Gladstone was naturally anxious to avoid being drawn out in this way, and so, in his reply, he attempted to shift the ground on to the basic question of whether or not he was to continue to lead the party.[17] Hartington remained insistent, however, that a meeting would be needed to decide whether 'the various sections of the party can acquiesce in the policy you propose to adopt', and he made it clear that his own desire for Liberal unity was dependent 'on what the party is likely to do, if in a majority after the election'.[18] This left Gladstone with little alternative but to resort to the use of a threat similar to the one he had made during the franchise crisis of December 1883, as the only way of asserting his view that the only question at stake was his leadership of the party. His letter of 11 September therefore contained a timely reminder of the hazards which Hartington would face in attempting to obstruct his path,

[15] Gladstone to Hartington, 3 Sept. 1885 (copy), BL Add. MSS 44148, fo. 114, in Holland, *Devonshire*, ii. 78–80.
[16] Hartington to Gladstone, 6 Sept. 1885, BL Add. MSS 44148, fo. 120, in Holland, *Devonshire*, ii. 80–1.
[17] Gladstone to Hartington, 8 Sept. 1885 (copy), BL Add. MSS 44148, fo. 127, in Holland, *Devonshire*, ii. 81–3.
[18] Hartington to Gladstone, 10 Sept. 1885, BL Add. MSS 44148, fo. 132, in Holland, *Devonshire*, ii. 83–5.

indicating that he might, after all, retire from politics before the general election, but that, if this happened, his 'sense of the obligations I owe to the party' would compel him to 'make some mention of the difficulties arising from divergences'.[19]

At the same time as he issued this almost routine warning of what would happen if Hartington tried to sabotage his plans, Gladstone was careful to reassure him of the limited extent of his objectives, by explaining that his references in earlier letters to 'certain historical cases', such as Norway and the debate of 1834, had 'no other purpose than that of promoting, what I think dangerously deficient in many quarters, an historical and therefore comprehensive view of the Irish question'. Gladstone maintained that he was looking no further than the footing on which the Liberal party might go into the general election, and that it was premature to consider the basis on which a Liberal government might afterwards be formed. As far as his election address was concerned, Gladstone explained:

What I say on Ireland is simply an expansion and adaptation of what I have already said often, namely, that Ireland may have all that is compatible with the unity of the Empire. When I said that it would have sufficed for you to declare the unity of the Empire, I meant it would have sufficed for *your* purpose. But I have had to say much more than you on the Irish question, and could not now hold back from what I have frequently promised.

Your letter obviously sets you free with regard to me and my proceedings. I hope that what I have now written may do something in the way of enabling you to define your course.

Nothing can be more unlikely according to *present* appearances than any effective or great legislative action for Ireland.[20]

This important qualification to Gladstone's intentions made Hartington's position considerably more comfortable, and he wrote, the following day, to express his relief that, whatever the direction Gladstone's own thinking was taking, this would not be reflected in the election address:

Of course, I know that you are, and have long been, in favour of granting to Ireland a larger measure of self-government than I think I could ever agree to. The knowledge that you do hold such opinions, and of the immense weight which they are likely to carry with them in the next Parliament, must

---

[19] Gladstone to Hartington, 11 Sept. 1885 (copy), BL Add. MSS 44148, fo. 136, in Holland, *Devonshire*, ii. 86–8.
[20] Ibid.

be a source of anxiety to me . . . But having made my protest, both in public and private, as to Ireland, the only point on which, as far as I know, there is likely to be a great difference of opinion between us, I do not know that I need say more.[21]

Gladstone's reply provides further confirmation of the under-standing that had been reached:

if I understand it right, the protest which you register signifies that you are not willing to be bound to the *extent* to which I bind myself in regard to Ireland, but that you do not on that account withdraw from the general opinion that under all the circumstances it is desirable that I should issue an Address, directed in my view to the election, and so framed as by no means to imply that I hold the party ripe for action.[22]

It is perfectly clear, then, that Hartington accepted Gladstone's leadership of the Liberal party on the basis that Ireland was to remain an open question, and that, whatever Gladstone's eventual conclu-sion might prove to be, no one was committed to it in advance. The formulation of a policy was to be deferred until after the general election, by which time the background against which political action had to be taken would be more sharply defined. This was as much as Hartington could reasonably expect, for the time being, and, in a letter to Goschen on 20 September, he expressed his satisfaction with the address which Gladstone had issued three days before. 'Even about Ireland', he noted, 'though, knowing his real opinion, I can read between the lines, there does not seem to be anything alarming.'[23]

Goschen's decision to follow Hartington in taking shelter under the Gladstonian 'umbrella' becomes easily intelligible when it is considered in this light. Contrary to Cooke and Vincent's assertion, Ireland was very much at the centre of Goschen's calculations. It was seen in Chapter 5 how the Gladstone ministry's Irish policies had provoked the Whig revolts of 1880–2 with which Goschen had become associated, and Whig alarm was revived in May 1885, when the Cabinet was wavering about the renewal of the crimes act, to the extent that Goschen and Albert Grey contemplated the formation of

---

[21] Hartington to Gladstone, 12 Sept. 1885, BL Add. MSS 44148, fo. 138, in Holland, *Devonshire*, ii. 88–9.
[22] Gladstone to Hartington, 13 Sept. 1885 (copy), BL Add. MSS 44148, fo. 141, in Holland, *Devonshire*, ii. 89.
[23] Hartington to Goschen, 20 Sept. 1885, in Elliot, *Goschen*, ii. 2.

a breakaway party.[24] Towards the end of July, Goschen still suspected that Gladstone was reserving himself as to the 'feasibility' of
Chamberlain's Central Board scheme, and that he was 'disposed to
move at the election in the direction which on more accurate
inspection he may find to be the most generally acceptable'. Thus, in
Goschen's opinion, 'If the bulk of the Liberal party go in for the
Chamberlain programme Gladstone will lead in that direction.'[25]
Indeed, as late as 11 September, Goschen expressed to Hartington
his 'general idea . . . that it is quite hopeless to look to carrying
anything till there has been a regular battle, or series of battles, with
the Irish', and he had wanted to know 'Is Chamberlain anxious for
union or quite ready for a split?'[26]

It was only when it became clear to Goschen, in the middle of
September, that Chamberlain had broken with Parnell, and that
Gladstone was going to lead the party without any specific reference
to Ireland, that he finally acquiesced in the 'umbrella strategy'. But,
even after making his decision to accept office in the next Liberal
ministry, so that he might establish himself as one of Gladstone's
political heirs, Goschen maintained the view that 'the next Parliament must be extremely short. The Parnellites will break it up, and if
not, Gladstone's retirement will break it up.'[27] The only reason why
Goschen was able to accept Gladstone's leadership of the party for
the general election, therefore, as he explained in a letter to Sir
Rowland Blennerhassett, was because Liberal policy towards
Ireland was to remain undefined:

[24] Goschen's diary, May 1885, ibid. i. 293. Cf. Goschen to Hartington, 25 May
1885, urging him to stand firm over the crimes act: Devonshire MSS, 340.1784, in
Elliot, *Goschen*, i. 298–9.
[25] W. C. Cartwright's diary, 27 July 1885, Cartwright MSS, 6/16. Goschen had
written to Gladstone on 10 July, urging him to take a clear line on Chamberlain's
Central Board plan: BL Add. MSS 46161, fo. 313. Four days later, the two had had a
long conversation on Ireland at dinner: see Sir Thomas Dyke Acland's memorandum,
14 July 1885, Bodleian MS Eng. Lett. d. 82, fo. 60. For Albert Grey's fear that
Gladstone might lead the Liberal party on the basis of Chamberlain's Central Board
scheme, see his letters to Earl Grey, 25 June, 3 July 1885, Grey MSS, Box 89.
[26] Goschen to Hartington, 11 Sept. 1885, Devonshire MSS, 340.1807.
[27] Goschen to Albert Grey, 20 Sept. 1885, Grey MSS, 211/3. Cf. Cartwright's
diary, 17 Oct. 1885, Cartwright MSS, 6/16, on Goschen: 'He himself (I hear from
Morier) is quite satisfied. He is confident Gladstone cannot avoid offering him office.
Will Chamberlain after his recent language sit in the same Cabinet? Goschen thinks
Chamberlain will accept and do so—but then how long can the Ministry last:
Morier tells me Goschen thinks not above a few months and that then a Coalition
administration must be formed.'

I have acted on this, and consider that otherwise I should not have been justified in supporting the Liberal Party. It would be something of a breach of faith if G. were to go in for [Chamberlain's plan] now . . . I fancy Hartington has expressed himself strongly enough on this point [at Belfast on 5 November] to prevent G. from going awry tho' he is sure to be ambiguous. He will certainly not pronounce against any concessions. His head is full of ideas which go in the direction of more concessions than I approve of but I think he can practically be kept straight. If I didn't think so, I could not have supported him.

Goschen concluded his letter to Blennerhassett by discussing the likely outcome of the general election, and its political aftermath:

I suppose it is certain that the Liberals will win and pretty heavily. Some policy as regards Ireland will have to be decided on. If it is a firm policy, the Irish will be quite unmanageable. If it is a policy going beyond the limits of safe concession, it must break *us* up.[28]

This letter reveals the third pillar supporting the consensus amongst Whigs and Radicals about Ireland. It was widely assumed that the Liberal party would have an overall majority in the next parliament,[29] and so would resume office in a position of independence from the bloc of Nationalist MPs, however large it might happen to be. Consequently, there were still grounds for hoping that it might be possible to restore the relations between the Liberal party and the Nationalists on their old footing, as they had been before the Conservatives' 'alliance' with Parnell. Spencer, for example, was hopeful that the extremists in Ireland could be undermined by the offer of a moderate local-government measure, and Northbrook similarly looked to a 'steady and gradual' introduction of 'local self-government'.[30] In a similar spirit, Hartington had spoken at Belfast on 5 November, urging the need for an independent Liberal majority able to deal with the Irish from a position of strength, but

[28] Goschen to Blennerhassett, 8 Nov. [1885], Cambridge University Library Add. 7486, E.53.
[29] Several examples of Liberal estimates have already been given in chs. 6 and 7. To these might be added Trevelyan's calculation of an overall majority of forty-five (i.e. 358 seats), which was revised, after Parnell's manifesto of 21 Nov., to an overall majority of twenty-five (i.e. 348 seats): W. C. Cartwright's diary, 18, 22 Nov. 1885, Cartwright MSS, 6/16.
[30] Spencer to Granville, 8 Aug. 1885, PRO 30/29/22A/5, also Edward Hamilton's diary, 26, 28 Sept. 1885, BL Add. MSS 48641; Northbrook to Hartington, 9 Nov. 1885, Devonshire MSS, 340.1828.

emphasizing that he 'contemplated very bold Irish reforms, all tending in the direction of decentralisation'.[31]

The Whigs therefore found themselves in the ambiguous position of wanting an overall parliamentary majority, so as to contain the Irish Nationalists, yet also of fearing such a majority for the impetus it would give to Chamberlain's Radical programme. As in 1880, it appeared that the price of independence from the Irish would be the loss of Whig influence over general Liberal policy. It was true that Gladstone's great authority could be relied upon to keep the Radicals in check, but then, it was his attitude towards home rule which most concerned the Whigs. What made the situation a little more tolerable was that Chamberlain happened, for the time being at least, to be in agreement with the Whigs that it was both desirable and practicable to bring the Nationalists to heel. Ironically, the same electoral assumptions which, as we saw in the last chapter, underpinned Gladstone's political strategy in the autumn of 1885 influenced the calculations of his Liberal colleagues in a quite different way, by encouraging the hope that, once the election was over, the Irish would have to accept what was offered to them.

II

In the event, of course, the general election of November–December 1885 did not produce the widely anticipated overall majority for the Liberals. The end result was a hung parliament, in which the eighty-six strong Parnellite contingent held the balance of power. An entirely new and unforeseen tactical situation was thus created, and the purpose of the remainder of this chapter is to examine the ways in which Gladstone and the Whigs adapted their strategies in accordance with the facts.

As in the past, the perceived strength of Whiggery seemed to grow in inverse proportion to the strength of the Liberal party as a whole, and, with the result of the election being regarded as a success for the Whigs, it was not to be expected that they would willingly choose this moment to play gratuitously into the hands of the Radicals by

[31] Hartington at Belfast, *The Times*, 6 Nov. 1885, p. 6. For praise of Hartington's speech from his Whig colleagues, cf. Spencer to Rosebery, 7 Nov. 1885, NLS MSS 10062; Kimberley to Granville, 11 Nov. 1885, PRO 30/29/28.

breaking away from Gladstone.[32] Hartington and Goschen were agreed that their principal objective, now that the prospect of an 'independent majority' for the Liberals had 'gone to smash',[33] had to be to forestall any opportunity for the formation of a Liberal government by a leader whose known Irish sympathies seemed only too likely to lead him into conceding the Nationalists' demand for home rule.[34] Bearing in mind the size of the Liberal majority over the Conservatives, however, the only realistic hope of stopping Gladstone lay in the possibility that the divisions among the Liberals might be too great even for him to overcome. Hartington and his supporters would do nothing to assist Gladstone in bringing down the Salisbury government for the purpose of constructing an alternative ministry on home-rule lines, and Chamberlain, after his venomous speech at Leicester on 3 December, in which he implicitly blamed the moderation of Gladstone's manifesto for the Liberal losses in the boroughs and hinted at a future election campaign fought on the disestablishment issue, appeared to have little interest in facilitating co-operation between the Radical and Whig sections.[35] In fact, privately, Chamberlain was just as anxious as Hartington and Goschen to 'sit' on Gladstone's 'Irish proposals' by making it impossible for him to attempt the formation of a government.[36] In these circumstances, Hartington was able to contemplate giving 'some promise of independent support' sufficient to keep the Conservatives in power, provided they dropped their alliance with Parnell, and to believe that 'A Liberal Government seems nearly an impossibility at present.'[37] So widespread was this opinion in Liberal circles, early in December 1885, that the

[32] 'I think we should make a mistake, if we played into the hands of the Radicals, who want to wait till Gladstone is gone and then break up our party in order to re-construct it on a Radical basis. This House of Commons is not Radical, and if the Irish difficulty could be tided over would support a Liberal Cabinet in settling many urgent questions in a reasonable manner', Kimberley to Derby, 14 Dec. 1885, Derby MSS.
[33] Hartington to Granville, 29 Nov. 1885, PRO 30/29/22A/3, in Holland, *Devonshire*, ii. 95.
[34] See Hartington to Goschen, 6 Dec. 1885, in Elliot, *Goschen*, ii. 2–3, and Goschen to Hartington, 7 Dec. 1885, Devonshire MSS, 340.1846, for the whole of this paragraph. Northbrook wrote to Granville on 3 Dec. that he was 'frightened in my heart at Mr. Gladstone's attitude to the Irish, and by the apprehension that he will make some demonstration in favour of some modified Home Rule', PRO 30/29/28.
[35] Chamberlain at Leicester, *The Times*, 4 Dec. 1885, p. 12. For Hartington's reaction, see his letter to Harcourt, 4 Dec. 1885, Harcourt MSS, Box 78.
[36] Chamberlain to Labouchere, 7 Dec. 1885, in Thorold, *Labouchere*, p. 246; Chamberlain to Harcourt, 6 Dec. 1885 (typescript), Harcourt MSS, Box 716.
[37] Hartington to Goschen, 6 Dec. 1885, in Elliot, *Goschen*, ii. 2–3.

immediate downfall of the Salisbury administration, when the new parliament met, was not thought to be a very probable outcome.[38]

Gladstone was clearly placed in a difficult position. Before the general election, it had seemed reasonable to base his strategy of gradually 'educating' the Liberal party into acceptance of the need for Irish home rule on the assumption that he would have an absolute majority in the new parliament. In that case, Gladstone's course would have been relatively simple, as he could have removed the Conservatives from office while avoiding any awkward vote relating to Ireland. As matters stood in December 1885, however, the Liberals, with at most 334 of the 670 seats in the new House of Commons, could not remove the Salisbury administration unless the Nationalists withdrew their support from it, but there was no obvious reason why the Nationalists should do this unless the Liberals were prepared to give an undertaking on home rule. Parnell would not be willing to relinquish his control of the House of Commons without a definite commitment from Gladstone;[39] but Gladstone, for his part, could give no such undertaking for fear of its effect on the unity of his own party, which had no wish to be ridden into office on Parnell's back.

The consequent ambiguity in Gladstone's dealings with his colleagues has led Cooke and Vincent to argue that, in fact, he had no definite objectives with regard to Ireland, and was prepared to keep his options open and lead his party in the pursuit of whatever policy could be agreed upon.[40] It is not easy to see how this view can be reconciled, however, with Gladstone's remark to Granville, made after he had seen two important colleagues, Spencer and Rosebery, at Hawarden on 8 December, that he expected 'a healthful, slow fermentation in many minds, working towards the final product'.[41] It becomes even more difficult when we consider hitherto unused material relating to the discussions at Hawarden, from 10 to 12 December, between Gladstone and two of his closest confidants,

[38] Cf. Hamilton's diary, 6 Dec. 1885, BL Add. MSS 48642; Lord Selborne to Sir Arthur Hamilton-Gordon, 10 Dec. 1885, 1st Earl Selborne MSS, 1874, fo. 51.
[39] The reasoning behind this was that, although Parnell had the power to deny office to the Liberals, once he had allowed them to have it he would no longer have had the power to remove them, except in the unlikely event of a renewed alliance with the Tories.
[40] Cooke and Vincent, *Governing Passion*, pp. 54–6.
[41] Gladstone to Granville, 9 Dec. 1885, in Agatha Ramm (ed.), *The Political Correspondence of Mr Gladstone and Lord Granville, 1876–1886* (Oxford, 1962), ii. 414.

Lord Wolverton and Sir Thomas Dyke Acland. A memorandum by Acland throws much interesting light on Gladstone's intentions, in the aftermath of the set-back at the elections:

> A long discussion on H.R. The two points alone reserved were the defence of the island army and navy . . . Some protection to the Landowners (and the minority?) . . . I asked how far support could be relied on—one answer was that the question had not been raised in the election therefore M.P.s were free—no fear of rank and file . . . One great point seems to be the need for not delaying. The main principle is the Constitutional voice of the representatives . . . As to the tactics—I understand the idea to be first find out whether the Conservatives and Parnell are acting together—whether either have a definite plan. If not then we should bring out a plan—I think first by disavowing to find out whether it will be accepted.[42]

Three important points emerge from this memorandum. Firstly, it shows that, in spite of the disappointment of the general election, Gladstone's thinking on home rule had not gone back in any way from the position he had outlined in his memorandum of 14 November 1885. Indeed, Acland provides further confirmation of this in another memorandum, written a few days later, in which he noted his impression that, subject to the reservations about the armed forces and the landowners, Gladstone's view was 'That any plan worthy of consideration involves the entire control of Irish affairs both Legislative and Administrative by an Irish Parliament or legislative assembly of some kind'.[43] Secondly, it indicates that Gladstone had reached the conclusion that he should make no move until the Conservatives had shown their hand. It was to facilitate this that his offer of support to Salisbury, if the latter was prepared to deal with home rule himself, was made. Whether Gladstone seriously expected Salisbury to do any such thing is impossible to tell,[44] but if the offer

---

[42] Sir Thomas Dyke Acland's memorandum, 12 Dec. 1885, Bodleian MS Eng. Lett. d. 82, fo. 101.

[43] Acland's memorandum, 20 Dec. 1885, ibid., fo. 105.

[44] Gladstone approached Salisbury via Arthur Balfour, whom he met at Eaton Hall on 15 Dec., and with whom he subsequently engaged in correspondence. See Hammond, *Gladstone and Irish Nation*, pp. 427–38, for a discussion of Gladstone's conduct at this time and for the evidence that might have encouraged him to think that Salisbury might take up home rule. It seems more probable that Gladstone's gesture was a purely tactical one, knowing that Salisbury was unlikely to attempt any initiative on home rule with his government in a minority in the Commons, but needing to make the Conservatives show their hand before taking action himself. Of course, simply by making it known to the Conservatives that he desired a settlement of the question of the government of Ireland, Gladstone effectively clarified the best course for them to take. In the event, the 'Hawarden Kite' achieved this anyway.

was declined, it would have been made clear that the only policy the Conservatives had was one of rigorous coercion, which would assuredly break up the Conservative–Parnell alliance, and perhaps also strengthen the feeling among the Liberals in favour of a policy of concession. In this way, it might have been possible to fulfil the requirements expressed by Wolverton, in a letter to Gladstone, just after the meeting at Hawarden: 'I am sure there must be a process of "education" for our men do not *realise* the *position* of the Irish question yet . . . To my mind the issue depends upon the party *clearly* understanding *your* position and feeling as you do the absolute necessity of the *immediate* settlement of the Irish question.'[45]

The third point relates to the so-called 'Hawarden Kite', the publication in the *Standard*, on 17 December, of the details of a home-rule scheme purporting to embody the views of Gladstone himself, together with less specific reports in other newspapers. It is now well known that these reports were the result of communications between Gladstone's son Herbert and Wemyss Reid of the *Leeds Mercury*, and of an unguarded interview given by Herbert to Dawson Rogers of the National Press Agency. Herbert had been stirred into action by a report, from Lyon Playfair, of Chamberlain and Dilke's view that his father had to be 'sat on', and by a plea for guidance from Wemyss Reid.[46] His intention, however, had been not to 'leak' his father's opinions, but merely to provide guidelines for the Liberal press to work along. As he explained to Lady Frederick Cavendish, in a letter intended to reach the eyes of Hartington, his interview with Dawson Rogers had been designed to 'guide him and his editors and prevent them from being absolutely at sea . . . My object was . . . a negative one—to give ideas for leading articles and to prevent friendly newspapers from falling into a trap.'[47] Acland's memorandum tends to reinforce this version, as the 'Kite' was flown before the intentions of the Conservatives were known, and indeed, both he and Wolverton were clearly surprised by the newspaper revelations.[48] A little-known account by William Jeans, a journalist

[45] Wolverton to Gladstone, 13 Dec. 1885, BL Add. MSS 44349, fo. 184.
[46] See Herbert Gladstone's *After Thirty Years* (1928), 306–14.
[47] Herbert Gladstone to Lady Frederick Cavendish, 31 Dec. 1885, BL Add. MSS 46046, fo. 56. This duly reached Hartington; see Lady Frederick's letter of 3 Jan. 1886, Devonshire MSS, 340.1879.
[48] Wolverton to Gladstone, 29 Dec. 1885, BL Add. MSS 44349, fo. 190. Acland wrote in his memorandum of 20 Dec., 'As to tactics I do not say anything. I am no judge', Bodleian MS Eng. Lett. d. 82, fo. 105.

working for the *Leeds Mercury*, also confirms that the 'Kite' was 'a matter of chance rather than design'. According to Jeans, Herbert Gladstone's conversation with Wemyss Reid in London on 15 December had been intended as confidential, to be used at the latter's discretion, and was therefore not used immediately. However, when Jeans discovered that Dawson Rogers intended to feed the information he had been given by Herbert to his client newspapers, Wemyss Reid felt obliged to publish too. There was a long-standing agreement between the *Leeds Mercury* and the *Standard* to share information, and it was as a result of this that the *Standard*, much to Wemyss Reid's disgust, published what appeared to be an authoritative statement of Gladstone's views on home rule.[49] The 'Kite' should be seen, therefore, not as a deliberate ploy by Gladstone aimed at capturing Irish support,[50] but as a well-meaning but bungled attempt by his son to assist in the process of 'fermentation in many minds'.

In fact, the newspaper revelations served only to make matters more difficult for Gladstone, for while he may have intended, as Acland's memorandum suggests, to leak a home-rule plan once the Conservatives had been forced into the open, such an idea was now rendered obsolete. Gladstone clearly needed more time for events to shape Liberal minds, but, with the premature disclosure of his views, he was forced into a defensive position. Communications with his colleagues virtually ceased during the second half of December, and he also refused to summon an early meeting of the ex-Cabinet for the purpose of discussing party policy.[51]

It was fortunate for Gladstone that, in spite of the 'Kite', Parnell showed no sign of wishing to ditch the government and throw in his lot with the Liberals. This meant that it might still be possible to gain more time by refraining from any attempt to turn out the Conservatives immediately. Thus, by 10 January, Edward Hamilton had gained the impression that Gladstone was 'determined not to join issue with the Government on the Address . . . finding that his party is not minded to follow him and that Parnell shows no outward

[49] William Jeans, *Parliamentary Reminiscences* (1912), 286–91. Cf. Wemyss Reid's letter to Herbert Gladstone, 17 Dec. 1885, disclaiming responsibility for the article in the *Standard*, BL Add. MSS 46041, fo. 75.

[50] As seems to be implied by J. R. Vincent, 'Gladstone and Ireland', *Proceedings of the British Academy*, 63 (1977), 224.

[51] Cf. Hartington to Gladstone, 1 Jan. 1886, BL Add. MSS 44148, fo. 192, Gladstone to Hartington, 2 Jan. 1886, Devonshire MSS, 340.1883, in Holland, *Devonshire*, ii. 106–9.

disposition to be reasonable, Mr G. is evidently inclined to keep in the background for the present at any rate'.[52] A few days earlier, in a letter to the Liberal chief whip, Gladstone had expressed his own opinion that 'there will be no ostensible breach between Tories and nationalists on the day of the Address', which would be 'at any rate a momentary relief and will afford time to cast about for more knowledge'. He had then proceeded to explain what he thought the party's course of action ought to be:

> we will wait to hear what the Government have to say, and give it a dispassionate consideration . . . Should I be unable to support their plan, I will bring forward another . . . And recommend the party to follow suit, keep its own counsel, turn over the subject from all points of view, and reserve its freedom of action until an occasion may arise when there may be a hope of acting usefully.[53]

This important letter suggests that what Gladstone was contemplating, in the weeks before the new parliament met, was a declaration of policy, once the government's own plans were known, similar to that which he had made in 1868 with regard to the Irish Church. Possibly he envisaged a similar outcome, with a measure eventually being passed after a general election in which the issue was prominent, though this must remain a matter for conjecture. At any rate, the letter provides interesting confirmation of Gladstone's resolve to carry a home-rule measure. Such was also the conclusion drawn by Lord Derby, who recorded in his diary a long conversation with Gladstone in London on 13 January. In Derby's opinion, there was:

> no doubt now possible about the fact, that he is a home ruler on conviction and principle, though using his discretion as to the time and manner of declaring himself. He seemed to think that he could avoid expressing an opinion on the subject early in the session, and wait for the Ministerial proposals . . . I left him with the conviction that his mind is made up about home rule, and that he will draw us all into support of it if he can.[54]

The main threat to Gladstone's strategy lay in the possibility that the Conservatives might seek to hold on to office by means of an arrangement with Hartington and the Whigs, and, by the middle of January, there were signs that the government was indeed trying to

[52] Hamilton's diary, 10 Jan. 1886, BL Add. MSS 48642.
[53] Gladstone to Lord Richard Grosvenor, 7 Jan. 1886, BL Add. MSS 44316, fo. 165.
[54] Lord Derby's diary, 13 Jan. 1886, Derby MSS.

engineer a split in the Liberal party. Reports were circulating that the
government intended to introduce new coercive legislation, that
Salisbury was willing to serve under Hartington, and that there had
been a reconciliation between Hartington and Lord Randolph
Churchill.[55] At the same time, Hartington wrote a letter to
Gladstone which provoked an indignant response from the Liberal
leader, in a letter to Granville, on the eighteenth:

Hartington writes to me a letter indicating the possibility that on Thursday
[the beginning of the parliamentary session], while I announce with reasons
a policy of silence and reserve, he may feel it his duty to declare his
determination to 'Maintain the Legislative Union', that is to proclaim a
policy (so I understand the phrase) of absolute resistance without examination to the demand made by Ireland through five-sixths of her members.

This is to play the Tory game with a vengeance. They are now, most rashly
not to say more, working the Irish question to split the Liberal party.

It seems to me that if a gratuitous declaration of this kind is made it must
produce an explosion: and that in a week's time Hartington will have to
consider whether he will lead the Liberal party himself or leave it to chaos.
He will make my position impossible . . . I do not see how I could, as leader,
survive a gratuitous declaration of opposition to me such as Hartington
appears to meditate.[56]

According to Lewis Harcourt, Granville showed this letter to
Hartington and Harcourt, with the result that Hartington was
persuaded to go and see Gladstone.[57] However, the meeting between
Hartington and Gladstone was less than cordial, and when Granville
called on Harcourt on the twentieth, he reported that 'they could not
have given worse advice than they did on Monday [the eighteenth] to
Hartington to go and see G. as he (Hartington) was most insolent in
his manner to G. and in Granville's phrase "He could not have
behaved worse to him if he (G.) had been the Duke of Devonshire"'.[58]

Nevertheless, the familiar threat contained in Gladstone's letter,
that he might be driven to retire and throw the responsibilities of

<hr />

[55] Cf. Lewis Harcourt's diary, 14 Jan. 1886, Harcourt MSS; Albert Grey to Earl
Grey, 15 Jan. 1886, Grey MSS, Box 90. Churchill had written a letter to Hartington
on the 13th apologizing for remarks made during the general election, Devonshire
MSS, 340.1902.

[56] Gladstone to Granville, 18 Jan. 1886, in Ramm (ed.), *Gladstone–Granville
Correspondence, 1876–1886*, ii. 422–3. Cf. Hartington to Gladstone, 15 Jan. 1886,
BL Add. MSS 44148, fo. 201, in Holland, *Devonshire*, ii. 111–12.

[57] Lewis Harcourt's diary, 18 Jan. 1886, Harcourt MSS.

[58] Ibid., 20 Jan. 1886.

leadership on to Hartington, appeared to have the desired effect of quietening the Whig leader.[59] When the new parliament assembled on 21 January, therefore, it was generally supposed that the Salisbury administration might survive for some time.[60] In the event, of course, the government did fall on the twenty-sixth, after an adverse vote on an amendment to the address, by Jesse Collings, relating to the provision of allotments for agricultural labourers, but it is clear that its fate had not been settled until almost the last moment. As late as the twenty-fourth, Gladstone refused to be drawn as to the course he would take on the Collings amendment,[61] and his decision to use this issue as a means of turning out the government was evidently arrived at suddenly. Lewis Harcourt recorded in his diary, on 25 January, that:

Gladstone arrived unexpectedly to see Father this morning. He had come to press the advisability of turning out the present Government at the very earliest opportunity, and wished to do so, if possible, on Jesse Collings' Amendment. Father said 'Have you considered whether you would be able to form a Government?' Gladstone replied 'Most certainly I should'. Father expressed doubts as to his being able to get six Cabinet Ministers for the House of Commons, but Gladstone would not hear of it and said he should easily do it . . . His great object in turning out the Government at once is to prevent W. H. Smith (the new Chief Secretary) from producing any scheme which might satisfy the Irish on the land question.[62]

Contrary to this typically Harcourtian interpretation, however, it is far more plausible to argue that Gladstone was motivated by the knowledge of a change in the attitude of the Parnellites towards a Liberal government, which seems to have stemmed from rumours of a Whig–Conservative combination. This suggestion would be logical, in so far as Gladstone's position since the election had been that nothing could happen until the Tory–Nationalist alliance was terminated, and it would also explain why Gladstone's decision to use the Collings amendment as a means of removing the government was

---

[59] Goschen wrote to his wife on 20 Jan. that Gladstone was 'very much annoyed with Hartington and is making things disagreeable, very disagreeable, for [him]': Elliot, *Goschen*, ii. 8–9.

[60] Cf. Brett's diary, 21 Jan. 1886, Esher MSS, 2/7; Lewis Harcourt's diary, 22 Jan. 1886, Harcourt MSS; Selborne to Sir Arthur Hamilton-Gordon, 21 Jan. 1886, 1st Earl Selborne MSS, 1874, fo. 55.

[61] Gladstone to Mrs O'Shea, 24 Jan. 1886 (copy), BL Add. MSS 56447.

[62] Lewis Harcourt's diary, 25 Jan. 1886, Harcourt MSS.

taken so late. The evidence for this interpretation comes mainly from the correspondence between Herbert Gladstone and Henry Labouchere, who acted as an intermediary between Hawarden and the Parnellites. As Herbert understood the situation on the twenty-third, 'Parnell will vote against Collings amendment, to keep the government safely in till they can be turned out with profit.'[63] Such information naturally reinforced the prevailing assumption that the Nationalists were not prepared to take the risk of putting Gladstone into power unfettered. However, a letter from Gladstone père to Mrs O'Shea, the following day, indicates that he may have suspected that the Nationalists were contemplating a change of strategy: 'It is difficult for me to determine my course about the motion of Mr. Jesse Collings, until I learn, probably from the debate, how far it is a matter of interest to the newly enfranchised rural labourers and their representatives. For the moment I will say no more.'[64] Of course, what he really meant was whether or not the amendment was likely to be a 'matter of interest' to Parnell. The appointment of W. H. Smith as the new chief secretary for Ireland, and the accompanying rumours about an anti-home rule coalition, were probably decisive in this respect. Labouchere reported to Herbert Gladstone on the twenty-fifth that the Nationalists were now 'very anxious to turn the Government out on Collings' Amendment. They are afraid of any truce', and similarly, on the twenty-sixth, he wrote that he had seen the Irish 'Lieutenants', who were 'certain that everything would go to pieces if time were given to Lord Salisbury and the Whigs to combine'.[65]

Thus, in the end, Gladstone was able to turn out the Conservative ministers and form a government of his own on the most favourable conditions that could be obtained. Once the Nationalists had resolved to withdraw their support from the Conservatives and take their chance with Gladstone, it became possible to use the Collings amendment as a device for defeating the government without even raising the question of Irish policy. Gladstone was therefore able to constitute an alternative government, unencumbered with specific Irish commitments, and with a brief simply to 'examine' the demand

---

[63]   Herbert Gladstone to Labouchere, 23 Jan. 1886, BL Add. MSS 46015, fo. 165. This impression was also reported by the London correspondent of the *Manchester Guardian*, 25 Jan. 1886, p. 5.

[64]   Gladstone to Mrs O'Shea, 24 Jan. 1886 (copy), BL Add. MSS 56447.

[65]   Labouchere to Herbert Gladstone, 25, 26 Jan. 1886, BL Add. MSS 46015, fos. 169, 170.

for home rule.[66] This method of procedure also helped to ensure that there was no immediate disruption of the Liberal party, and even those like Hartington, who could not agree to serve in the new ministry, felt obliged to promise a dispassionate consideration of Gladstone's Irish policy, when it assumed a more definite shape.[67]

III

If there is nothing in the tactics adopted by Gladstone, in the weeks preceding the formation of his third ministry, to support the contention that he was not at that stage resolved to pursue a policy of home rule, a question mark still remains over the intentions of Hartington. His behaviour was so enigmatic that, between 23 and 27 January, according to several independent sources, he was contemplating a measure which amounted to a 'Repeal of the Union', and Cooke and Vincent have used this evidence to support their suggestion that Hartington may have been planning to pre-empt Gladstone with a home-rule policy of his own.[68]

A closer examination of what Hartington was saying makes it clear, however, that what he had in mind was not a home-rule measure of the kind demanded by the Nationalists, but a policy designed to remove the Irish members from parliament and turn Ireland into a 'subject province'. That this was his meaning is confirmed by the text of Albert Grey's letter of 24 January, in which the phrase 'Repeal of the Union' was used,[69] and is further supported

---

[66] For the memorandum by Gladstone outlining the basis on which the new government was being formed, see John Morley, *Life of William Ewart Gladstone* (1903), iii. 292.

[67] Hartington to Gladstone, 30 Jan. 1886, BL Add. MSS 44148, fo. 212, in Holland, *Devonshire*, ii. 124–5.

[68] Cooke and Vincent, *Governing Passion*, pp. 95–7.

[69] Albert Grey to Hartington, 24 Jan. 1886: 'It appears to me, after long consideration, that such a Repeal of the Union as you contemplated when you spoke of getting rid of the Irish members from the House of Commons must lead to eventual separation. If Ireland is not to keep her place as an equal and integral part of the United Kingdom, she will, unless she sets up as a separate independent entity, be reduced to the miserable position of a subject Province . . . Irish dignity will be insulted, so long as a foreign legislature in which she has no part exercises Sovereign powers over her, and once reduced to the degraded position of a mercenary Province, nothing will satisfy Irish sentiment until complete separation is accomplished, or until she is taken back within the fold of the Union on equal terms.' Devonshire MSS, 340.1915. Cf. the partial quotation by Cooke and Vincent, *Governing Passion*, p. 96.

by an entry in the diary kept by Lord Derby, who had also seen
Hartington on 23 January:

> He dwelt on the impossibility of any business being done in parliament while
> the Irishmen sat there ... He thought it absolutely necessary that they
> should be turned out. 'Then', I said, 'you must give them full control over
> their own affairs in a local parliament'. He did not see that, thought it did not
> follow, was not for making concessions to them, would get rid of them for
> our sake, not for theirs, assumed that in any case there must be a power in the
> English parliament to override a local legislature set up in Dublin—in short,
> he would restore the Irish parliament as it was before Grattan and 1780.
> 'Did he suppose that would satisfy the Irish? would they not be worse off
> than before?' He could not tell and did not much care. 'But will Gladstone
> agree to a plan quite different from his own?' 'No, certainly not'.[70]

The question that still has to be answered, of course, is why was
Hartington talking in these terms in the first place? Derby's record of
his conversation on the twenty-third suggests a solution: Hartington
'distinctly assured me that he would not take office on the mere
chance of being able to agree on Irish policy afterwards, but would
insist on knowing what was proposed'.[71] He was obviously determined to avoid another 'sell-out', and was not prepared to join a
government formed by Gladstone unless there was a clear understanding as to the Irish policy which would be pursued. But such a
stand was likely to render the formation of a Gladstone administration impossible, and though Hartington would obviously have
preferred, in this case, to give an independent support to a Conservative government,[72] he had also to take into account the naked threat
made by Gladstone, in his letter to Granville on the eighteenth, that if
he was prevented from forming a government, he might throw the
responsibility for constructing an alternative administration with an
alternative Irish policy on to Hartington. An additional problem for
Hartington, which has been almost completely overlooked by other
historians, was the attitude of the Queen, who was more than usually
averse to the prospect of having Gladstone as her first minister. This
raised the possibility that, when the Salisbury administration fell,
Her Majesty might choose to summon Hartington rather than
Gladstone. It is not entirely clear when Hartington first became

---

[70] Lord Derby's diary, 24 Jan. 1886, Derby MSS.
[71] Ibid.
[72] Ibid.

aware of this potential complication, but it was certainly no later than 25 January, when he related to Sir Henry James a conversation with General Ponsonby, the Queen's private secretary, which had presumably taken place that day.[73] The rumour that Hartington might be asked to form a ministry, or, according to an alternative version, that the Queen might seek to impose conditions as to policy which Gladstone would find impossible to accept, became widespread in political circles during the following few days—even Gladstone was aware of it.[74] Consequently, right up until 30 January, when Gladstone finally received the royal summons, Hartington had to contend with the possibility of being called upon to attempt to carry out a policy of his own.[75] A letter to his mistress, the Duchess of Manchester, provides a clear indication of how uncertain the situation was: 'I hope the Queen won't ask me but I am afraid she may . . . if I hear nothing I shall hardly be able to come to K[imbolton] on Saturday, as it is so likely that I may be sent for to Osborne either on Saturday or Sunday.'[76]

There is no reason to suppose, however, that Hartington had any desire to implement his own policy, let alone that he was considering competing with Gladstone. On the contrary, his decision to vote against the Collings amendment, which brought down the Conservatives on the twenty-sixth, was clearly intended to emphasize his differences with the Liberal party in order, hopefully, to render him

---

[73] Sir Henry James's memoir, 25 Jan. 1886, in Lord Askwith, *Lord James of Hereford* (1930), 153. The basis for the irregular step of summoning a person who was not the recognized leader of his party was apparently the fact that Gladstone had spoken to the Queen in the sense of finally taking his leave, when resigning the previous June. Ibid. In an intriguing letter to the Queen on 24 Jan., Salisbury reported that he had heard 'that the apprehension which keeps Mr. Gladstone from attacking us is the fear lest your Majesty should send in that case for Lord Hartington', G. E. Buckle (ed.), *The Letters of Queen Victoria*, 3rd series (1930), i. 17. Whether under the influence of Salisbury's letter is not clear, but it was on the same day that Ponsonby consulted Rosebery about the possibility of the Queen sending for Hartington: Robert Rhodes James, *Rosebery* (1963), 178.

[74] For Gladstone's awareness that the Queen might demand impossible conditions, see Sir Henry James's memoir, 27 Jan. 1886, in Askwith, *James of Hereford*, p. 157. Cf. Edward Hamilton's diary, 26 Jan. 1886, BL Add. MSS 48642; Lewis Harcourt's diary, 28 Jan. 1886, Harcourt MSS.

[75] It was for this reason that, even on 27 Jan., after the defeat of the Conservative government, Hartington's 'mind seemed to be dealing with the details of some scheme to secure partial legislative independence', Sir Henry James's memoir, 27 Jan. 1886, in Askwith, *James of Hereford*, p. 155.

[76] Hartington to the Duchess of Manchester, 28 Jan. 1886, Devonshire MSS, Uncalendered.

ineligible as a Liberal Prime Minister. As he wrote to the Duchess of Manchester, that same night: 'Mr. Gladstone must try and form a Government now, and I daresay he will succeed; but I foresee a most awful crisis with the Queen.'[77] The fact that he had done nothing to encourage his followers to vote with him against the Collings amendment,[78] with the result that the number of Liberal dissentients totalled only eighteen, was also surely intended to facilitate the formation of a Gladstone ministry without him. To Hartington's immense relief, the Queen was finally persuaded by Goschen, who had set himself up as Her Majesty's Liberal confidant, that she must take Gladstone as her first minister.[79]

The arrangement whereby Hartington promised to give an impartial consideration to the policy that finally emerged from the Gladstone ministry's 'examination' of the Irish demand for home rule undoubtedly saved him from what would have become a politically disastrous position. Hartington was only too well aware, after his experiences during the leadership crisis of April 1880, that any attempt by him to obey the Queen's wishes and form a government in defiance of Gladstone's ambitions was likely to do irreparable damage to his political career, for even if he did succeed in putting together a ministerial team, it was almost certain to collapse ignominiously under the pressure of having a rival leader with a rival policy waiting in the wings. As he observed to the Duchess of Manchester, 'Mr G. with an undeveloped plan in his pocket would be a terrible force against us.'[80] Consequently, it seemed positively advantageous, from Hartington's point of view, to allow Gladstone to try his hand, while he remained in an independent position:

I think that now that he has gone as far as he has, it is necessary that he should have a fair trial and should show his hand. If he fails and if either the English or Irish won't have his plan there may be some chance of governing Ireland in some other way; but if he is prevented from having a fair chance by premature opposition and obstruction, then I don't believe that the Country

---

[77] Hartington to the Duchess of Manchester, 26 [Jan.] 1886, ibid.
[78] Arthur Elliot's diary, 26 Jan. 1886, Elliot MSS.
[79] See Hartington to the Duchess of Manchester, 28, 29 Jan. 1886, Devonshire MSS, Uncalendered; Goschen to the Queen, 29 Jan. 1886, in Buckle (ed.), *Victoria's Letters* (3rd series), i. 29–31.
[80] Hartington to the Duchess of Manchester, 27 Jan. 1886, Devonshire MSS, Uncalendered.

will be governable at all. At all events, I think I shall be able to take my own line about this.[81]

Hartington's belief that it was desirable to allow Gladstone to proceed with his plan must be understood within the context of the great uncertainty, felt in political circles, about the likely disposition of the new electorate towards the alternative policy of coercion. For this reason, there was little confidence among leading Liberals, after the general election, that it would be possible to establish a Liberal government on a coercionist basis until Gladstone had been given a chance to devise a policy of conciliation. This attitude had been articulated most forcefully by Harcourt, who pressed on Hartington the view that if a government was formed which rejected Gladstone's plan, or which acted contrary to what was believed to be Gladstone's plan, it was certain to be confronted with an Irish agitation of unprecedented violence, with a revival of outrages, a breakdown of law and order, and a strike against the payment of rent. 'I confess I doubt if the resistance could be overcome. The name and authority of Mr G. would be appealed to as showing that reasonable demands had been refused and would be regarded as a palliation if not a justification of the violence and outrages of a nation unable to obtain its just rights.'[82] Britain, the argument continued, thanks to the Conservatives' volte-face on the crimes act, in July 1885, lacked the 'moral resources' with which to carry the necessary measures of coercion, and as the general public was not sufficiently appreciative of the dangers of home rule to 'feel that it must be repelled at *all cost*', there was little hope of establishing a government with the requisite determination and public support to be able to survive.[83]

Given the prevailing attitude in Liberal minds, Hartington had found it impossible to rouse his colleagues into any kind of organized resistance to Gladstone. A letter published in *The Times*, shortly after the flying of the Hawarden Kite, had been intended to emphasize

[81] Hartington to the Duchess of Manchester, 30 Jan. 1886, ibid. Cf. Sir Henry James's memoir, 30 Jan. 1886, in Askwith, *James of Hereford*, p. 164.

[82] Harcourt to Hartington, 20 Dec. 1885, Devonshire MSS, 340.1859. At this time, Harcourt was staying with Chamberlain at Highbury.

[83] Harcourt to Hartington, 24 Dec. 1885, ibid. 340.1866. For a similar view, see the copy of the memorandum, dated 13 Dec. 1885, embodying the views of Northbrook and Spencer, in 1st Earl Selborne MSS, 1869, fo. 95. The difficulty of securing support from the Liberal party for a coercion policy was later used as an argument by Hartington in his letters to the Duchess of Manchester, 27, 28 Jan. 1886, Devonshire MSS, Uncalendered.

that his own position on home rule had not changed,[84] but when Hartington attempted to organize a conclave of leading Liberals, to discuss their position, the response was disappointing. Granville, Spencer, and Rosebery all stayed away from the meeting at Devonshire House, on New Year's Day 1886, and those who did attend, Chamberlain, Harcourt, and Dilke, were all of the opinion that it was necessary to 'have out' Gladstone's plan.[85] It was particularly ominous that Chamberlain was now contemplating a home-rule policy of his own,[86] and, later in the month, the choice of the Collings amendment as the instrument for bringing down the Salisbury administration appeared to confirm the Radical leader's inclination towards a *rapprochement* with Gladstone over Ireland.

However, it was not simply the doubtful reliability of the British people or his own party that Hartington had to bear in mind in January 1886. Another possibility which needed to be considered seriously, was that Gladstone might not, after all, come out in favour of a policy of home rule for Ireland. Gladstone remained as ambiguous as ever about his real intentions, and, during the week preceding the opening of parliament, a number of those who were particularly close to him gained the impression that, whatever his own opinions might be, Gladstone was likely to conclude that home rule was impracticable in the prevailing circumstances, and that he might even be forced into a policy of coercion.[87] Lord Spencer—the wish no doubt being father to the thought—believed that Gladstone was about to ditch home rule, and Granville had received a letter from Gladstone referring to 'Home Rule (which indeed the social state of Ireland may effectually thrust aside for the time)'.[88] Furthermore, there is evidence to suggest that Gladstone used similar language during his interview with Hartington on 30 January. Three

[84] *The Times*, 21 Dec. 1885, p. 8. Cf. Hartington to Derby, 20 Dec. 1885, Derby MSS; Goschen to Hartington, n.d. [20–1 Dec. 1885], Devonshire MSS, 340.1864.
[85] Lewis Harcourt's diary, 1 Jan. 1886, Harcourt MSS.
[86] 'His idea is this—give Ireland a constitution, an upper and a lower House of Assembly; reserve to England the power and the duty of protecting her ... all representation in the Imperial Parliament to cease.' Ibid.
[87] Mrs Gladstone maintained that if the Irish proved unmanageable, her husband might even be driven to disfranchisement: Edward Hamilton's diary, 14 Jan. 1886, BL Add. MSS 48642.
[88] Lewis Harcourt's diary, 14 Jan. 1886, Harcourt MSS. Gladstone to Granville, 18 Jan. 1886, in Ramm (ed.), *Gladstone–Granville Correspondence, 1876–1886*, ii. 422–3.

days afterwards, Reginald Brett, Hartington's former private secretary, had a long conversation with his old chief, whom he found to be:

satisfied with his position, and glad to be free from the ties of unsympathetic comradeship. He said that he felt in an altogether too favourable position. Whatever the result of Mr. Gladstone's experiment, whether success or failure, he, Hartington, would reap the benefit without the risk of responsibility. There was an unfairness about this which struck him. Although he could not join the Government upon the basis of 'examination', there was no reason why men should not serve it in a subordinate capacity, or support it. But *he* could not take the responsibility of joining a *Cabinet* upon an invitation to 'examine' the question of Home Rule. Mr. Gladstone laid great stress upon this phrase and the idea which it contains. Hartington will form no cave at present. He will support the Government, and give them a fair field upon which to launch their experiment.[89]

The implication that, during his interview with Hartington, Gladstone, who was as unwilling as ever to contemplate anything more than the immediate future, conveyed the impression that the government's 'examination' of the question of home rule might not lead to the introduction of a home-rule measure[90] is confirmed by Brett's subsequent advice to Hartington: 'As Mr G. seems inclined to vary his programme, and as his declarations, when Parliament meets, may possibly not chime with his personal explanations to you, I think, in view of the future, it would be desirable for you to write a memorandum (if you have not already done so) of your interview with him.'[91] Unfortunately, there is no trace of a memorandum by Hartington, but it seems clear from the evidence here that he had been encouraged to believe that there was a role for him to play, by standing aside from the government's 'examination' of home rule, as the focus for an eventual reconstruction of the ministry, when Gladstone retired, presumably on alternative lines.

This continuing uncertainty about the ultimate policy of the Gladstone ministry shows why there was no insincerity about the conduct of those, including Selborne and James, who were clearly tempted by offers of Cabinet posts, or of those who, without any discouragement from Hartington, did actually take office under

[89] Brett's diary, 3 Feb. 1886, Esher MSS, 2/7.
[90] It might be noted that, when taking office, Gladstone admitted to the Queen that the odds against success were '49 to 1': Buckle, *Victoria's Letters* (3rd series), i. 36–7. He reputedly told the Prince of Wales that he 'would be out of office "with ignominy" in three months': Brett's diary, 5 Feb. 1886, Esher MSS, 2/7.
[91] Brett to Hartington, 3 Feb. 1886 (copy), Esher MSS, 2/7.

Gladstone.[92] Indeed, for a brief period in the early weeks of February 1886, a mood of cautious optimism prevailed among the Liberal opponents of home rule that the issue might never come to a head. Goschen, for instance, remarked to Morier that, since the formation of the new government, a reaction had set in and home rule appeared to have 'gone back'.[93] Albert Grey's opinion was that, as Gladstone needed to gain the support of either the Nationalists or the Conservatives for his Irish policy, 'he will discover that Principle and Justice require him to disappoint the Parnellites and to work upon the Tories to support him in a national policy'.[94] Similarly, Edward Heneage, who had joined the government, believed that when the Cabinet produced its policy, it would 'not be Home Rule'.[95] They were soon to be proved wrong.

[92] Gladstone's memoranda on the construction of his third ministry are printed in John Brooke and Mary Sorensen (eds.), *The Prime Minister's Papers: W. E. Gladstone*, iv: *Autobiographical Memoranda, 1868–1894* (1981), 33–8. For an analysis, see Cooke and Vincent, *Governing Passion*, pp. 341–6, 365–8. Hartington was clearly anxious that Gladstone should succeed in forming a government, and was fearful that if others, like James, did decline offers from Gladstone, he might give up the attempt: Hartington to the Duchess of Manchester, 30 Jan. 1886, Devonshire MSS, Uncalendered. Gladstone did, in the event, experience some difficulty in filling up the Household offices, since a number of peers like the Duke of Westminster were unwilling to serve. See the correspondence between Gladstone and Granville, 1–16 Feb. 1886, in Ramm (ed.), *Gladstone–Granville Correspondence, 1876–1886*, ii. 427–31.

[93] Goschen to Morier, 10 Feb. 1886, in Elliot, *Goschen*, ii. 14–16.

[94] Albert Grey to W. C. Cartwright, 10 Feb. 1886, Cartwright MSS, Box 16, unmarked bundle.

[95] Heneage to Cartwright, 14 Feb. 1886, ibid.

Conclusion

Though the outcome of the government's 'examination' of the question of Irish home rule was not formally revealed to the House of Commons until 8 April 1886, it had become increasingly clear, from the middle of March, what the conclusion was going to be. During the early weeks of the administration, Gladstone had been able to keep the work of devising possible Irish measures largely in his own hands, but when Chamberlain provoked a confrontation in Cabinet on 13 March, he was forced to state that it was his intention to legislate for a parliament in Dublin.[1] Cooke and Vincent have seen Gladstone's ambiguity up to this point as proof that he had not settled on any policy, and was simply waiting for circumstances to shape his proposals.[2] They point to the fact that a land-purchase bill was for some time expected to be the government's principal measure, and that a resort to coercion was still considered a possibility.[3] Consequently, in their view, Gladstone's declaration for home rule on 13 March was made purely for tactical reasons, with the object of uniting the Liberal party around his leadership in the face of Chamberlain's challenge.[4]

This interpretation is not borne out, however, by the evidence in the diary kept by Sir Edward Hamilton, Gladstone's former private secretary, who, in his new capacity as a Treasury official, was 'borrowed' by his old chief to assist with the financial aspects of the Irish schemes. From an early stage, Hamilton was in little doubt as to where the Prime Minister's plans were leading: he noted on 11 February, for instance, that 'What he has in view for the Constitution of Ireland he calls "central organ" or "Irish authority", but though he avoids the name, it will evidently fall but little short of a Parliament.'[5] A proposal submitted by Chamberlain for a land-purchase measure, to be administered by an Irish Central Board, was

---

[1] For an account of this incident, see A. B. Cooke and John Vincent, *The Governing Passion: Cabinet Government and Party Politics in Britain, 1885–86* (Hassocks, 1974), 383–4.
[2] Ibid. 54–5.
[3] Ibid. 54.
[4] Ibid. 55–6.
[5] Hamilton's diary, 11 Feb. 1886, BL Add. MSS 48643.

'put . . . on one side as utterly impracticable'.[6] But the crucial point
which emerges is that the process whereby land purchase was
gradually subordinated to a home-rule bill had clearly begun before
Chamberlain's confrontation with Gladstone. As early as 2 March,
Gladstone was talking of separating the two measures,[7] and by the
twelfth, the day before the critical Cabinet meeting, he was proposing, to the dismay of Spencer, that the work of converting tenants
into proprietors should be left to the new Irish authority.[8] Cooke and
Vincent, it seems, failed to ask the obvious question: why was
Chamberlain provoked into bringing the matter to a head when he
did?

It is difficult to resist the conclusion that Gladstone had known all
along what he was aiming for, and that he simply used land purchase
as a means of securing the support of key Whig ministers, like
Spencer, while gaining time in which to effect that process of
'fermentation in many minds, working towards the final product',
which seems to have been the essence of his strategy from the autumn
of 1885. The effect of the passage of time, in a period of great
uncertainty and perplexity such as this, was always likely to be to
create an air of inevitability about home rule,[9] with this solution
winning the day perhaps by default.[10] Certainly, by late March the
suggestion of a home-rule measure seemed likely to receive a far
more favourable reception than would previously have been possible, as Hamilton observed: 'the idea of Home Rule, which was
formerly looked upon as a forbidden subject for even discussion, is
now considered a fairly "open question" . . . the *pros* for and *cons*
against it are a legitimate matter of argument'.[11]

Indeed, there is nothing to suggest that, between the formation of
his government and the confrontation on 13 March, Gladstone ever
regarded Chamberlain as a serious threat to his plans. Chamberlain's
reputation with the Radical section of the party had been damaged
by the general election, and it was not unreasonable for Gladstone to
assume that he would fall into line with his Irish proposals, along

[6] Ibid., 19 Feb. 1886. For Chamberlain's proposal, see J. L. Garvin, *Life of Joseph Chamberlain*, ii. (1933), 182–3.
[7] Hamilton's diary, 2 Mar. 1886, BL Add. MSS 48643. See also the entry for 9 Mar.
[8] Ibid., 12 Mar. 1886.
[9] Ibid., 27, 29 Feb. 1886, for the idea that the country was coming round to home rule.
[10] Cf. Lord Derby's diary, 20 Feb. 1886, Derby MSS, for this fear.
[11] Hamilton's diary, 26 Mar. 1886, BL Add. MSS 48643.

with the rest of the Cabinet. It is certainly difficult to see how Gladstone could have calculated on Chamberlain's resignation, for although Chamberlain had been averse, in the aftermath of the elections, to the idea of dealing with Parnell on home-rule lines, he had also appreciated the dangers of standing out against Gladstone, and had seemed reconciled, by the time the new parliament met, to the need for co-operation with the Liberal leader. The choice of Collings's amendment as the instrument for bringing down the Salisbury administration was rightly seen as a sign that Chamberlain was aligning himself with Gladstone on the Irish question in order to tie him to the Radical programme.[12] John Morley actually claimed that Chamberlain had been converted to home rule,[13] though it appears more likely, from his correspondence, that he was still hoping to establish a revised version of his own Irish proposals as the official policy of the government.[14] For instance, he indicated to John Bright that his continued membership of the government depended on Gladstone's acceptance of his view that 'the land business is at the bottom of everything',[15] while to Reginald Brett he wrote more bluntly that the essential question was 'will Mr G.—at 76—frankly lean on the Radicals for the last steps of his journey'.[16] By early March, however, it had become clear to Chamberlain that the government's 'examination' was a sham, that Gladstone had no intention of compromising on his Irish plans and was gradually drawing his colleagues into the home-rule solution.[17] At the Cabinet on 13 March, therefore, Chamberlain finally unleashed his pent-up frustration at the way his position as the natural intermediary between the Liberal party and the Irish Nationalists had been destroyed by the (imagined) treachery of Parnell and the opportunism

[12] Kate Courtney's diary, 25, 26 Jan. 1886, Courtney MSS.
[13] Brett's diary, 29 Jan. 1886, Esher MSS, 2/7.
[14] See Brett's diary, 16 Jan. 1886, ibid., for Chamberlain's determination to force down Parnell's demands. On 22 Jan., Chamberlain made overtures to Parnell on the basis of a land-purchase measure, in the hope of obtaining Nationalist support for the Collings amendment: Garvin, *Chamberlain*, ii. 166–7.
[15] Chamberlain to Bright, 5 Feb. 1886, BL Add. MSS 43387, fo. 200.
[16] Chamberlain to Brett, 8 Feb. 1886, Esher MSS, 5/4.
[17] For Chamberlain's mounting suspicions, see his letter to John Morley, 5 Mar. 1886, Chamberlain MSS, JC5/54/686. Cf. W. T. Stead's diary, 8 Mar. 1886: 'Brett says Gladstone's Home Rule scheme very nearly elaborated, and that there is to be a Parliament in Dublin—Knew the exact phrase it would go by, but did not like to tell me. Thought Chamberlain must leave the Cabinet: Mr. Gladstone had led him to believe that there is nothing decided upon. The Grand Old Man's tactical skill marvellous—almost too smart', F. Whyte, *Life of W. T. Stead* (1925), i. 217.

of the 'Grand Old Man'. Infuriated by his own manifest impotence, Chamberlain's pride made it impossible for him to swallow any scheme initiated and devised by Gladstone.[18]

Gladstone seems to have been equally confident of his ability to secure Hartington's acquiescence in a home-rule policy. He was reported by Hamilton as being 'much pleased and even touched by Hartington's behaviour', at the time of the formation of the new government,[19] and his optimism that Hartington would prove amenable survived right up until the parliamentary debate on the home-rule bill in April. The details of the bill were confided to Hartington the day before the debate began, and Gladstone was evidently taken aback by the resolute manner in which the Whig leader subsequently spoke against it.[20] However, the cautious approach to Gladstone's 'experiment' which Hartington had adopted in January should not lead us to suppose that he was ever likely to fall in with the Prime Minister's plans, or to accept Cooke and Vincent's argument that it was only the knowledge of the breach between Chamberlain and Gladstone which caused Hartington to come out against home rule before Chamberlain pre-empted his position.[21]

After the great uncertainty of the period leading up to the formation of the new administration, Hartington's interview with Gladstone on 30 January had seemed to revitalize the traditional Whig strategy of remaining within the Liberal fold in the hope of exerting an influence upon future developments. It was not clear that Gladstone would, in the end, produce a home-rule measure, and even if he did, the difficulties involved in carrying it were certain to be formidable. The prospect of a Hartingtonian succession was therefore still quite genuine, and it was reflected in his conversation with Lord Ebrington on 25 February: 'He said he was pretty confident that Gladstone would retire into private life if his Cabinet broke up on the Irish question, or if he was beaten on it.'[22] Hartington may well have

---

[18] Such was also Hamilton's view, diary, 28 Mar. 1886, BL Add. MSS 48643.
[19] Ibid., 29 Jan. 1886, BL Add. MSS 48642.
[20] Ibid., 7, 10 Apr. 1886, BL Add. MSS 48643.
[21] Cooke and Vincent, *Governing Passion*, pp. 106–8.
[22] Ebrington's diary, 25 Feb. 1886, Fortescue MSS. One of the young Whig dissentients seems to have had a similar idea: 'You ask as to [Hartington's] and Goschen's chances of getting enough support to form a ministry. I don't think while Gladstone and Chamberlain work together there is any possibility of a strong Liberal Government without them. Men won't vote against Gladstone. If the latter falls, then I should hope Hartington would be able to rally enough men round him to get on', Arthur Elliot to W. C. Cartwright, 3 Mar. 1886, Cartwright MSS, Box 16, unmarked bundle.

been attracted by the idea, urged upon him by Harcourt and James, of an eventual reconstruction of the Liberal party, under his leadership, after a period of Conservative rule. Lewis Harcourt noted in his diary on 20 March that his father had 'spoken to Hartington on the subject and told him that it would be a great mistake for him (Hartington) to come in after Gladstone but that if he bides his time the whole of the Liberal party will rally round him and after Salisbury has been in a short time he will be able to form a strong Government. Hartington seems to see this but [father] is much amused at the way Hartington talks already of "my Government".'[23] Three days later, Lewis added that 'James looks forward to the early smash of this Government, the formation of a Salisbury administration to coerce Ireland followed by a Hartington Government which is to unite all sections of the Liberal party: of course he sees as all Liberals do the folly of Hartington rising at once out of the ashes of Mr. Gladstone's Government under which circumstances none of the present Cabinet could join him (Hartington).'[24] We need not necessarily assume that Hartington ever entirely gave up hope of an eventual reconstruction of this sort, although the vehemence of Gladstone's response, when he came out against the home-rule bill in April, must have made such an outcome appear increasingly less likely.

The possibility of a reconstructed Liberal ministry would certainly explain why Hartington was reluctant to engage himself in any way with the Conservatives. However, it should be noted that, when he was approached by Salisbury early in March, Hartington did 'express the hope that they might act together in defeating any proposition for a separate Irish Parliament',[25] and he had already taken the decision to organize regular meetings of a group of his own supporters.[26] The implication that Hartington was preparing to resist a proposal for Irish home rule, if it was made, is reinforced by his letter to John Bright, dated 5 March—when rumours about

[23] Lewis Harcourt's diary, 20 Mar. 1886, Harcourt MSS.
[24] Ibid., 23 Mar. 1886. Cf. James's memoir, 22 Mar. 1886, in Askwith, *James of Hereford*, pp. 172–3, recording a conversation with Hartington.
[25] James's memoir, 4 Mar. 1886, in Askwith, *James of Hereford*, p. 171.
[26] Albert Grey to Earl Grey, 1 Mar. 1886, Grey MSS, Box 90. Cooke and Vincent, *Governing Passion*, p. 115, try to play this point down. Earlier, on 19 Feb., Ebrington recorded in his diary that Goschen 'was all in favour of expanding the anti-Home Rule movement, and that if necessary to oppose, Hartington should find a ready made party behind him', Fortescue MSS.

Gladstone's intentions were beginning to spread, but still more than a week before Chamberlain precipitated the Cabinet crisis:

I don't think from all you have said on the subject that you are likely to be in favour of giving to the Irish a separate Parliament, which in some form or other I conceive will be Mr. Gladstone's proposal . . . I think . . . that the time is approaching when all those who are in an independent position and feel any doubts as to the course which the government are likely to take ought to come to an understanding with each other.[27]

Cooke and Vincent's argument that Hartington's opposition was motivated simply by the fear of being pre-empted by Chamberlain relies, in any case, upon the assumption that, after the general election of 1885, Chamberlain recognized that his version of Radicalism was played out, and that he was therefore looking for a new 'role' to perform.[28] The evidence produced earlier, however, suggests that until March 1886 Chamberlain was still trying to tie Gladstone to his Radical policies, and it would seem more plausible to argue, for this reason, that Hartington's concern, up to this point, was that by moving into an immediate and irreconcilable opposition to Gladstone, he might tempt Chamberlain to accept home rule as a way of consolidating the rift between Gladstone and the Whigs.[29] Furthermore, even when Chamberlain did resign, he was determined to emphasize his willingness to go further than Hartington in terms of concession to the Irish (he favoured some kind of federal arrangement), and the Whig leader was prepared for the possibility that he might 'have to differ from [Chamberlain] as well as from Gladstone'.[30] Chamberlain's resignation was undoubtedly a significant turning-point, but in a quite different sense from Cooke and Vincent's, for it had the effect of placing Gladstone's Irish plans unequivocally in the forefront of the political conflict, and thus put

[27] Hartington to Bright, 5 Mar. 1886, B L Add. MSS 43387, fo. 238. When Bright called on Hartington on 10 Mar., he thought him 'very reasonable and his course greatly to his credit': R. A. J. Walling (ed.), *The Diaries of John Bright* (1930), 535.
[28] Cooke and Vincent, *Governing Passion*, pp. 14–15.
[29] It is worth noting that some sympathizers feared that Hartington had thrown the game away by voting against the Collings amendment: e.g. Charles Cooper to Rosebery, 27 Jan. 1886, NLS MSS 10011; Lord Edmond Fitzmaurice to W. C. Cartwright, 1 Feb. 1886, Cartwright MSS, Box 6, bundle marked '1886–1903'. Evidently, they believed that Hartington should have taken office under Gladstone, as the best way of curbing his home-rule tendencies.
[30] Hartington to Goschen, 8 Apr. 1886, in Elliot, *Goschen*, ii. 38. For Chamberlain's position, see Garvin, *Chamberlain*, ii. 199–206.

an end to any remaining hopes that they might be shelved altogether.[31] Thereafter, Hartington seems to have shown little interest in facilitating a compromise with Gladstone, in spite of the fact that, in the middle of May, extensive negotiations were being conducted, involving moderate Gladstonians like Kay Shuttleworth and Whitbread (along with Sir Edward Hamilton), and dissentient Liberals like James, Sir Hussey Vivian, and Bright.[32] Hartington expressed the fear that Gladstone would simply exploit any signs of wavering on the part of the dissentient Liberals,[33] and it is significant that, on 18 May, at Bradford, he should have delivered what a dismayed Hamilton described as a 'very *ultra*' speech, effectively putting a damper on the compromise negotiations.[34] Hartington's conduct in May 1886 was hardly that of a man bent on securing the succession to Gladstone at any cost, in terms of policy.

As far as Gladstone's motives are concerned, there remains the question of what he expected to achieve by introducing a bill which, in view of the inevitable opposition of the House of Lords, had no realistic chance of being passed into law during the 1886 session. It has recently been argued that he was motivated solely by the short-term need to 'recapture control of his party', and that the home-rule bill 'was and had to be, a trial run whose genuinely Irish purpose lay at most in forging a link of expediency between Gladstone and the Parnellites'.[35] However, if it is accepted that, for some time after the formation of his third ministry, Gladstone believed in the possibility of securing a united Liberal support, including both Hartington and Chamberlain, for a home-rule measure, and that indeed he had pursued this strategy consistently since the autumn of 1885, then an alternative perspective is available to us. It was shown in an earlier chapter how Gladstone had developed an instinctively

[31] See Lewis Harcourt's diary, 23 Mar. 1886, Harcourt MSS, for his father's view of Chamberlain's resignation.
[32] Cooke and Vincent, *Governing Passion*, pp. 419–23.
[33] Hartington to James, 12 May 1886 (typescript), Hereford and Worcester Record Office, M45/1664, in Askwith, *James of Hereford*, p. 183.
[34] Hamilton's diary, 19 May 1886, BL Add. MSS 48643. For Hartington's speech, see *The Times*, 19 May 1886, p. 11. Chamberlain was also involved in negotiations with Gladstone at this time, but, as Richard Jay has suggested, it is unlikely that either man really wanted an agreement: *Joseph Chamberlain: A Political Study*, (Oxford, 1981), 124, 137–44. It is interesting to note Hartington's letter to James, on 22 May: 'Chamberlain says that my Bradford speech killed conciliation, and that he is sorry for it; but I don't think he seems very unhappy', Hereford and Worcester Record Office, M45/199. Cooke and Vincent make no mention of the Bradford speech.
[35] Cooke and Vincent, *Governing Passion*, p. 163.

short-term personal outlook which constantly appealed to the circumstances of the present for justification and refused to look to the
too-distant future. In guiding the Liberal party towards a policy of
home rule for Ireland, therefore, Gladstone was able to separate his
personal position from the ultimate political objective, believing as
he did that his own leadership might continue for no more than a few
months, and this made it possible for him to make light of considerations which might otherwise have proved overwhelming, such as
the attitude of the House of Lords.[36]

Gladstone conceived of his task, therefore, in terms of laying the
foundations for eventual action by a united Liberal party, and
hopefully a united country, on a policy of home rule for Ireland. The
question of who would be the leader to carry the final measure did
not concern him, and it was congenial to hint at the possibility of
leaving this work to his successors.[37] At a point such as this, it
becomes impossible to assess the 'real' motivating force behind the
man. To deny the influence of ambition and the urge to meet a great
political challenge would be extremely foolish, but not more so than
to refuse to recognize the validity of other impulses. After all, even
when Hartington and Chamberlain declared their opposition, it did
not follow that the home-rule cause was hopelessly lost. It was
always on the cards that the bill might be given its second reading by
the House of Commons,[38] and though it could have gone no further
at that time, the moral victory thus gained would have provided the
home-rule movement with a considerable impetus. Speculation here
could be endless, but we need to envisage only one possible line of
development in order to grasp the point: a decision, after securing the

[36] Gladstone's lack of concern for the obstacle posed by the House of Lords is
illustrated by his letter to Rosebery, 13 Nov. 1885, NLS MSS 10023, fo. 112, and by
his conversation with Lord Derby, recorded in the latter's diary, 13 Jan. 1886, Derby
MSS.

[37] Cf. Walling (ed.), *Bright Diaries*, pp. 448–9, for Bright's memorandum of a
conversation with Gladstone on 20 Mar. For a long time after his conversation with
Gladstone, when resigning from the government in Mar., Edward Heneage believed
that the Prime Minister was willing to withdraw his bills in order to avert a split in the
Liberal party, and that he desired Hartington to succeed him: Heneage to Wintringham, 17 May 1886, Heneage MSS, 2 HEN 5/13, fo. 42. Gladstone's attitude had
changed markedly, however, when Hartington came out against the home-rule bill in
April, and he began to speak of fighting a general election on the issue: Hamilton's
diary, 12 Apr. 1886, BL Add. MSS 48643.

[38] This was especially so after Gladstone's meeting of Liberal MPs at the Foreign
Office on 27 May, which led to doubts about the intentions of Chamberlain and his
group of supporters: Albert Grey to Earl Grey, 29 May 1886, Grey MSS, Box 90.

second reading, to defer the issue until the next session so as to avoid the need for a dissolution of parliament; an autumn filled with demonstrations by obedient Liberal organizations; immense pressure on individual MPs from the (now) Gladstonian-dominated caucus, and perhaps, in the end, a 'compromise' solution, substantially along Gladstone's original lines, but with sufficient flexibility on points of detail to save a few faces? To accept that the home-rule bill of 1886 was a 'trial run' need not devalue its 'genuinely Irish purpose'.

In the event, of course, the home-rule bill was defeated at the second-reading stage, in the early hours of 8 June, and a divided Liberal party was plunged into a general election battle which inevitably served to widen the rift between the Gladstonian and Unionist Liberals. This rift was never to be healed, and for all but three of the following twenty years, the Gladstonian Liberals found themselves on the opposition benches, encumbered with an Irish policy which many regarded as a serious political liability. The influence of Gladstone's commitment to home rule on the character of the post-1886 Liberal party was therefore profound, and deserves to be considered at some length.

Professor Shannon, in a famous book, has suggested that the ultimate result of Gladstone's leadership was the 'ruin of Radicalism', with the Liberal party, after Chamberlain's defection in 1886, being 'diverted . . . from its logical path' of becoming a party 'under predominantly Radical inspiration and control'.[39] It is obvious that Gladstone had no intention of becoming a puppet of Chamberlainite Radicalism, and his efforts to secure an alliance of his own with Parnell illustrate clearly his determination to keep the initiative in his own hands. However, I would argue that the collapse of Chamberlain's Radical position and the desertion of old associates like John Morley were the culmination of a process which had begun before the general election of 1885.[40] Indeed, the capture of the National Liberal Federation by supporters of Gladstone in May 1886 reflected rivalries and tensions which had been present since the foundation of

[39] R. T. Shannon, *Gladstone and the Bulgarian Agitation 1876* (1975 edn., Hassocks), 273. Similar views have been expressed by Donald Southgate, *The Passing of the Whigs, 1832–1886* (1962), 418, and D. A. Hamer, *Liberal Politics in the Age of Gladstone and Rosebery* (Oxford, 1972), 116.

[40] This point was discussed in ch. 6. At Christmas 1885, John Morley predicted to W. T. Stead that the Radicals would 'have to undergo eclipse—and perhaps extinction (not painless)', Whyte, *Stead*, i. 217.

that organization in 1877.[41] The fact was that Radicalism, even in the 1880s, identified itself more intimately with that appeal to moral sentiment so characteristic of Gladstone's style of leadership (exemplified by the plea for trust in the Irish people, and the sense of making amends for past wrongs), than with the more efficient, programmatic style offered by Chamberlain. It was this inherent weakness in Radicalism itself, as Professor Shannon seems at one point to recognize,[42] that prevented it from becoming the force which Chamberlain wanted to make it. 'Gladstonian Liberalism' provided the Radicals with an identity which they could never have found for themselves.

A far stronger case may be made for the view that the schism in 1886 damaged the Whigs rather than the Radicals. In fact, Radicalism almost certainly gained by the defection of some of the most illustrious names from the counterbalancing Whig section of the party,[43] and by the increasing dependence of the Liberal front bench, after 1886, on the rank and file, with all their crotchets.[44] But it is by no means clear that the schism need inevitably have happened, had it not been for the strain placed on the Whigs' sense of party loyalty by Gladstone's political methods. Hartington's conduct does not suggest that he wished to relinquish that controlling influence over Radical movements expected of him as a matter of family tradition, and it was shown in an earlier chapter that his supporters had not given up hope of securing control of the post-Gladstonian Liberal party. Over a period of several years, however, since before the

[41] For the prominent part played by Leeds in the May coup, see M. Ostrogorski, *Democracy and the Organisation of Political Parties* (1902), i. 289–94.

[42] Shannon, *Bulgarian Agitation*, pp. 273–4.

[43] It is not easy to measure the effect of the Liberal schism on the House of Lords in 1886, since Gladstone's bill was defeated in the Commons, but by 1893 the Liberal peerage was dangerously close to extinction, as only forty-one voted for the second home-rule bill. The consequences of the Liberal schism for the House of Commons may be seen from a brief summary of the respective compositions of the Gladstonian Liberal and Liberal Unionist parties after the 1886 general election. At that time, there were 189 Gladstonians, of whom sixty-six (34.9 per cent) had backgrounds in industry and commerce, fifty-five (29.1 per cent) were from the legal profession, and only forty-five (23.8 per cent) were from the aristocratic and landowning class. By comparison, of the seventy-seven Liberal Unionists, thirty-four (44.1 per cent) were from the aristocratic and landowning class, twenty-six (35 per cent) were from industry and commerce, and nineteen (24.7 per cent) were members of the legal profession. The overlap between members of the aristocratic and landowning class and the other social groups was very small in the case of the Gladstonian Liberals, but there was still a significant overlap in the case of the Liberal Unionist lawyers.

[44] Cf. Hugh Berrington, 'Partisanship and Dissidence in the Nineteenth Century House of Commons', *Parliamentary Affairs*, 21 (1967–8), 338–74.

general election of 1880, the question of the relations between the Liberal party and the Irish Nationalists had been a central point of conflict, with Hartington and many other Liberals being determined to resist the efforts of Chamberlain and some of the Radicals (often with Gladstone's connivance) to establish an alliance with Parnell. Consequently, Gladstone's seemingly machiavellian bid for the support of the eighty-six nationalist MPs returned at the 1885 general election was a move which many Liberals found impossible to accept.

It is important to emphasize that while the Liberal Unionists of 1886 had no faith in the character of the Irish people and the moderation of their representatives, and therefore believed that the home-rule measure proposed by Gladstone was incompatible, given the existing circumstances, with the preservation of the Union, this did not mean that they were opposed to the granting of some degree of autonomy to the Irish when the conditions were right. On the contrary, all Liberals were bound to believe in the efficacy of local self-government,[45] and some of the Liberal Unionists were clearly prepared to contemplate setting up an Irish legislature in Dublin.[46] The advantages of getting rid of the Irish representatives from Westminster altogether were an important consideration for some.[47] But there was an almost unanimous agreement that a comprehensive measure of land purchase was an essential pre-condition to any institutional changes, and this sequence of measures was hardly something that Gladstone could be expected to implement in the short space of time presumed to be left to him.[48] It is indicative of the general attitude that, prior to the formation of the third Gladstone

[45] Cf. Albert Grey to Earl Grey, 25 June 1885, Grey MSS, Box 89; Arthur Elliot to Albert Grey, 22 Dec. 1885, Grey MSS, 217/5; Lord Lorne to Elliot, 8 Jan. 1886, Elliot MSS.

[46] Cf. Lord Wolmer to Earl of Selborne, 23 Jan. 1886, 1st Earl of Selborne MSS, 1869, fo. 127; Selborne to Wolmer, 26 Jan. 1886, 2nd Earl of Selborne MSS, 91, fo. 127; Lansdowne to Rosebery, 22 Feb. 1886, NLS MSS 10085, fo. 83; Heneage to Thomas Wintringham, 7 June 1886, Heneage MSS, 2 HEN 5/13, fo. 49.

[47] e.g. Selborne to Wolmer, 26 Jan. 1886, 2nd Earl of Selborne MSS, 91, fo. 127. The Duke of Argyll wrote to Albert Grey, on 21 Mar. 1886, that he would willingly vote for the removal of the Irish MPs if 'Honour' permitted it—unfortunately it did not. Grey MSS 239/4.

[48] See Albert Grey to Earl Grey, 25 June 1885, Grey MSS, Box 89, and Wolmer to Selborne, 29 Jan. 1886, 1st Earl of Selborne MSS, 1869, fo. 143, for the view that land purchase must come first. Cf. Selborne to Wolmer, 26 Jan. 1886, 2nd Earl of Selborne MSS, 91, fo. 127, and Lansdowne to Lord Morley, 2, 15 Apr. 1886, BL Add. MSS 48267, fos. 37, 39, for doubts about Gladstone's ability to effect such a settlement.

ministry, both Hartington and Goschen expressed their support for a large measure of land purchase,[49] and Goschen was actually reported as being 'not averse from some measure of Home Rule but violently opposed to Gladstone and Parnellites.'[50]

In fact, the beliefs of the Liberal Unionists with regard to Ireland in no way set them apart from those of the bulk of the Gladstonians, for whom blind obedience to Gladstone (perhaps reinforced by fear of their constituents), in spite of their own misgivings, seems to have been the predominant influence. It was his powerful advocacy of home rule which alone convinced the Liberal rank and file that the measure could be safely conceded. John Bright was probably not far wrong in asserting that, but for Gladstone, no more than twenty Liberal MPs would have supported a proposal for an Irish parliament; and Lord Ebrington was able to produce a telling article, based on an analysis of election addresses, showing that only fourteen Liberal MPs had favoured the Parnellite demand for legislative independence during the 1885 general election.[51]

At the Cabinet level, with the exception of Gladstone himself, it is doubtful whether anyone genuinely believed that a safe and satisfactory settlement of the Irish question was attainable at that time along home-rule lines. John Morley, Gladstone's new Irish chief secretary, seems to have doubted whether the offer of home rule would succeed or be beneficial to the Irish—he had told the Harcourts that it would turn Ireland into 'a squalid little state like Iowa'—but felt that it was unavoidable, and Lord Spencer, a key convert to Gladstone's policy, was similarly despairing of the situation, adopting a '"what else can you do" tone'.[52] It is also noticeable how little enthusiasm for home

[49] Lewis Harcourt's diary, 13 Jan. 1886, Harcourt MSS; Arthur Elliot's diary, 13 Jan. 1886, Elliot MSS. Hartington had earlier written to Lansdowne of his desire for a land-purchase measure, though he thought this would have to be coupled with a local government bill, which he did not think would succeed: Hartington to Lansdowne, 4 Jan. 1886 (copy), Devonshire MSS, 340.1884.

[50] Lord Morley's diary, Jan. 1886, BL Add. MSS 48292. Cf. Spencer to Granville, 17 Dec. 1885, PRO 30/29/22A/5.

[51] Bright to W. H. Northy, 27 July 1886, BL Add. MSS 44877, fo. 106; Ebrington, 'Liberal Election Addresses', *Nineteenth Century*, 19 (Apr. 1886), 606–19. Of the three Liberal MPs elected for Leicestershire in 1885, Paget and Ellis had declared their opposition to home rule, and Johnson Ferguson expressed no opinion. The following year, all three supported Gladstone's bill, *Victoria County History of Leicestershire*, ii. 135–6.

[52] For Morley, cf. Lewis Harcourt's diary, 14 Jan. 1886. Harcourt MSS; Kate Courtney's diary, 18 Apr. 1886, Courtney MSS. For Spencer, see A. Ponsonby, *Henry Ponsonby: His Life from his Letters* (1942), 209.

rule was to be found among many of the younger Liberals who were to figure prominently in the post-Gladstonian era. R. T. Reid, for example, who was to become Lord Chancellor in 1905, wrote to Herbert Gladstone early in January 1886 that:

I am very anxious about the Irish question. If I could believe in the honesty and purpose of the Parnellites I should feel very happy. What I fear is that they would use the Executive power, if they got it, to inaugurate a reign of terror in Ireland . . . My anxiety is as to the *time* . . . Would it not be better to give them local self-government first and educate them to the use of power?[53]

James Bryce, who was to have a brief and unhappy spell as Irish chief secretary from 1905, expressed the view that home rule had not been adequately discussed in England, and that Gladstone was unlikely to secure a majority of Liberal MPs sufficient to carry a measure.[54] Moreover, Henry Campbell-Bannerman, a former Irish chief secretary who was to become Prime Minister in 1905, felt that, as a home-rule measure was unlikely to be carried, the question ought not to be raised at all: 'It is not as if any of us thought it a good thing in itself, or beneficial either to Ireland or England . . . We regard Home Rule only as a dangerous and damaging *pis aller*.'[55] Support for Gladstone's home-rule initiative clearly involved a gigantic act of faith, and many of his followers later expressed their misgivings about his tactics, which they felt had brought about an unnecessary split in the party.[56] For some, acquiescence in home rule reflected a sense of hopelessness about the possibility of any alternative

[53] Reid to Herbert Gladstone, 7 Jan. 1886, BL Add. MSS 46018, fo. 104. Reid had good reason to be prejudiced against the Irish, having lost his seat in the 1885 general election because of them.

[54] Bryce to Herbert Gladstone, 11 Dec. 1885, 11 Jan. 1886, BL Add. MSS 46019, fos. 8, 10.

[55] Campbell-Bannerman to Spencer, 8 Jan. 1886 (copy), BL Add. MSS 41228, fo. 309. Lord Acton, one of Gladstone's closest confidants, also had grave doubts about the efficacy of a home-rule measure: 'I am not sanguine about success in Ireland. Arguments founded on the presumed good qualities of the Irish do not go very far with me, and I am ready to find the vices of the national character incurable. Especially in a Country where religion does not work, ultimately, in favour of morality. Therefore I am not hopeful, and it is with a mind prepared for failure and even disaster that I persist in urging the measure', Acton to Mary Gladstone, 14 Apr. 1886, Acton MSS.

[56] Cf. Robert Farquharson, *In and Out of Parliament* (1911), 225; Alfred E. Pease, *Elections and Recollections* (1932), 110; Coleridge to Grant Duff, 16 Nov. 1886, in E. H. Coleridge, *Life . . . of John Duke, Lord Coleridge, Lord Chief Justice of England* (1904), ii. 353–4. This view was also expressed by a prominent Nonconformist: J. Guinness Rogers, *An Autobiography* (1903), 230.

policy.[57] One Liberal MP, who supported home rule in both 1886 and 1893, later felt 'free to admit . . . that it was better Mr. Gladstone's Bills did not pass'.[58]

Furthermore, it is undoubtedly a mistake to assume that the Unionist Liberals were necessarily more reactionary than their Gladstonian counterparts in general political terms. Even a cynical back-bench Radical like Sir Wilfrid Lawson confessed his surprise at the way many MPs voted: 'a good number of the men of my acquaintance whom I looked upon as almost too matter-of-course supporters of Gladstone went against him; while those who I half expected would not be sorry to desert him in a difficulty became his strongest supporters on Home Rule'.[59] Professor Lubenow's recent work on the parliamentary Liberal party in 1886 has indeed suggested that the division on the home-rule bill was not reflected in other issues, and that it cut across pre-existing social divisions within the party.[60] My own analysis of the social basis of the home-rule division on 8 June 1886, though somewhat different from Professor Lubenow's, largely reinforces his conclusion. For instance, if we look at the voting of the 105 Liberal MPs defined, in Chapter 6, as belonging to the 'aristocratic-landowning' section of the Liberal party after the general election of 1885, it emerges that forty-three (41 per cent) opposed Gladstone's bill, though we should add to these Grosvenor (elevated to the peerage), and Speaker Peel and the Hon. C. P. Villiers (who did not vote, but subsequently sat as Liberal Unionists), making a total of forty-six (43.8 per cent). The forty-three voting MPs represented 45.7 per cent of the group of ninety-four Liberals (including Sir Edward Watkin) who defied Gladstone, at a time when the 'aristocratic-landowning' section accounted for 31.7 per cent of

[57] Cf. Eleanor F. Rathbone, *William Rathbone: A Memoir* (1905), 412–13; Helen C. Colman, *Jeremiah James Colman: A Memoir* (privately printed, 1905), 308–9.

[58] Samuel Smith, MP, *My Life Work* (1902), 231.

[59] G. W. E. Russell (ed.), *Sir Wilfrid Lawson: A Memoir* (1909), 186.

[60] W. C. Lubenow, 'Irish Home Rule and the Great Separation in the Liberal Party in 1886: The Dimensions of Parliamentary Liberalism', *Victorian Studies*, 26 (1982–3), 161–80, and 'Irish Home Rule and the Social Basis of the Great Separation in the Liberal Party in 1886', *Historical Journal*, 28 (1985), 125–42. Another recent study based on an analysis of parliamentary division lists has concluded that the voting behaviour of the Liberal Unionist peers betrays continuing Liberal tendencies: Gregory D. Phillips, 'The Whig Lords and Liberalism, 1886–1893', ibid. 24 (1981), 167–73. A practical illustration of the Liberality of the Whig peers is provided by R. J. Moore, 'The Twilight of the Whigs and the Reform of the Indian Councils, 1886–1892', ibid. 10, (1967), 400–14.

the parliamentary party, which suggests that, while the notion of a 'revolt of the Whigs' is not entirely without foundation, it does not tell the whole story. In fact, thirty-one of the ninety-four rebels (33 per cent) can be categorized in the 'industrialists and merchants' group, and twenty-one (22.3 per cent) were lawyers.[61] Moreover, of the ninety-four Liberal Unionists, only fifteen had a previous record of rebellion against their own government on the Irish legislation of 1880–1 (in other words, they are listed in Appendix II), thirty-two were men who had not sat in the 1880 parliament (though six of them had sat before 1880), and the remaining forty-six were members of that parliament with no previous record of rebellion on Irish issues.[62] Even after allowing for the presence in this last figure of aristocratic Whigs like Lord Ebrington and Lord Edward Cavendish, one is bound to conclude that Gladstone, in 1886, lost the support of a significant portion of the Liberal 'centre'. The intense bitterness generated by the Liberal schism, which divided families and led to social ostracism and blackballing, is a strong indication that there was nothing 'inevitable' about it.[63]

In electoral terms, the schism of 1886 was undoubtedly a disaster for the Liberal party. Most of the successful Liberal Unionist candidates in the subsequent general election were sitting MPs, who benefited from an electoral pact with the Conservatives, and in the agricultural counties of England, their defection often left the Liberal party leaderless. The impact of Liberal Unionism was magnified by the heavy concentration of its representatives in certain regions, notably Devon and Cornwall, the West Midlands, and Scotland.[64] Meanwhile, the Conservatives made further gains in the English boroughs and recovered much of the ground lost in the English

[61] The overlap between these two categories and the aristocratic-landowning group was six in each case, so that the figures given are the maximum possible for each of the categories.

[62] As an additional check, the voting record of the group of forty-six was examined in relation to another separate rebellion, that on the vote of censure against the Gladstone ministry for its handling of the situation in the Sudan, on 27 Feb. 1885, and it was found that all either voted for the government or were paired in its favour. The possibility that many of the forty-six might be 'Radicals' was also considered, but even if the list produced by Dr Heyck, in his study of *The Dimensions of British Radicalism* (Illinois, 1974), 242–4, were to be accepted, only ten were 'Radicals'.

[63] Cf. Pease, *Elections and Recollections*, p. 137; Henry Broadhurst, *M.P.: The Story of his Life . . . Told by Himself* (1901), 195–6.

[64] Michael Kinnear, *The British Voter: An Atlas and Survey since 1885* (1968), 17–19, 98–9; Neal Blewett, *The Peers, the Parties and the People: The General Elections of 1910* (1972), 11–16.

counties in 1885, leaving the Gladstonian Liberals largely dependent on their support in traditional strongholds like Wales, Yorkshire, the north-east of England, and rural Scotland, which was never going to be sufficient to provide an overall parliamentary majority. Furthermore, the Liberal party was weakened by defections in the press, which, as Professor Koss has recently argued, represented a genuine political realignment rather than simply the clarification of a long-term trend. The result was that whereas, up to 1886, the Liberal press had been in the majority, this now ceased to be the case: Liberal losses were spread over both daily and weekly publications, and were most serious in London and Scotland, but the provincial and the Nonconformist press were also divided.[65] Encumbered with an unpopular and 'unpatriotic' policy, reduced to a narrow geographical basis of support, and deprived of allies particularly in the metropolitan press, the Liberal party was less than convincing when it tried to present itself in its traditional guise as a 'national' party, capable of transcending 'class' interests.

Gladstone, it is therefore suggested, by prematurely forcing the issue of Irish home rule and staking his own political career upon it, succeeded in creating an artificial division among the Liberals, and enabled the Conservatives, with their Liberal Unionist allies, to establish themselves as the 'natural' majority party. His failure of leadership was concealed, however, behind an interpretation of the alignment of the 'classes' against the 'masses', expressed publicly in his manifesto to the electors of Midlothian on 1 May 1886,[66] which has had an enduring influence upon the historiography of the Liberal party. It was from this that the belief grew that the Liberals had been a chronically divided party, held together in the early 1880s only by the great cohesive powers of Gladstone himself, and that the split in 1886 had simply been the culmination of an inevitable process, 'the revolt of the Whigs', whereby the propertied classes set their face

[65] Stephen Koss, *The Rise and Fall of the Political Press in Britain*, i (1981), 286–92.
[66] *The Times*, 4 May 1886, p. 5. Gladstone was becoming increasingly intolerant of opposition to him, as a family friend noted after the general election: 'I fear that the time has passed when he can listen as he used to do. Generally, disagreement with him produces sorrow that people can be so blind as not to see the truth, then he warms up, is shocked at your want of all moral feeling and overpowers you with a speech which reduces you to silence', Lord Arthur Russell to Lady Blennerhassett, 30 Aug. 1886, Cambridge University Library Add. 7486, E.52.

against the 'progressive spirit' in social questions which had supposedly infused the rest of the party.[67]

For Gladstone personally, '1886' completed the process by which his motivations were being unconsciously secularized, as his earlier concept of 'religious nationality' gave way to a vague Liberal humanitarianism.[68] By investing 'the people' with a superior morality to that of the 'upper ten thousand', and by employing the language of 'class', Gladstone succeeded in transforming a bankrupt religious ideology into a serviceable political creed. Yet his personal identification with the 'masses' existed far more in the realm of sentiment than in that of reality, and it would be a mistake to regard Gladstone in his last years as a Radical.[69] His interest in social questions, after 1886, was both half-hearted and motivated entirely by tactical considerations. Indeed the tragedy for the Liberal party, as a whole, was that it acquired an unreal image as a party of the working man which it was scarcely capable of living up to, and which it had assumed quite independently of those social developments in the late 1880s and 1890s that gave rise to the demand for a separate working-class party. Whether a Liberal party enjoying a firm tenure of power after 1886 could have absorbed the pressures emanating from the spread of trade unionism and socialist thinking, and so prevented a separate 'Labour' party from gaining a foothold in parliament, is impossible to tell, but it is clear that its only chance of doing so was by remaining what at heart it always wanted to be—a broadly based party representative of all classes. In this sense, the triumph of 'Gladstonian Liberalism', in 1886, may be seen as an important stage in the Liberal party's decline.

---

[67] Interesting examples of the 'class' interpretation of the Liberal schism expounded by Gladstone and Harcourt are cited in Hamer, *Liberal Politics*, pp. 147, 210–11. Herbert Gladstone expanded on this view in *After Thirty Years* (1928), 166–78, 195–7, 379. It was he who wrote of the 'progressive spirit' within the Liberal party.

[68] Cf. H. C. G. Matthew, 'Gladstone, Vaticanism and the Question of the East', in D. Baker (ed.), *Studies in Church History*, xv (Oxford, 1978), 441–2.

[69] Cf. K. O. Morgan, *Wales in British Politics, 1868–1922* (3rd edn., Cardiff, 1980), 133–4; Michael Barker, *Gladstone and Radicalism: The Reconstruction of Liberal Policy in Britain, 1885–94* (Hassocks, 1975), 87–96, 195–9.

APPENDIX I

The Liberal Party and the Eastern Question in 1878

This appendix should be understood not as an analysis of two permanent 'wings' of the parliamentary Liberal party, but rather as a 'snapshot' of the way the Liberals were divided at a time of exceptional political stress, when the 'Eastern Question' threatened to lead to war between Britain and Russia.

Parliamentary division lists have been taken from *Hansard's Parliamentary Debates* and the *Parliamentary Buff Book* for 1878, supplemented by Ross's *Parliamentary Record* for 1878. Personal details are derived from *Dod's Parliamentary Companion*. An MP listed as a member of the nobility was either the heir, younger son, or brother of a peer of the realm. A landowner is defined as someone with an entry in John Bateman's *Great Landowners of Great Britain and Ireland* (1879 and 1883 editions). Those described as gentry are listed in *Burke's Landed Gentry* (1879 and 1886 editions). Irish home rulers have not been included.

A positive vote for the Whig or Radical line is indicated by a +, a negative vote by a −, and absence without pair by an *.

THE WHIGS

Key to divisions

1. A vote for the government's emergency vote of credit (7 February).
2. A vote for the government's emergency vote of credit (8 February).
3. Opposition to Lawson's amendment opposing the calling out of the reserves (9 April).
4. Opposition to Hartington's resolution on the movement of Indian troops to Malta (23 May).
5. Opposition to Hartington's resolutions on the treaty of Berlin (2 August).

A blank space on divisions 1–3 indicates that the MP followed the official leadership line of abstention. Similarly, a − vote on divisions 4 and 5 indicates that the MP was supporting the official leaders.

Name	Constituency	Background	1	2	3	4	5
W. B. Beaumont	S. Northumberland	Landowner	+	+		*	*
H. A. Brassey	Sandwich	Landowner			+	−	−
T. Brassey	Hastings	Landowner (Bar)			+	−	−

Name	Constituency	Background	1	2	3	4	5
T. Cave	Barnstaple	Ex-merchant		−	+	−	−
Lord G. Cavendish	N. Derbyshire	Nobility		+		−	−
Sir T. E. Colebrooke	N. Lanarkshire	Baronet (Land)			+	−	−
J. Corbett	Droitwich	Landowner (Salt Works)	+			−	−
C. Cotes	Shrewsbury	Landowner			+	−	−
J. Cowen	Newcastle	Manufacturer	+	+	+	*	+
R. W. Duff	Banffshire	Landowner			+	−	−
Lord E. Fitzmaurice	Calne	Nobility			+	−	−
Hon. C. Fitzwilliam	Malton	Nobility				+	−
F. J. Foljambe	East Retford	Landowner		+	+	−	−
W. H. Foster	Bridgnorth	No Information			+	+	+
Lord de Grey	Ripon	Nobility	+			−	−
Sir F. Goldsmid	Reading	Baronet (Land) (QC)			+		
				[died 2 May]			
T. Hankey	Peterborough	Ex-merchant		+	+	−	−
H. A. Herbert	Kerry	Landowner			+	+	*
Lord Lorne	Argyllshire	Nobility		+	+	+	*
Lord Macduff	Elgin and Nairn	Nobility			+	−	−
C. F. Mackintosh	Inverness Burghs	Ex-solicitor	−	−	+	−	−
W. F. Maitland	Breconshire	Landowner		+		*	*
Colonel Mure	Renfrewshire	Landowner		+	+	*	*
A. W. Peel	Warwick	Son of Baronet			+	−	−
P. Ralli	Bridport	Merchant			+	−	−
H. W. Ripley	Bradford	Manufacturer	+	+		+	+
J. A. Roebuck	Sheffield	QC				+	+
N. M. de Rothschild	Aylesbury	Banking	+		+	+	+
J. D'A. Samuda	Tower Hamlets	Engineer	+	+	+	+	+
T. E. Smith	Tynemouth	Merchant		+		−	*
Lord Stafford	Sutherland	Nobility	+	+	+	*	*
C. R. M. Talbot	Glamorganshire	Landowner				+	*
Lord Tavistock	Bedfordshire	Nobility	−	−	+	−	−
J. Walter	Berkshire	Landowner (Prop. of *Times*)	+	+		−	*
Sir E. Watkin	Hythe	Railway Director			+	+	*
W. Whitworth	Newry	Merchant				*	+
J. Yeaman	Dundee	Merchant	+	+	+	+	+

A total of thirty-seven MPs appear on this list of 'Whigs', or about 15.5 per cent of the parliamentary Liberal party (approx. 238). Of these thirty-seven, twenty-three (62 per cent) may be classified as members of the 'aristocratic-landowning' section, while ten (27 per cent) had backgrounds in industry and trade.

The predominance of aristocrats and landowners is reflected in the types of constituency represented by the MPs on this list. Only six members were representatives of urban or major industrial constituencies, whereas fourteen represented smaller English boroughs (and one an agricultural borough), and twelve sat for English, Welsh, and Scottish counties.

It should be noted that by 1880, three of the MPs on this list, Foster, Ripley, and Yeaman, had become Conservatives.

THE RADICALS

The following list is based on two parliamentary divisions: 1. Lawson's amendment against the calling out of the reserves, on 9 April; 2. the opposition, organized by Fawcett and Rylands on 27 May, to the grant of funds required for the upkeep of the Indian troops moved to Malta, by voting against the Speaker leaving the chair at the end of the second-reading stage. Those who acted as tellers for these divisions are considered to have voted. It should be added that all but eight of the MPs below had also rebelled against the official party leaders on one or both of the divisions on the government's emergency vote of credit (7–8 February). The eight who did not so vote were Amory, A. C. Barclay, Howard, Hughes, Milbank, Morley, Russell, and Williams.

Name	Constituency	Background	1	2
Sir J. H. Amory	Tiverton	Baronet (land) (Lace Manufacturer)		+
E. Backhouse	Darlington	Banker	+	
A. C. Barclay	Taunton	No Information	+	
J. W. Barclay	Forfarshire	Shipowner	+	+
J. Barran	Leeds	Merchant and Manufacturer	+	
T. Blake	Leominster	Ex-accountant and Estate Agent	+	+
Jacob Bright	Manchester	Manufacturer	+	+
John Bright	Birmingham	Manufacturer	+	
A. Brogden	Wednesbury	Ironmaster	+	
T. Burt	Morpeth	Miner	+	+
C. Cameron	Glasgow	Medicine	+	+
Sir G. Campbell	Kirkcaldy Burghs	Gentry (Bar)	+	
J. Chamberlain	Birmingham	Ex-manufacturer	+	+

Name	Constituency	Background	1	2
J. C. Clarke	Abingdon	Railway Director	+	
L. H. Courtney	Liskeard	Professor	+	+
J. Cowan	Edinburgh	Manufacturer	+	
J. K. Cross	Bolton	Manufacturer	+	+
R. Davies	Anglesey	Landowner	+	
Sir C. W. Dilke	Chelsea	Baronet (Bar)	+	
L. L. Dillwyn	Swansea Boroughs	Gentry	+	+
J. Dodds	Stockton-on-Tees	Solicitor		+
P. E. Eyton	Flint Boroughs	Attorney		+
H. Fawcett	Hackney	Professor	+	+
R. Ferguson	Carlisle	Manufacturer	+	+
I. Fletcher	Cockermouth	Coal and Iron (Gentry)	+	
Sir C. Forster	Walsall	Ex-barrister	+	
W. E. Gladstone	Greenwich	Son of Baronet	+	
W. H. Gladstone	Whitby	Landowner	+	
E. T. Gourley	Sunderland	Merchant and Shipowner	+	
Hon. E. F. L. Gower	Bodmin	Nobility (Bar)	+	
C. Harrison	Bewdley	No Information	+	
J. F. Harrison	Kilmarnock Burghs	Barrister	+	
S. Holland	Merionethshire	Quarryowner	+	
J. Holms	Hackney	Manufacturer	+	
C. H. Hopwood	Stockport	Q C	+	+
E. S. Howard	E. Cumberland	Barrister	+	
W. B. Hughes	Caernarvon Boroughs	Landowner (Bar)	+	
E. Jenkins	Dundee	Barrister		+
Sir W. Lawson	Carlisle	Baronet (Land)	+	
E. A. Leatham	Huddersfield	Banker	+	+
G. J. Shaw Lefevre	Reading	Barrister	+	
J. F. Leith	Aberdeen	Q C	+	
J. A. Lush	Salisbury	Medicine	+	+
A. McArthur	Leicester	Merchant	+	+
A. MacDonald	Stafford	Miner		+
D. McLaren	Edinburgh	Merchant	+	+
J. Maitland	Kirkcudbrightshire	Barrister	+	
F. A. Milbank	Yorks, N. Riding	Landowner	+	
C. J. Monk	Gloucester	Barrister		+
G. O. Morgan	Denbighshire	Q C		+
S. Morley	Bristol	Manufacturer	+	
A. J. Mundella	Sheffield	Manufacturer	+	
P. H. Muntz	Birmingham	Merchant		+

Name	Constituency	Background	1	2
J. W. Pease	S. Durham	Coal and Iron (Land)	+	+
F. Pennington	Stockport	Ex-merchant	+	+
R. N. Phillips	Bury	Manufacturer (Land)		+
S. Plimsoll	Derby	Coal Merchant	+	
T. B. Potter	Rochdale	Merchant	+	
J. Ramsay	Falkirk Burghs	Merchant (Land)	+	
H. Richard	Merthyr Tydfil	Ex-nonconformist Minister	+	+
Lord A. Russell	Tavistock	Nobility	+	
P. Rylands	Burnley	Coal and Iron		+
H. B. Samuelson	Frome	No Information	+	
H. B. Sheridan	Dudley	Barrister	+	
J. Simon	Dewsbury	Barrister		+
Sir J. G. T. Sinclair	Caithness	Baronet (Land)	+	
R. Smyth	Co. Londonderry	Professor		+
P. A. Taylor	Leicester	No Information	+	+
G. O. Trevelyan	Hawick Burghs	Son of Baronet	+	+
Sir S. Waterlow	Maidstone	Baronet (Wholesale Stationer)	+	+
J. Whitwell	Kendal	Manufacturer	+	
C. J. W. Williams	Denbigh Boroughs	Barrister	+	
C. H. Wilson	Kingston-upon-Hull	Merchant (Land)	+	
A. W. Young	Helston	Lawyer (Australia)	+	

A total of seventy-four MPs appear on this list of 'Radicals', or about 31 per cent of the parliamentary Liberal party. Of these seventy-four, thirty (40.5 per cent) can be classified as members of the 'industrialists and merchants' group (although six also had aristocratic or landed connections, usually representing converted wealth). Of the remainder, twelve (16.2 per cent) were from the aristocratic-landowning section (even if the six who overlap were to be added, the figure would still only be 24.3 per cent), whereas fifteen (20 per cent) were connected with the legal profession. The social diversity of Radicalism is illustrated by the three professors, two doctors of medicine, two miners, two bankers, the ex-accountant and estate agent, and the ex-Nonconformist minister.

An analysis of the types of constituency represented by these 'Radical' MPs shows that an overwhelming majority came from the boroughs. Thirty-three were members for urban and industrial constituencies in England, and seventeen represented smaller English boroughs, while a further fourteen came from Welsh and Scottish boroughs. In other words, sixty-four of the seventy-four 'Radicals' sat for boroughs, whereas only three, for example, represented English counties (two of these being areas with a mining population).

APPENDIX II

'The Young Whig Party'

The following list of 'Whig' M Ps in the parliament of 1880–5 is not intended to be comprehensive, and it does not consist entirely of men who would be defined as Whigs in a social sense. What it seeks to establish are the approximate dimensions and the social composition of a group of M Ps with a record of being prepared to oppose their own government on the crucial question of Irish land legislation, during the sessions of 1880 and 1881.

It would have been easy to produce a much larger list by including the names of those M Ps known to have been absent without pair from the divisions under consideration. For instance, about seventy members were thus absent from the vote on the second reading of the Compensation for Disturbance Bill in July 1880, and it is fairly certain that a substantial number of these men were registering a protest, but unfortunately it is impossible to assess the extent of this protest in a satisfactory way. The difficulty here is a serious one which clearly applies to the other divisions, notably that on the Heneage amendment. It was claimed that about fifteen M Ps were absent without pair on this occasion, including Lord Edward Cavendish, the Hon. E. F. Leveson-Gower, and the Hon. H. F. Cowper, all of whom were the brothers of senior government ministers.[1] Furthermore, according to Albert Grey, 'There were a good few curs like Tavistock who wouldn't vote against Gladstone, there were others like . . . Sir Arthur Lusk who wished to vote with us but were out of the way, and there were a good number who voted with the Government but who to quote Broadhurst 'ad their 'eads in one lobby and their seats in another.'[2] In the case of another division, not used for this analysis, in which the government was defeated on an amendment to its Prevention of Crimes Bill, in July 1882, it was alleged that as many as fifty members walked out of the House.[3] In addition to the forty-nine names in the list below, then, there were perhaps as many again who were silently sympathetic to the rebels' views.

[1] Cf. W. C. Cartwright's diary, 17 June 1881, Cartwright MSS, 6/15.
[2] Albert Grey to Earl Grey, 17 June 1881, Grey MSS, Box 89.
[3] For Cartwright's claim, see Herbert Gladstone's diary, 9 July 1882, Glynne–Gladstone MSS. Albert Grey reported to Lord Halifax that a substantial number of M Ps had walked out: 7 July 1882, Hickleton MSS, A4/84. On this occasion, twenty-four Liberals opposed their own government, ten of whom do not appear in this appendix, namely: W. B. Beaumont, J. Corbett, R. Creyke, Sir A. Fairbairn, C. Flower, P. H. Muntz, A. W. Peel, J. Pender, C. S. Roundell, and G. W. E. Russell. It might be noted that twenty-three of the M P's on the list below were absent from this division.

The list of 'Whig' MPs consists of those members who cast at least one positive vote in the following four divisions:

1. Opposition to the second reading of the Compensation for Disturbance Bill (5 July 1880).
2. Opposition to the third reading of the Compensation for Disturbance Bill (26 July 1880).
3. Support for Heneage's amendment to the Irish Land Bill (16 June 1881).
4. Support for Fitzmaurice's amendment to the Irish Land Bill (26 July 1881).

Division lists have been taken from *Hansard's Parliamentary Debates*, with supplementary information provided by Ross's *Parliamentary Record* for 1880 and 1881 and the *Parliamentary Buff Book* for 1880 and 1881. Personal details have been derived from *Dod's Parliamentary Companion* and F. W. S. Craig's *British Parliamentary Election Results, 1832–85* and 1885–1918. An MP listed as a member of the nobility was either the heir, younger son, or brother of a peer of the realm. A landowner is defined as someone with an entry in John Bateman's *Great Landowners of Great Britain and Ireland* (1883 edition). Those described as gentry are listed in *Burke's Landed Gentry* (1886 edition). The term Liberal Unionist is abbreviated throughout as 'LU', and the Liberal Unionist Association as 'LUA'. The heading 'Entry' refers to the date at which the individual was first elected to the House of Commons, but does not necessarily imply that he sat continuously from that time.

A 'Whig' vote is indicated by a +, a vote against the 'Whig line' is indicated by a −, and an * denotes a member who was absent without pair. Sir Edward Watkin, who was paired *against* the third reading of the Compensation for Disturbance Bill, is considered to have cast a vote. Those who acted as tellers for the Heneage and Fitzmaurice divisions are also considered to have voted.

Name	Constituency	Born	Entry	Background	1	2	3	4	Subsequent Career
H. G. Allen	Pembroke Boroughs	1815	1880	Barrister	—	*	+		Opposed home-rule bill.
M. Bidulph	Herefordshire	1834	1865	Gentry (Banker)	*	*	+	+	Opposed home-rule bill.
Sir R. Blennerhassett	Kerry	1839	1865	Baronet and Landowner	*	*	+	+	Defeated 1885. Member of LUA general committee.
H. R. Brand	Stroud	1841	1868	Son of Speaker Brand	*	*	*	+	Opposed home-rule bill.
H. A. Brassey	Sandwich	1840	1868	Landowner	—	*	—	—	Retired 1885.
F. W. Buxton	Andover	1847	1880	Son of Baronet (Banker)	*	*	+	—	Defeated 1885. Member of LUA general committee.
Lord C. Campbell	Argyllshire	1853	1878	Nobility	—	*	—		Retired 1885.
Sir G. Campbell	Kirkcaldy Burghs	1824	1875	Gentry (Barrister)	—	—	—	+	Supported home-rule bill.
W. C. Cartwright	Oxfordshire	1826	1868	Landowner	+	*	+	+	Retired 1885, defeated LU candidate 1886.
Sir T. E. Colebrooke	Lanarkshire, North	1813	1842	Baronet and Landowner	*	+	+	+	Retired 1885, defeated LU candidate 1886.
D. Davies	Cardigan Boroughs	1818	1874	Colliery owner, etc.	*	—	+	+	Opposed home-rule bill.
Hon. J. C. Dundas	Richmond	1845	1873	Nobility (Barrister)	+	+	+	+	Retired 1885, defeated LU candidate 1886.
Hon. A. R. D. Elliot	Roxburghshire	1846	1880	Nobility (Barrister)	*	*	+		Opposed home-rule bill.
T. W. Evans	Derbyshire, South	1821	1857	Landowner	*	*	+	+	Retired 1885, defeated LU candidate 1886.
Sir W. H. B. Ffolkes	Lynn Regis	1847	1880	Landowner	*	*	+		Defeated 1885, defeated LU candidate 1900.
Lord E. Fitzmaurice	Calne	1846	1868	Nobility			+	+	Retired 1885, Liberal MP 1898–1906.
Hon. C. W. Fitzwilliam	Malton	1826	1852	Nobility	+	+	+	+	Retired 1885.
Hon. W. H. Fitzwilliam	Yorks, W. Riding (S)	1840	1868	Nobility	+	+	+		Retired 1885. LU MP 1888–92.
Hon. W. J. Fitzwilliam	Peterborough	1852	1878	Nobility	+	*	+		Opposed home-rule bill.
F. J. S. Foljambe	East Retford	1830	1857	Landowner	—	—	+	+	Defeated 1885, defeated LU candidate 1886.

Name	Constituency	Born	Entry	Background	1	2	3	4	Subsequent Career
W. Fowler	Cambridge	1826	1868	Barrister	*	*	+	–	Retired 1885, defeated LU candidate 1886.
Hon. Sir A. H. Gordon	Aberdeenshire, East	1817	1875	Nobility	–	–	+	+	Retired 1885.
G. J. Goschen	Ripon	1831	1863	Banking Family			+	+	Opposed home-rule bill.
A. H. G. Grey	Northumberland, South	1851	1880	Nobility	+	+	+	+	Opposed home-rule bill.
M. J. Guest	Wareham	1839	1869	Son of Baronet	+	+			Retired 1885, LU member of Dorset county council.
J. G. C. Hamilton	Lanarkshire, South	1829	1857	Landowner	–	–		+	Supported home-rule bill.
E. Heneage	Great Grimsby	1840	1865	Landowner	–	*	+	+	Opposed home-rule bill.
Sir H. Johnstone	Scarborough	1829	1869	Baronet and Landowner	+				Resigned, 23 July 1880, cr. Baron Derwent, 1881, Unionist peer.
Col. R. N. F. Kingscote	Gloucestershire, West	1830	1852	Landowner	+	+	+	+	Resigned, February 1885.
Hon. F. W. Lambton	Durham, South	1855	1880	Nobility	+	+	+	+	Retired 1885, LU MP 1900–10.
Hon. B. Lawley	Chester	1818	1880	Nobility	+				Unseated on petition, 17 July 1880, succ. later that year, LU peer.
W. H. Leatham	Yorks, W. Riding (S)	1815	1865	Gentry (Ex-banker)	–	–	+	–	Retired 1885.
Hon. G. H. C. Leigh	Warwickshire, South	1851	1880	Nobility	*	*	+	+	Died October 1884.
Lord Lymington	Barnstaple	1856	1880	Nobility	+	*	+		Opposed home-rule bill.
P. McLagan	Linlithgowshire	1823	1865	Gentry	–	–	+		Abstained on home-rule bill, but subsequently supported the measure.
Lord Moreton	Gloucestershire, West	1857	1880	Nobility	+	–	+		Retired 1885.
W. Nicholson	Petersfield	1824	1866	Landowner	–	–	+	+	Seceded, April 1885.
C. M. Norwood	Hull	1825	1866	Merchant and Shipowner	+	*	+		Defeated 1885, defeated LU candidate 1886.
Hon. W. H. B. Portman	Dorset	1829	1852	Nobility	+	+	+		Retired 1885, succ. 1888, LU peer.

Name	Constituency	Born	Entry	Background	1	2	3	4	Subsequent Career
P. Ralli	Wallingford	1845	1875	Merchant	–	–	+	+	Defeated 1885, defeated LU candidate 1892.
J. Ramsay	Falkirk Burghs	1814	1868	Merchant (Landowner)	–	*	+	+	Opposed home-rule bill.
Sir J. W. Ramsden	Yorks, W. Riding (E)	1831	1853	Baronet and Landowner	+	+	+	+	Opposed home-rule bill.
Sir N. de Rothschild	Aylesbury	1840	1865	Baronet and Landowner (Banking Family)	+	+	+	+	cr. Baron Rothschild, 1885, LU peer.
C. Seely	Lincoln	1803	1861	Landowner	+	+	+		Retired 1885.
Sir J. G. T. Sinclair	Caithness	1825	1869	Baronet and Landowner	+	+		+	Retired 1885.
Lord Stafford	Sutherland	1851	1874	Nobility	*	+	–	+	Opposed home-rule bill.
C. R. M. Talbot	Glamorganshire	1803	1830	Landowner	+	+	–	–	Opposed home-rule bill, supporter of Gladstone.
Sir E. W. Watkin	Hythe	1819	1864	Baronet (Railway Dir.)	*	+	+		Opposed home-rule bill.
E. W. B. Willyams	Truro	1836	1857	Landowner	+	*		–	Retired 1885, defeated LU candidate 1887.

The following points emerge from this list:

1. Of this group of forty-nine MPs, nineteen were no more than 40 years of age in 1880, and of those nineteen, eight were aged under 30. The fact that all eight of those under the age of 30 and four of those under the age of 40 were the sons of peers lends credence to the idea of a 'young Whig party'.

2. Only nine of the forty-nine had been elected for the first time in 1880 (Lymington was returned at a by-election in February 1880), but seven of those nine MPs were no more than 40 years of age in 1880 (as was Lymington).

3. A breakdown of the types of constituency represented by these forty-nine MPs shows that twelve sat for English counties and twenty-three for English boroughs. Most of these English borough members represented small electorates: sixteen of the twenty-three boroughs concerned disappeared after the redistribution of 1885, and five of the remainder lost one seat. The other main source of 'Whiggery' appears to have been the Scottish counties, which provided eight members of this group. Two MPs sat for Scottish boroughs, two for Welsh boroughs, one for a Welsh county, and one for an Irish county. Of the forty-nine 'Whig' members, twelve represented constituencies which, in Professor Hanham's estimation, were under the control of a patron (this includes Chester, where Lawley was unseated, and Glamorganshire, where C. R. M. Talbot held a predominant interest).

4. An analysis of the social composition of this 'Whig' group shows it to have been drawn overwhelmingly from the aristocratic and landowning classes. Sixteen members were related to the peerage (and H. R. Brand was also to become so when his father was elevated in 1884), six were baronets, two were the sons of baronets, fourteen were landowners (ten of these were also listed as gentry), and four were gentry. In all, therefore, forty-two (forty-three if Brand were to be included) of the forty-nine were connected to the aristocratic and landowning classes, 85.7 per cent (87.6 per cent including Brand) of the group. Of course it is true that nine of these MPs had other interests, four in banking and three in law, but it is significant that only Ramsay and Watkin were connected with industry or trade. The six MPs not mentioned so far may be classified as follows: industry and trade (three), law (two), banking (one).

5. By 1885, Leigh had died, Nicholson had seceded from the party, and Kingscote had resigned from the House of Commons on accepting a crown appointment. Three others (including the unseated Lawley) had been elevated to the Lords, leaving forty-three in their seats at the dissolution of parliament. Of these forty-three, nineteen did not contest the 1885 general election, and six others did but were defeated, so that only eighteen of the original forty-nine were members of the House of Commons which met in January 1886.

6. Of the eighteen survivors, fifteen voted against the second reading of the Irish home-rule bill, in the early hours of 8 June 1886, Sir George Campbell and J. G. C. Hamilton supported the bill, and Peter McLagan walked out of the House but subsequently remained on the Gladstonian side. C. R. M. Talbot was among the fifteen who opposed the bill, but he did not become a Liberal Unionist.

7. All three members of the original group who had been elevated to the peerage by 1885 were subsequently Liberal Unionists. Furthermore, of the six who were defeated in the 1885 elections, four later reappeared as Liberal Unionist candidates and the other two were members of the general committee of the Liberal Unionist Association; while of the nineteen who 'retired' in 1885, eight later stood as Liberal Unionist candidates, Guest became a Liberal Unionist county councillor, and Portman became a Liberal Unionist peer. No information has been found regarding the views on Irish home rule of Hamilton-Gordon, Leatham, and Seely (who were all dead by 1890), nor of the Hon. Charles Fitzwilliam, Lord Moreton, Lord Colin Campbell, Sinclair, and Brassey (though it might be noted that the heads of the families to which Fitzwilliam, Moreton, and Campbell belonged were all Liberal Unionists). This leaves Lord Edmond Fitzmaurice, who, by 1886, had come to the conclusion that home rule was unavoidable, though he doubted Gladstone's ability to settle the question,[4] and who eventually returned to the Commons in 1898 as a Liberal.

8. In other words, Leigh, Nicholson, and Kingscote must be excluded from consideration. Of the remaining forty-six, the opinions on home rule of eight are unknown, four ultimately supported Gladstone's initiative, C. R. M. Talbot was an independent Liberal, supporting Gladstone's leadership but opposed to home rule, and thirty-three had definite Liberal Unionist connections.

---

[4] Fitzmaurice felt that home rule had been made inevitable by previous Liberal legislation, which had destroyed or weakened the old bases of the Protestant ascendancy—the Irish Church, the Land system, and the education system—but failed to reconcile the Catholic majority. He saw no possibility of one democracy governing another against its will. However, he regretted that the task of dealing with home rule had fallen to Gladstone. Cf. Fitzmaurice to Arthur Elliot, 20 Dec. 1885, Elliot MSS; Fitzmaurice to W. C. Cartwright, 1 Feb. 1886, Cartwright MSS, Box 16, bundle marked '1886–1903'.

APPENDIX III

Gladstone's Notes on Irish Home Rule, 14 November 1885

The following documents are to be found in B L Add. M S S 56446, part of a collection of Gladstone's papers rediscovered in 1969 and deposited in 1970. Whether John Morley had seen them before they were sent to Macmillan's for transcription (and never returned) is not clear, but he was, at any rate, unable to use them in his biography of Gladstone. J. L. Hammond certainly did not know about them when he was writing *Gladstone and the Irish Nation*. It is extraordinary, however, that Cooke and Vincent, who did consult this collection of papers, should (apparently) have overlooked these home-rule notes, and thus missed the important fact that Gladstone was jotting down the outlines of a bill *before* the general election (cf. *The Governing Passion*, p. 52). When considered in conjunction with Gladstone's letter to Rosebery, dated 13 November 1885, in which he explained his tactical reasons for not announcing a scheme at that time, the significance of his notes made the following day seems clear.

It should be added, however, that the actual home-rule measure which Gladstone proposed to the House of Commons on 8 April 1886 discarded a number of the safeguards contained in the 'sketch' of 14 November 1885. For instance, there was to be no Irish representation at Westminister. Furthermore, there were to be no nominated members in the Irish chamber: instead, there were to be two 'orders' of Irish representatives, both elected, one by household suffrage, the other by a propertied franchise. The special provision for minority representation also disappeared.

Bases 1. Irish Chamber for Irish affairs. 2. Prerogative of the Crown and oath of allegiance as for Imperial Parliament. 3. Protection of minority and nominated members. 4. Equitable share of Imperial charges, first charge on revenue of Ireland. 5. Schedule A. Imperial subjects reserved. 6. Schedule B. Imperial charges shared. 7. Except as to defences Imperial Authority suspended in Ireland. 8. Irish representatives in Imperial Houses to remain, for Imperial purposes only. N 14 85.

Or, *more* briefly. 1. Irish Chamber for Irish affairs. 2. Irish representation to remain as now for Imperial affairs. 3. Equitable division of Imperial charges by fixed proportions. 4. Protection of minority. 5. Suspension of Imperial Authority for all civil purposes whatsoever. N 14 85.

Sketch

Establish an Irish Chamber to deal with all Irish, as distinct from Imperial questions.

To sit for — years.

Subject to the same prerogatives of the Crown, as the Imperial Parliament.

Provisions for securing to minority a proportionate representation.

Provision for Imperial charges to be made by appointing a due, fixed proportion thereof to be the first charge on Irish Consolidated Fund.

Imperial Charges to be set out in Schedule: Royalty, the Debt, Army and Navy, the Chief.

One third of House to be named in Act, two thirds to be the present representation duplicated: except Dublin University to remain as now, Royal University to have two members.

Nominated members to sit until Parliament otherwise provide (vacancies to be filled by the Crown?).

Offices of State and Civil functionaries in Ireland to cease to be subject to any British authority, except as herein provided, to be suspended in Ireland so long as the conditions of this Act are fulfilled.

Matters of defence remain under Imperial authority as now.

Crown Property held for civil purposes to be at the disposal of the Chamber.

Irish representation in both Houses of the Imperial Parliament to remain as now for Imperial subjects only.

If speech or vote be challenged, question to be decided by the House or the Speaker thereof.

Schedule of subjects withdrawn as Imperial from the Irish Chamber.

Irish representatives to share in all questions of grievances and Ministerial responsibility which touch the reserved subjects only.

Specify parts of Act alterable by Chamber including particulars of representation, except such as secure proportionate representation of Minority.

With regard to all civil establishments whatever it is presumed that Irish officers of State will be under the sole control of the Chamber and advise the Crown for Irish purposes (as e.g. in Canada. Canadian officers of State).

A seat in the Imperial Parliament not to disqualify for sitting in the Irish Chamber.

Seat in Irish Chamber not to disqualify for holding office in G.B.

Auxiliary forces to be charged on Ireland and only raised by authority of Chamber but when raised to be under the control of the Crown. N 14 85.

BIBLIOGRAPHY

This bibliography is divided into the following sections:

I. Works of Reference
II. Newspapers and Periodicals
III. Manuscript Sources
IV. Printed Primary Sources
V. Biographies, Memoirs, etc
VI. Secondary Literature
VII. Articles

The place of publication of all printed works is London unless otherwise stated.

I. WORKS OF REFERENCE

Annual Register.
Bateman, John, *Great Landowners of Great Britain and Ireland* (1883 edn.).
Burke's Landed Gentry (1879 and 1886 edns.).
Burke's Peerage, Baronetage and Knightage.
Craig, F. W. S., *British Parliamentary Election Results, 1832–1885* (1977).
—— *British Parliamentary Election Results, 1885–1918* (1974).
Dictionary of National Biography.
Dod's Parliamentary Companion.
Hansard's Parliamentary Debates, 3rd series.
Roberts, T. N., *Parliamentary Buff Book* (1875–81).
Ross, C., *Parliamentary Record* (1877–85).

II. NEWSPAPERS AND PERIODICALS

Daily News
Daily Telegraph
Edinburgh Review
Fortnightly Review
Gentleman's Magazine
Leeds Mercury
Manchester Guardian
Nineteenth Century
Nonconformist
Pall Mall Gazette

Scotsman
Spectator
The Economist
The Times

III. MANUSCRIPT SOURCES

British Library Additional Manuscripts series

41206–52	Sir Henry Campbell-Bannerman papers.
43383–92	John Bright papers.
43510–644	1st Marquess of Ripon papers.
43874–967	Sir Charles Dilke papers.
44086–835,	
56444–53	W. E. Gladstone papers.
44900–2	Lord Kilbracken (J. A. Godley) papers.
45724–5	Henry Ponsonby papers.
45985–6118	Herbert Gladstone papers.
46219–71	Mary Gladstone-Drew papers.
48265–300	3rd Earl of Morley papers.
48599–699	Sir Edward Hamilton papers.
48777	Letters of John Bright to W. H. Northy.
49199–285	Lord Stanmore (Sir Arthur Hamilton-Gordon) papers.
49561	1st Viscount Halifax papers.
49638–81	Lord Avebury (Sir John Lubbock) papers.
57934–41	M. J. Guest papers.
58774–801	T. H. S. Escott papers.
62114A	W. H. O'Shea papers.

British Library of Political and Economic Science

Henry Broadhurst MSS.
Leonard Courtney MSS (including Kate Courtney's diary).
Frederic Harrison MSS.

Bodleian Library

James Bryce MSS.
G. J. Goschen MSS.
Sir William Harcourt MSS.
Lewis Harcourt MSS.
Alfred Milner MSS.
Monk Bretton (J. G. Dodson) MSS.
J. E. Thorold Rogers MSS.
2nd Earl of Selborne MSS.
Sir Thomas Dyke Acland MSS (MS Eng. Lett. d. 81, 82, 89).

Cambridge University Library

Lord Acton MSS.
Sir Rowland and Lady Blennerhassett MSS.
1st Viscount Halifax MSS ('Hickleton MSS', microfilm copy).

National Library of Scotland

Hon. Arthur Elliot MSS.
3rd and 4th Earl of Minto MSS.
R. B. Haldane MSS.
5th Earl of Rosebery MSS.

Other Collections

W. P. Adam MSS (Scottish Record Office).
James Beal MSS (Greater London Record Office).
W. C. Cartwright MSS (Northampton CRO).
Joseph Chamberlain MSS (Birmingham University Library).
H. C. E. Childers MSS (Royal Commonwealth Society, London).
15th Earl of Derby MSS (Liverpool Record Office).
8th Duke of Devonshire MSS (Chatsworth House, Derbyshire).
Ashton Dilke MSS (Churchill College, Cambridge).
2nd Viscount Esher (Reginald Brett) MSS (Churchill College, Cambridge).
3rd and 4th Earl Fortescue MSS (Devon CRO, Exeter).
Glynne–Gladstone MSS (Clwyd CRO).
2nd Earl Granville MSS (Public Record Office).
3rd and 4th Earl Grey MSS (University of Durham).
1st Viscount Hampden MSS (House of Lords Record Office).
Edward Henage MSS (Lincoln CRO).
Sir Henry James MSS (Hereford and Worcester CRO).
Colonel R. N. F. Kingscote MSS (Gloucester CRO).
A. J. Mundella MSS (Sheffield University Library).
Mundella–Leader Correspondence (Sheffield University Library).
2nd Earl of Northbrook MSS (India Office Library, London).
Lyon Playfair MSS (Library of Imperial College, London).
Sir John Ramsden MSS (Sheepscar Library, Leeds).
1st Earl of Selborne MSS (Lambeth Palace Library).
Strachie (Lord Carlingford and Lady Waldegrave) MSS (Somerset CRO).

IV. PRINTED PRIMARY SOURCES

The following selection of published works includes convenient editions of existing documentary material (some of which is not at present available to scholars) together with volumes based on materials which can no longer be located. Published speeches and pamphlets have also been included. All may therefore be regarded as 'primary' sources. Some volumes of primary material which proved to be of limited value for this study have been excluded, however, and are listed instead in Section V.

Aberdare, Lord, *Letters of the Rt. Hon. Henry Austin Bruce, G.C.B., Lord Aberdare of Dufferyn* (2 vols., privately printed, Oxford, 1902).

Acland, A. H. D. (ed.), *Memoir and Letters of the Right Honourable Sir Thomas Dyke Acland* (privately printed, Oxford, 1902).

Argyll, Duchess of (ed.), *George Douglas, 8th Duke of Argyll (1823–1900): Autobiography and Memoirs* (2 vols., 1906).

Bahlman, D. W. R. (ed.), *The Diary of Sir Edward Walter Hamilton, 1880–1885* (2 vols., Oxford, 1972).

Bailey, John (ed.), *The Diary of Lady Frederick Cavendish* (2 vols., 1927).

Bassett, A. Tilney (ed.), *Gladstone to his Wife* (1936).

Brooke, John, and Mary Sorensen (eds.), *The Prime Minister's Papers: W. E. Gladstone* (4 vols., 1971–81).

Buckle, G. E. (ed.), *The Letters of Queen Victoria*, 2nd series, *1862–1885* (3 vols., 1926–8).

—— *The Letters of Queen Victoria*, 3rd series, *1886–1901* (3 vols., 1930).

Carlisle, Henry E. (ed.), *A Selection from the Correspondence of Abraham Hayward, Q.C., from 1834 to 1884* (2 vols., 1886).

Cooke, A. B., and John Vincent (eds.), *Lord Carlingford's Journal: Reflections of a Cabinet Minister, 1885* (Oxford, 1971).

Cowper, Countess (ed.), *Earl Cowper, K.G.: A Memoir* (privately printed, 1913).

Drus, Ethel (ed.), *A Journal of Events during the Gladstone Ministry, 1868–74, by John, First Earl of Kimberley* (Camden Miscellany, 21; 1958).

Foot, M. R. D., and H. C. G. Matthew (eds.), *The Gladstone Diaries* (9 vols.–, Oxford, 1968–).

Gladstone, W. E., *A Chapter of Autobiography* (1868).

—— *The Irish Question, i: History of an Idea; ii: Lessons of the Election* (1886).

—— *Political Speeches in Scotland, November and December 1879* (reprinted Leicester, 1971, with an introduction by M. R. D. Foot).

Gordon, Peter (ed.), *The Red Earl: The Papers of the Fifth Earl Spencer, 1835–1910, i: 1835–1885* (Northants Record Society, 31; 1981).

Goschen, G. J., *Address to the Philosophical Institution at Edinburgh on Laissez Faire and Government Interference* (1883).

—— *Political Speeches Delivered during the General Election 1885* (Edinburgh, 1886).

Guedalla, P. (ed.), *The Queen and Mr. Gladstone* (2 vols., 1933).

Hamer, D. A. (ed.), *The Radical Programme 1885* (Hassocks, 1971).

Harcourt, Sir William, 'A Speech Addressed to his Constituents in the Corn Exchange, at Oxford, on December 21, 1874' (1875).

Hartington, Marquis of, *An Address Delivered before the University of Edinburgh on his Inauguration as Lord Rector, Jan. 31, 1879* (1879).

—— *Election Speeches in 1879 and 1880: With Address to the Electors of North East Lancashire* (1880).

Hirst, F. W. (ed.), *Early Life and Letters of John Morley* (2 vols., 1927).

Howard, C. H. D. (ed.), *A Political Memoir 1880–92, by Joseph Chamberlain* (1953).

Lathbury, D. C. (ed.), *Correspondence on Church and Religion of William Ewart Gladstone* (2 vols., 1910).

Mallock, W. H., and Lady Gwendolen Ramsden (eds.), *Letters, Remains and Memoirs of Edward Adolphus Seymour, Twelfth Duke of Somerset, K.G.* (1893).

Paul, Herbert (ed.), *Letters of Lord Acton to Mary Gladstone* (1904).

Ponsonby, Arthur, *Henry Ponsonby: His Life from his Letters* (1942).

Ramm, Agatha (ed.), *The Political Correspondence of Mr Gladstone and Lord Granville, 1868–1876*, (Camden, 3rd series, 81–2; 1952).

—— *The Political Correspondence of Mr Gladstone and Lord Granville, 1876–1886* (2 vols., Oxford, 1962).

Walling, R. A. J. (ed.), *The Diaries of John Bright* (1930).

V. BIOGRAPHIES, MEMOIRS, ETC.

Anderson, Mosa, *Henry Joseph Wilson: Fighter for Freedom 1833–1914* (1953).

Armytage, W. H. G., *A. J. Mundella 1825–1897: The Liberal Background to the Labour Movement* (1951).

Askwith, Lord, *Lord James of Hereford* (1930).

Bagehot, Walter, *Biographical Studies* [ed. R. H. Hutton] (1881).

Bassett, A. Tilney, *The Life of the Rt. Hon. John Edward Ellis, M.P.* (1914).

Battersea, Lady, *Reminiscences* (1922).

Begbie, Harold, *Albert Grey: A Last Word* (1917).

Bonner, Hypatia Bradlaugh, *Charles Bradlaugh: A Record of his Life and Work* (2 vols., 1895).

Brett, M. V. (ed.), *Journals and Letters of Reginald, Viscount Esher, i* (1934).

Broadhurst, Henry, *Henry Broadhurst, M.P.: The Story of his Life . . . Told by Himself* (1901).

Brodrick, G. C., *Memories and Impressions, 1831–1900* (1900).

Bryce, James, *Studies in Contemporary Biography* (1903).

Buchan, John, *Memoir of Lord Minto* (1924).

Burt, Thomas, *An Autobiography* (1924).

Channing, F. A., *Memories of Midland Politics, 1885–1910* (1918).

Chapman, J. K. (ed.), 'A Political Correspondence of the Victorian Era: The Letters of Lady Sophia Palmer and Sir Arthur Gordon, 1884–1889', *Transactions of the American Philosophical Society*, 61 (Mar. 1971).

Childers, Spencer, *The Life and Correspondence of the Right Hon. Hugh C. E. Childers, 1827–1896* (2 vols. 1901).

Coleridge, E. H., *Life and Correspondence of John Duke, Lord Coleridge, Lord Chief Justice of England* (2 vols., 1904).

Collings, J. and Green, J. L., *Life of the Right Hon. Jesse Collings* (1920).

Colman, Helen C., *Jeremiah James Colman: A Memoir* (privately printed, 1905).

Corder, Percy, *The Life of Robert Spence Watson* (1914).

Crewe, Marquis of, *Lord Rosebery* (2 vols., 1931).

Davidson, J., *Eminent Radicals In and Out of Parliament* (1880).

Denholm, A., *Lord Ripon 1827–1909: A Political Biography* (1982).

Duff, M. E. Grant, *Some Brief Comments on Passing Events, 1858–1881* (Madras, 1884).

Edwards, J. Passmore, *A Few Footprints* (privately printed, 1905).

Elliot, Hon. A. D., *The Life of George Joachim Goschen, First Viscount Goschen, 1831–1907* (2 vols., 1911).

Escott, T. H. S. *Politics and Letters* (1886).

Esher, Viscount, *Extracts from Journals 1872–1881* (privately printed, Cambridge, 1908).

—— *Extracts from Journals 1880–95* (privately printed, Cambridge, 1914).

Farquharson, R., *In and Out of Parliament: Reminiscences of a Varied Life* (1912).

Fisher, H. A. L., *James Bryce (Viscount Bryce of Dechmont, O.M.)* (2 vols., 1927).

Fitzmaurice, Lord Edmond, *The Life of Granville George Leveson-Gower, Second Earl of Granville, K.G. 1815–1891* (2 vols., 1905).

Fowler, Edith H., *The Life of Henry Hartley Fowler, First Viscount Wolverhampton, C.C.S.I.* (1912).

Fraser, Peter, *Joseph Chamberlain; Radicalism and Empire, 1868–1914* (1966).

—— *Lord Esher: A Political Biography* (1973).

Gardiner, A. G., *The Life of Sir William Harcourt* (2 vols. 1923).

Garvin, J. L., and Julian Amery, *The Life of Joseph Chamberlain* (6 vols., 1932–69).

Gladstone, Viscount, *After Thirty Years* (1928).

Goldsmid, Louisa S., *Memoir of Sir Francis Henry Goldsmid* (1879).

Gooch, G. P.., *Life of Lord Courtney* (1920).

—— (ed.), *The Later Correspondence of Lord John Russell, 1840–1878* (2 vols., 1925).

Gower, Hon E. F. Leveson-, *Bygone Years* (1905).

Gower, Sir George Leveson-, *Years of Content 1858–1886* (1940).
Gwynn, S., and G. M. Tuckwell, *The Life of the Rt. Hon. Sir Charles W. Dilke, Bart, M.P.* (2 vols., 1917).
Haldane, Viscount, *An Autobiography* (1929).
Hamer, D. A., *John Morley: Liberal Intellectual in Politics* (Oxford, 1968).
Hamer, F. E. (ed.), *The Personal Papers of Lord Rendel* (1931).
Hammond, J. L. and Barbara, *James Stansfeld: A Victorian Champion of Sex Equality* (1932).
Harris, S. H., *Auberon Herbert: Crusader for Liberty* (1943).
Haultain, A. (ed.), *A Selection from Goldwin Smith's Correspondence* (1913).
Hewett, O. W., *Strawberry Fair: A Biography of Frances, Countess Waldegrave, 1821–1879* (1956).
Hodder, Edwin, *The Life of Samuel Morley* (1887).
Holland, Bernard, *The Life of Spencer Compton, Eighth Duke of Devonshire, 1833–1908* (2 vols. 1911).
Huntly, Marquis of, *Milestones* (1926).
Hutchinson, H. G., *Life of Sir John Lubbock, Lord Avebury* (2 vols., 1914).
—— *Portraits of the Eighties* (1920).
Huxley, Gervas, *Victorian Duke: The Life of Hugh Lupus Grosvenor, First Duke of Westminster* (1967).
Innes, A. Taylor, *Chapters of Reminiscence* (1913).
James, R. R., *Rosebery* (1963).
Jay, Richard, *Joseph Chamberlain: A Political Study* (Oxford, 1981).
Jeans, William, *Parliamentary Reminiscences* (1912).
Jones, E. R., *Life and Speeches of Joseph Cowen, M.P.* (1885).
Kilbracken, Lord, *Reminiscences* (1931).
Kirkby, M. W., *Men of Business and Politics: The Rise and Fall of the Quaker Pease Family of North East England, 1700–1943* (1984).
Koss, S. E., *Sir John Brunner: Radical Plutocrat 1842–1919* (Cambridge, 1970).
Laughton, J. K., *Memoirs of the Life and Correspondence of Henry Reeve* (2 vols., 1898).
Leach, Henry, *The Duke of Devonshire* (1904).
Leader, R. E., *Life and Letters of John Arthur Roebuck* (2 vols., 1897).
Leventhal, F. M., *Respectable Radical: George Howell and Victorian Working Class Politics* (1971).
Lucy, Henry, *A Diary of Two Parliaments, 1874–1885* (2 vols. 1885–6).
—— *Memories of Eight Parliaments* (1908).
—— *Sixty Years in the Wilderness* (1909).
Lyall, Sir Alfred, *The Life of the Marquess of Dufferin and Ava* (2 vols., 1905).
McCabe, J., *Life and Letters of G. J. Holyoake* (2 vols. 1908).
McCullagh, T., *Life of Sir William McArthur* (1891).

MacInnes, Anna G., *Recollections of the Life of Miles MacInnes* (1911).
Mackie, J. B., *Life and Work of Duncan McLaren* (2 vols., Edinburgh, 1888).
Magnus, P., *Gladstone: A Biography* (1954).
Mallet, Bernard, *Thomas George, Earl of Northbrook: A Memoir* (1908).
Mallet, Sir Charles, *Herbert Gladstone: A Memoir* (1932).
Marindin, G. E. (ed.). *Letters of Frederic, Lord Blachford* (1896).
Edward Marjoribanks, Lord Tweedmouth, K. T. 1849–1909: Notes and Recollections (1909).
Martin, A. P., *Life and Letters of the Right Honourable Robert Lowe, Viscount Sherbrooke* (2 vols., 1893).
Masterman, Lucy (ed.), *Mary Gladstone—Mrs Drew: Her Diaries and Letters* (1930).
Maurice, Sir F., *The Life of Viscount Haldane of Cloan* (2 vols., 1937–9).
Miall, C. S., *Henry Richard, M.P.: A Biography* (1889).
Morley, John, *The Life of William Ewart Gladstone* (3 vols., 1903).
Morley, (John) Viscount, *Recollections* (2 vols., 1917).
Newton, J., *W. S. Caine, M.P.: A Biography* (1907).
Newton, Lord, *Lord Lansdowne: A Biography* (1929).
Pease, Alfred E., *Elections and Recollections* (1932).
Peel, Albert (ed.), *Letters to a Victorian Editor: Henry Allon—Editor of the British Quarterly Review* (1929).
Rathbone, Eleanor F., *William Rathbone: A Memoir* (1905).
Reid, Andrew (ed.), *Why I am a Liberal* (1885).
Reid, S. J. (ed.), *Memoirs of Sir Wemyss Reid 1842–1885* (1905).
Reid, T. Wemyss, *Life of the Right Honourable W. E. Forster* (2 vols., 1888).
—— *The Life, Letters and Friendships of Richard Monckton Milnes, First Lord Houghton* (2 vols., 1890).
—— *Memoirs and Correspondence of Lyon Playfair, First Lord Playfair of St. Andrews* (1899).
—— *Politicians of Today* (2 vols., 1880).
Robbins, Keith, *John Bright* (1979).
Rogers, J. Guinness, *An Autobiography* (1903).
Russell, G. W. E. (ed.), *Letters of Matthew Arnold, 1848–1888* (2 vols., 1901).
—— (ed.), *Sir Wilfrid Lawson: A Memoir* (1909).
—— (ed.), *Malcolm MacColl: Memoirs and Correspondence* (1914).
—— *Portraits of the Seventies* (1916).
Rylands, L. G., *Correspondence and Speeches of Mr. Peter Rylands, M.P.: With a Sketch of his Life* (2 vols., Manchester, 1890).
Selborne, Roundell, Earl of, *Memorials: Personal and Political, 1865–1895* (2 vols., 1898).
Shannon, Richard, *Gladstone*, i (1982).

Simpson, P.C., *The Life of Principal Rainy* (2 vols., 1909).
Smalley, G., *Life of Sir Sydney H. Waterlow, Bart* (1909).
Smith, Goldwin, *My Memory of Gladstone* (1904).
Smith, Samuel, *My Life Work* (1902).
Spender, J. A., *The Life of the Right Hon. Sir Henry Campbell Bannerman, G.C.B.* (2 vols., 1923).
Spinner, T. J., *George Joachim Goschen: The Transformation of a Victorian Liberal* (Cambridge, 1973).
Stansky, Peter, *Gladstone: A Progress in Politics* (1981).
Stephen, Leslie, *Life of Henry Fawcett* (1885).
Thorold, A. L., *The Life of Henry Labouchere* (1913).
Tollemache, Hon. L. A., *Talks with Mr. Gladstone* (1898).
Torrens, W. M., *Twenty Years in Parliament* (1893).
Trevelyan, G. M., *The Life of John Bright* (1913).
—— *Grey of Falloden: Being the Life of Sir Edward Grey, afterwards Viscount Grey of Falloden* (1937).
—— *Sir George Otto Trevelyan: A Memoir* (1932).
West, Sir Algernon, *Recollections, 1832 to 1886* (2 vols., 1899).
Whyte, F., *Life of W. T. Stead* (2 vols., 1925).
Williams, J. F., *et al.*, *Memories of John Westlake* (1914).
Wilson, John, *CB: A Life of Sir Henry Campbell Bannerman* (1973).
Wolf, Lucien, *Life of the First Marquess of Ripon* (2 vols., 1921).

VI. SECONDARY LITERATURE

Adams, Francis, *History of the Elementary School Contest in England [1882]* (reprinted, Hassocks, 1972, with an introduction by Asa Briggs).
Adelman, Paul, *Victorian Radicalism* (1984).
Barker, Michael, *Gladstone and Radicalism: The Reconstruction of Liberal Policy in Britain, 1885–94* (Hassocks, 1975).
Bentley, J., *Ritualism and Politics in Victorian Britain: The Attempt to Legislate for Belief* (Oxford, 1978).
Bentley, Michael, *Politics without Democracy, 1815–1914 (1984)*.
Butler, Perry, *Gladstone: Church, State and Tractarianism—A Study of his Religious Ideas and Attitudes, 1809–1859* (Oxford, 1982).
Clayden, P. W., *England under Lord Beaconsfield* (1880).
Cooke, A. B., and John Vincent, *The Governing Passion: Cabinet Government and Party Politics in Britain, 1885–86* (Hassocks, 1974).
Cowling, Maurice, *1867: Disraeli, Gladstone and Revolution: The Passing of the Second Reform Bill* (Cambridge, 1967).
Davis, R. W., *Political Change and Continuity 1760–1885: A Buckinghamshire Study* (Newton Abbot, 1972).
Ensor, R. C. K., *England 1870–1914* (Oxford, 1936).
Guttsman, W. L., *The British Political Elite* (1963).

Hamer, D. A., *Liberal Politics in the Age of Gladstone and Rosebery* (Oxford, 1972).

—— *The Politics of Electoral Pressure: A Study in the History of Victorian Reform Agitations* (Hassocks, 1977).

Hammond, J. L., *Gladstone and the Irish Nation*, (1964 reprint, with an introduction by M. R. D. Foot).

Hanham, H. J., *Elections and Party Management: Politics in the Time of Disraeli and Gladstone* (1978 edn., Hassocks).

Harrison, Henry, *Parnell, Joseph Chamberlain and Mr. Garvin* (1938).

Harvie, Christopher, *The Lights of Liberalism: University Liberals and the Challenge of Democracy 1860–86* (1976).

Heyck, T. W., *The Dimensions of British Radicalism: The Case of Ireland, 1874–1895* (Illinois, 1974).

Hilton, Boyd, 'Gladstone's Theological Politics', in M. Bentley and J. Stevenson (eds.), *High and Low Politics in Modern Britain* (Oxford, 1983), 28–57.

Hurst, M. C., 'Joseph Chamberlain and West Midland Politics, 1886–1895', Dugdale Society Occasional Papers No. 15 (Oxford, 1962).

—— *Joseph Chamberlain and Liberal Reunion: The Round Table Conference of 1887* (1967).

Jones, Andrew, *The Politics of Reform 1884*, (Cambridge, 1972).

Kinnear, Michael, *The British Voter: An Atlas and Survey since 1885* (1968).

Knaplund, Paul, *Gladstone and Britain's Imperial Policy* (reprinted, 1966).

—— *Gladstone's Foreign Policy* (reprinted, 1970).

Koss, Stephen, *The Rise and Fall of the Political Press in Britain*, i (1981).

Lloyd, T. O., *The General Election of 1880* (Oxford, 1968).

Low, Sidney, *The Governance of England* (1904).

Lowell, A. L., *The Government of England* (2 vols., 1908).

Maccoby, S., *English Radicalism 1853–1886* (1938).

—— (ed.), *The English Radical Tradition, 1763–1914* (1952).

Matthew, H. C. G., *The Liberal Imperialists: The Ideas and Policies of a Post-Gladstonian Elite* (Oxford, 1973).

—— 'Gladstone, Vaticanism and the Question of the East', in D. Baker (ed.), *Studies in Church History*, (Oxford, 1978), 417–42.

Morgan, K. O., *Wales in British Politics, 1868–1922* (3rd edn., Cardiff, 1980).

O'Brien, C. C., *Parnell and his Party 1880–90* (2nd edn., Oxford, 1964).

Olney, R. J., *Lincolnshire Politics, 1832–1885* (Oxford, 1973).

Ostrogorski, Moisei, *Democracy and the Organisation of Political Parties*, trans. F. Clarke (2 vols. 1902).

Pelling, Henry, *The Origins of the Labour Party 1880–1900* (2nd edn., Oxford, 1965).

—— *Social Geography of British Elections 1885–1910* (1967).

—— *Popular Politics and Society in Late Victorian Britain* (2nd edn., 1979).

Rossi, John P., 'The Transformation of the British Liberal Party: A Study of the Tactics of the Liberal Opposition, 1874–1880', *Transactions of the American Philosophical Society*, 68, (Dec. 1978).

Saunders, William, *The New Parliament 1880* (1880).

Schreuder, D. M., *Gladstone and Kruger: Liberal Government and Colonial 'Home Rule' 1880–1885*, (1969).

—— 'Gladstone and the Conscience of the State', in P. Marsh (ed.), *The Conscience of the Victorian State* (Hassocks, 1979), 73–130.

Shannon, Richard, *Gladstone and the Bulgarian Agitation 1876* (1975 edn., Hassocks).

—— 'Midlothian: 100 Years After', in Peter J. Jagger (ed.), *Gladstone, Politics and Religion: A Collection of Founder's Day Lectures delivered at St Deiniol's Library, Hawarden, 1967–83* (1985), 88–103.

Southgate, D., *The Passing of the Whigs, 1832–1886* (1962).

Stansky, P., *Ambitions and Strategies: The Struggle for the Leadership of the Liberal Party in the 1890s* (Oxford, 1964).

Steele, E. D., *Irish Land and British Politics: Tenant Right and Nationality 1865–1870* (Cambridge, 1974).

Swartz, Marvin, *The Politics of British Foreign Policy in the Era of Disraeli and Gladstone* (1985).

The History of The Times, ii: The Tradition Established, 1841–1884 (1939).

Thomas, J. A., *The House of Commons 1832–1901: A Study of its Economic and Functional Character* (Cardiff, 1939).

Thompson, F. M. L., *English Landed Society in the Nineteenth Century* (1963).

Thompson, G. C., *Public Opinion and Lord Beaconsfield 1875–1880* (2 vols., 1886).

Thompson, P., *Socialists, Liberals and Labour: The Struggle for London 1885–1914* (1967).

Thornley, David, *Issac Butt and Home Rule* (1964).

Vidler, A. R., *The Orb and the Cross: A Normative Study in the Relations of Church and State with Reference to Gladstone's Early Writings* (1945).

Vincent, John, *The Formation of the British Liberal Party, 1857–68* (1976 edn., Hassocks).

—— *Pollbooks: How Victorians Voted* (Cambridge, 1967).

Watson, R. Spence, *The National Liberal Federation* (1907).

Watson, R. W. Seton-, *Disraeli, Gladstone and the Eastern Question* (reprinted, 1962).

VII. ARTICLES

Berrington, Hugh, 'Partisanship and Dissidence in the Nineteenth Century House of Commons', *Parliamentary Affairs*, 21 (1967–8), 338–74.

Blewett, Neal, 'The Franchise in the United Kingdom 1885–1918', *Past and Present*, 32 (1965), 27–56.

Bristow, E., 'The Liberty and Property Defence League and Individualism', *Historical Journal*, 18 (1975), 761–89.

Chadwick, M. E. J., 'The Role of Redistribution in the Making of the Third Reform Act', *Historical Journal*, 19 (1976), 665–83.

Cowling, Maurice, 'Derby, Disraeli and Fusion, October 1865 to July 1866', *Historical Journal*, 8 (1965), 31–71.

Davis, Peter, 'The Liberal Unionist Party and the Irish Policy of Lord Salisbury's Government, 1886–1892', *Historical Journal*, 18 (1975), 85–104.

Dunbabin, J. P. D., 'Parliamentary Elections in Great Britain, 1868–1900: A Psephological Note', *English Historical Review*, 71 (1966), 82–99.

Ensor, R. C. K., 'Some Political and Economic Interactions in Late-victorian England', *Transactions of the Royal Historical Society* (4th series), 21 (1949), 17–28.

Fair, J. D., 'Royal Mediation in 1884: A Reassessment', *English Historical Review*, 88 (1973), 100–13.

Fraser, Peter, 'The Liberal Unionist Alliance: Chamberlain, Hartington and the Conservatives, 1886–1904', *English Historical Review*, 77 (1962), 53–78.

Glaser, J. F., 'English Nonconformity and the Decline of Liberalism', *American Historical Review*, 63 (1958), 352–63.

Goodman, Gordon L., 'Liberal Unionism: The Revolt of the Whigs', *Victorian Studies*, 3 (1959–60), 173–89.

Hamer, D. A., 'Gladstone: The Making of a Political Myth', *Victorian Studies*, 22, (1978–9), 29–50.

Hanham, H. J., 'British Party Finance 1868–80', *Bulletin of the Institute of Historical Research*, 27 (1954), 69–90.

Harvie, C., 'Ideology and Home Rule: James Bryce, A. V. Dicey and Ireland, 1880–1887', *English Historical Review*, 91, (1976), 298–314.

Herrick, F. H., 'The Origins of the National Liberal Federation', *Journal of Modern History*, 17, (1945), 116–29.

Howard, C. H. D., 'The Parnell Manifesto of 21 November 1885, and the Schools Question', *English Historical Review*, 62, (1947), 42–51.

—— 'Joseph Chamberlain and the Unauthorised Programme', *English Historical Review*, 65 (1950), 477–91.

—— 'Joseph Chamberlain, Parnell and the Irish "Central Board" Scheme, 1884–5', *Irish Historical Studies*, 8 (1952–3), 324–61.

Howarth, Janet, 'The Liberal Revival in Northamptonshire 1880–1895: A Case Study in Late nineteenth Century Elections', *Historical Journal*, 12, (1969), 78–118.

Hurst, M. C., 'Joseph Chamberlain, the Conservatives and the Succession to John Bright, 1886–9', *Historical Journal*, 7 (1964), 64–93.

—— 'Liberal versus Liberal: The General Election of 1874 in Bradford and Sheffield', *Historical Journal*, 15 (1972), 669–713.

—— 'Liberal versus Liberal 1874: A Rebuttal', *Historical Journal*, 17 (1974), 162–4.

—— 'Liberal versus Liberal 1874: A Surrebuttal', *Historical Journal*, 19 (1976), 1001–4.

Ingham, S. M., 'The Disestablishment Movement in England, 1868–74', *Journal of Religious History*, 3 (1964–5), 38–60.

Kellas, J. G., 'The Liberal Party and the Scottish Church Disestablishment Crisis', *English Historical Review*, 79 (1964), 31–46.

—— 'The Liberal Party in Scotland, 1876–1895', *Scottish Historical Review*, 14 (1965), 1–16.

Lubenow, W. C., 'Irish Home Rule and the Great Separation in the Liberal Party in 1886: The Dimensions of Parliamentary Liberalism', *Victorian Studies*, 26, (1982–3), 161–80.

—— 'Irish Home Rule and the Social Basis of the Great Separation in the Liberal Party in 1886', *Historical Journal*, 28 (1985), 125–42.

McGill, Barry, 'Francis Schnadhorst and Liberal Party Organisation', *Journal of Modern History*, 34 (1962), 19–39.

Machin, G. I. T., 'Gladstone and Nonconformity in the 1860s: The Formation of an Alliance', *Historical Journal*, 17, (1974), 347–64.

Maelh, W. H., 'Gladstone, the Liberals and the Election of 1874', *Bulletin of the Institute of Historical Research*, 36 (1963), 53–69.

Moore, R. J., 'The Twilight of the Whigs and the Reform of the Indian Councils, 1886–1892', *Historical Journal*, 10 (1967), 400–14.

Parry, J. P., 'Religion and the Collapse of Gladstone's First Government, 1870–1874', *Historical Journal*, 25 (1982), 71–101.

Phillips, Gregory D., 'The Whig Lords and Liberalism, 1886–1893', *Historical Journal*, 24, (1981), 167–73.

Quinault, Roland, 'John Bright and Joseph Chamberlain', *Historical Journal*, 28 (1985), 623–46.

Ramm, Agatha, 'Gladstone's Religion', *Historical Journal*, 28 (1985), 327–40.

Savage, D. C., 'Scottish Politics 1885–6', *Scottish Historical Review*, II (1961), 118–35.

Simon, Alan, 'Joseph Chamberlain and Free Education in the Election of 1885', *History of Education*, 2 (1973), 56–78.

—— 'Church Disestablishment as a Factor in the General Election of 1885', *Historical Journal*, 18 (1975), 791–820.

Steele, E. D., 'Gladstone and Ireland', *Irish Historical Studies*, 17 (1970–1), 58–88.

Temmel, M. R., 'Liberal versus Liberal 1874: W. E. Forster, Bradford and Education', *Historical Journal*, 18 (1975), 611–22.

—— 'Gladstone's Resignation of the Liberal Leadership, 1874–1875', *Journal of British Studies*, 16, (Fall 1976), 153–77.

Thompson, F. M. L., 'Land and Politics in England in the Nineteenth Century', *Transactions of the Royal Historical Society* (5th series), 15 (1965), 23–44.

Vincent, John, 'Gladstone and Ireland', *Proceedings of the British Academy*, 63 (1977), 193–238.

Warren, A. J., 'Gladstone, Land and Social Reconstruction in Ireland, 1881–1887', *Parliamentary History*, 2 (1983), 153–73.

Weston, C. C., 'The Royal Mediation in 1884', *English Historical Review*, 82 (1967), 296–322.

Wright, D. G., 'Liberal versus Liberal, 1874: Some Comments', *Historical Journal*, 16 (1973), 597–603.

Index